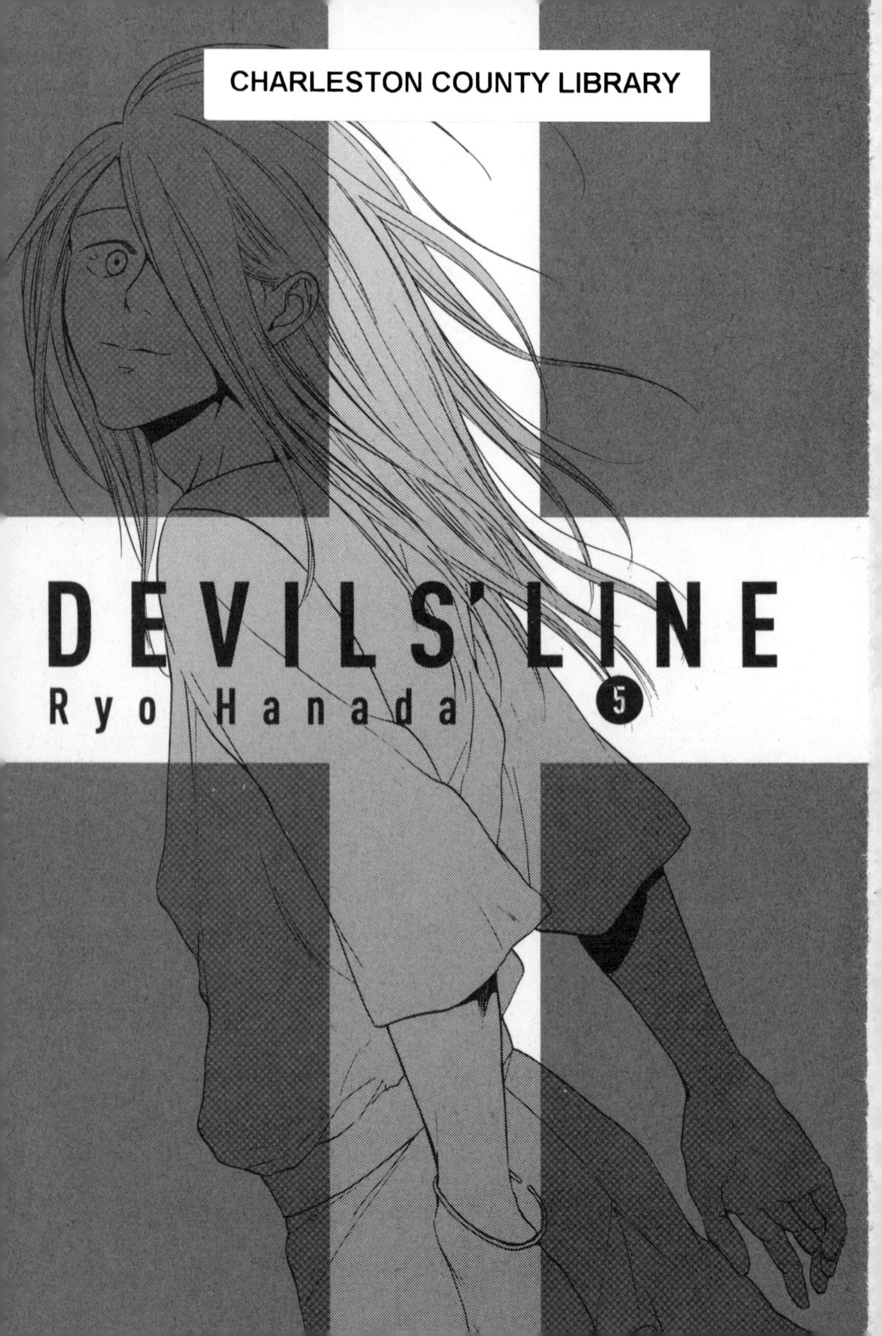
DEVILS' LINE
Ryo Hanada
5

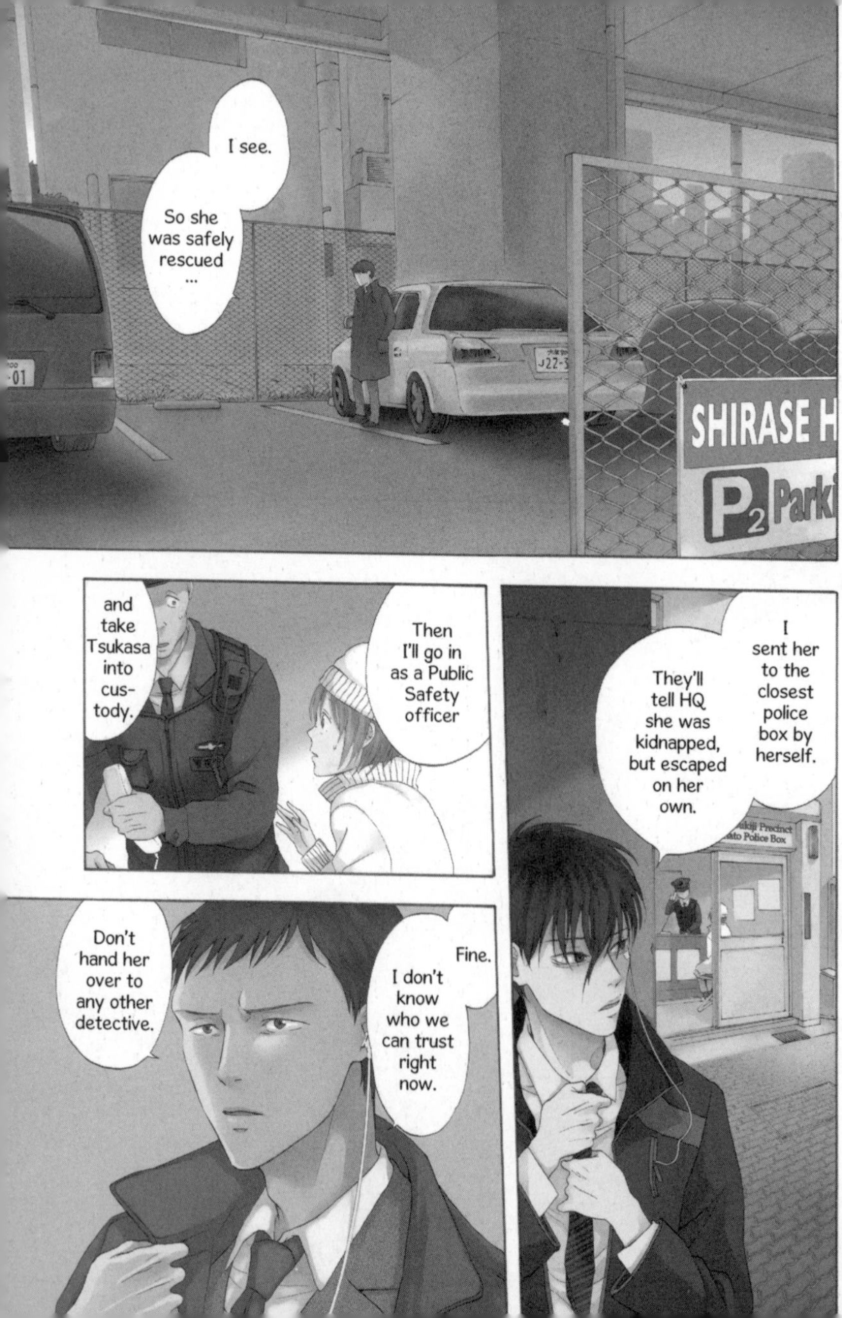
I see.
So she was safely rescued ...
SHIRASE H
Parki
I sent her to the closest police box by herself.
They'll tell HQ she was kidnapped, but escaped on her own.
Then I'll go in as a Public Safety officer
and take Tsukasa into custody.
Fine.
I don't know who we can trust right now.
Don't hand her over to any other detective.

Line 23
Copy

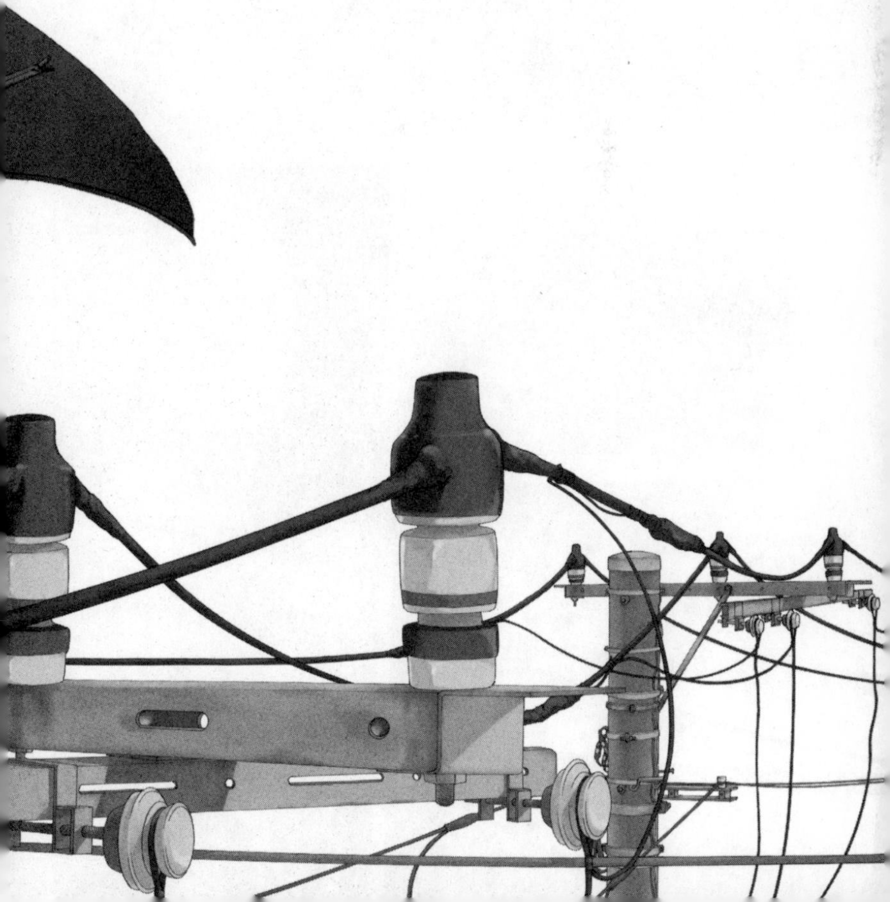

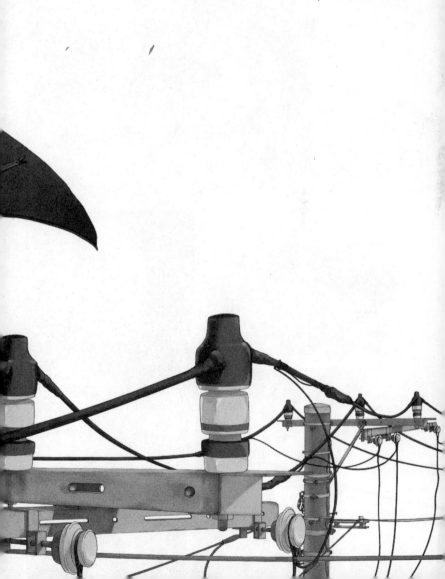

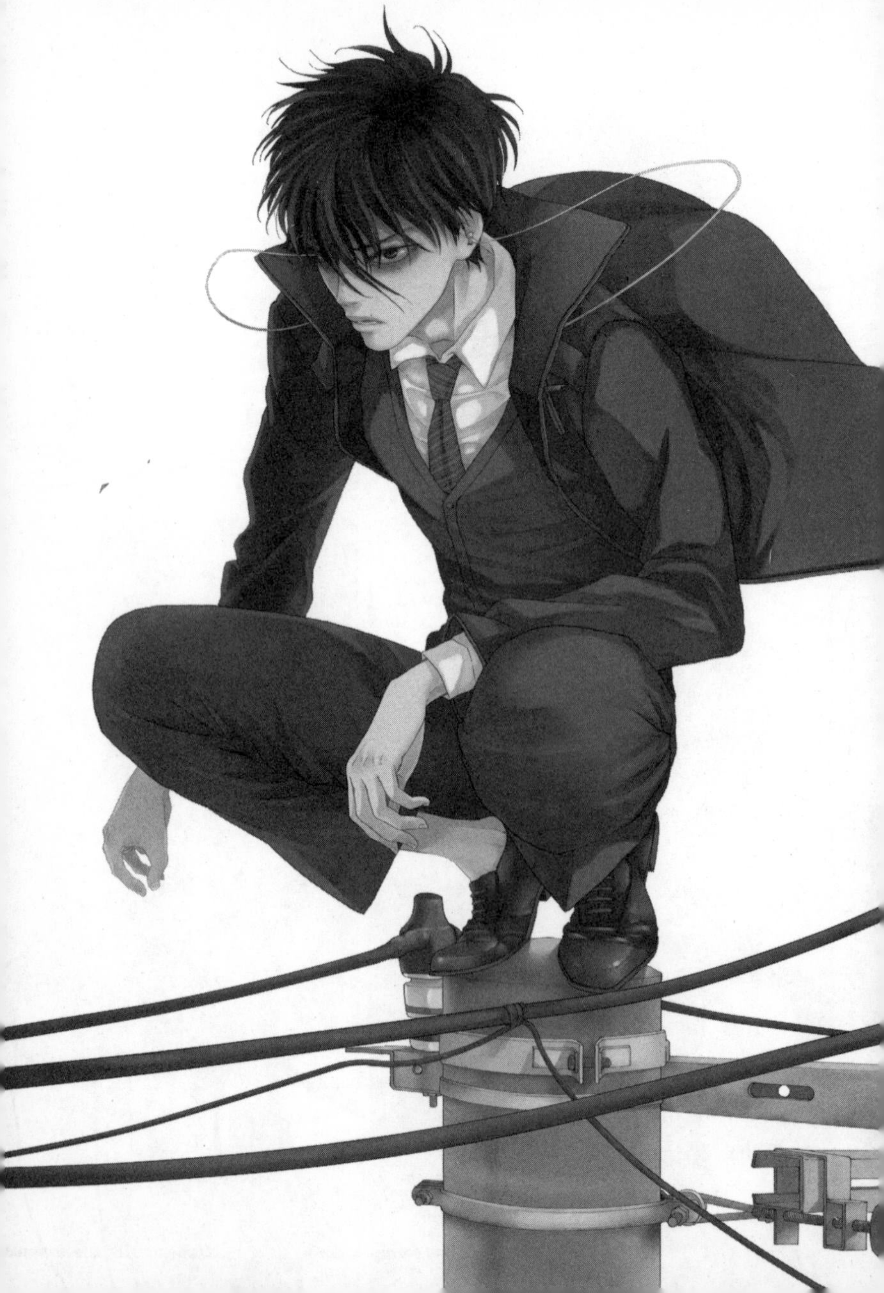

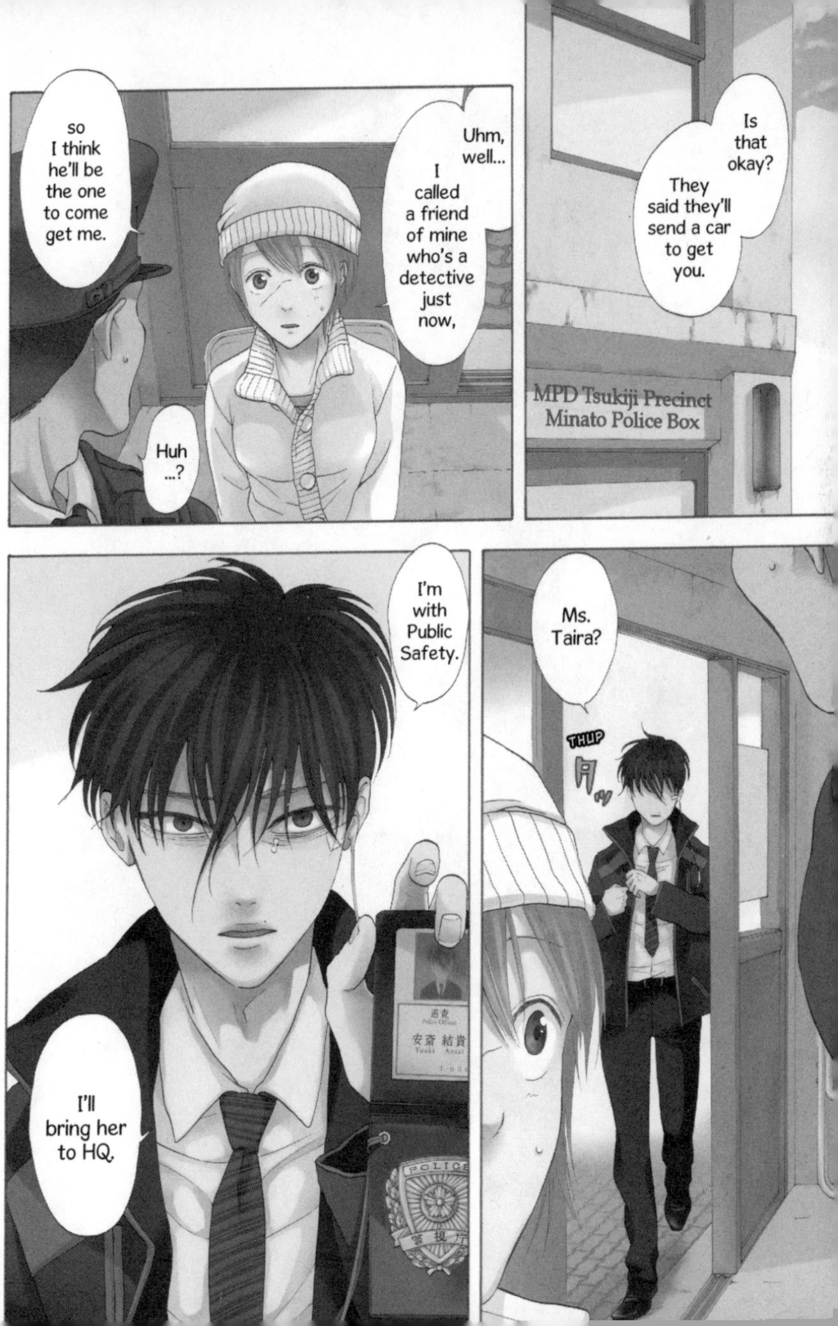
Is that okay?
They said they'll send a car to get you.
MPD Tsukiji Precinct
Minato Police Box
Uhm, well...
I called a friend of mine who's a detective just now,
so I think he'll be the one to come get me.
Huh ...?
Ms. Taira?
THUP
I'm with Public Safety.
I'll bring her to HQ.

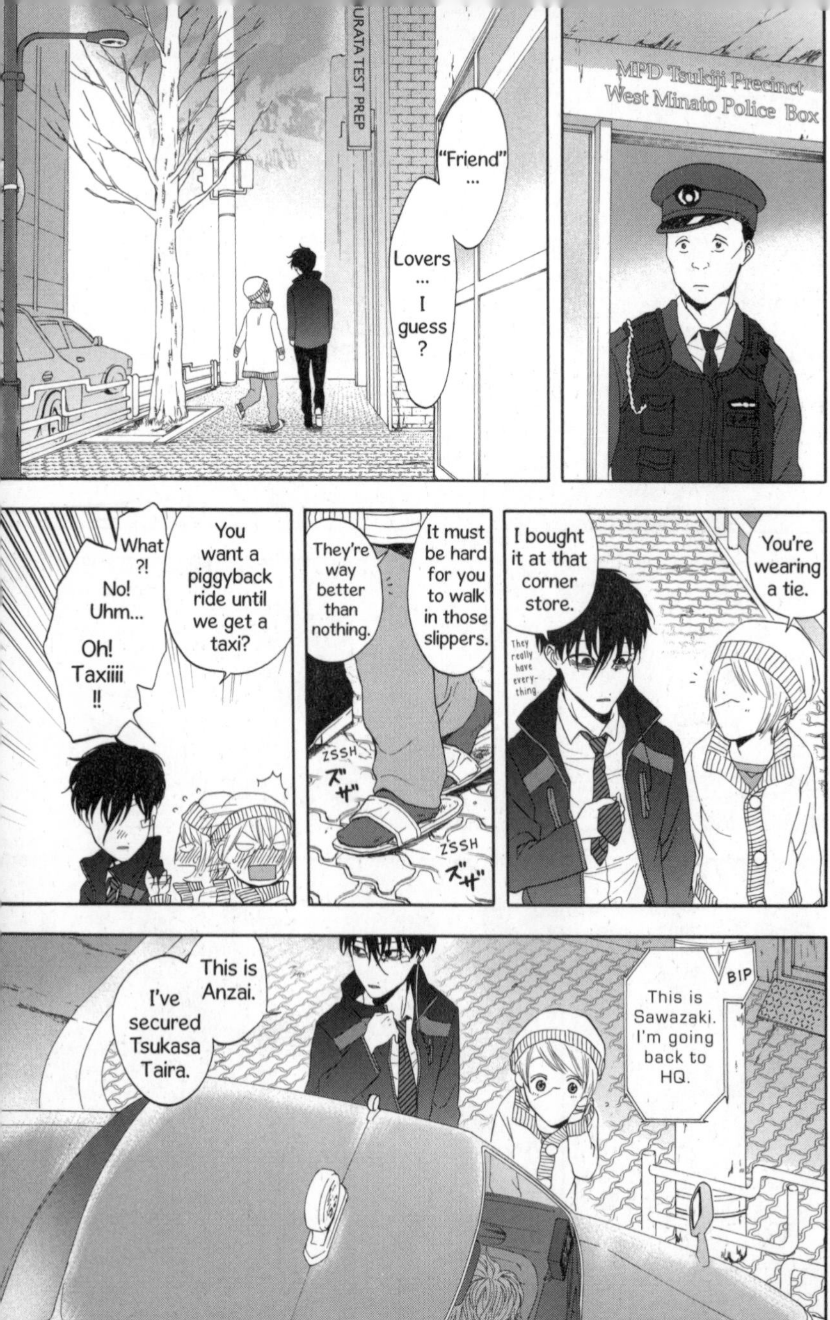
MPD Tsukiji Precinct
West Minato Police Box
URATA TEST PREP
"Friend"...
Lovers... I guess?
You're wearing a tie.
I bought it at that corner store.
They really have everything
It must be hard for you to walk in those slippers.
They're way better than nothing.
ZSSH
ズザ
ZSSH
ズザ
You want a piggyback ride until we get a taxi?
What?! No! Uhm... Oh! Taxiiii!!
BIP
This is Sawazaki. I'm going back to HQ.
This is Anzai. I've secured Tsukasa Taira.

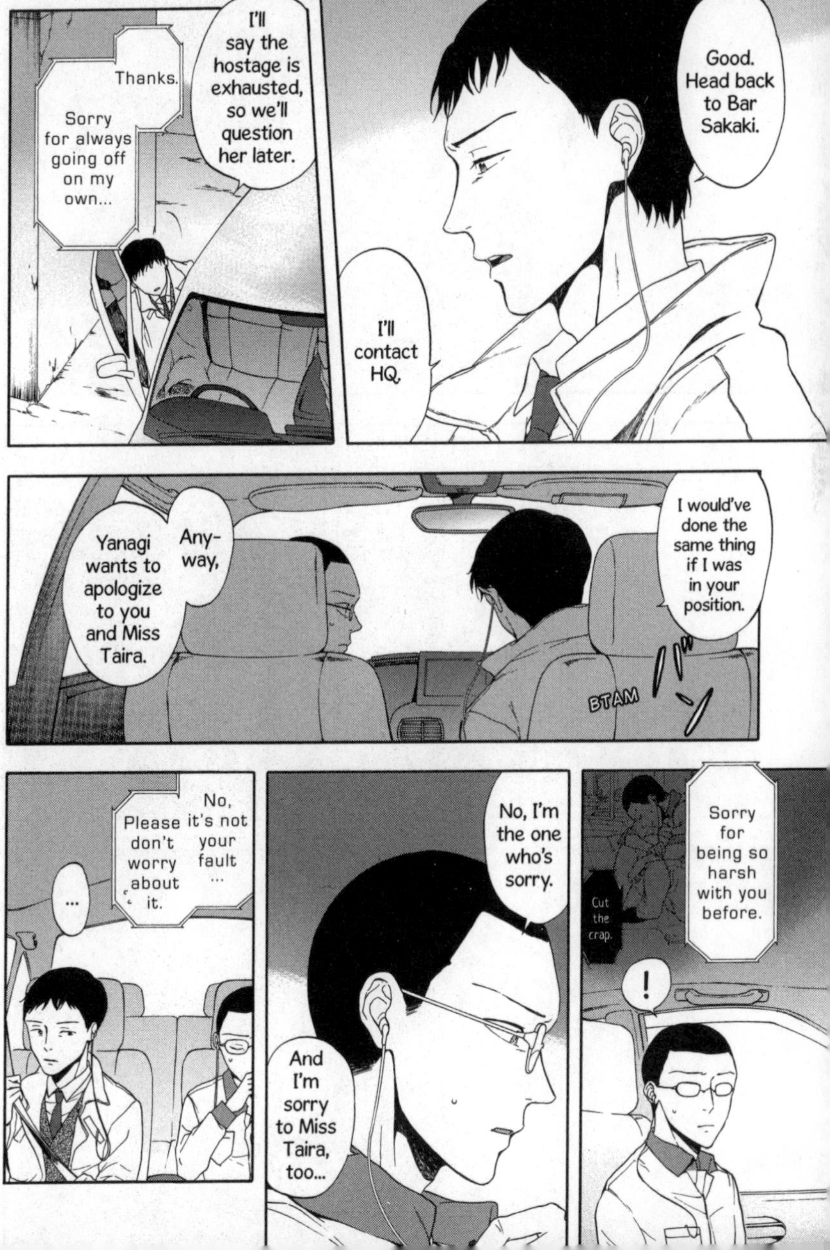
Good. Head back to Bar Sakaki.
I'll contact HQ.
I'll say the hostage is exhausted, so we'll question her later.
Thanks.
Sorry for always going off on my own...
I would've done the same thing if I was in your position.
BTAM
Anyway,
Yanagi wants to apologize to you and Miss Taira.
Sorry for being so harsh with you before.
Cut the crap.
!
No, I'm the one who's sorry.
And I'm sorry to Miss Taira, too...
No, it's not your fault...
Please don't worry about it.
...

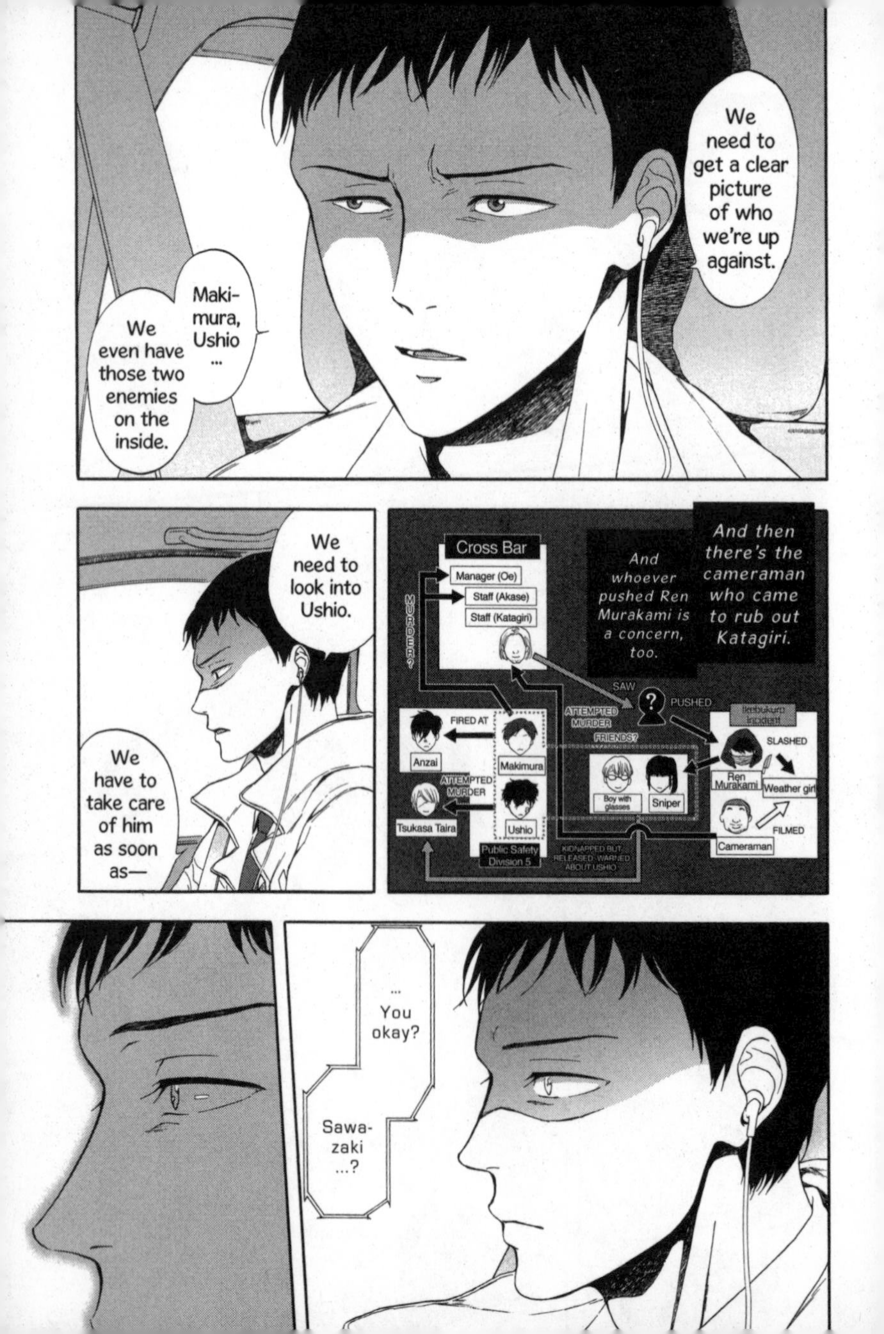
We need to get a clear picture of who we're up against.
Maki-mura, Ushio ...
We even have those two enemies on the inside.
And then there's the cameraman who came to rub out Katagiri.
And whoever pushed Ren Murakami is a concern, too.
Cross Bar
Manager (Oe)
Staff (Akase)
Staff (Katagiri)
MURDER?
SAW
PUSHED
ATTEMPTED MURDER
FRIENDS?
SLASHED
FIRED AT
Anzai
Makimura
ATTEMPTED MURDER
Tsukasa Taira
Ushio
Public Safety Division 5
Boy with glasses
Sniper
Ren Murakami
Weather girl
FILMED
Cameraman
KIDNAPPED BUT RELEASED. WARNED ABOUT USHIO
We need to look into Ushio.
We have to take care of him as soon as—
... You okay?
Sawa-zaki ...?

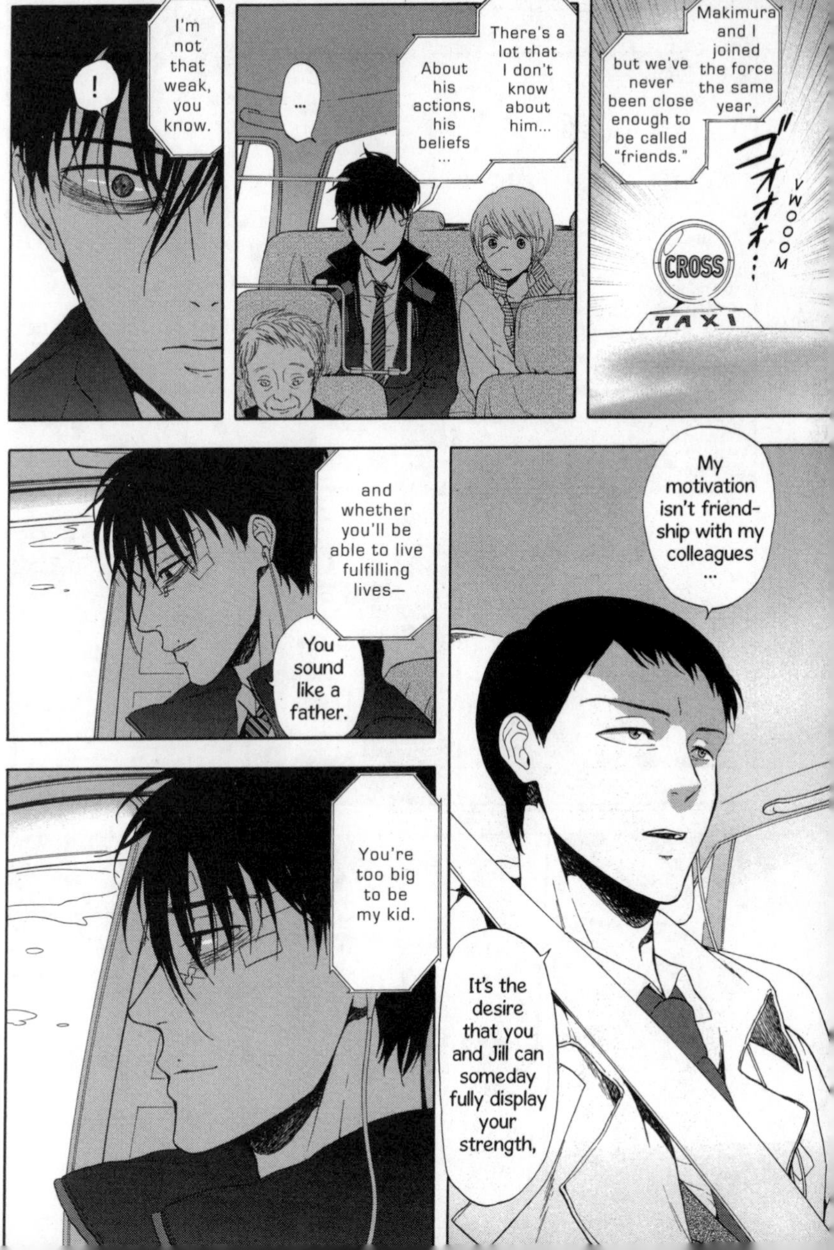
Makimura and I joined the force the same year,
but we've never been close enough to be called "friends."
ゴオオオ…
VWOOOM
CROSS
TAXI
There's a lot that I don't know about him...
About his actions, his beliefs...
...
I'm not that weak, you know.
!
My motivation isn't friendship with my colleagues...
It's the desire that you and Jill can someday fully display your strength,
and whether you'll be able to live fulfilling lives—
You sound like a father.
You're too big to be my kid.

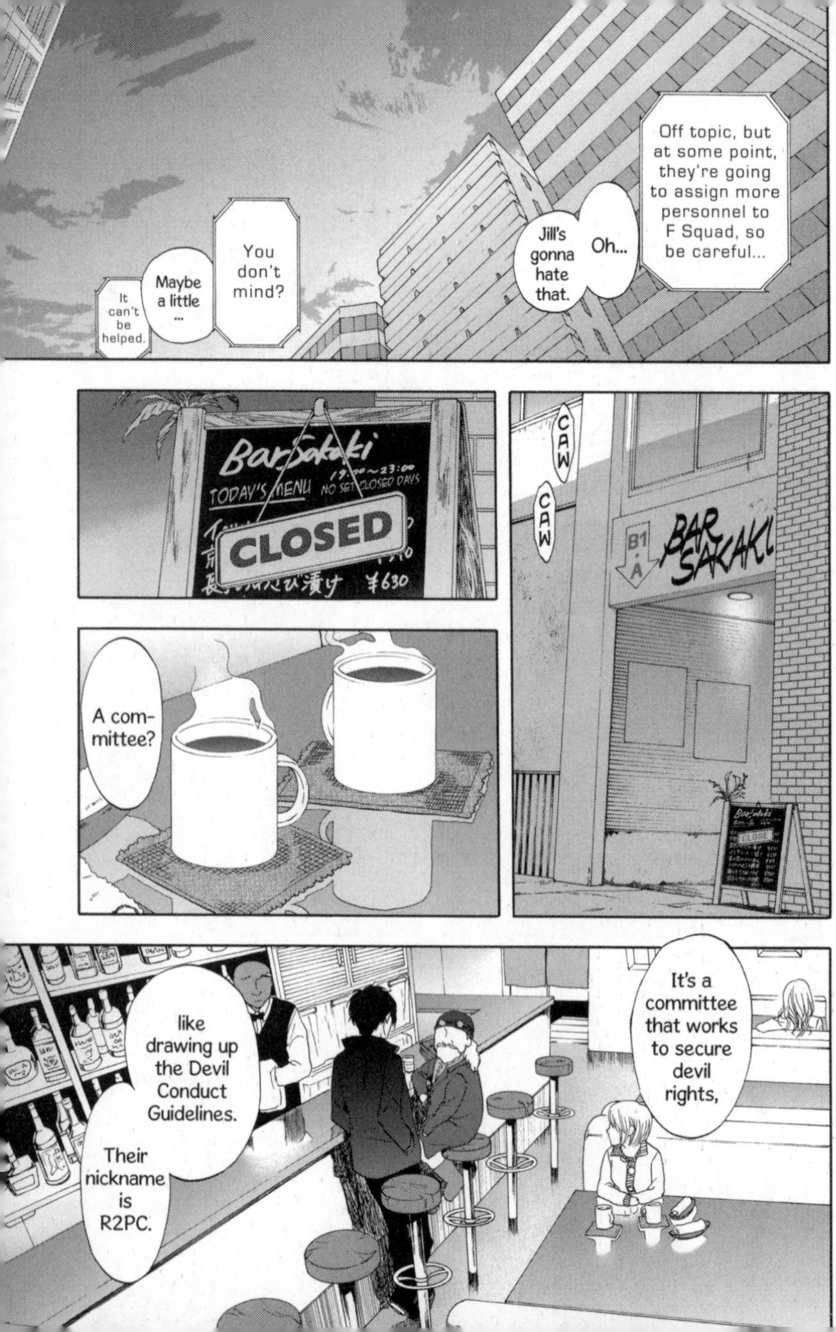
Off topic, but at some point, they're going to assign more personnel to F Squad, so be careful...
Oh...
Jill's gonna hate that.
You don't mind?
Maybe a little ...
It can't be helped.
CAW
CAW
B1 A
BAR SAKAKI
Bar Sakaki
TODAY'S MENU
NO SET CLOSED DAYS
CLOSED
¥630
A committee?
It's a committee that works to secure devil rights,
like drawing up the Devil Conduct Guidelines.
Their nickname is R2PC.

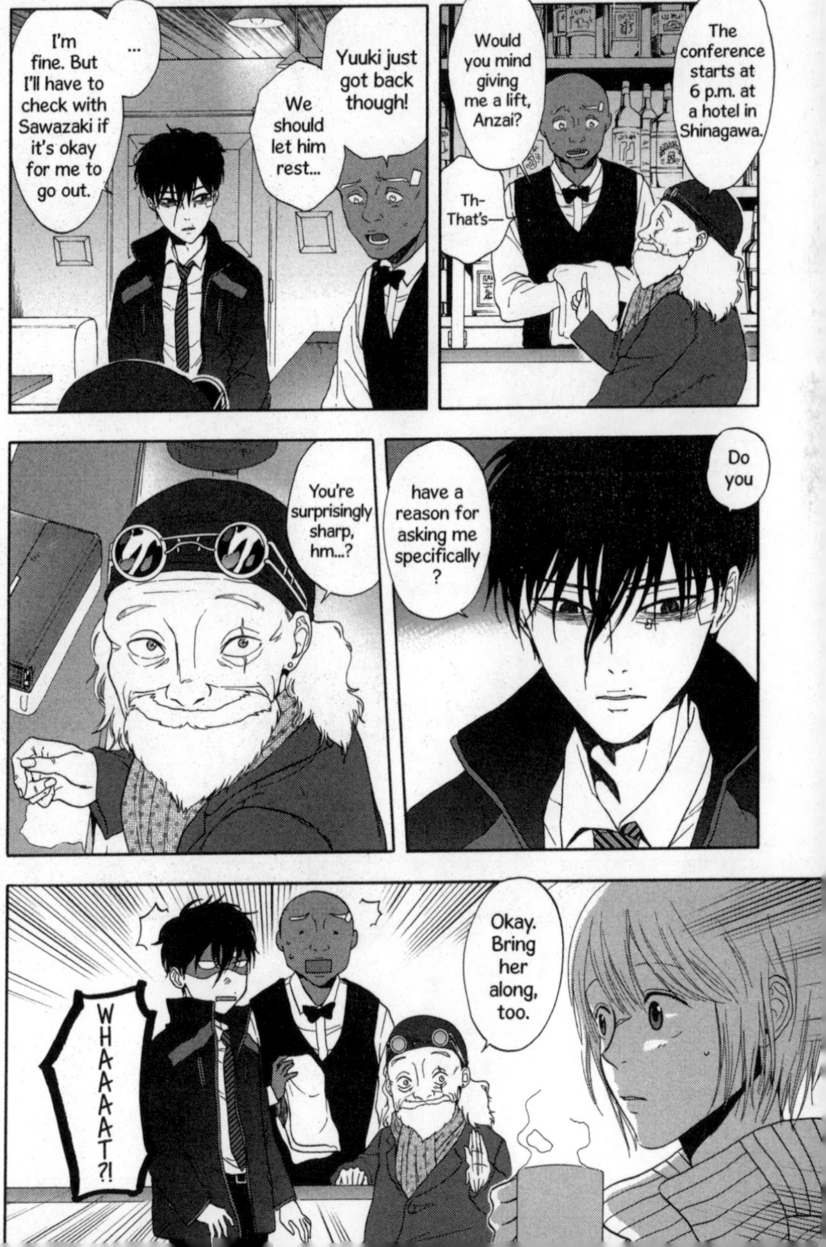
The conference starts at 6 p.m. at a hotel in Shinagawa.
Would you mind giving me a lift, Anzai?
Th- That's—
Yuuki just got back though!
We should let him rest...
...
I'm fine. But I'll have to check with Sawazaki if it's okay for me to go out.
Do you
have a reason for asking me specifically?
You're surprisingly sharp, hm...?
Okay. Bring her along, too.
WHAAAAAT?!

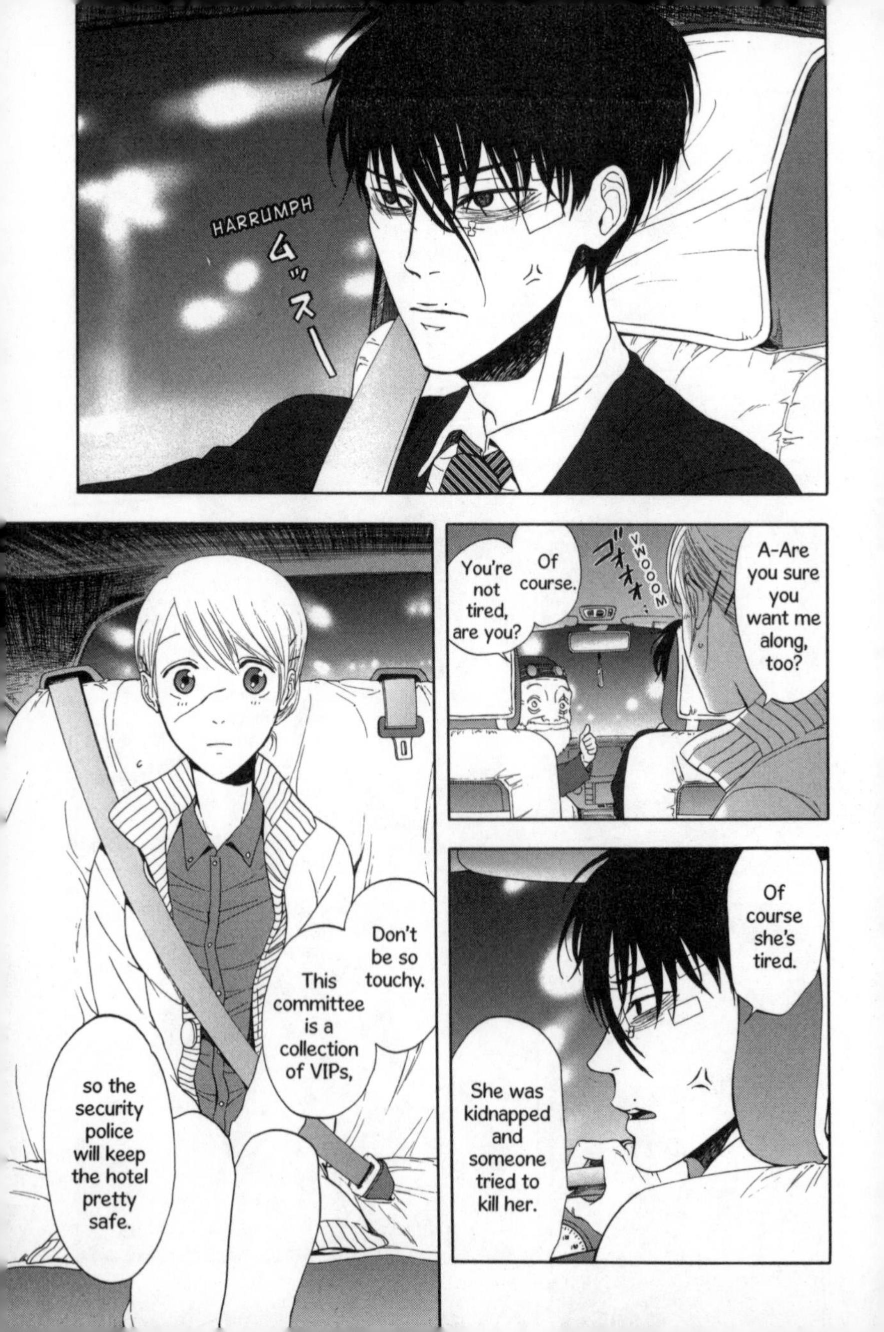
HARRUMPH
ムッスー
A-Are you sure you want me along, too?
VWOOOM
ゴォォォ
Of course.
You're not tired, are you?
Of course she's tired.
She was kidnapped and someone tried to kill her.
Don't be so touchy.
This committee is a collection of VIPs,
so the security police will keep the hotel pretty safe.

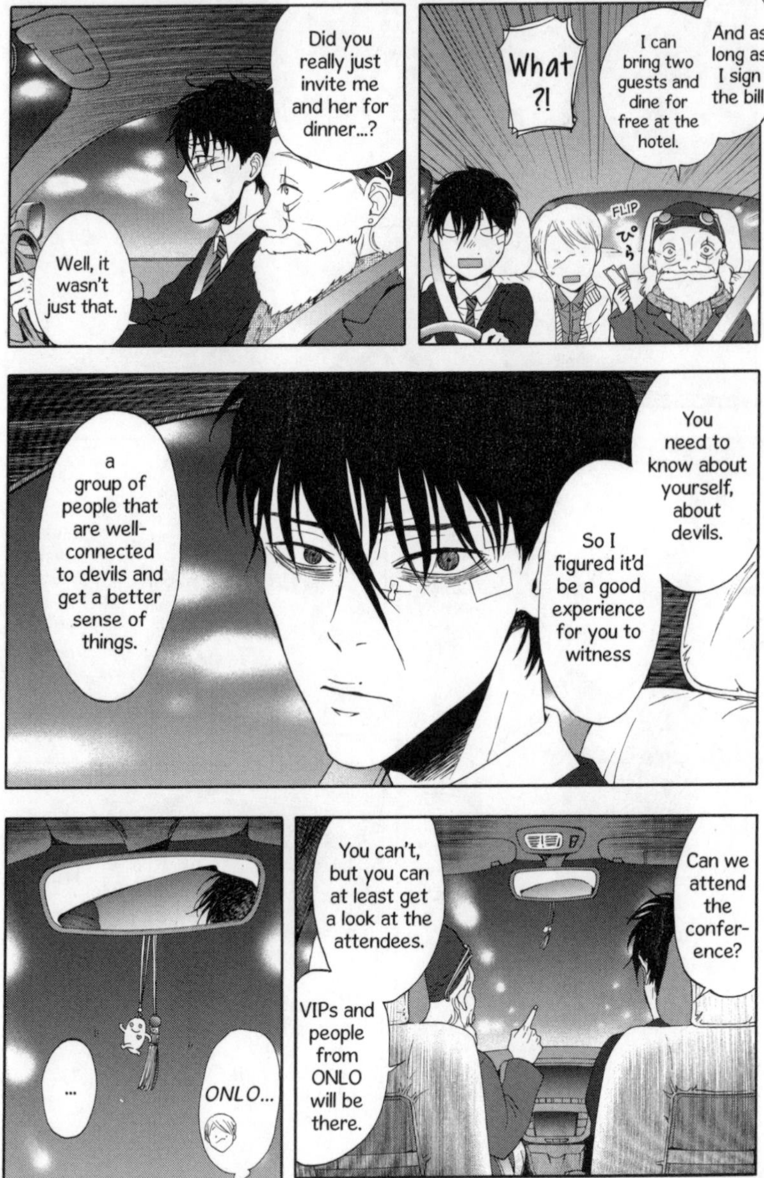
And as long as I sign the bill,
I can bring two guests and dine for free at the hotel.
What?!
FLIP
ぴら
Did you really just invite me and her for dinner...?
Well, it wasn't just that.
You need to know about yourself, about devils.
So I figured it'd be a good experience for you to witness
a group of people that are well-connected to devils and get a better sense of things.
Can we attend the confer-ence?
You can't, but you can at least get a look at the attendees.
VIPs and people from ONLO will be there.
...
ONLO...

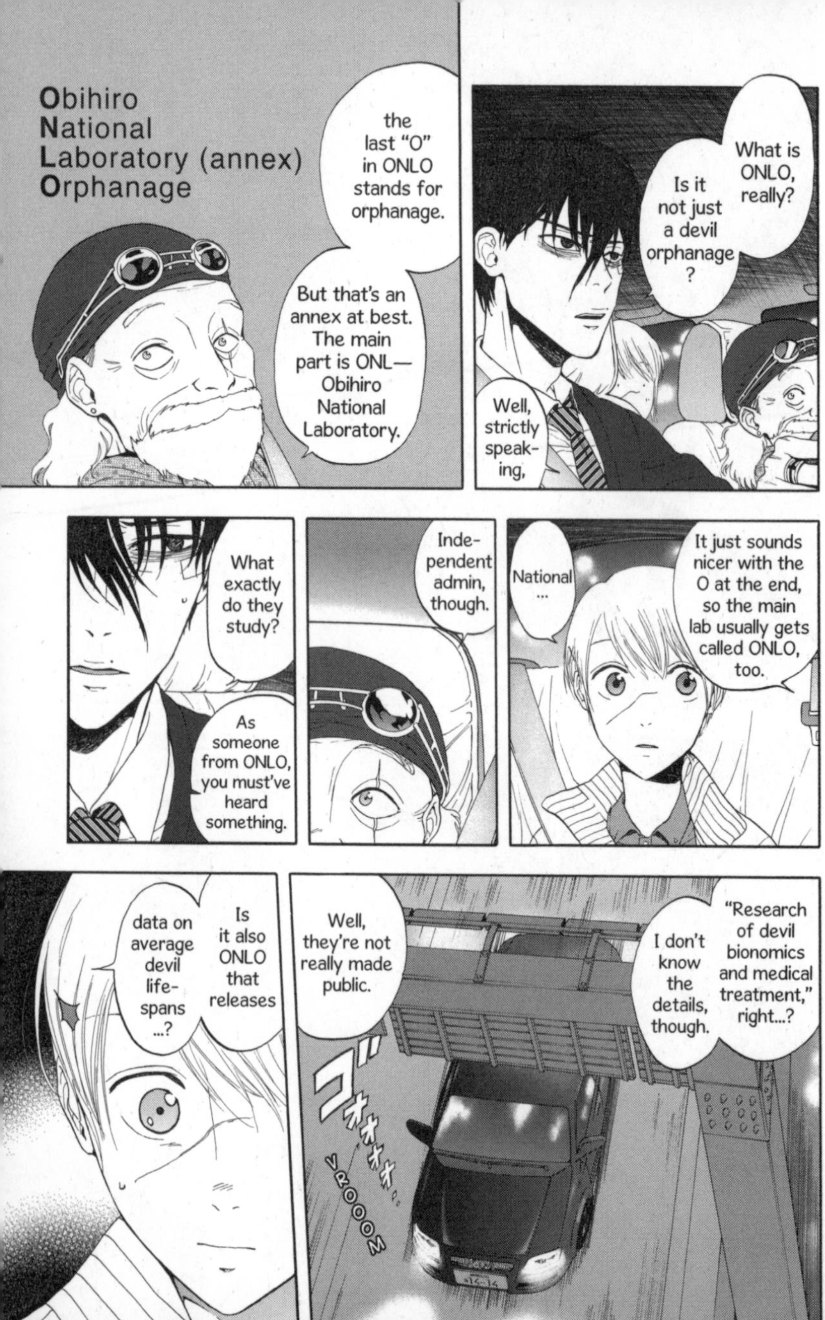
What is ONLO, really?
Is it not just a devil orphanage?
Well, strictly speaking,
the last "O" in ONLO stands for orphanage.
Obihiro National Laboratory (annex) Orphanage
But that's an annex at best. The main part is ONL—Obihiro National Laboratory.
It just sounds nicer with the O at the end, so the main lab usually gets called ONLO, too.
National...
Independent admin, though.
What exactly do they study?
As someone from ONLO, you must've heard something.
"Research of devil bionomics and medical treatment," right...?
I don't know the details, though.
Well, they're not really made public.
VROOOM
Is it also ONLO that releases
data on average devil life-spans...?

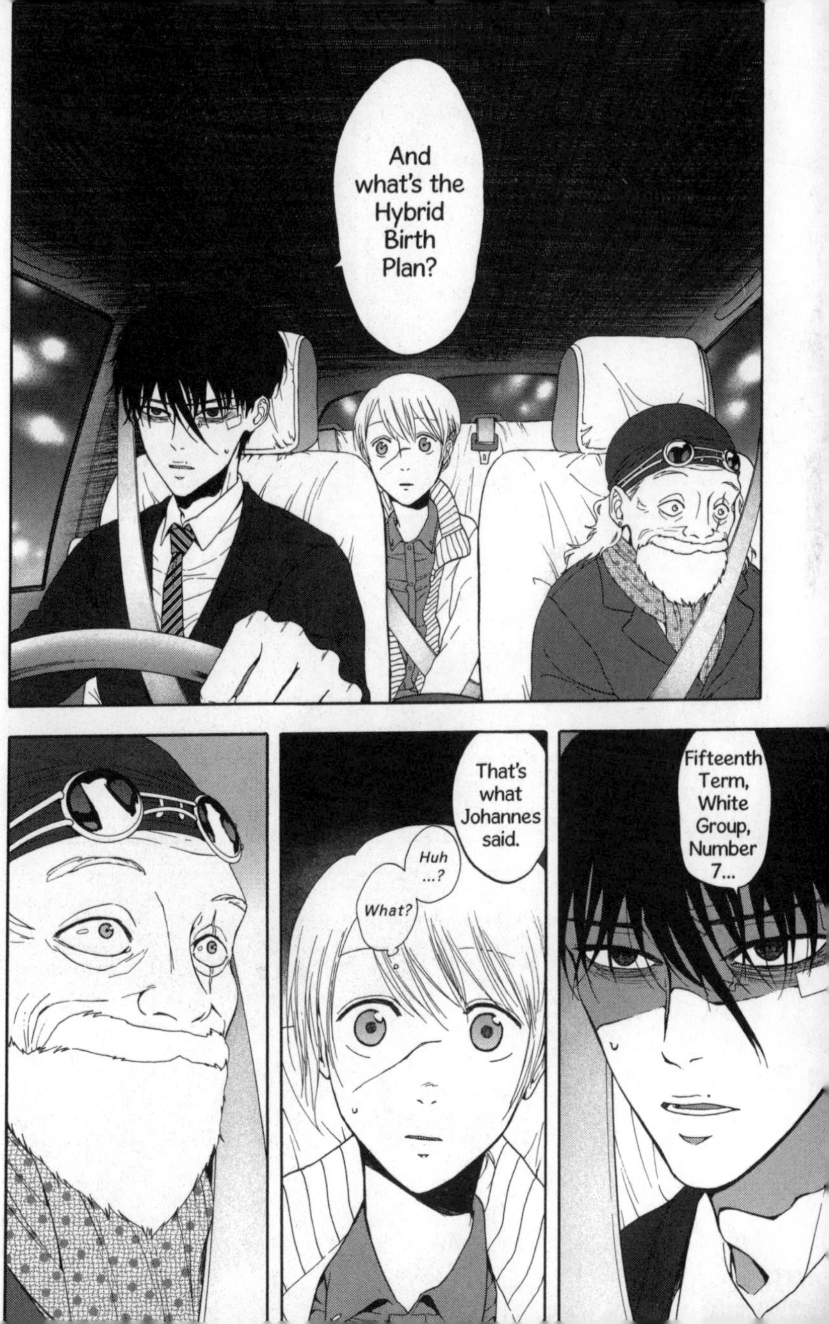
And what's the Hybrid Birth Plan?
Fifteenth Term, White Group, Number 7...
That's what Johannes said.
Huh ...?
What?

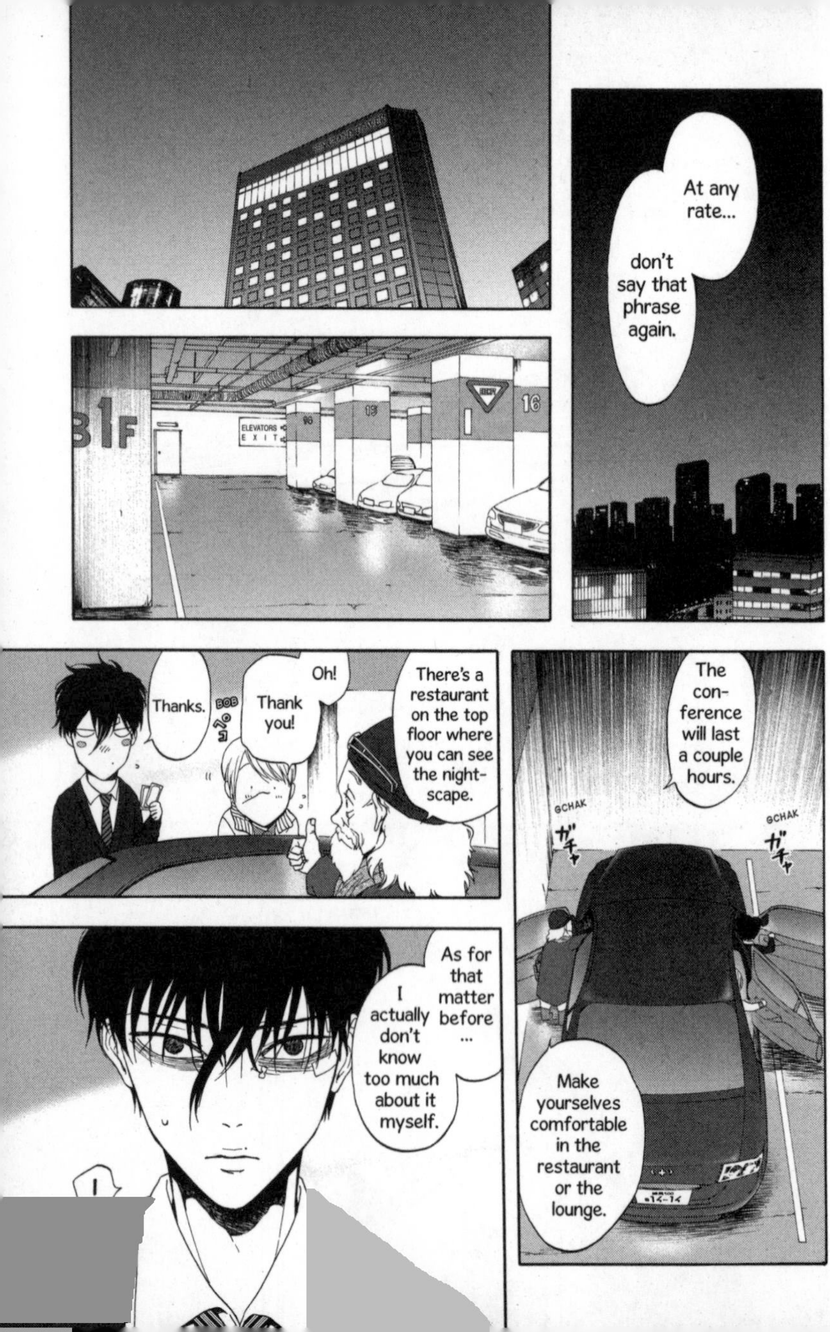
At any rate...
don't say that phrase again.
B1F
ELEVATORS EXIT
16
The conference will last a couple hours.
GCHAK
GCHAK
Make yourselves comfortable in the restaurant or the lounge.
There's a restaurant on the top floor where you can see the night-scape.
Oh!
Thank you!
BOB
Thanks.
As for that matter before ...
I actually don't know too much about it myself.

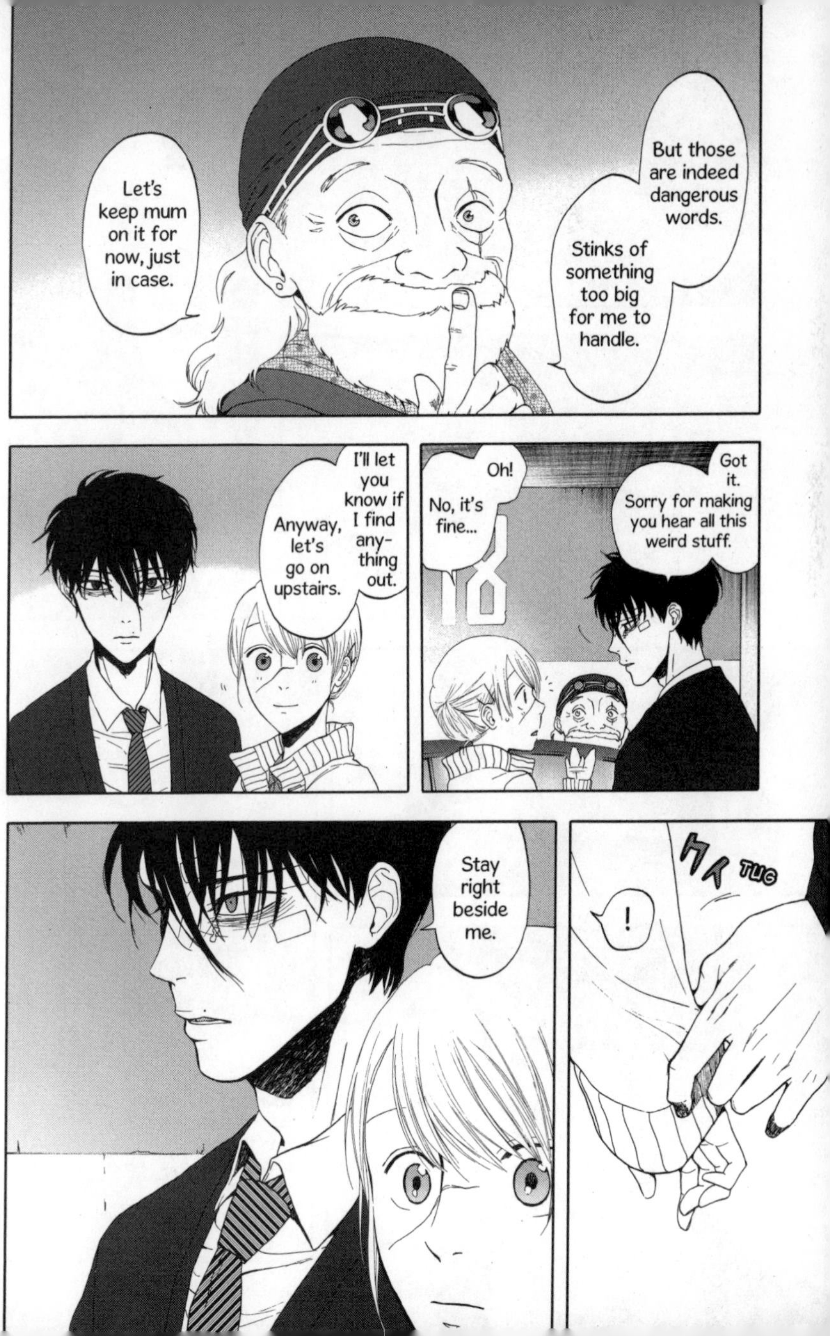
But those are indeed dangerous words.
Stinks of something too big for me to handle.
Let's keep mum on it for now, just in case.
Got it. Sorry for making you hear all this weird stuff.
Oh!
No, it's fine...
I'll let you know if I find any-thing out.
Anyway, let's go on upstairs.
クイ
TUG
!
Stay right beside me.

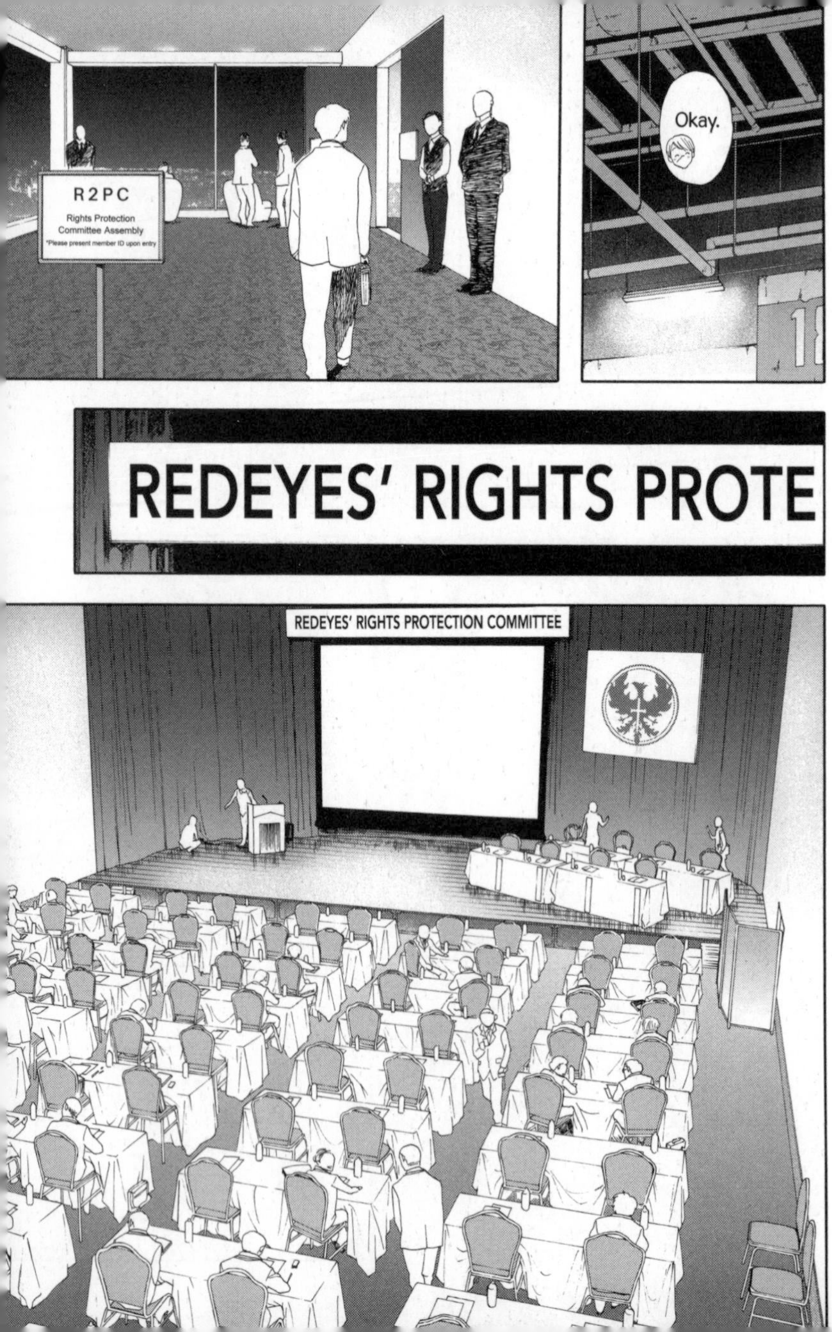
Okay.
R2PC
Rights Protection
Committee Assembly
*Please present member ID upon entry
REDEYES' RIGHTS PROTE
REDEYES' RIGHTS PROTECTION COMMITTEE

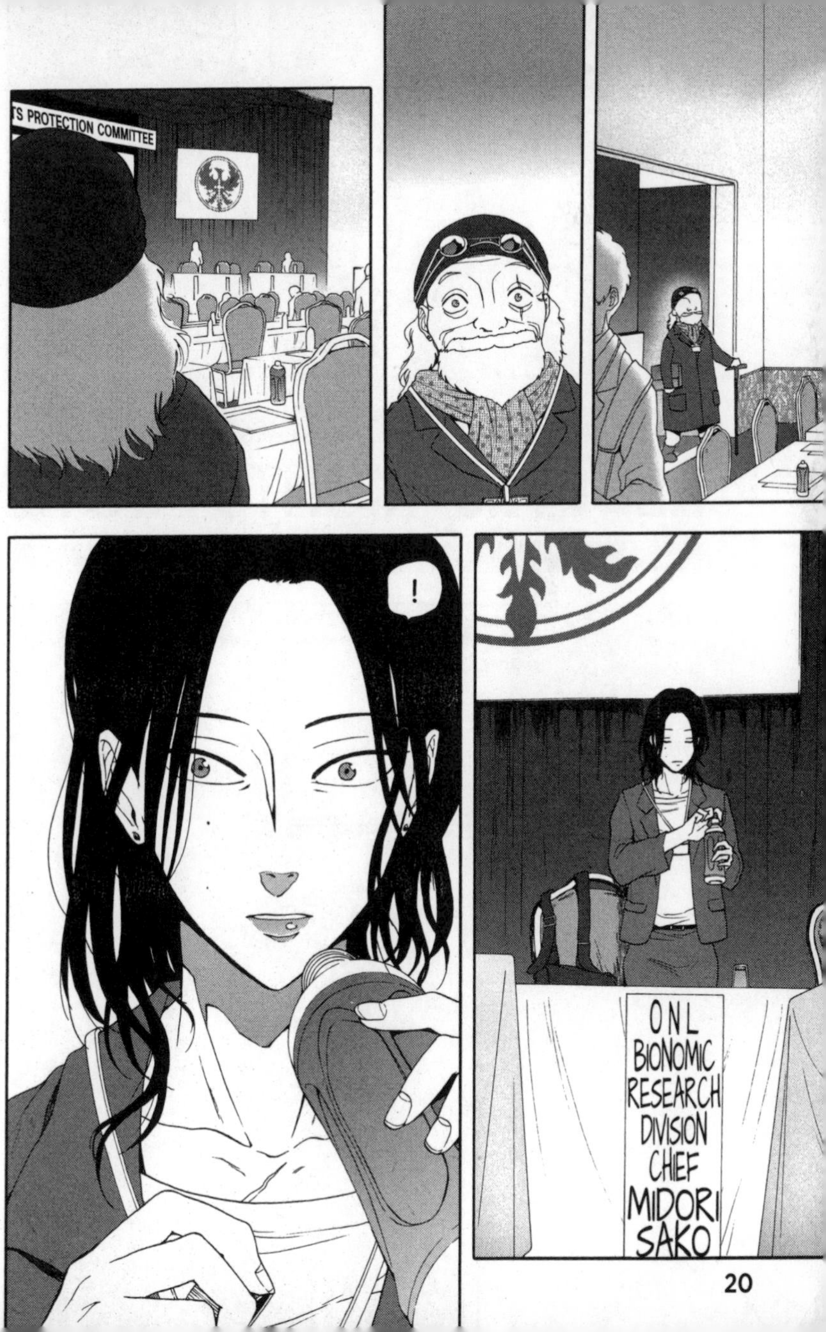
TS PROTECTION COMMITTEE
ONL BIONOMIC RESEARCH DIVISION CHIEF MIDORI SAKO
!

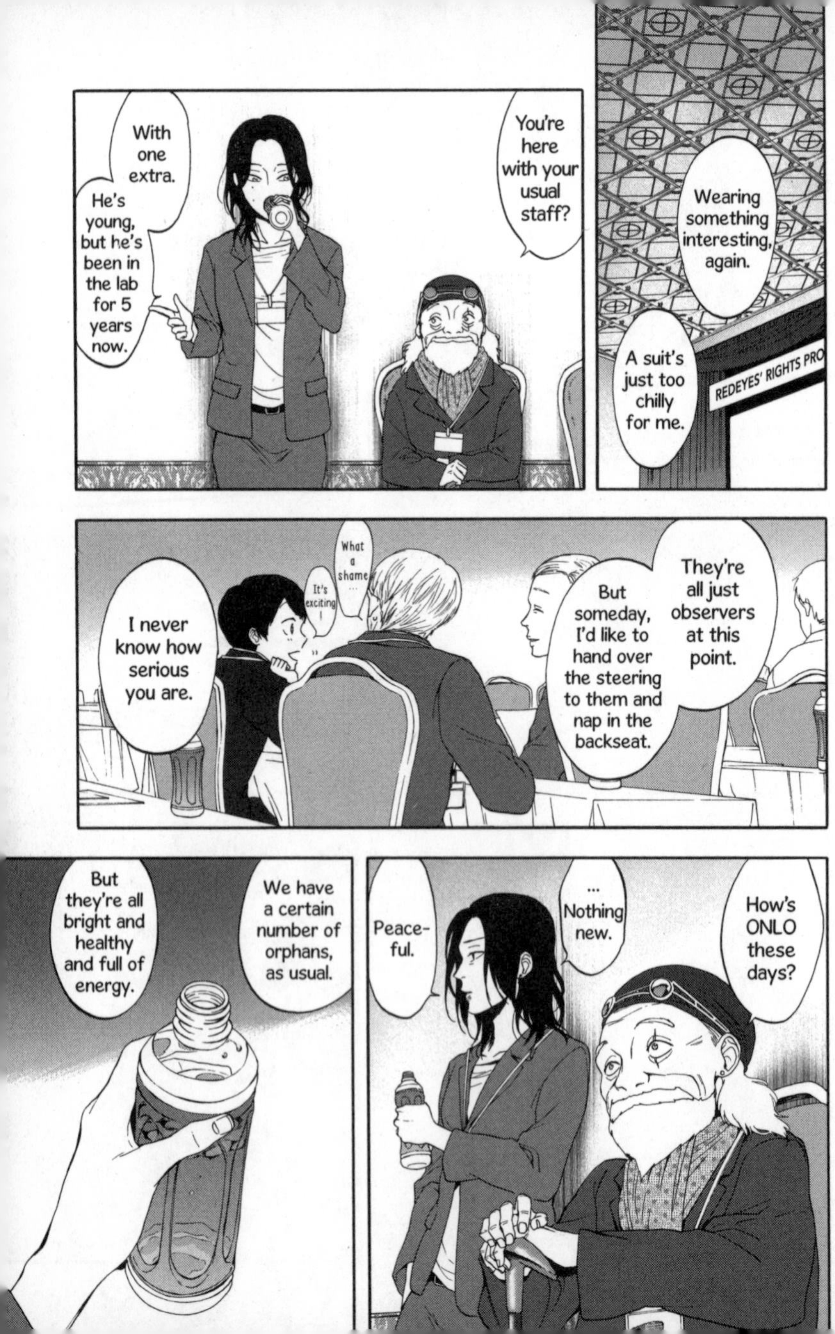
Wearing something interesting, again.
A suit's just too chilly for me.
REDEYES' RIGHTS PRO
You're here with your usual staff?
With one extra.
He's young, but he's been in the lab for 5 years now.
They're all just observers at this point.
But someday, I'd like to hand over the steering to them and nap in the backseat.
What a shame ...
It's exciting!
I never know how serious you are.
How's ONLO these days?
... Nothing new.
Peace-ful.
We have a certain number of orphans, as usual.
But they're all bright and healthy and full of energy.

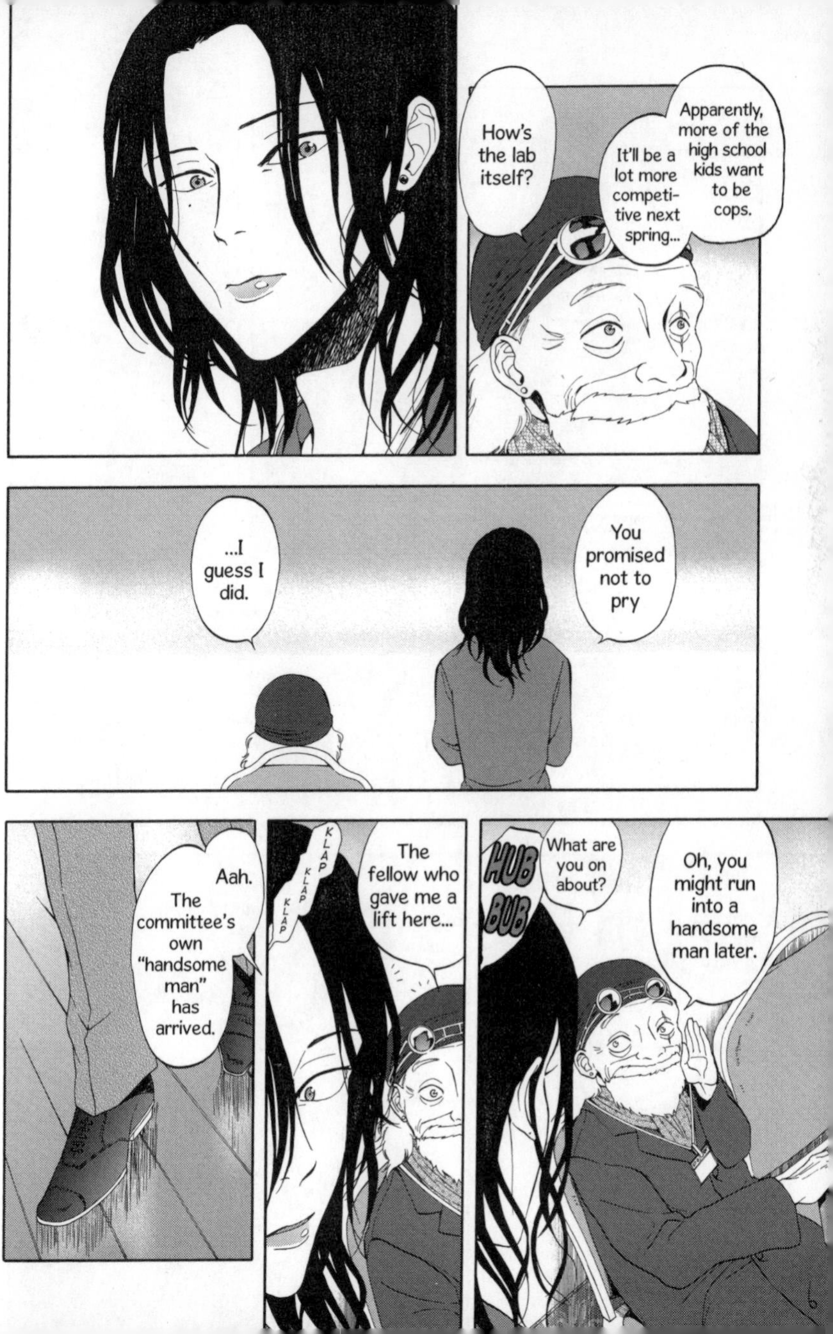
Apparently, more of the high school kids want to be cops.
It'll be a lot more competitive next spring...
How's the lab itself?
You promised not to pry
...I guess I did.
Oh, you might run into a handsome man later.
What are you on about?
HUB BUB
The fellow who gave me a lift here...
KLAP KLAP KLAP
Aah. The committee's own "handsome man" has arrived.

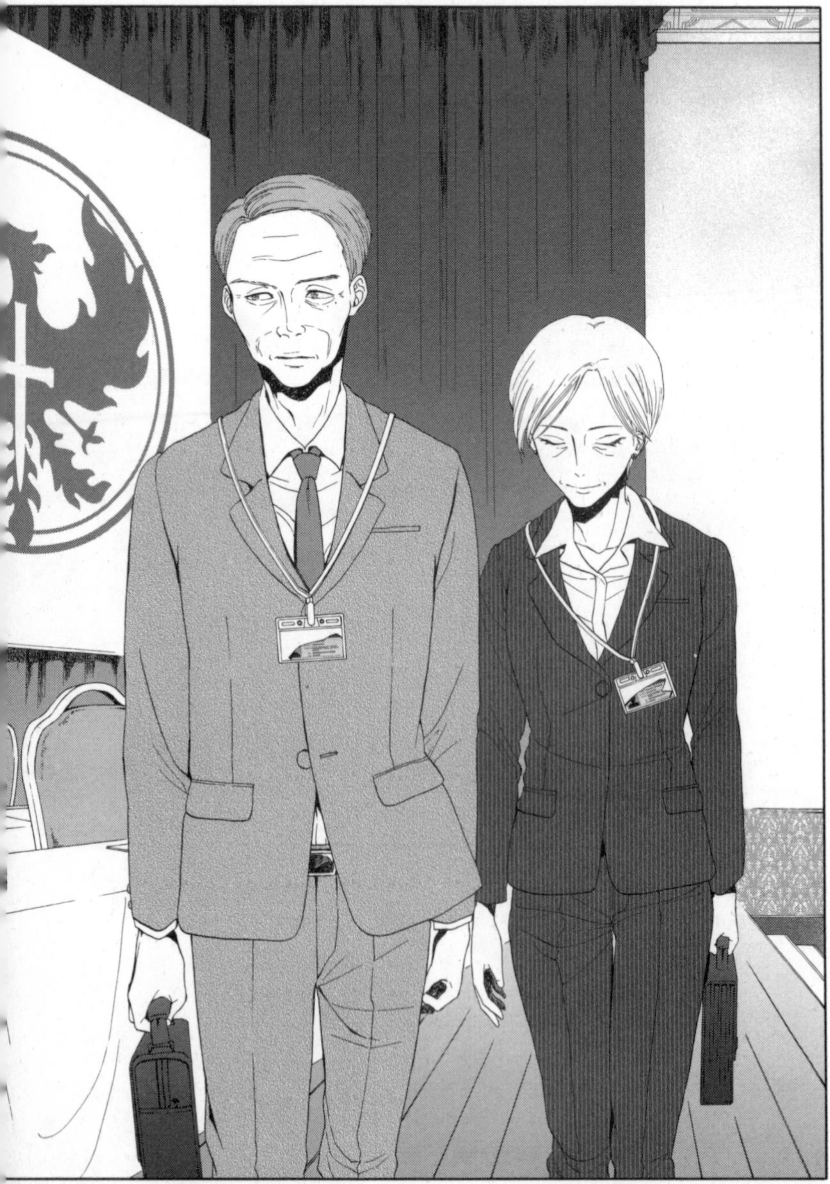

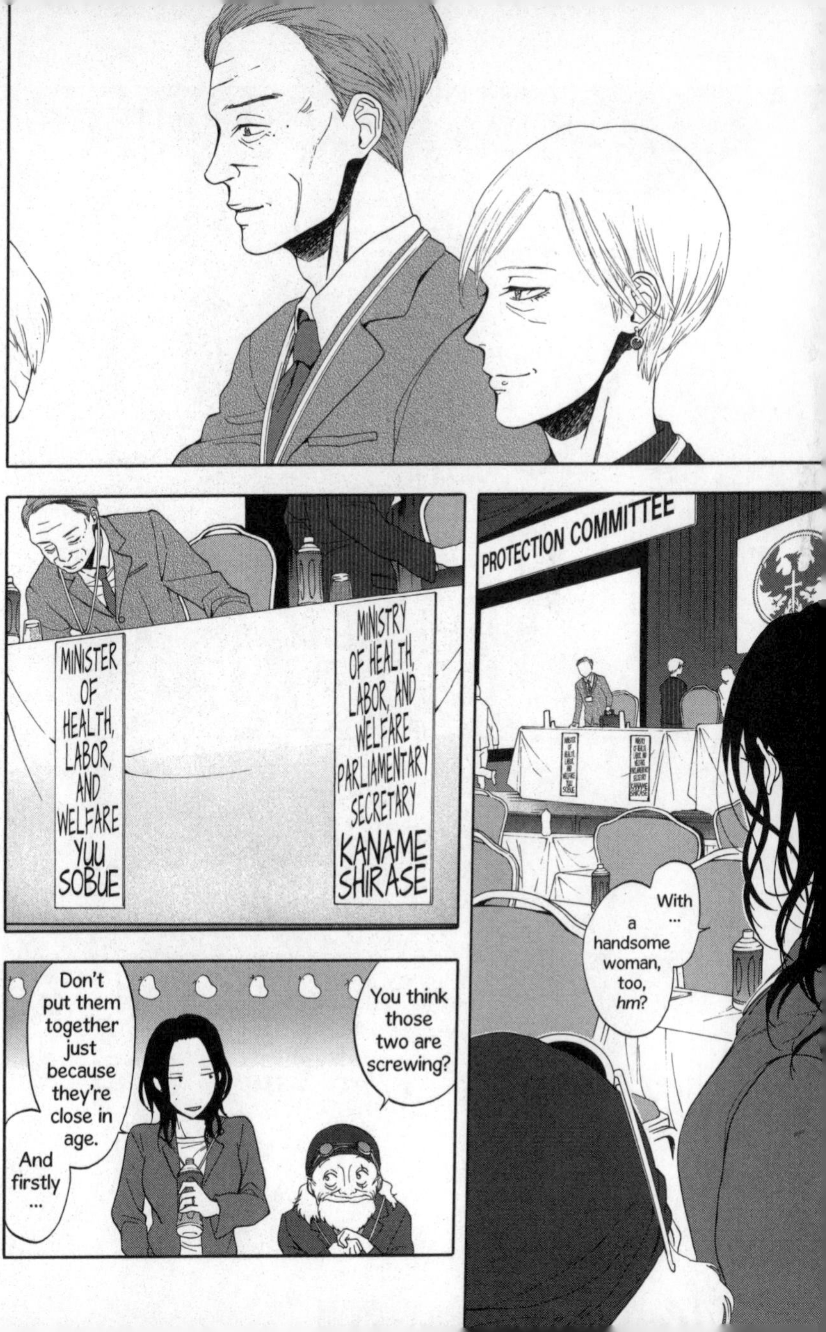
PROTECTION COMMITTEE
With ... a handsome woman, too, *hm*?
MINISTRY OF HEALTH, LABOR, AND WELFARE PARLIAMENTARY SECRETARY KANAME SHIRASE
MINISTER OF HEALTH, LABOR, AND WELFARE YUU SOBUE
You think those two are screwing?
Don't put them together just because they're close in age.
And firstly ...

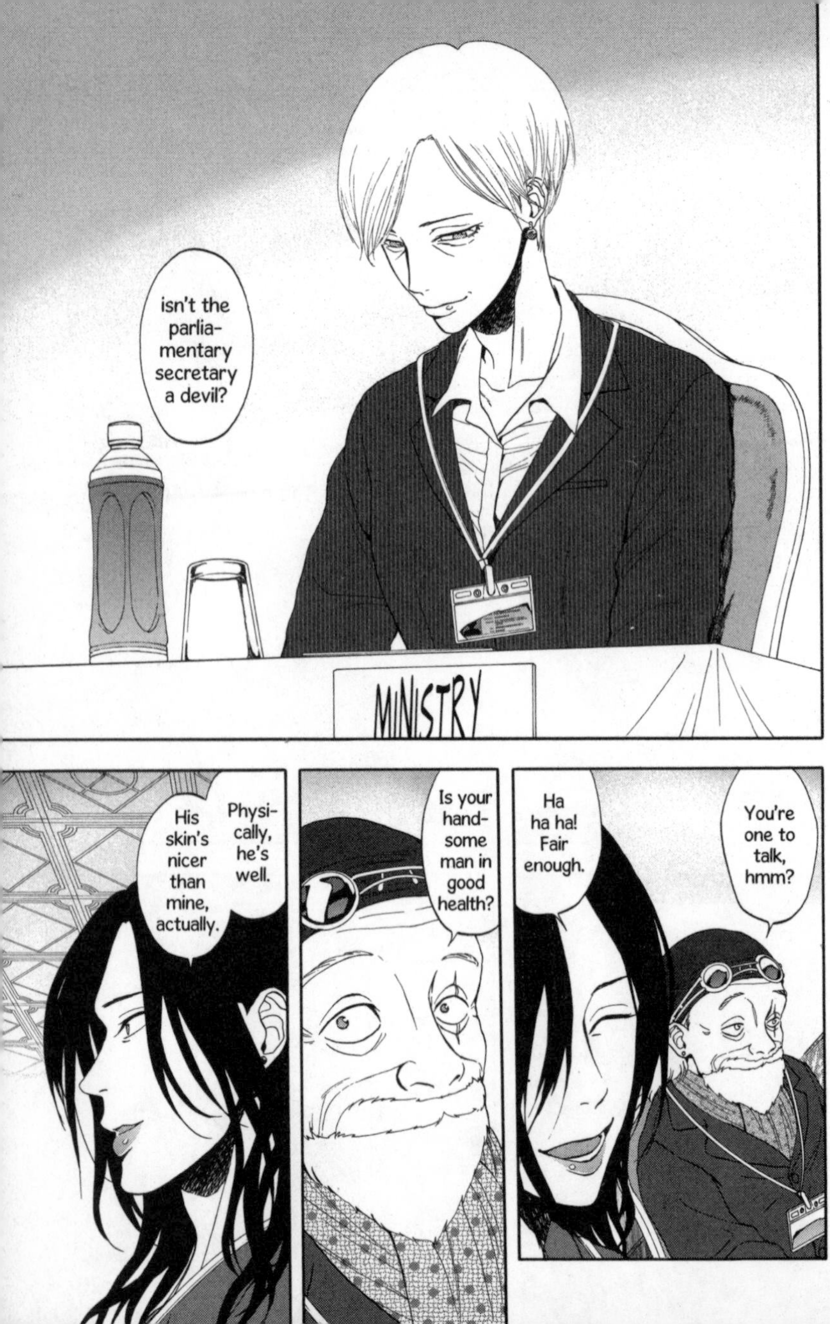
isn't the parliamentary secretary a devil?
MINISTRY
You're one to talk, hmm?
Ha ha ha! Fair enough.
Is your handsome man in good health?
Physically, he's well.
His skin's nicer than mine, actually.

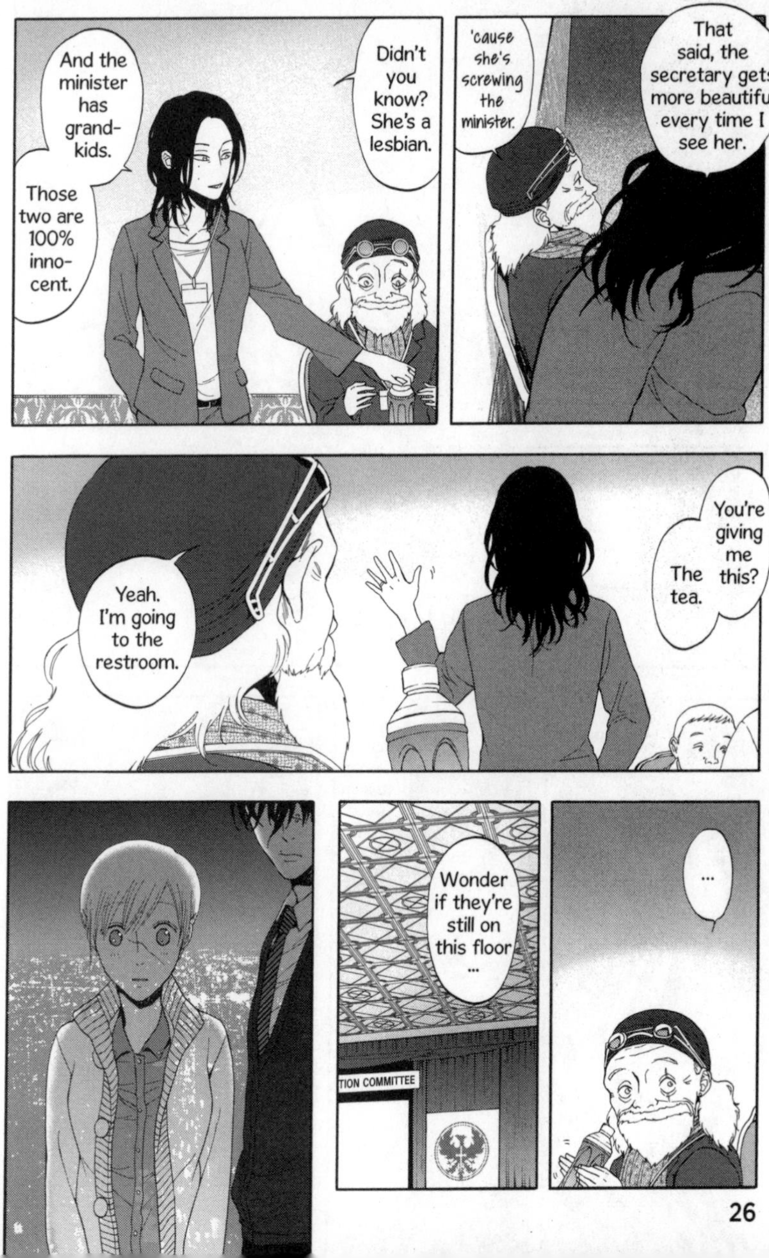
That said, the secretary gets more beautiful every time I see her.
'cause she's screwing the minister.
Didn't you know? She's a lesbian.
And the minister has grand-kids.
Those two are 100% inno-cent.
You're giving me this?
The tea.
Yeah. I'm going to the restroom.
...
Wonder if they're still on this floor...
TION COMMITTEE

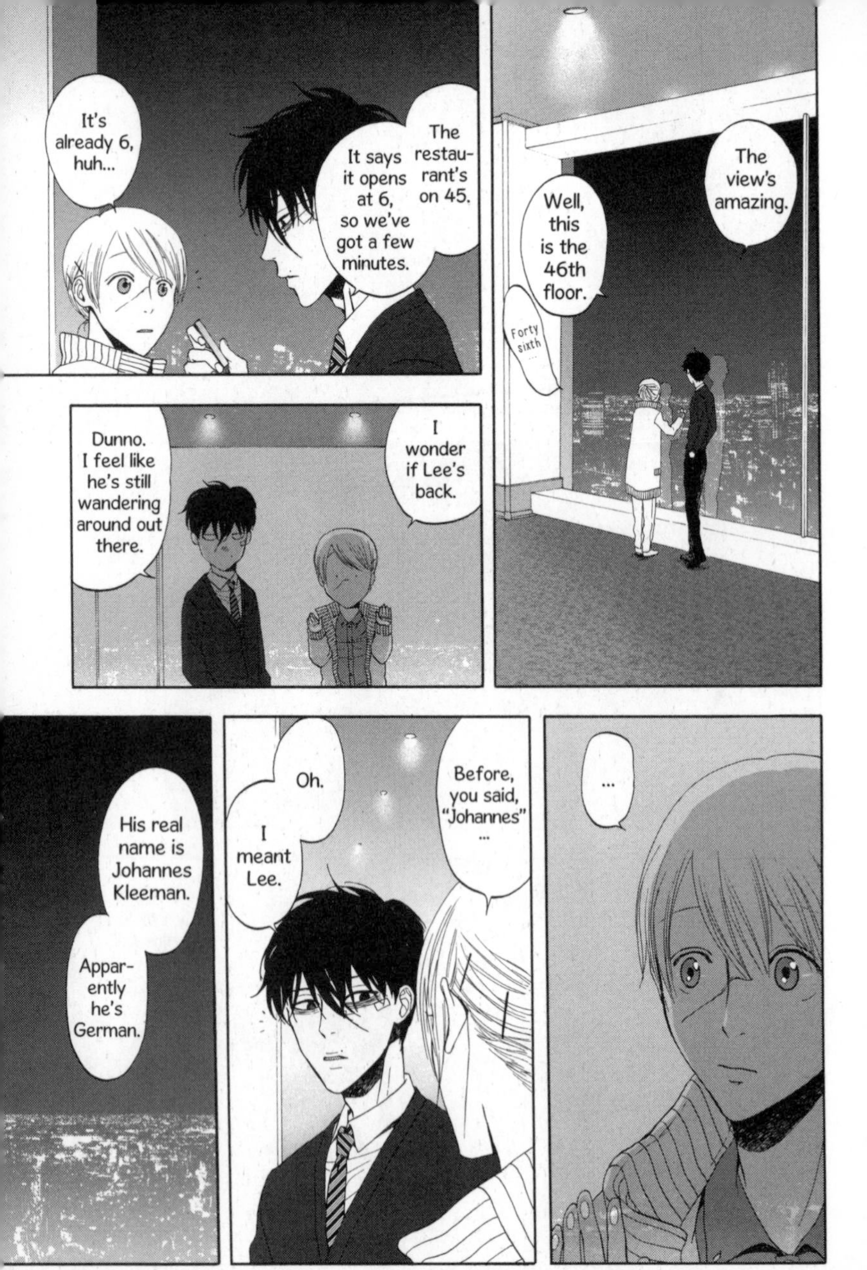
The view's amazing.
Well, this is the 46th floor.
Forty sixth...
The restaurant's on 45.
It says it opens at 6, so we've got a few minutes.
It's already 6, huh...
I wonder if Lee's back.
Dunno. I feel like he's still wandering around out there.
...
Before, you said, "Johannes"...
Oh.
I meant Lee.
His real name is Johannes Kleeman.
Apparently he's German.

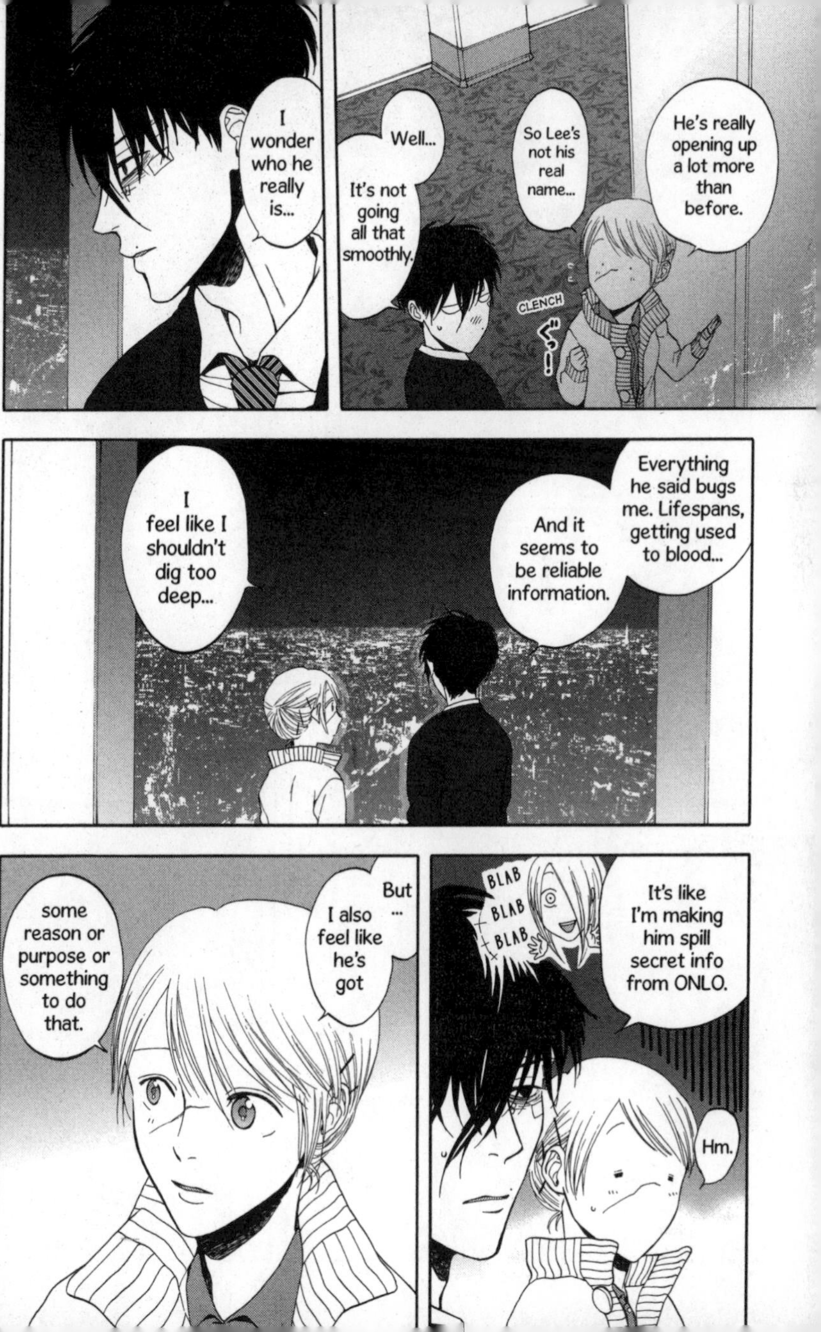
He's really opening up a lot more than before.
CLENCH
So Lee's not his real name...
Well...
It's not going all that smoothly.
I wonder who he really is...
Everything he said bugs me. Lifespans, getting used to blood...
And it seems to be reliable information.
I feel like I shouldn't dig too deep...
BLAB BLAB BLAB
It's like I'm making him spill secret info from ONLO.
Hm.
But...
I also feel like he's got
some reason or purpose or something to do that.

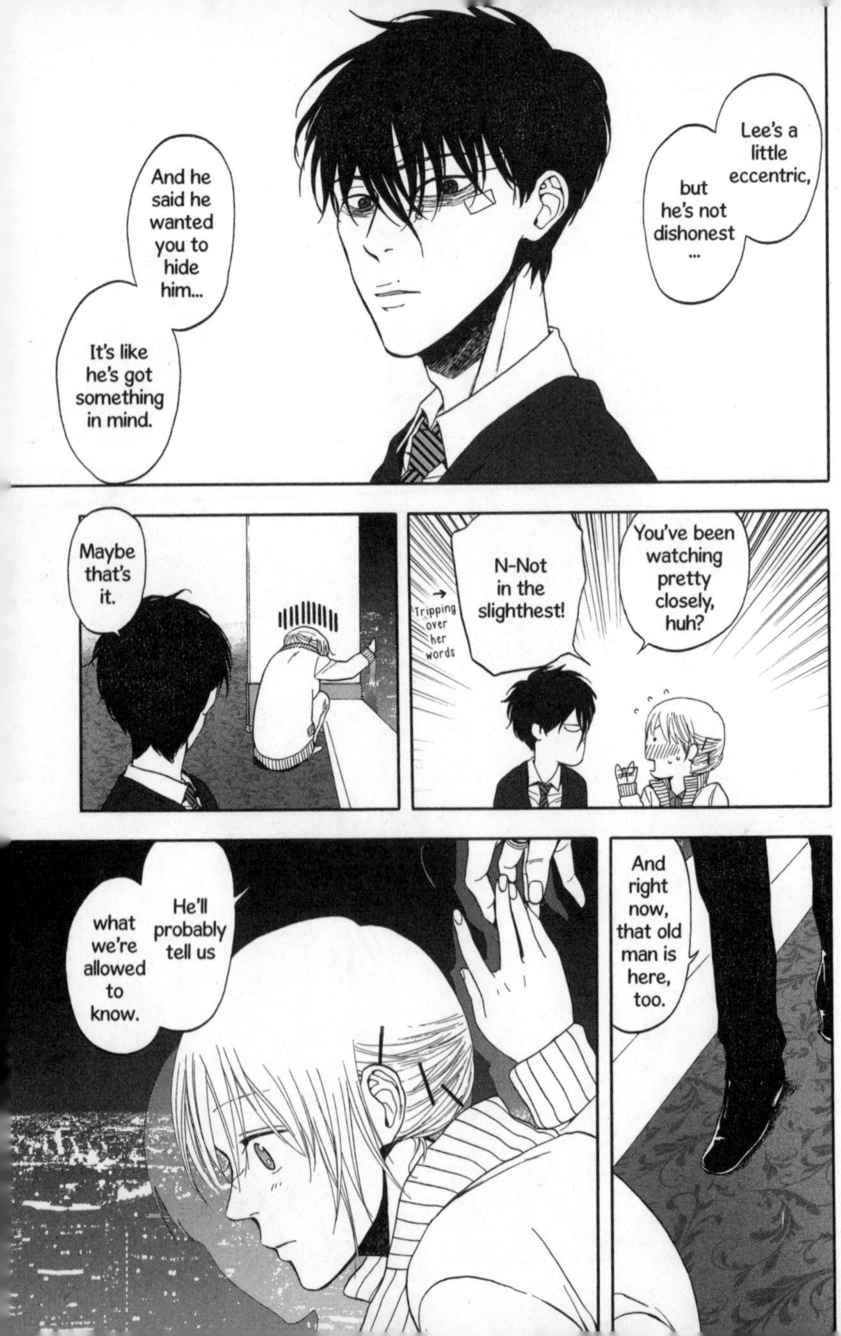
Lee's a little eccentric, but he's not dishonest ...
And he said he wanted you to hide him...
It's like he's got something in mind.
You've been watching pretty closely, huh?
N-Not in the slightest!
→ Tripping over her words
Maybe that's it.
And right now, that old man is here, too.
He'll probably tell us what we're allowed to know.

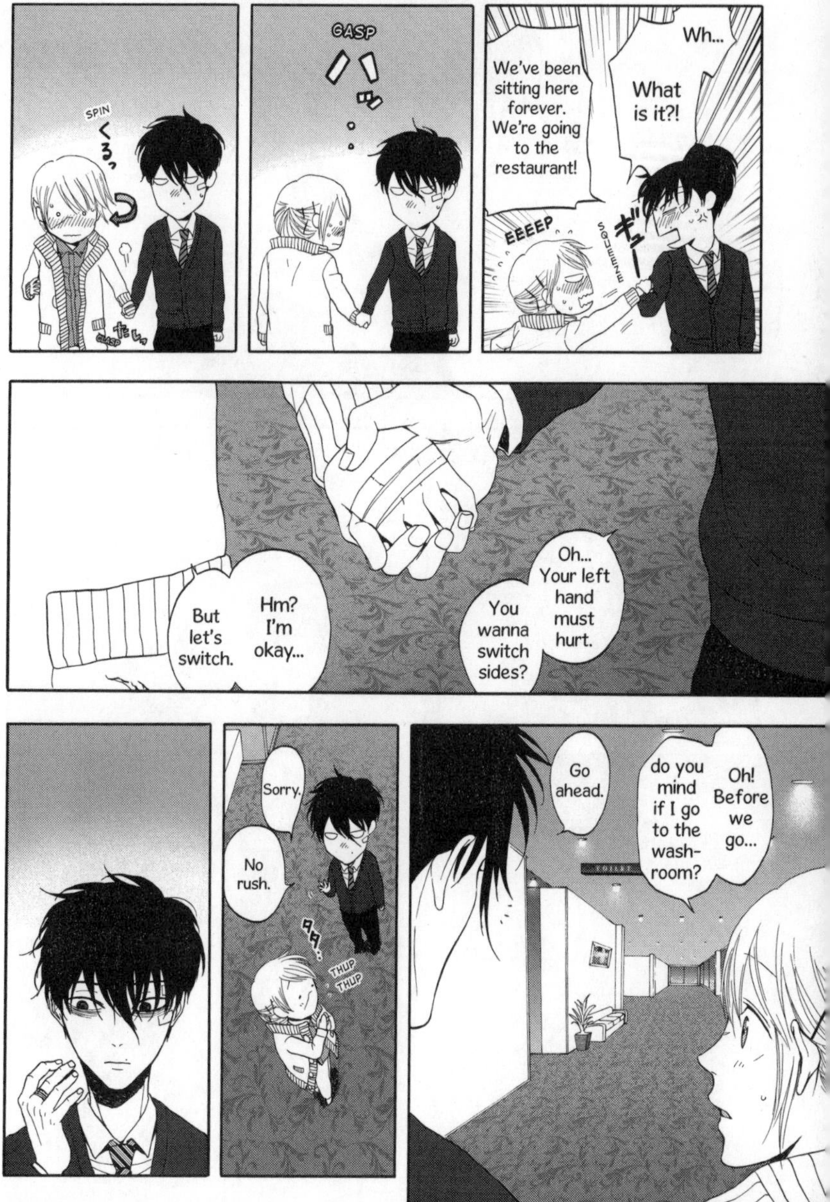
Wh...
What is it?!
We've been sitting here forever. We're going to the restaurant!
EEEEP
SQUEEZE
ギュー
GASP
ハッ
SPIN
GASP
Oh... Your left hand must hurt.
You wanna switch sides?
Hm? I'm okay...
But let's switch.
Oh! Before we go...
do you mind if I go to the wash-room?
Go ahead.
Sorry.
No rush.
タタ…
THUP THUP

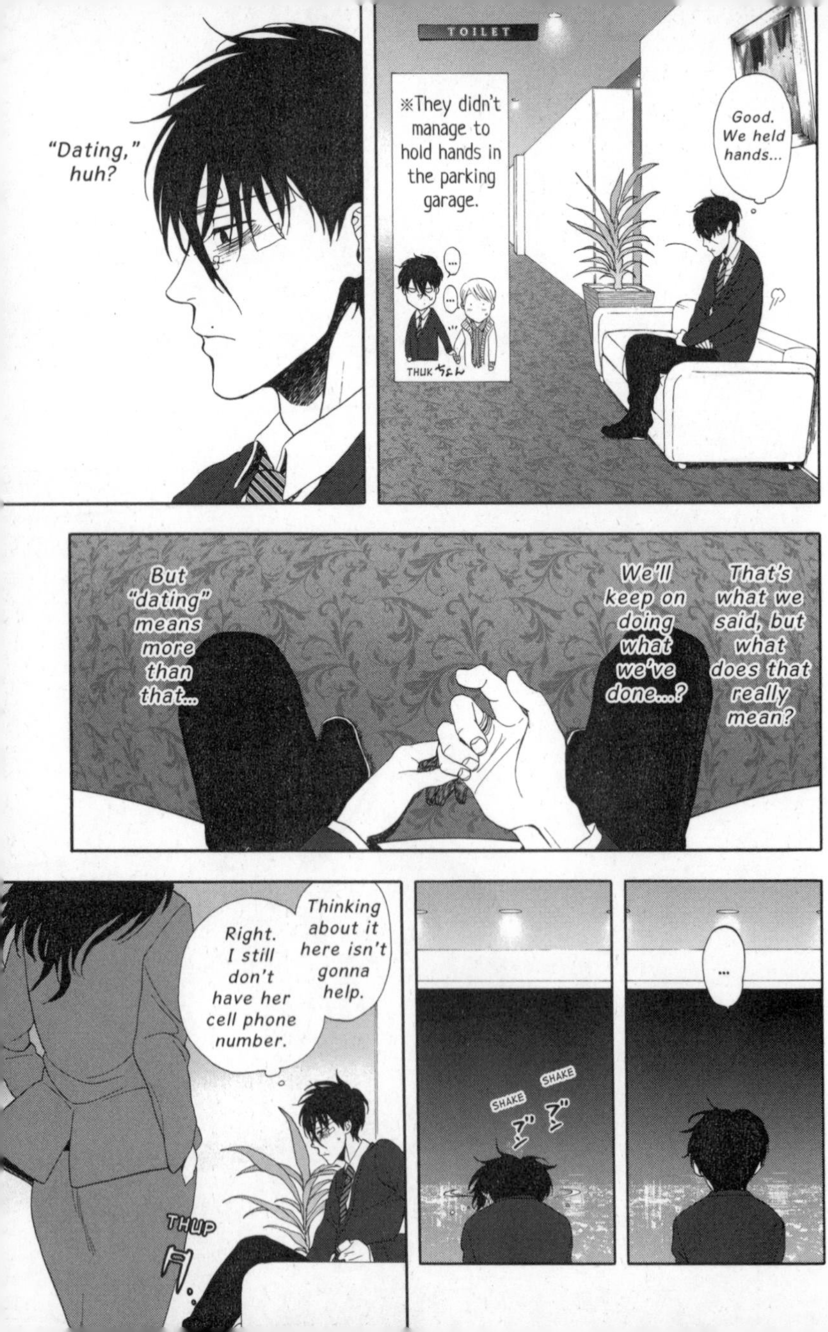
TOILET
Good. We held hands...
※They didn't manage to hold hands in the parking garage.
...
...
THUK
"Dating," huh?
That's what we said, but what does that really mean?
We'll keep on doing what we've done...?
But "dating" means more than that...
...
SHAKE
SHAKE
Thinking about it here isn't gonna help.
Right. I still don't have her cell phone number.
THUP

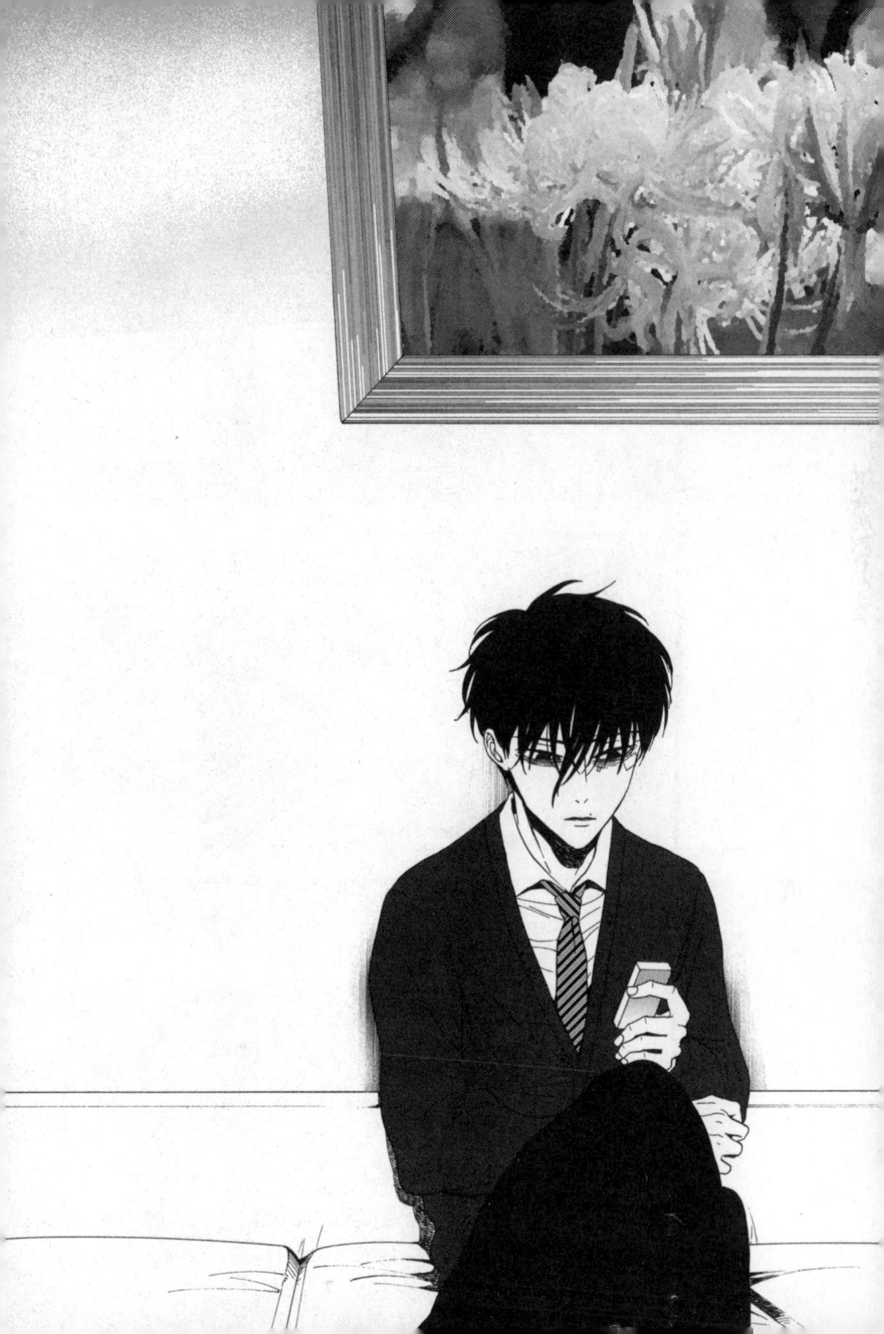

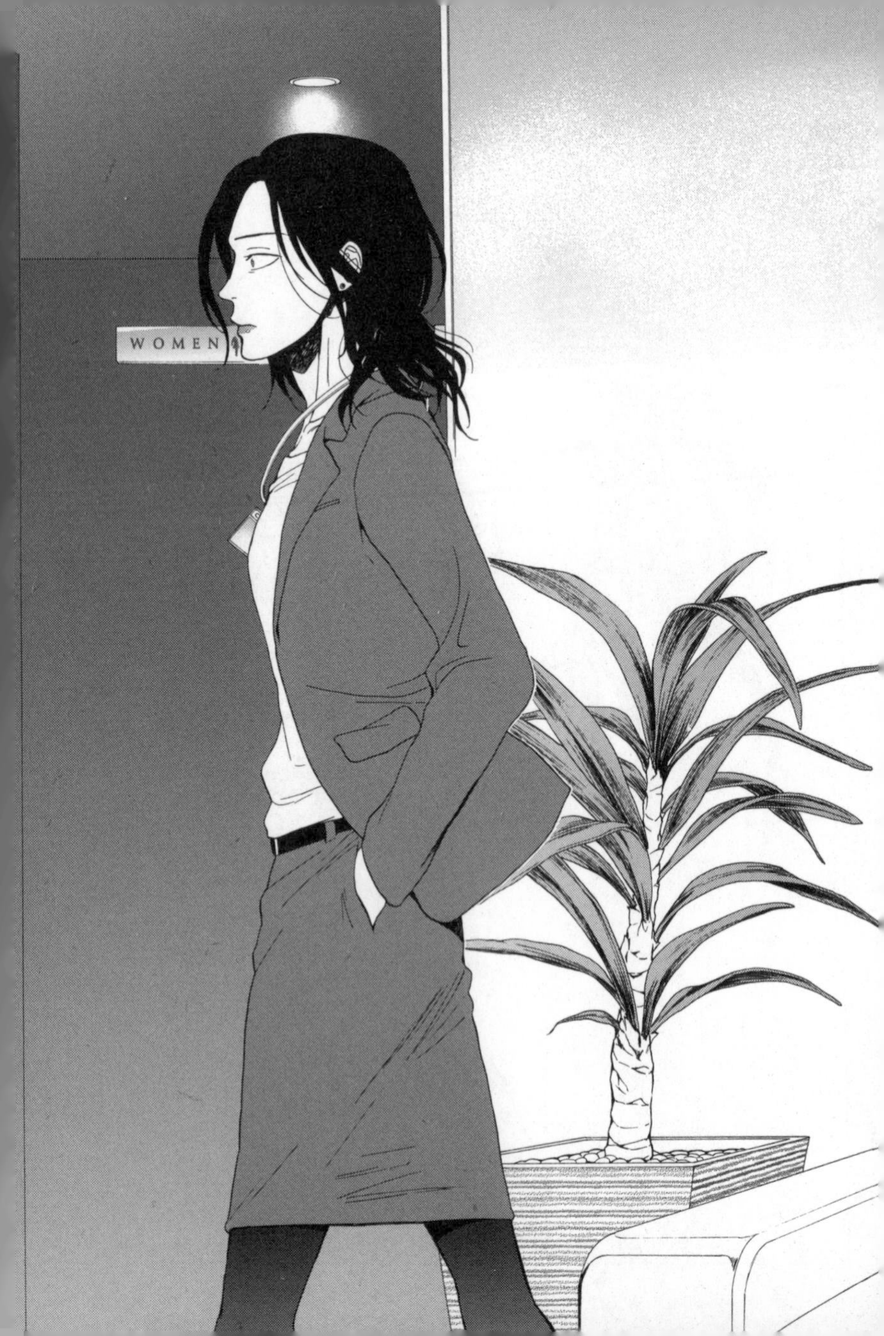
WOMEN

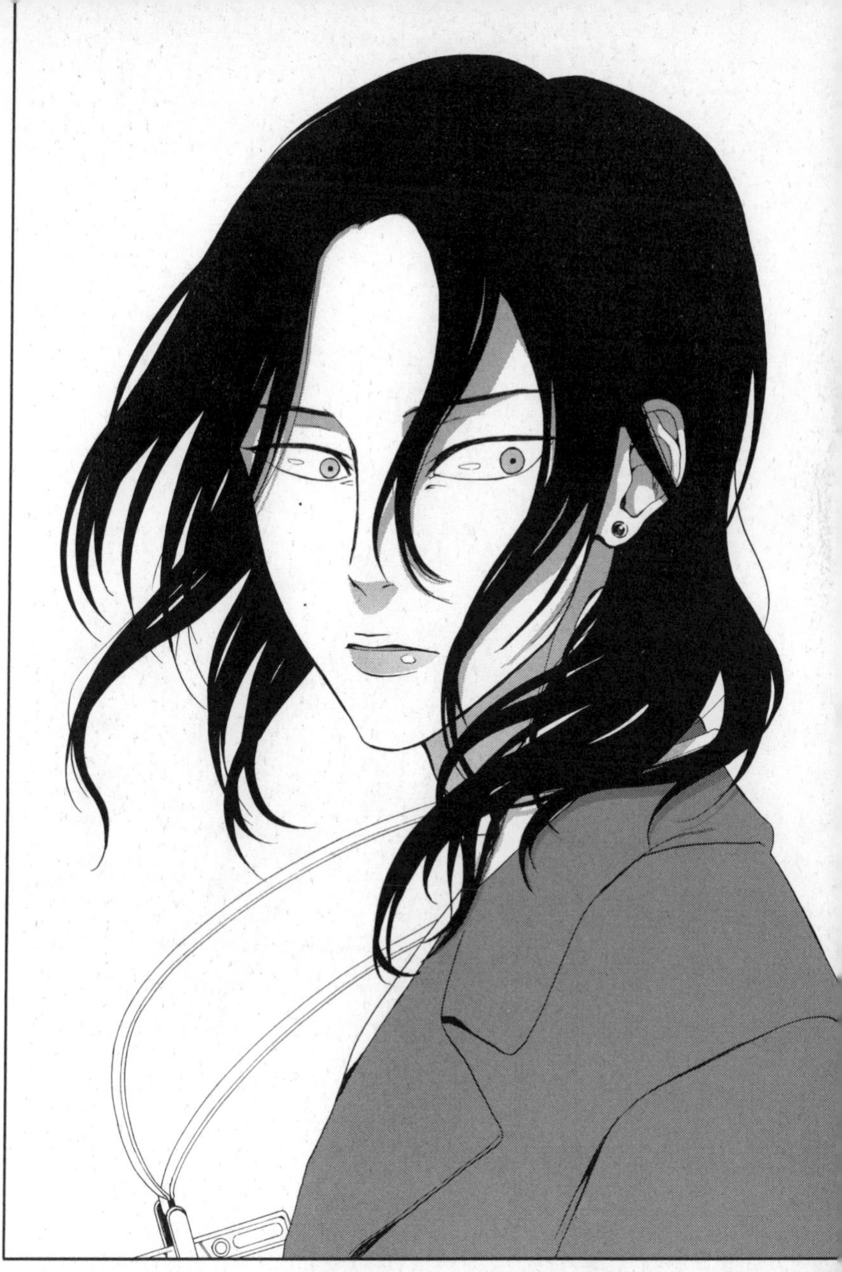

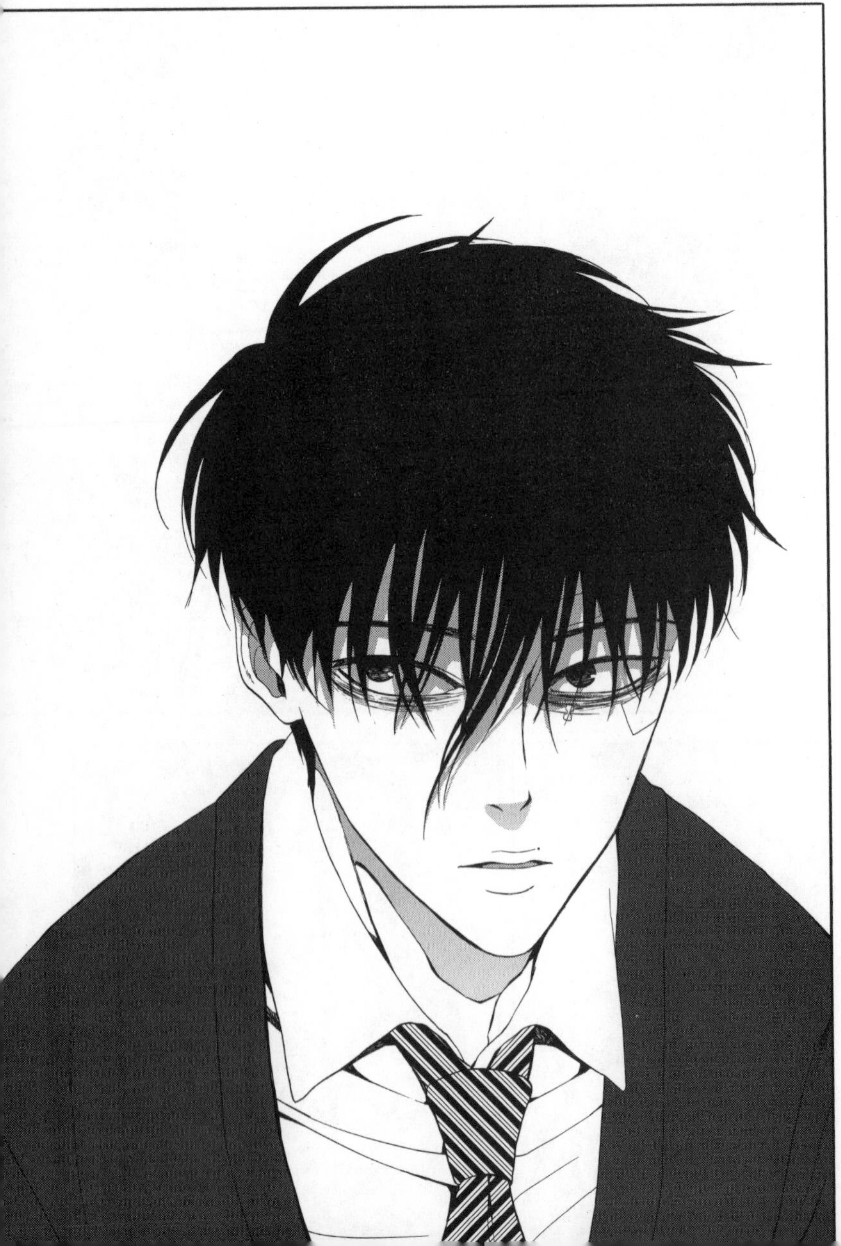

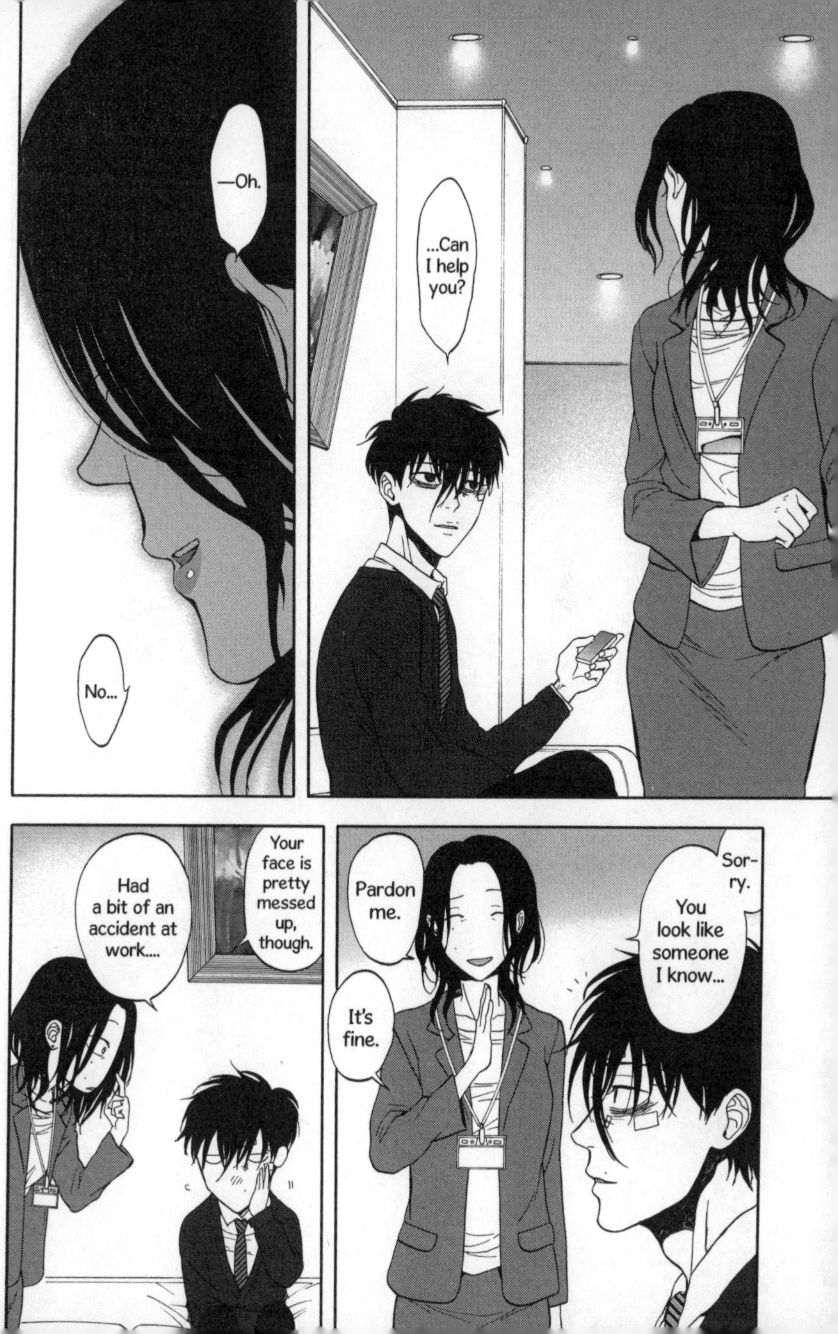
...Can I help you?
—Oh.
No...
Sor-ry. You look like someone I know...
Pardon me.
It's fine.
Your face is pretty messed up, though.
Had a bit of an accident at work....

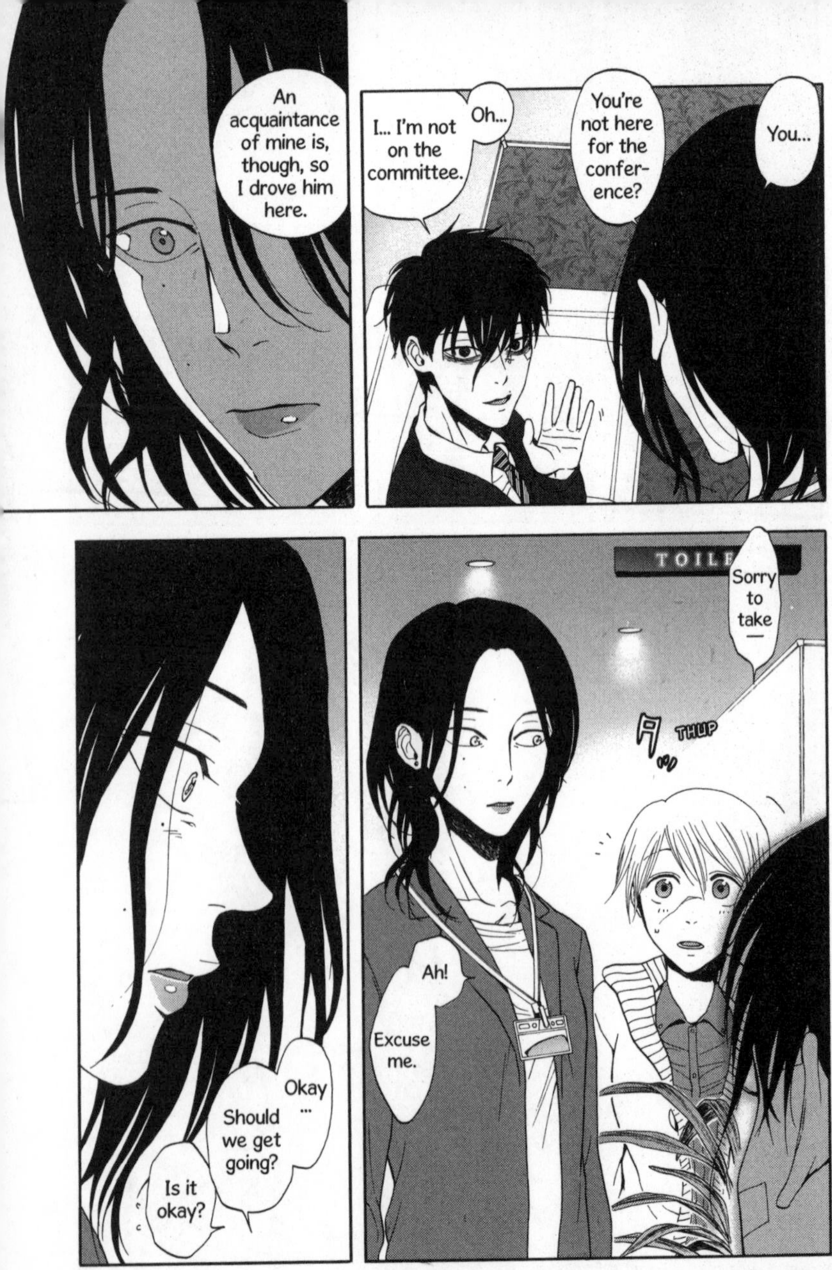
You...
You're not here for the confer-ence?
Oh...
I... I'm not on the committee.
An acquaintance of mine is, though, so I drove him here.
TOILE
Sorry to take —
THUP
Ah!
Excuse me.
Okay ...
Should we get going?
Is it okay?

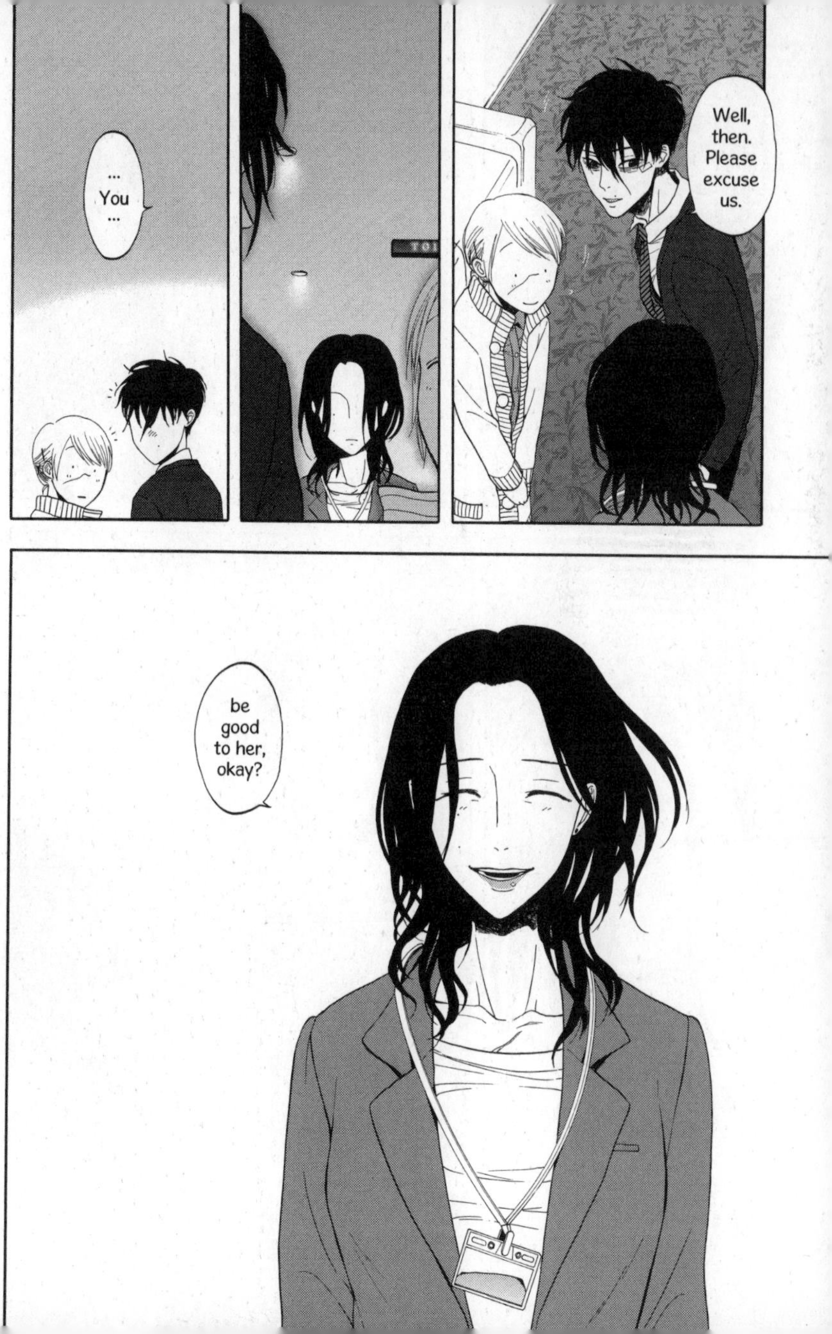
Well, then. Please excuse us.
... You ...
be good to her, okay?

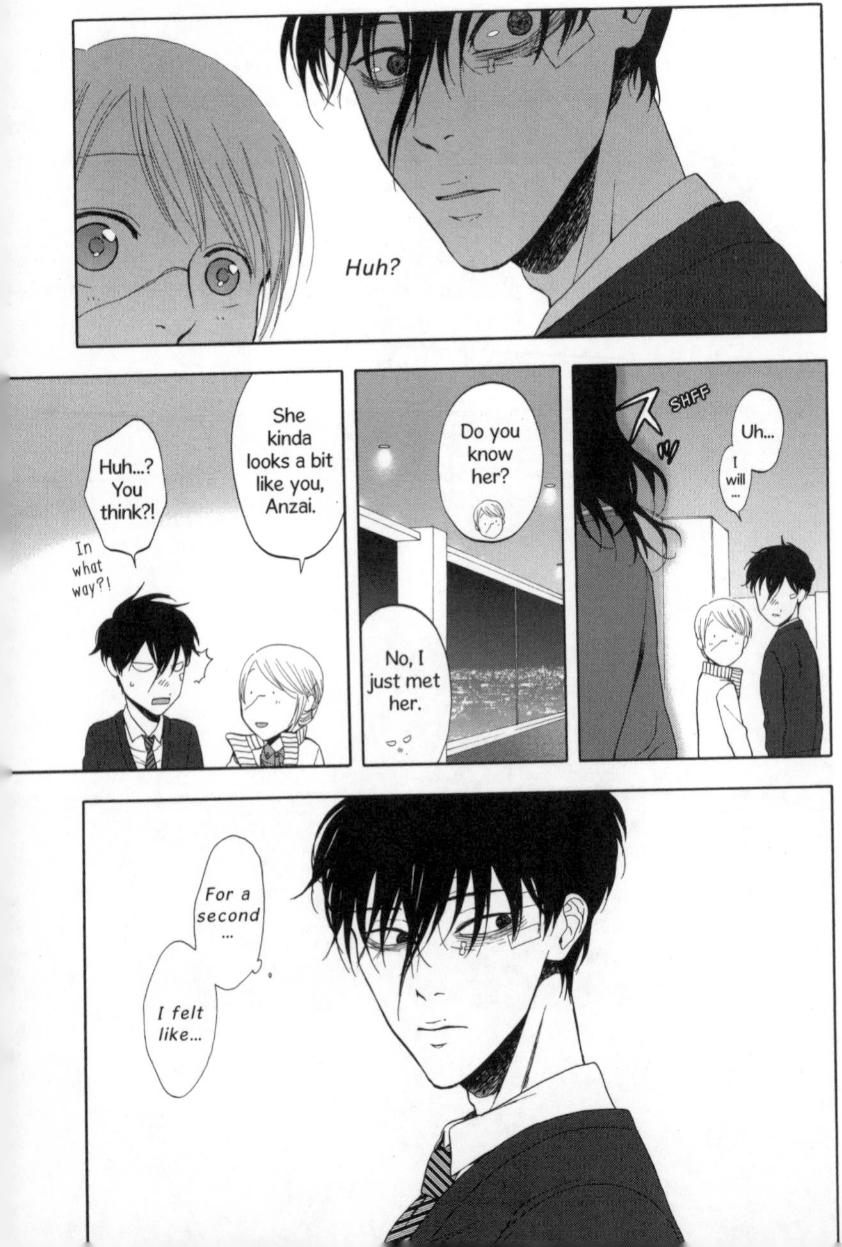
Huh?
SHFF
Uh...
I will ...
Do you know her?
No, I just met her.
She kinda looks a bit like you, Anzai.
Huh...? You think?!
In what way?!
For a second ...
I felt like...

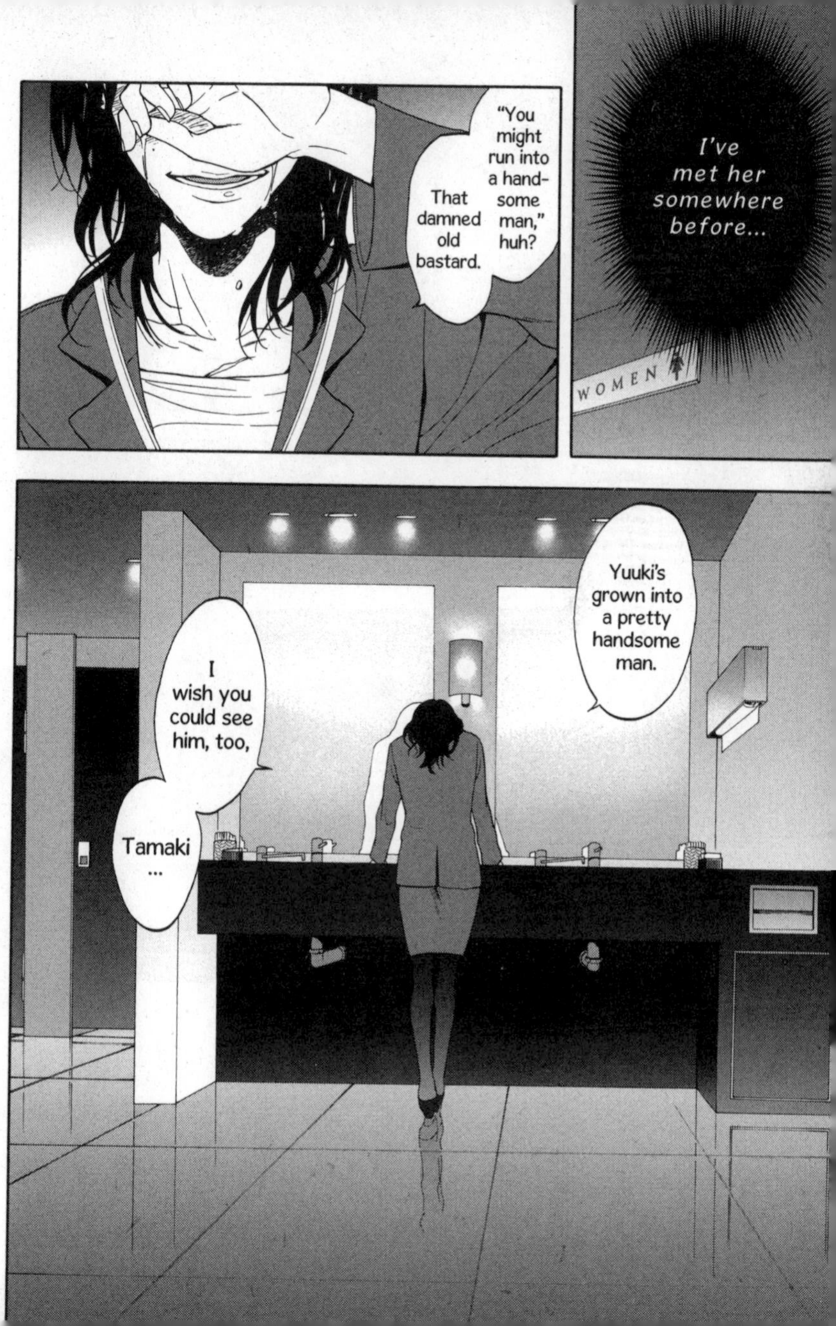
I've met her somewhere before...
WOMEN
"You might run into a hand-some man," huh?
That damned old bastard.
Yuuki's grown into a pretty handsome man.
I wish you could see him, too,
Tamaki...

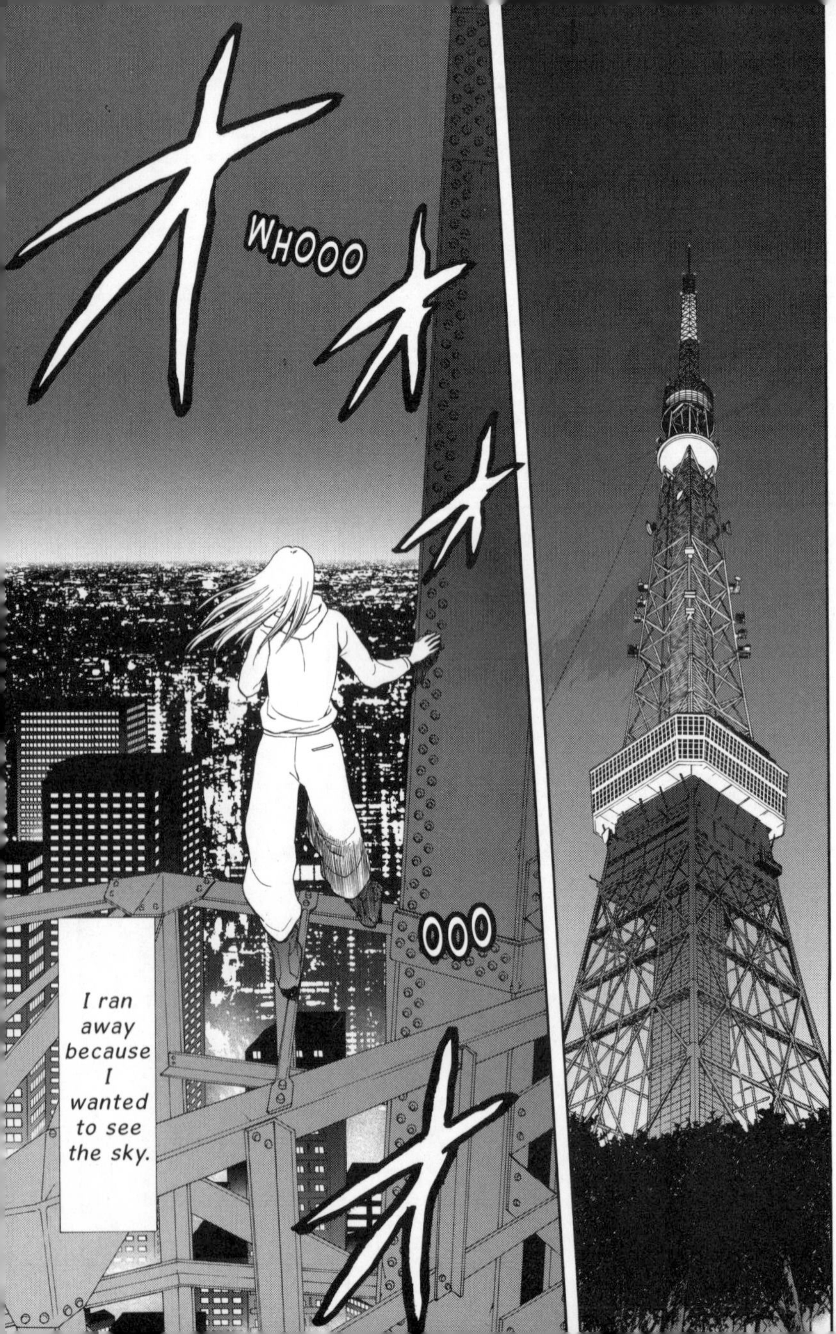
WHOOO
OOO
I ran away because I wanted to see the sky.

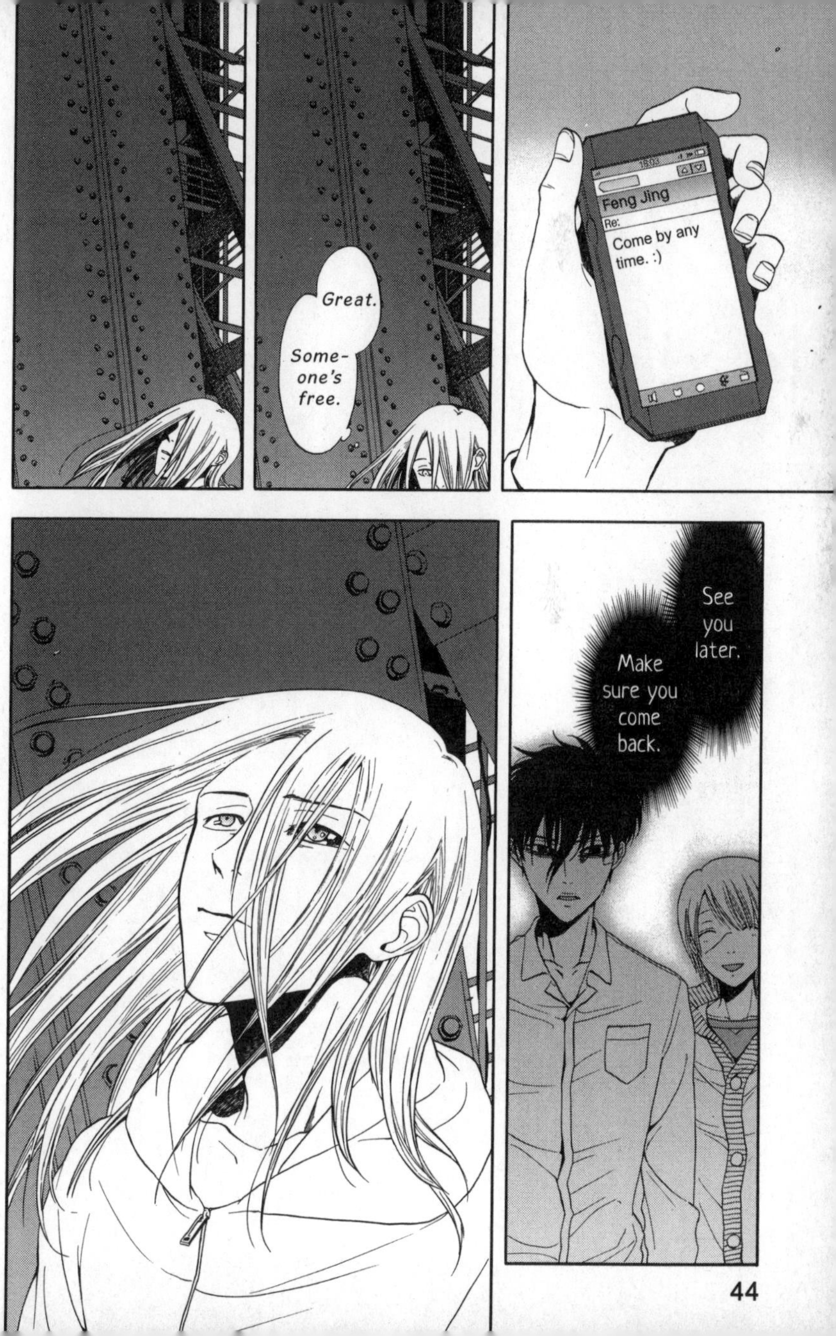
Feng Jing
Re:
Come by any time. :)
Great.
Some-one's free.
See you later.
Make sure you come back.

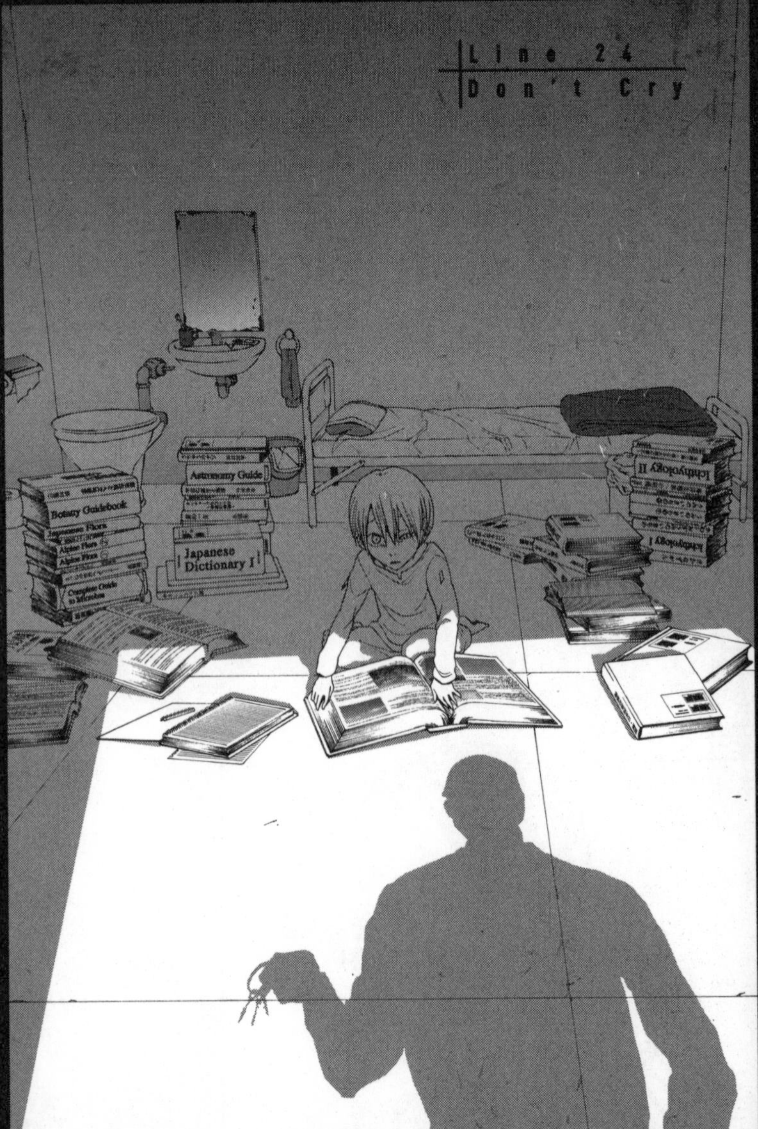
Line 24
Don't Cry
Astronomy Guide
Botany Guidebook
Japanese Dictionary I
Ichthyology II

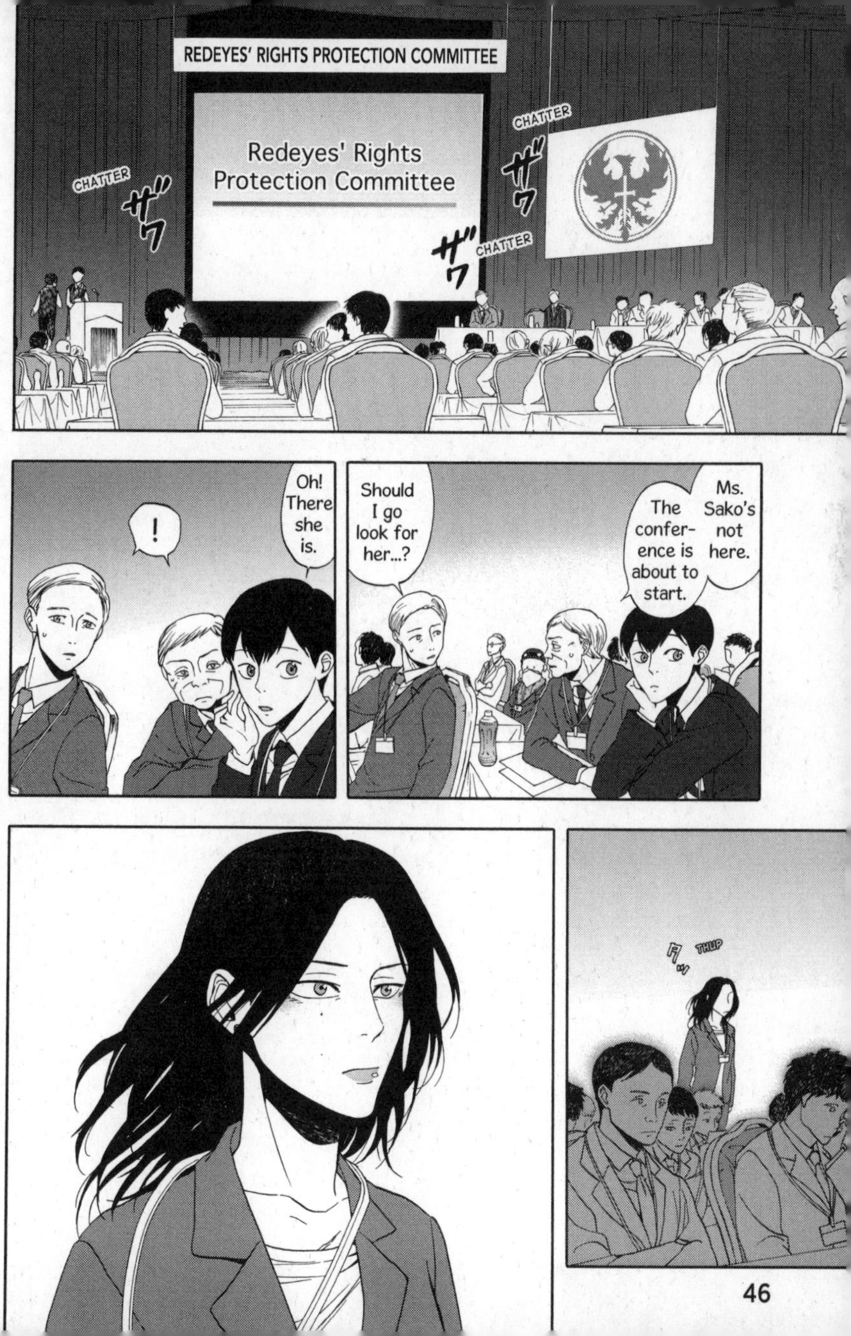
REDEYES' RIGHTS PROTECTION COMMITTEE
Redeyes' Rights Protection Committee
ザワ CHATTER
ザワ CHATTER
ザワ CHATTER
Ms. Sako's not here.
The confer-ence is about to start.
Should I go look for her...?
Oh! There she is.
!
THUP

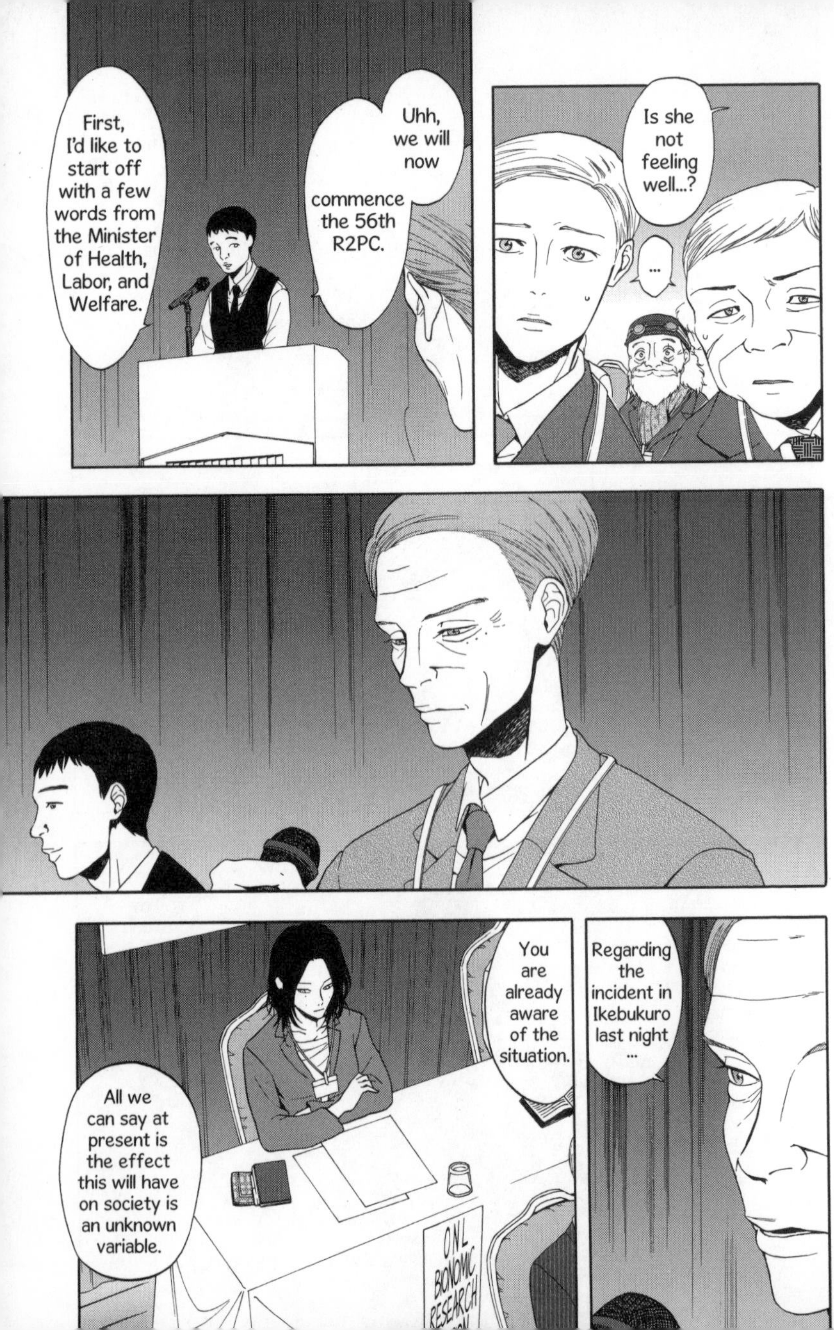
Is she not feeling well...?
...
Uhh, we will now
commence the 56th R2PC.
First, I'd like to start off with a few words from the Minister of Health, Labor, and Welfare.
Regarding the incident in Ikebukuro last night ...
You are already aware of the situation.
All we can say at present is the effect this will have on society is an unknown variable.
ONL BIONOMIC RESEARCH

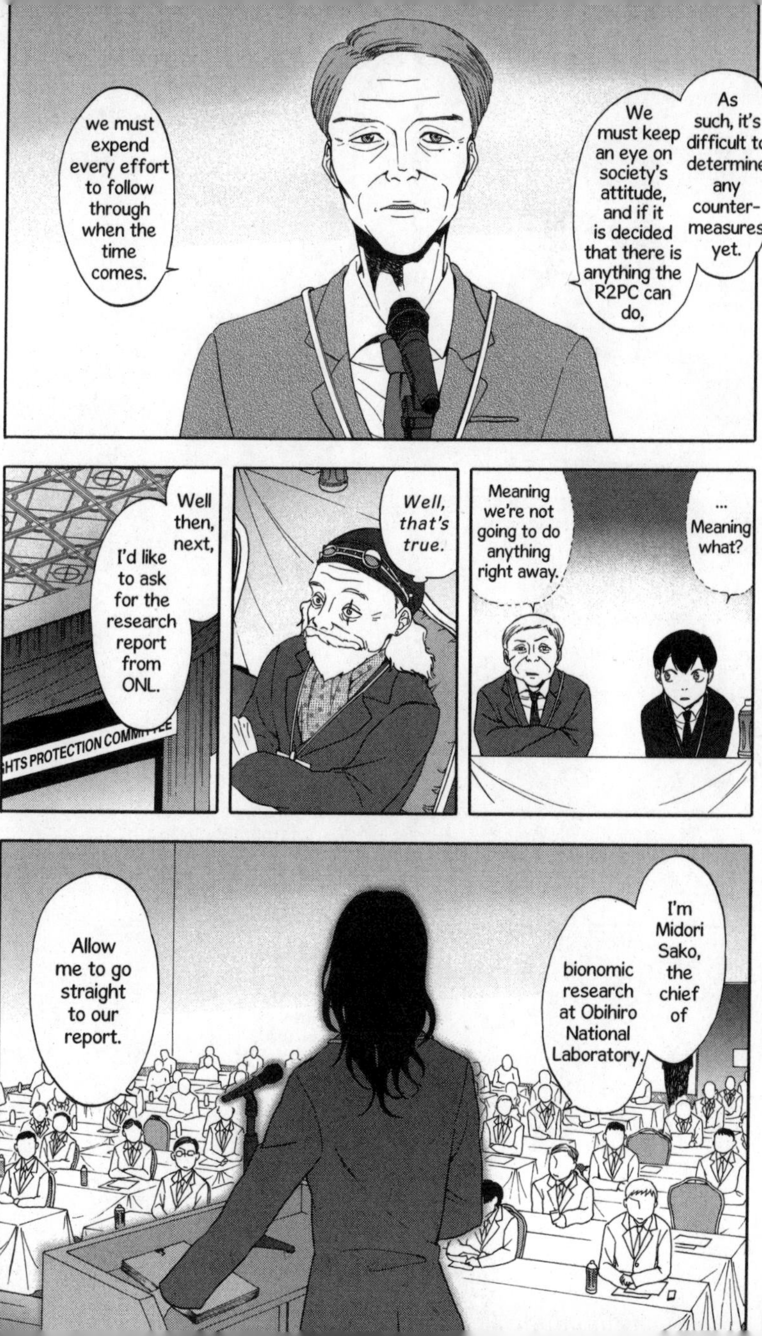
As such, it's difficult to determine any counter-measures yet.
We must keep an eye on society's attitude, and if it is decided that there is anything the R2PC can do,
we must expend every effort to follow through when the time comes.
...Meaning what?
Meaning we're not going to do anything right away.
Well, that's true.
Well then, next,
I'd like to ask for the research report from ONL.
I'm Midori Sako, the chief of bionomic research at Obihiro National Laboratory.
Allow me to go straight to our report.

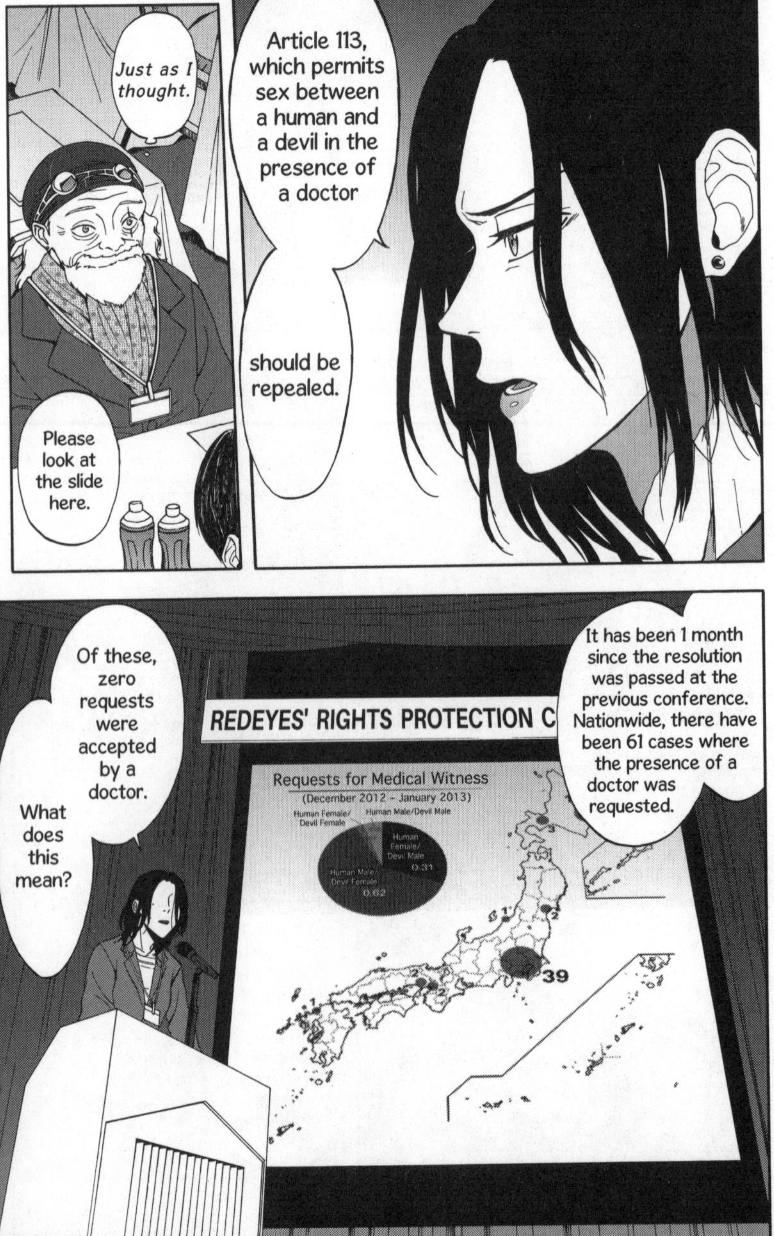

Article 113, which permits sex between a human and a devil in the presence of a doctor
should be repealed.
Just as I thought.
Please look at the slide here.
It has been 1 month since the resolution was passed at the previous conference. Nationwide, there have been 61 cases where the presence of a doctor was requested.
REDEYES' RIGHTS PROTECTION C
Requests for Medical Witness
(December 2012 – January 2013)
Human Female/ Devil Female
Human Male/Devil Male
Human Female/ Devil Male
0.31
Human Male/ Devil Female
0.62
39
Of these, zero requests were accepted by a doctor.
What does this mean?

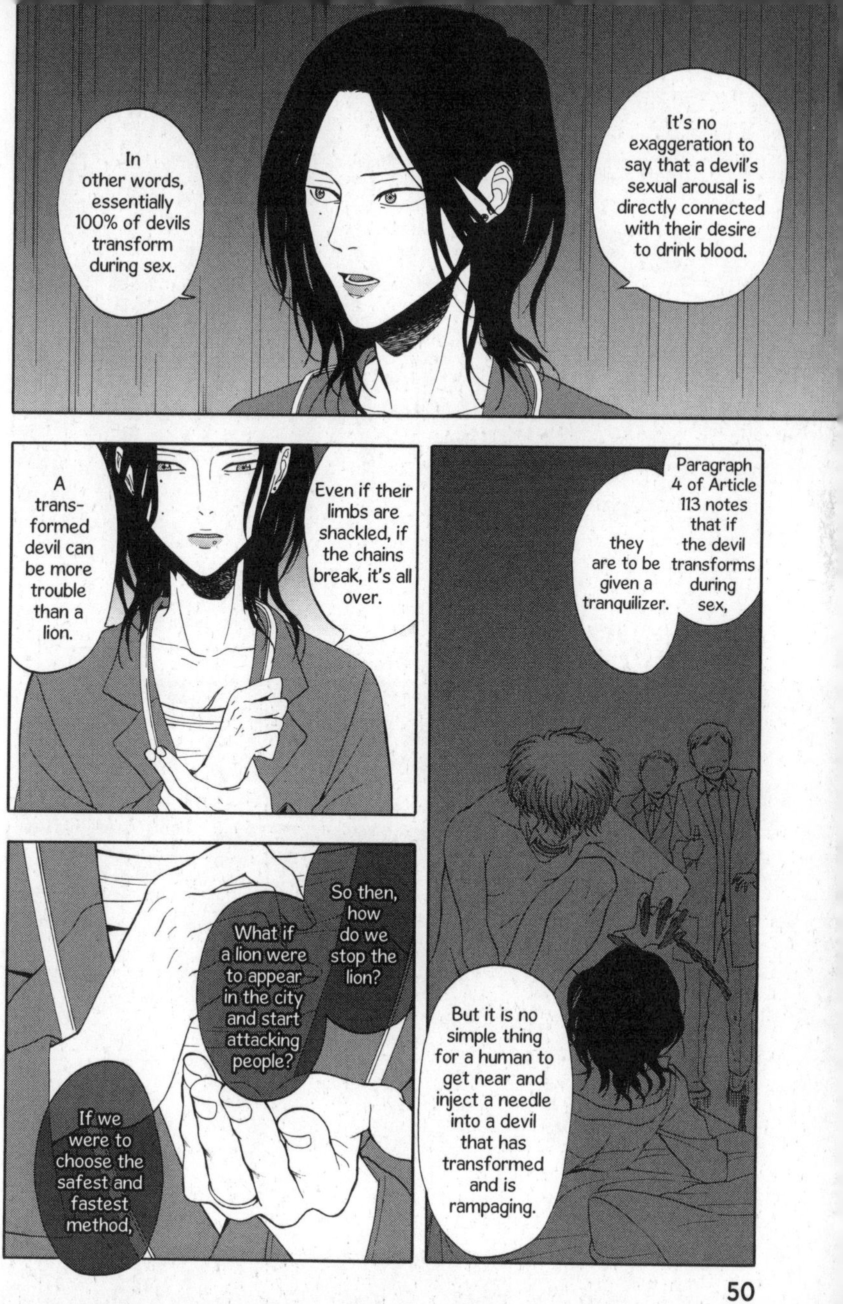
It's no exaggeration to say that a devil's sexual arousal is directly connected with their desire to drink blood.
In other words, essentially 100% of devils transform during sex.
Paragraph 4 of Article 113 notes that if the devil transforms during sex,
they are to be given a tranquilizer.
But it is no simple thing for a human to get near and inject a needle into a devil that has transformed and is rampaging.
Even if their limbs are shackled, if the chains break, it's all over.
A trans-formed devil can be more trouble than a lion.
So then, how do we stop the lion?
What if a lion were to appear in the city and start attacking people?
If we were to choose the safest and fastest method,

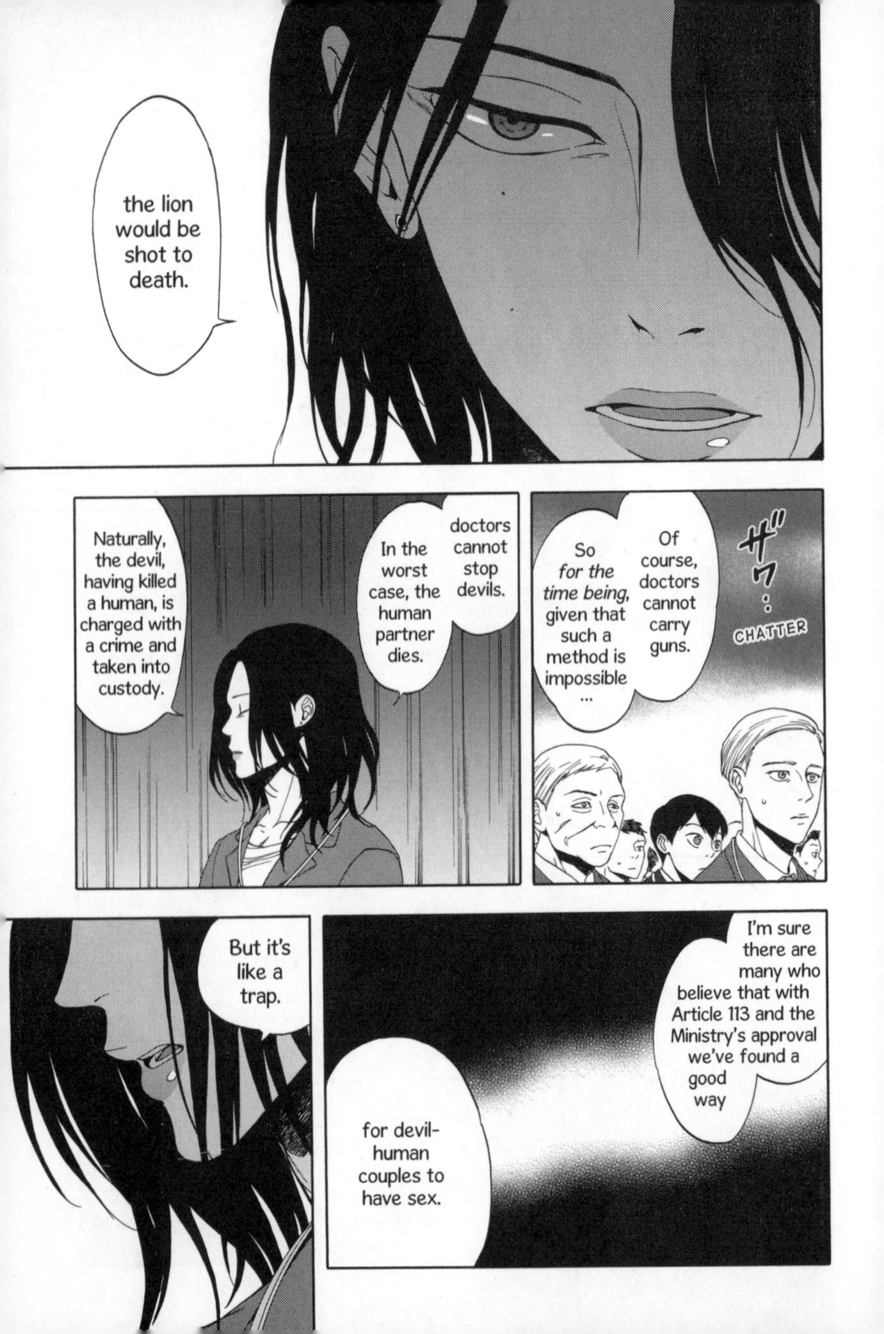
the lion would be shot to death.
ザワ…
CHATTER
Of course, doctors cannot carry guns.
So *for the time being,* given that such a method is impossible …
doctors cannot stop devils.
In the worst case, the human partner dies.
Naturally, the devil, having killed a human, is charged with a crime and taken into custody.
I'm sure there are many who believe that with Article 113 and the Ministry's approval we've found a good way
for devil-human couples to have sex.
But it's like a trap.

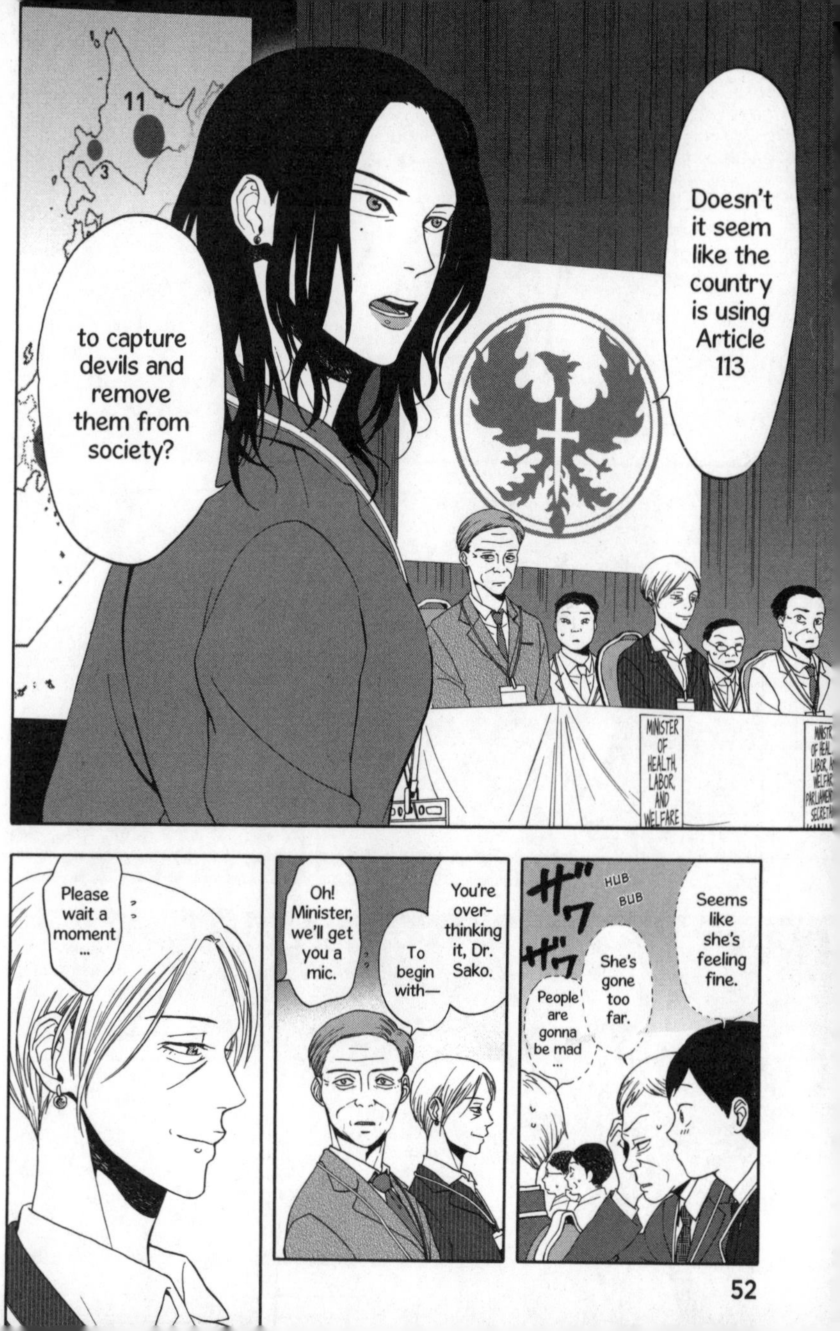
Doesn't it seem like the country is using Article 113
to capture devils and remove them from society?
MINISTER OF HEALTH, LABOR, AND WELFARE
ザワ
ザワ
HUB BUB
Seems like she's feeling fine.
She's gone too far.
People are gonna be mad ...
You're over-thinking it, Dr. Sako.
To begin with—
Oh! Minister, we'll get you a mic.
Please wait a moment ...

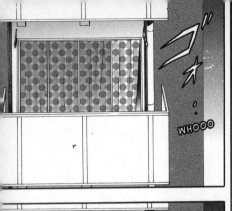

WHOOO

JUMP

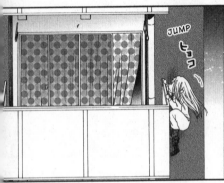

That was fast!

WHIP

Meow!

Window's open.

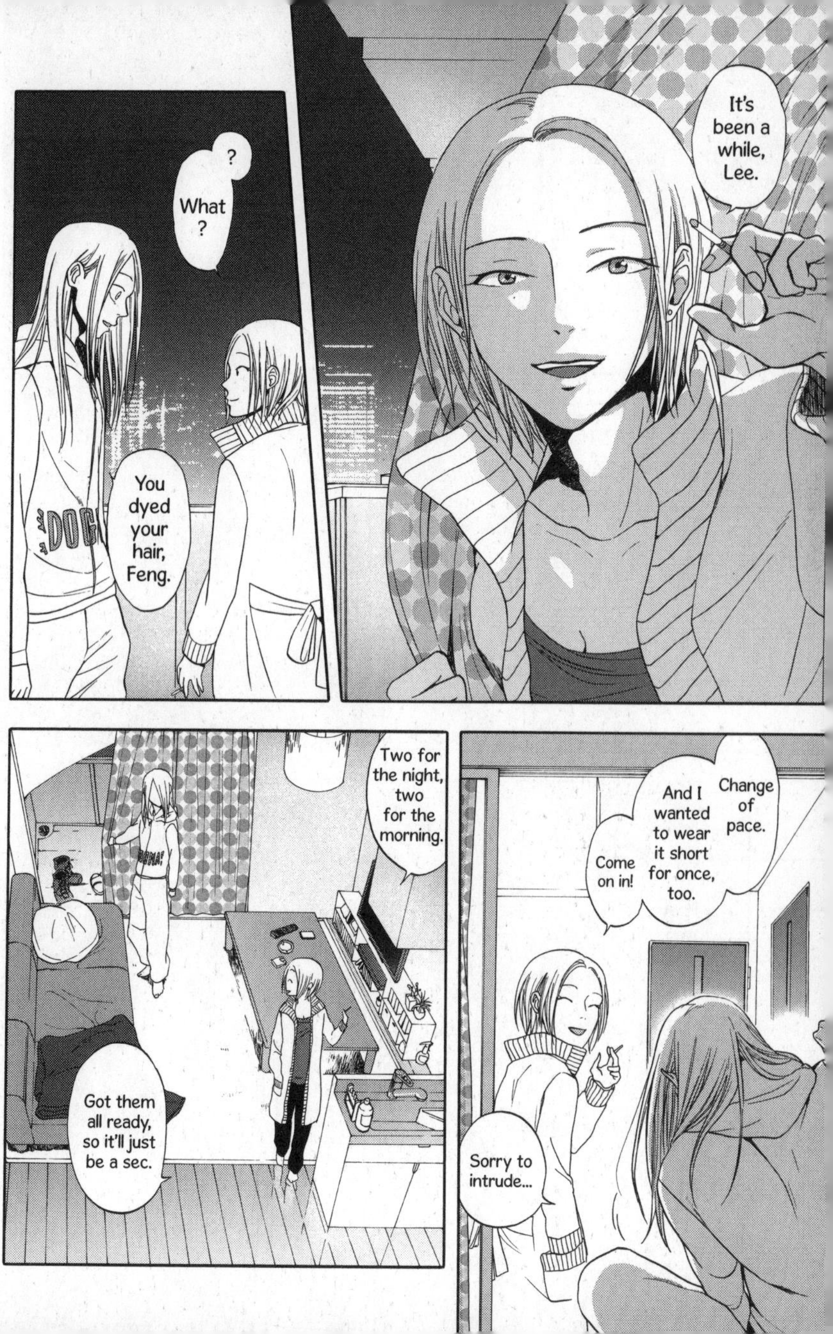
It's been a while, Lee.
? What ?
You dyed your hair, Feng.
Change of pace.
And I wanted to wear it short for once, too.
Come on in!
Sorry to intrude...
Two for the night, two for the morning.
Got them all ready, so it'll just be a sec.

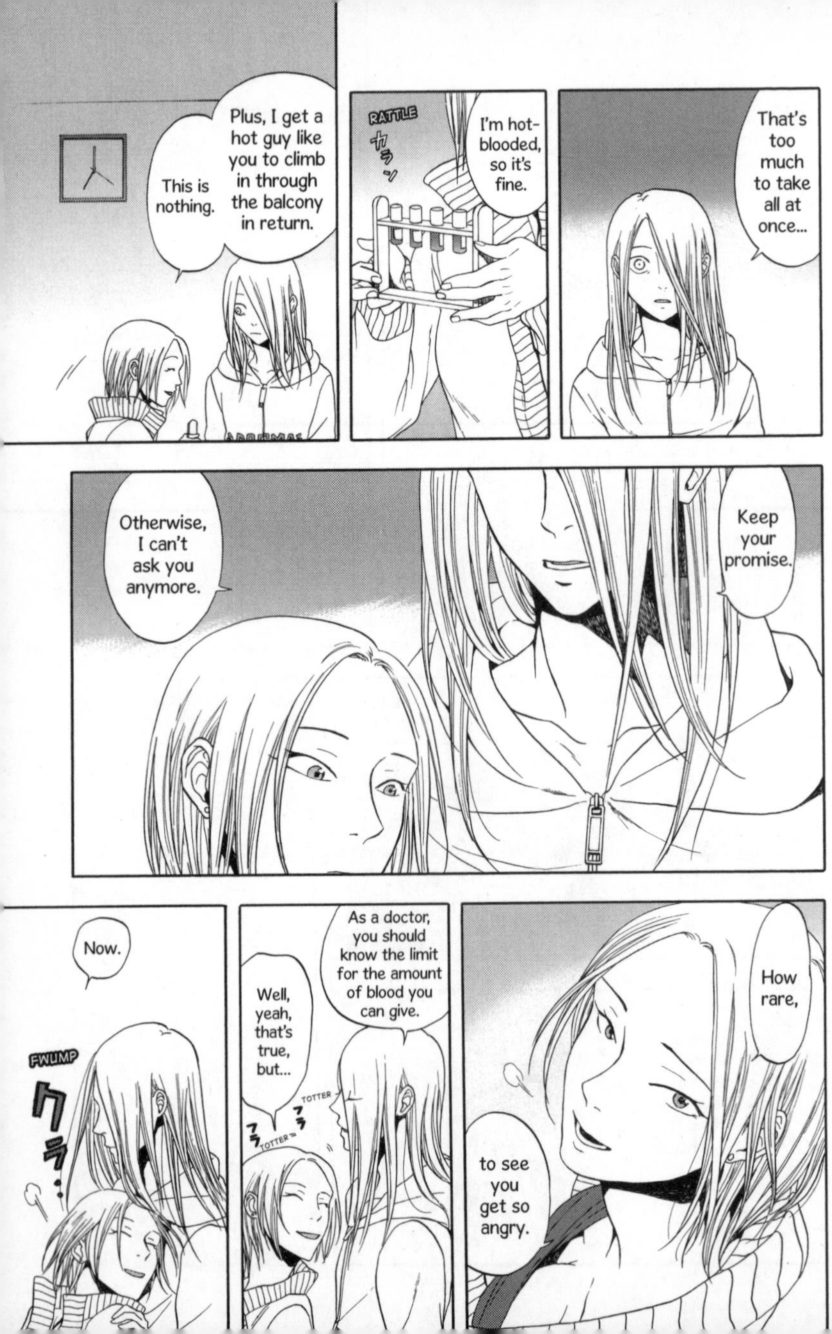

That's too much to take all at once...
RATTLE
I'm hot-blooded, so it's fine.
Plus, I get a hot guy like you to climb in through the balcony in return.
This is nothing.
Keep your promise.
Otherwise, I can't ask you anymore.
How rare,
to see you get so angry.
As a doctor, you should know the limit for the amount of blood you can give.
Well, yeah, that's true, but...
TOTTER
TOTTER
Now.
FWUMP

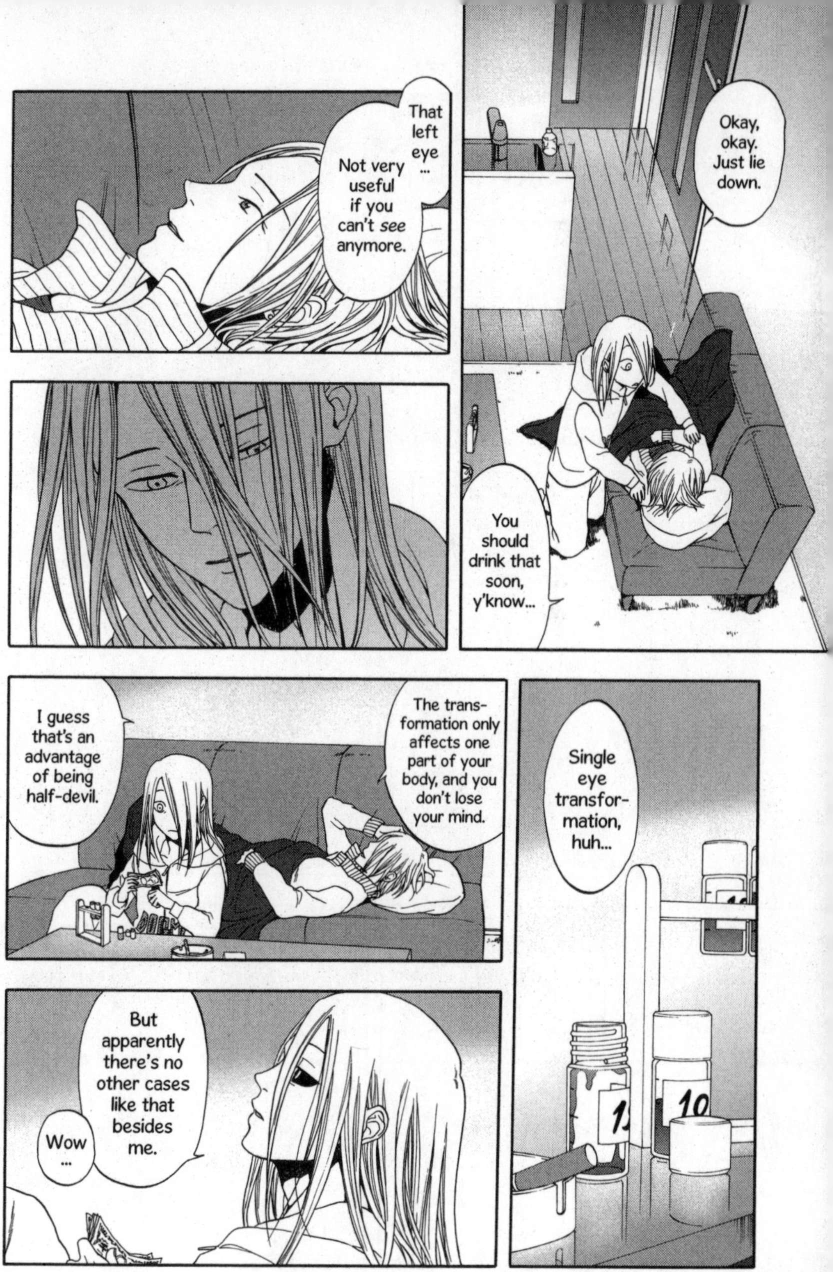
Okay, okay. Just lie down.
You should drink that soon, y'know...
That left eye ...
Not very useful if you can't *see* anymore.
Single eye transformation, huh...
The transformation only affects one part of your body, and you don't lose your mind.
I guess that's an advantage of being half-devil.
But apparently there's no other cases like that besides me.
Wow ...

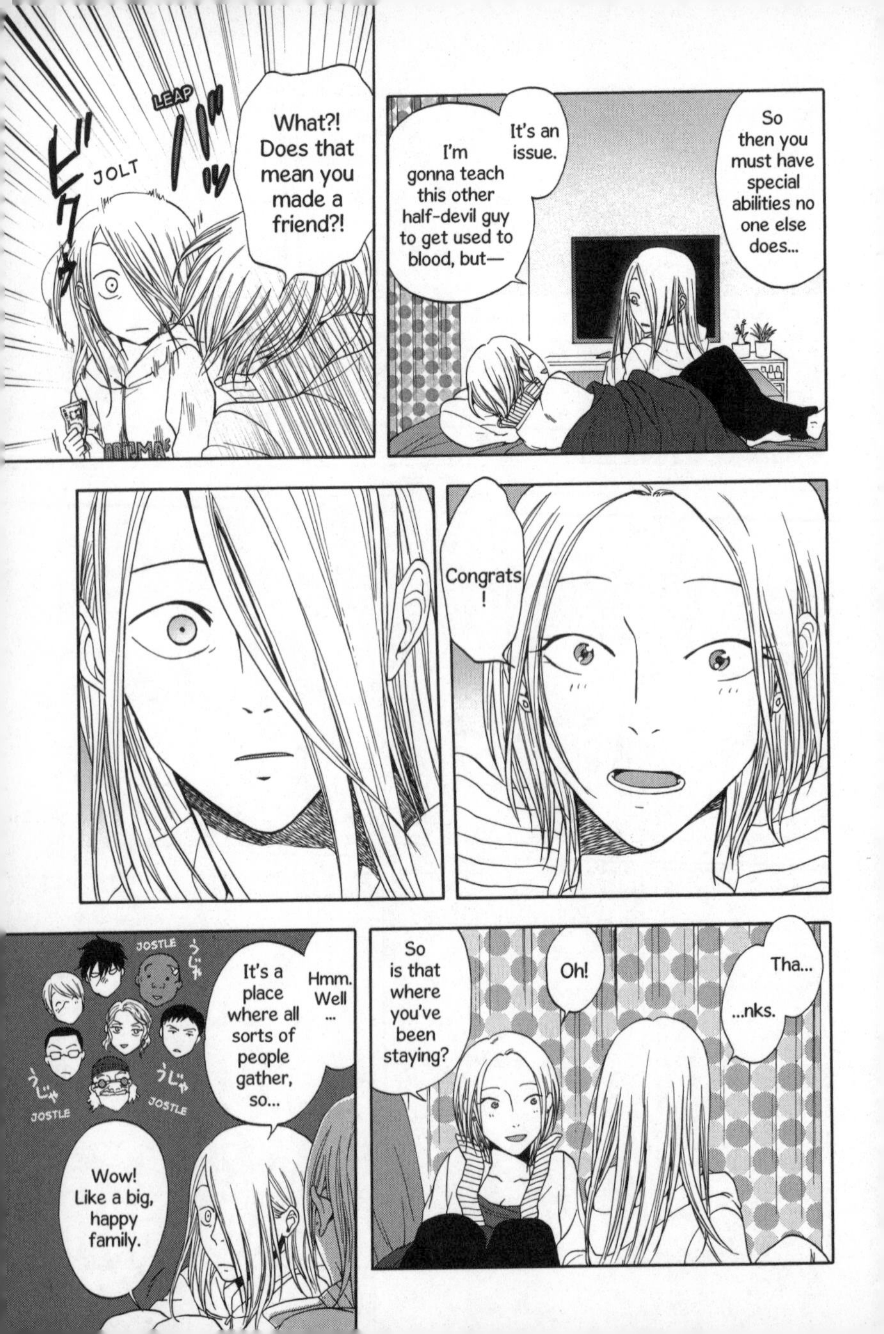
So then you must have special abilities no one else does...
It's an issue.
I'm gonna teach this other half-devil guy to get used to blood, but—
LEAP
JOLT
What?! Does that mean you made a friend?!
Congrats!
Tha...
...nks.
Oh!
So is that where you've been staying?
Hmm. Well ...
It's a place where all sorts of people gather, so...
JOSTLE
JOSTLE
JOSTLE
Wow! Like a big, happy family.

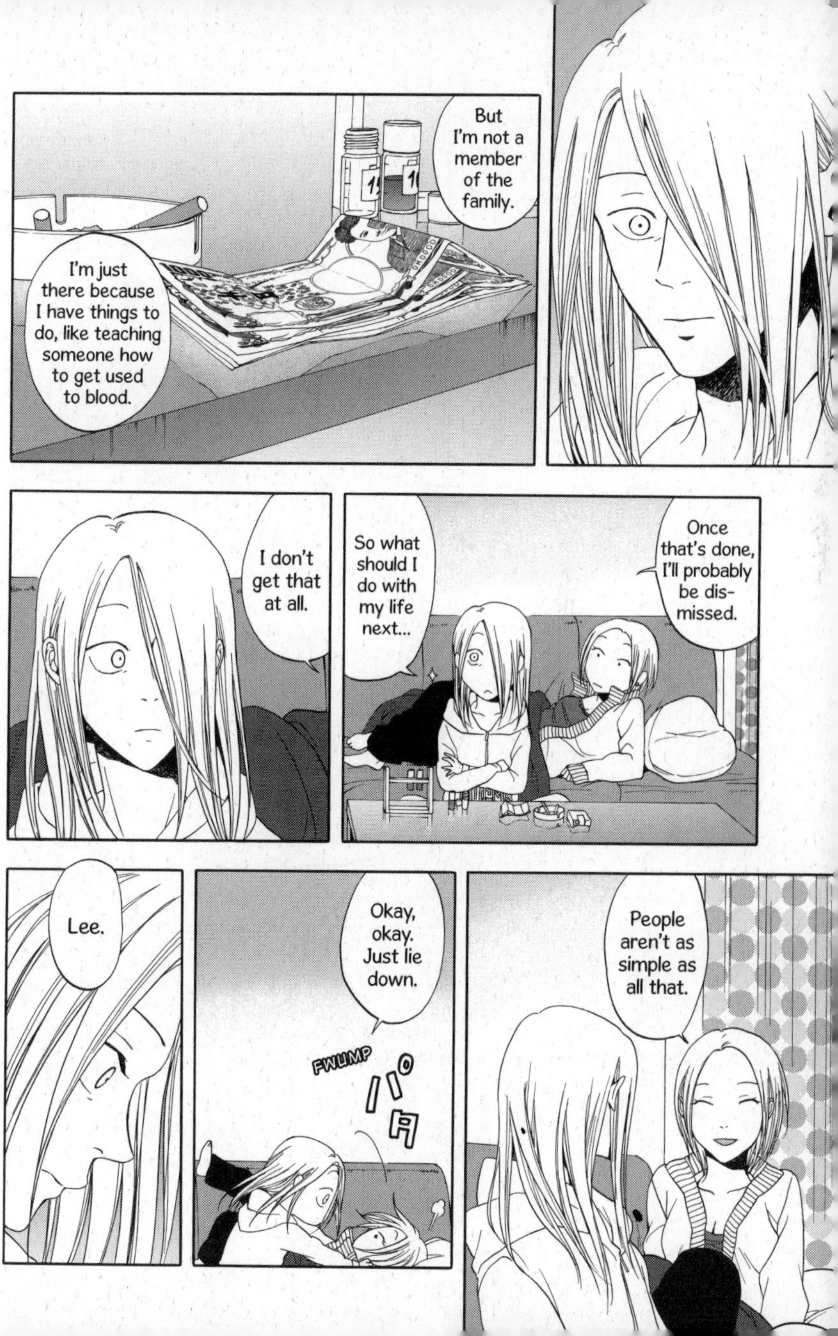
But I'm not a member of the family.
I'm just there because I have things to do, like teaching someone how to get used to blood.
Once that's done, I'll probably be dis- missed.
So what should I do with my life next...
I don't get that at all.
People aren't as simple as all that.
Okay, okay. Just lie down.
FWUMP
Lee.

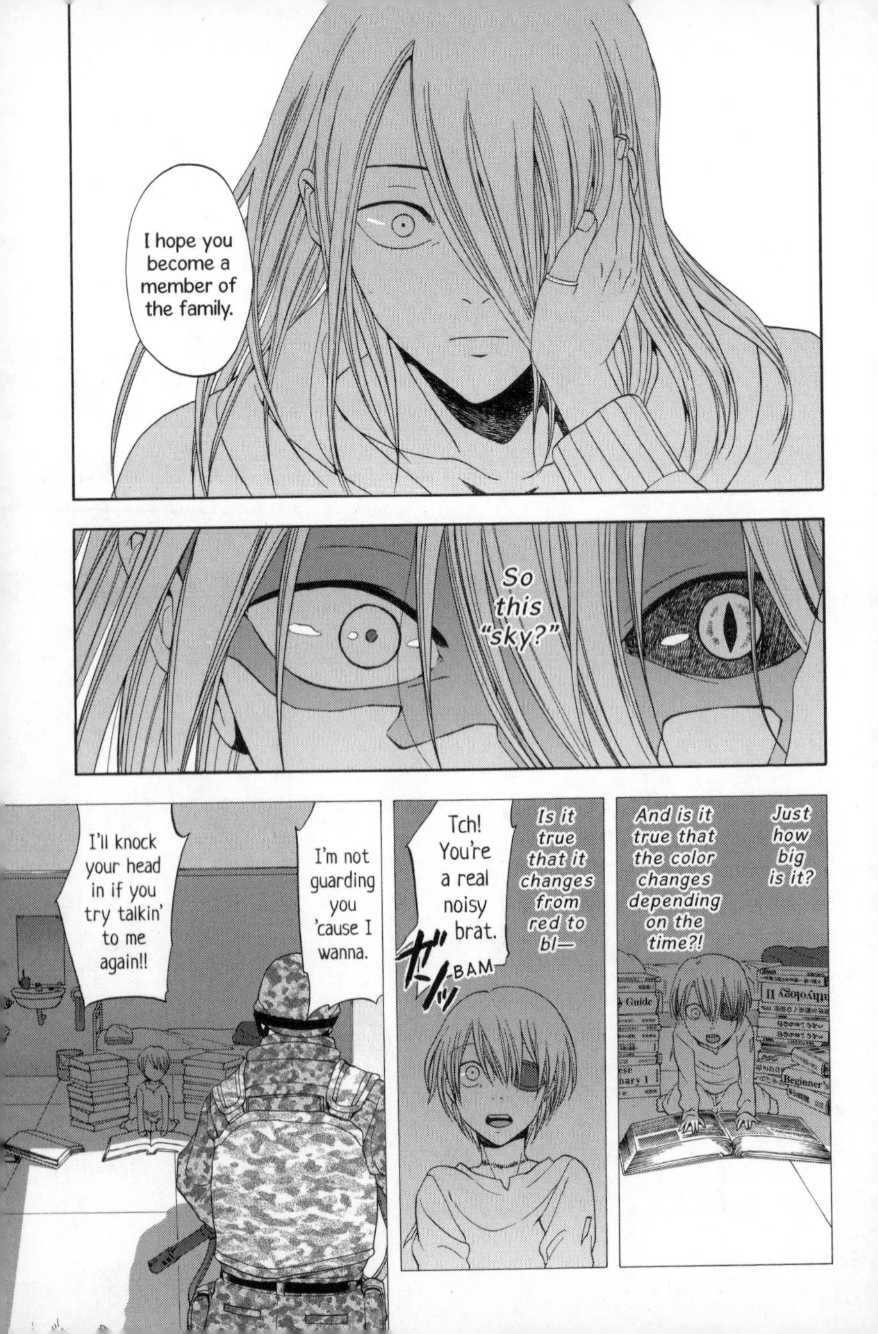
I hope you become a member of the family.
So this "sky?"
Just how big is it?
And is it true that the color changes depending on the time?!
Is it true that it changes from red to bl—
Tch! You're a real noisy brat.
BAM
I'm not guarding you 'cause I wanna.
I'll knock your head in if you try talkin' to me again!!

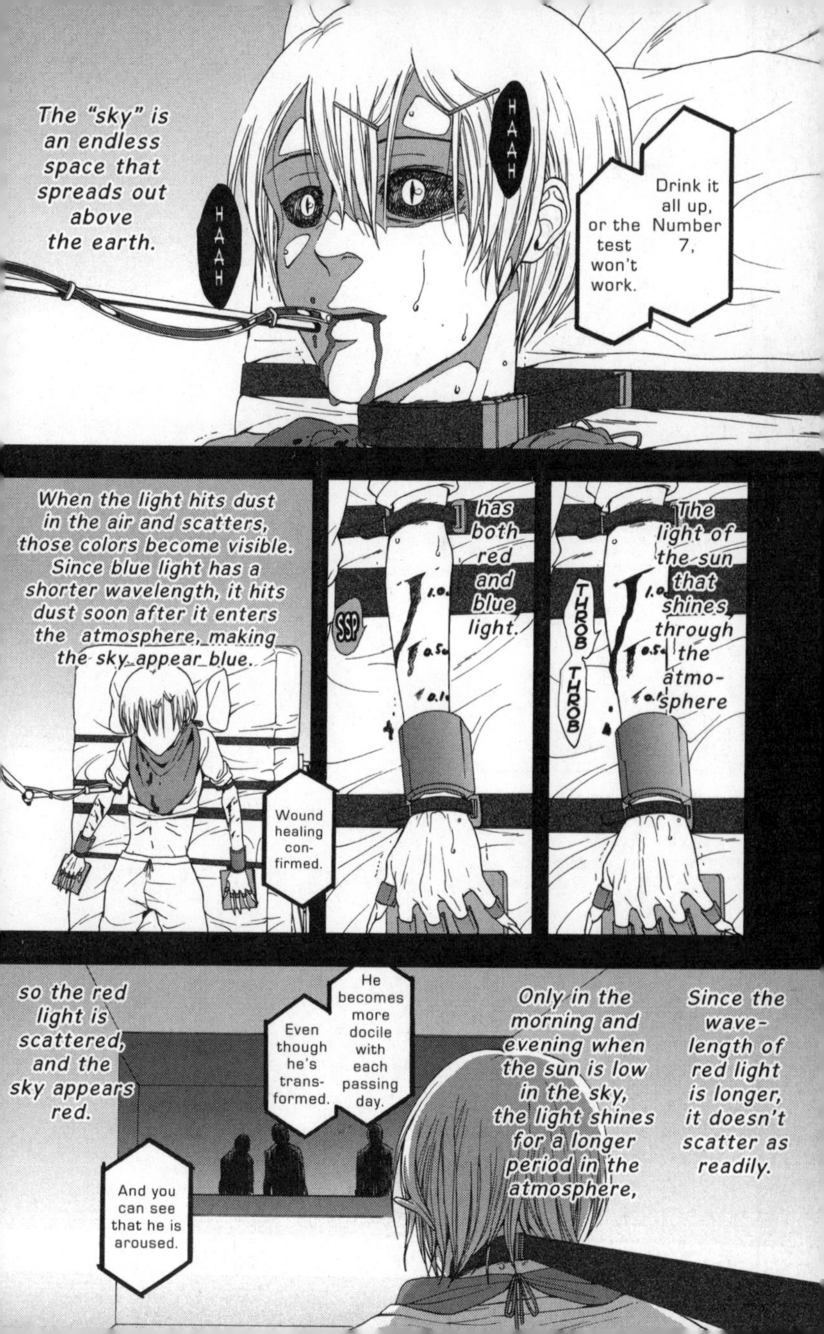

Drink it all up, Number 7, or the test won't work.
HAAH
HAAH
The "sky" is an endless space that spreads out above the earth.
The light of the sun that shines through the atmosphere
THROB THROB
has both red and blue light.
SSP
When the light hits dust in the air and scatters, those colors become visible. Since blue light has a shorter wavelength, it hits dust soon after it enters the atmosphere, making the sky appear blue.
Wound healing confirmed.
Since the wavelength of red light is longer, it doesn't scatter as readily.
Only in the morning and evening when the sun is low in the sky, the light shines for a longer period in the atmosphere,
He becomes more docile with each passing day.
Even though he's transformed.
so the red light is scattered, and the sky appears red.
And you can see that he is aroused.

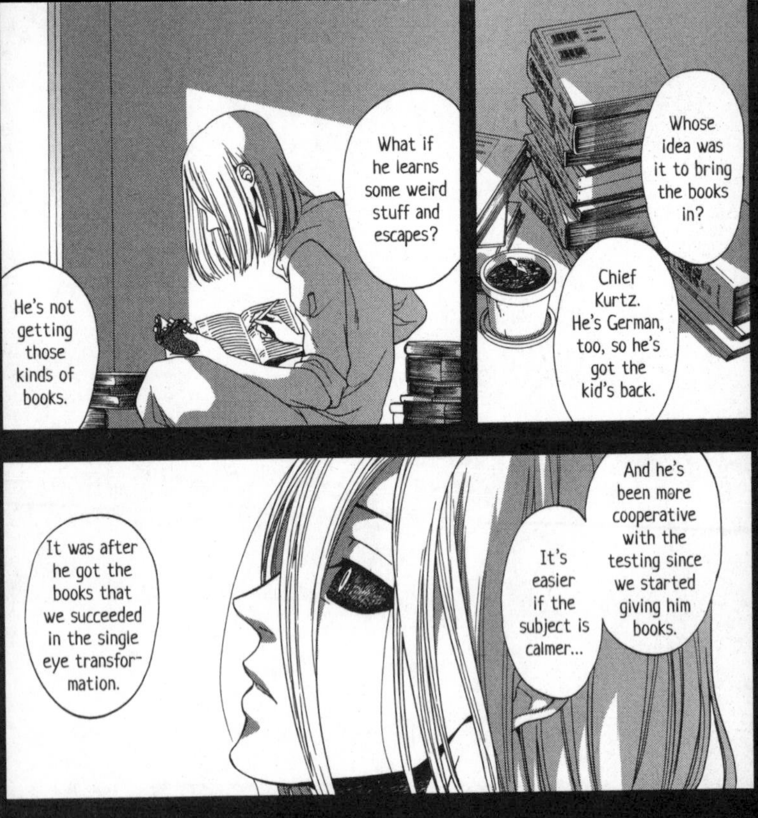
Whose idea was it to bring the books in?
Chief Kurtz. He's German, too, so he's got the kid's back.
What if he learns some weird stuff and escapes?
He's not getting those kinds of books.
And he's been more cooperative with the testing since we started giving him books.
It's easier if the subject is calmer...
It was after he got the books that we succeeded in the single eye transformation.

The "sky" is

an endless space

that spreads out above the earth...

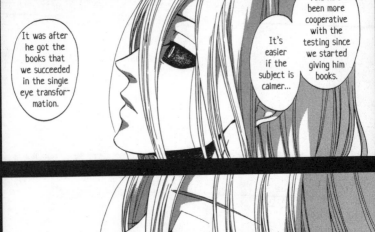

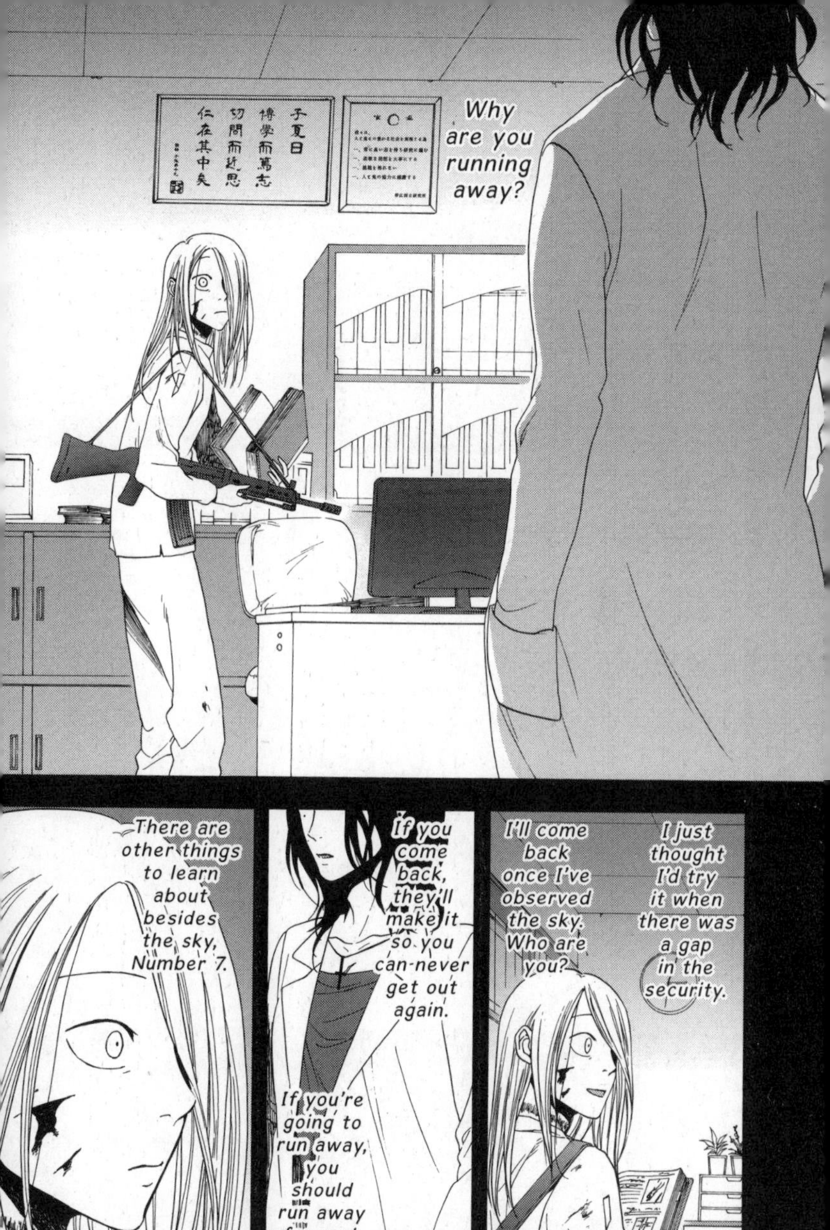

子夏曰 博學而篤志 切問而近思 仁在其中矣
Why are you running away?
I just thought I'd try it when there was a gap in the security.
I'll come back once I've observed the sky. Who are you?
If you come back, they'll make it so you can never get out again.
If you're going to run away, you should run away for real.
There are other things to learn about besides the sky, Number 7.

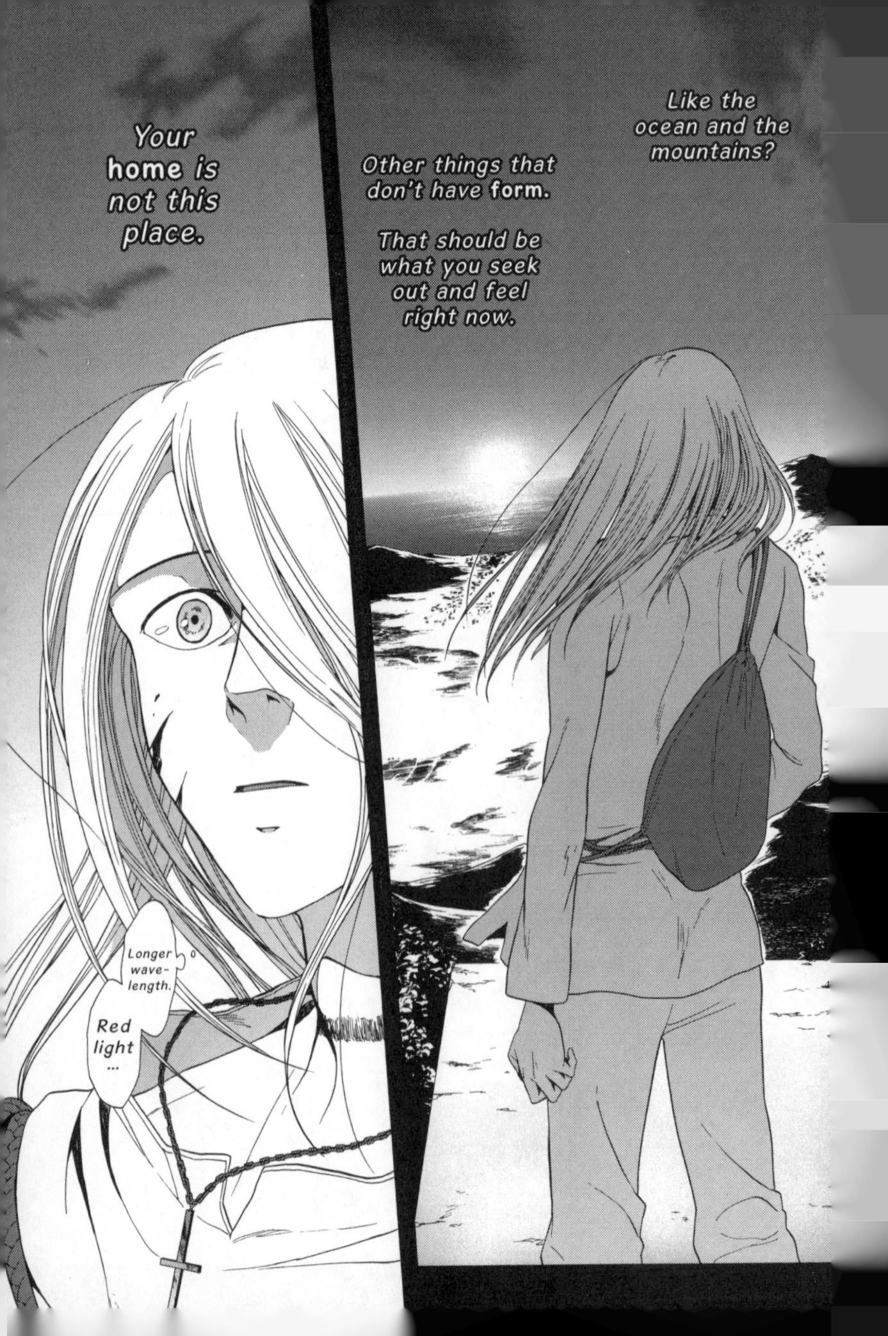
Like the ocean and the mountains?
Other things that don't have form.
That should be what you seek out and feel right now.
Your home is not this place.
Longer wave-length.
Red light ...

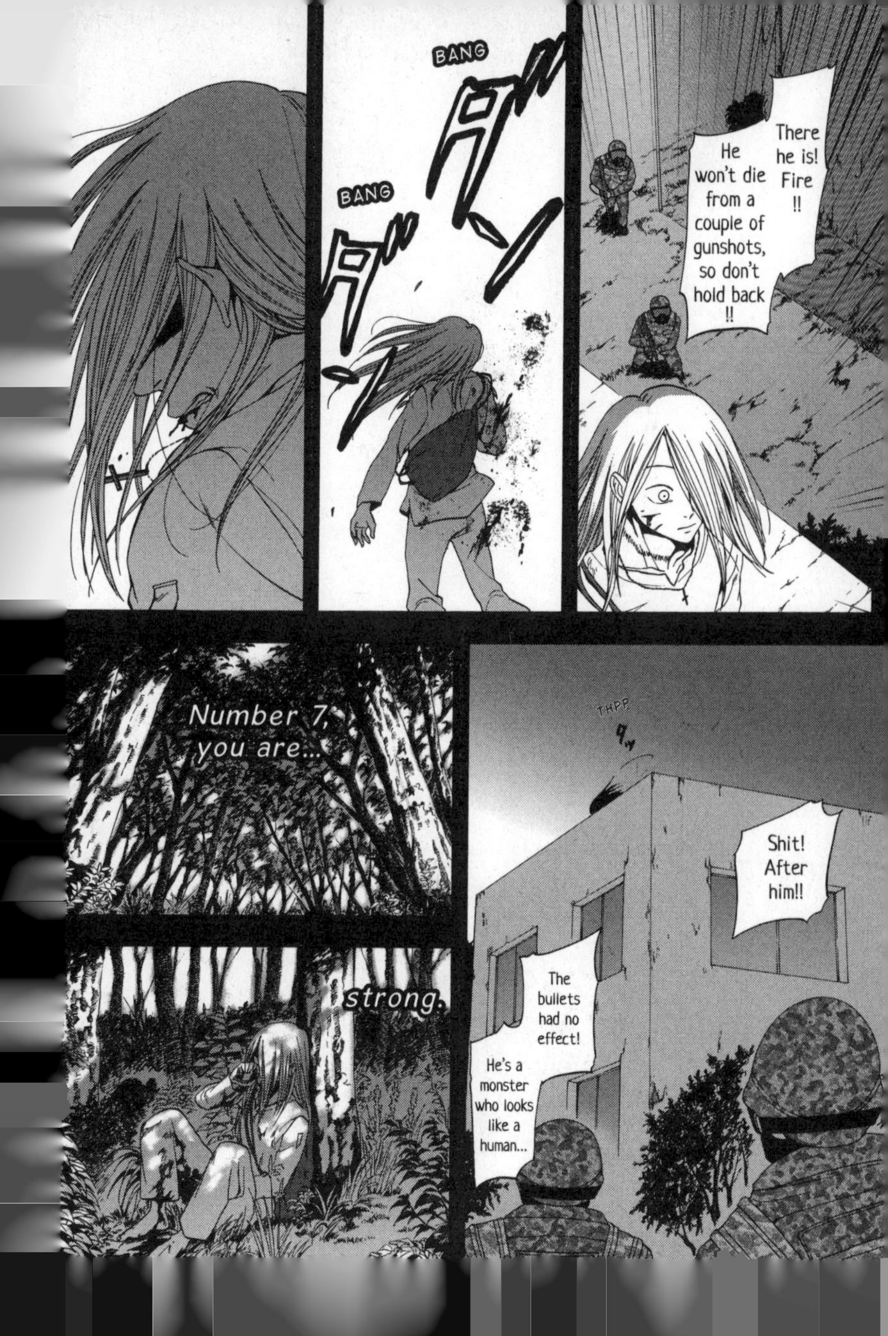
There he is! Fire !!
He won't die from a couple of gunshots, so don't hold back !!
BANG
BANG
THPP
Shit! After him!!
The bullets had no effect!
He's a monster who looks like a human...
Number 7, you are...
strong.

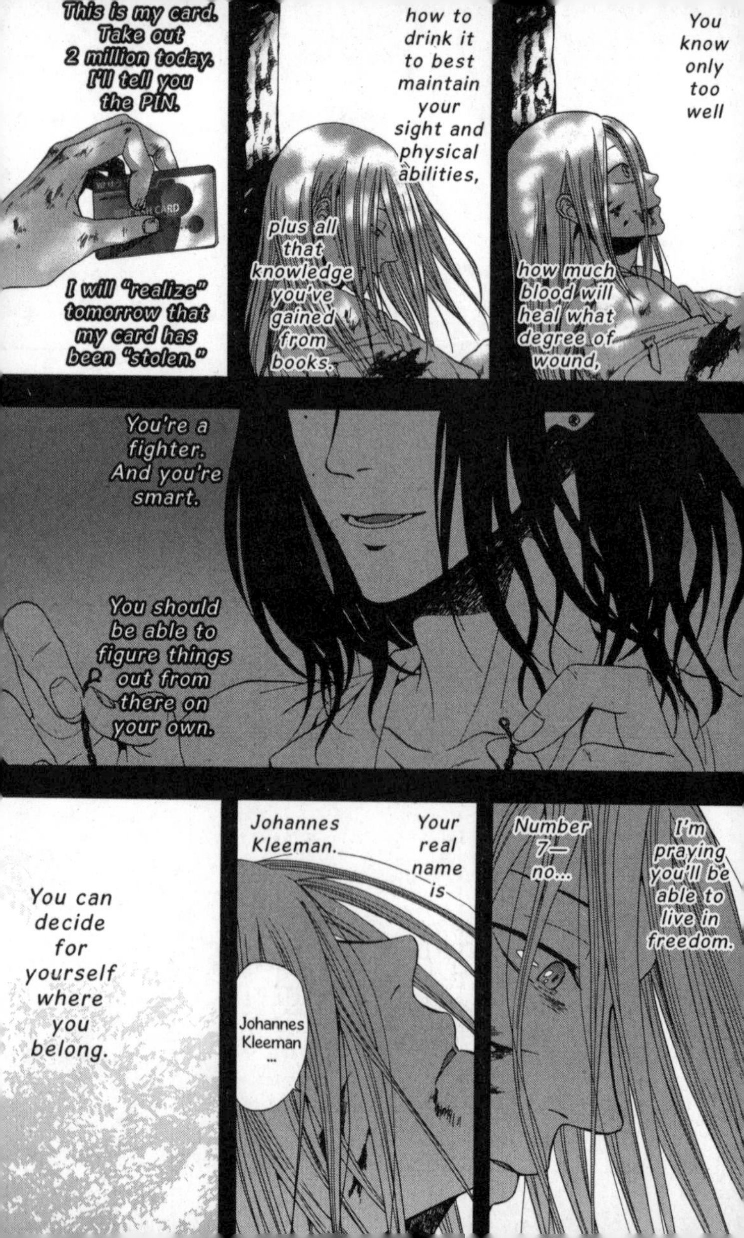
You know only too well
how much blood will heal what degree of wound,
how to drink it to best maintain your sight and physical abilities,
plus all that knowledge you've gained from books.
This is my card. Take out 2 million today. I'll tell you the PIN.
I will "realize" tomorrow that my card has been "stolen."
You're a fighter. And you're smart.
You should be able to figure things out from there on your own.
I'm praying you'll be able to live in freedom.
Number 7— no...
Your real name is
Johannes Kleeman.
Johannes Kleeman ...
You can decide for yourself where you belong.

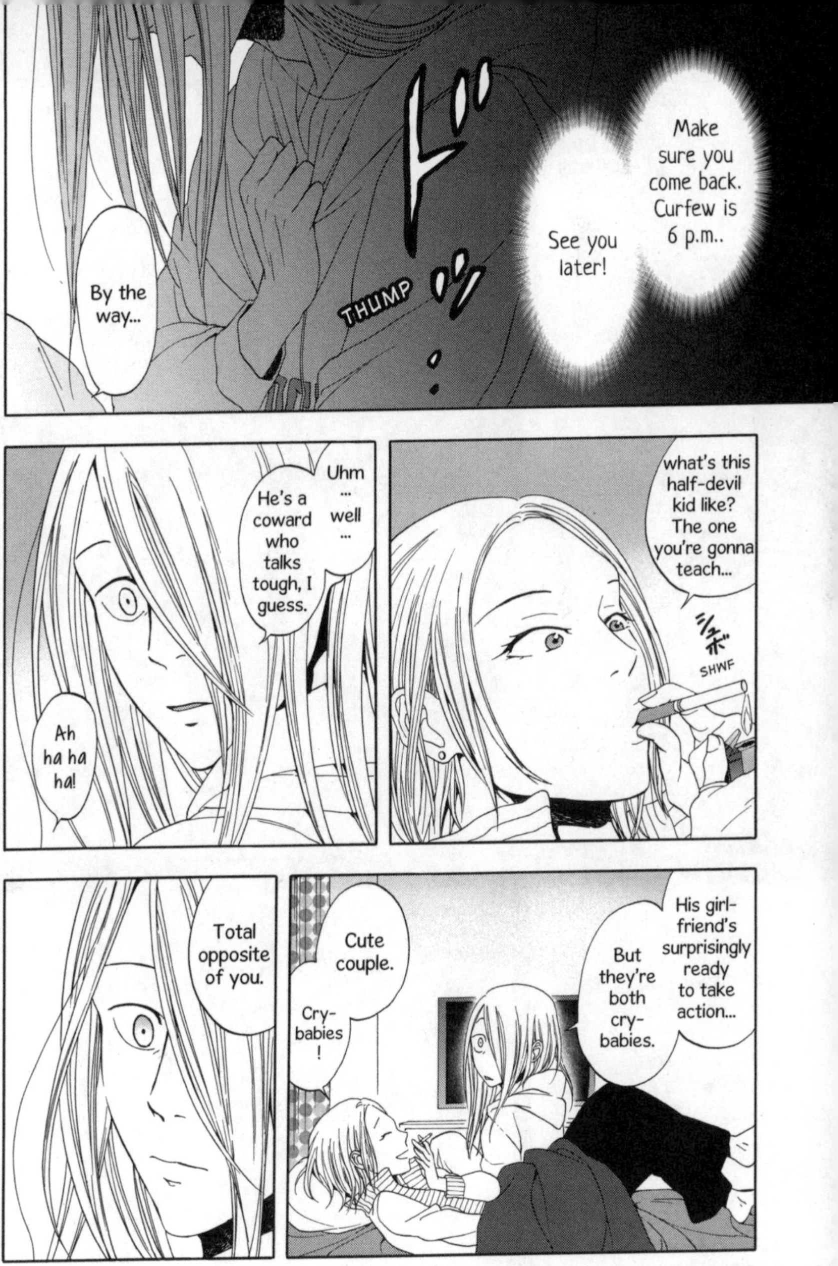
Make sure you come back. Curfew is 6 p.m..
See you later!
ドッ
THUMP
By the way...
what's this half-devil kid like? The one you're gonna teach...
シュボ
SHWF
Uhm ... well ...
He's a coward who talks tough, I guess.
Ah ha ha ha!
His girl-friend's surprisingly ready to take action...
But they're both cry-babies.
Cute couple.
Cry-babies!
Total opposite of you.

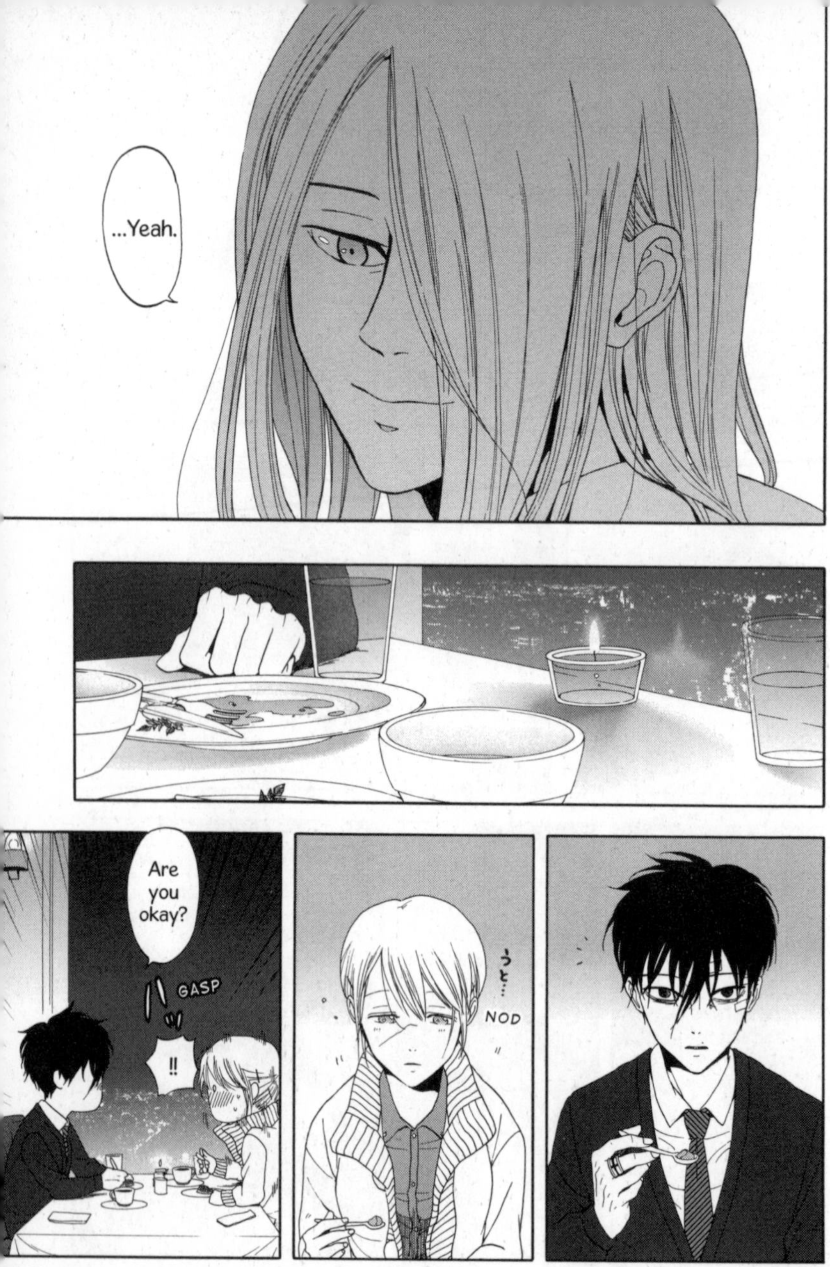
...Yeah.
うと…
NOD
Are you okay?
GASP
!!

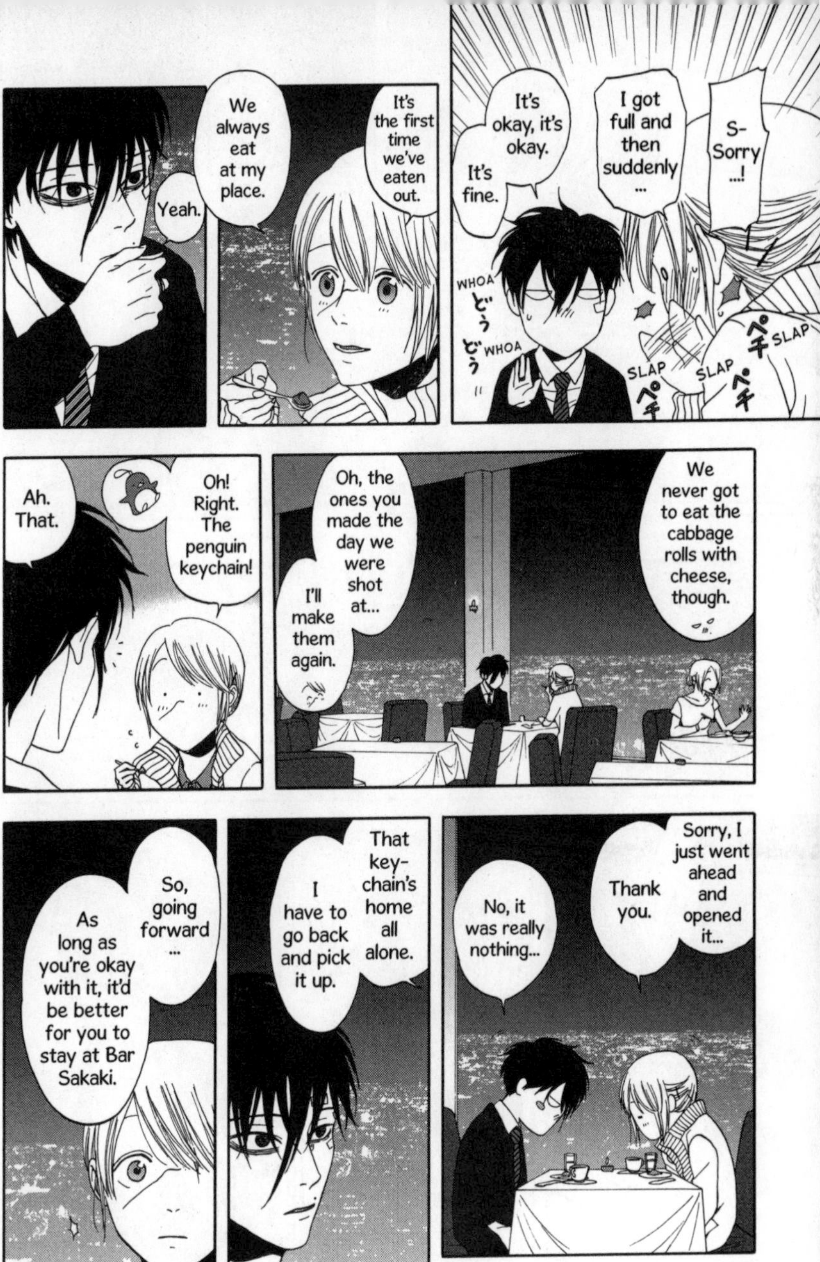
S- Sorry ...!
I got full and then suddenly ...
It's okay, it's okay.
It's fine.
WHOA
WHOA
SLAP
SLAP
SLAP
It's the first time we've eaten out.
We always eat at my place.
Yeah.
We never got to eat the cabbage rolls with cheese, though.
Oh, the ones you made the day we were shot at...
I'll make them again.
Oh! Right. The penguin keychain!
Ah. That.
Sorry, I just went ahead and opened it...
Thank you.
No, it was really nothing...
That key-chain's home all alone.
I have to go back and pick it up.
So, going forward ...
As long as you're okay with it, it'd be better for you to stay at Bar Sakaki.

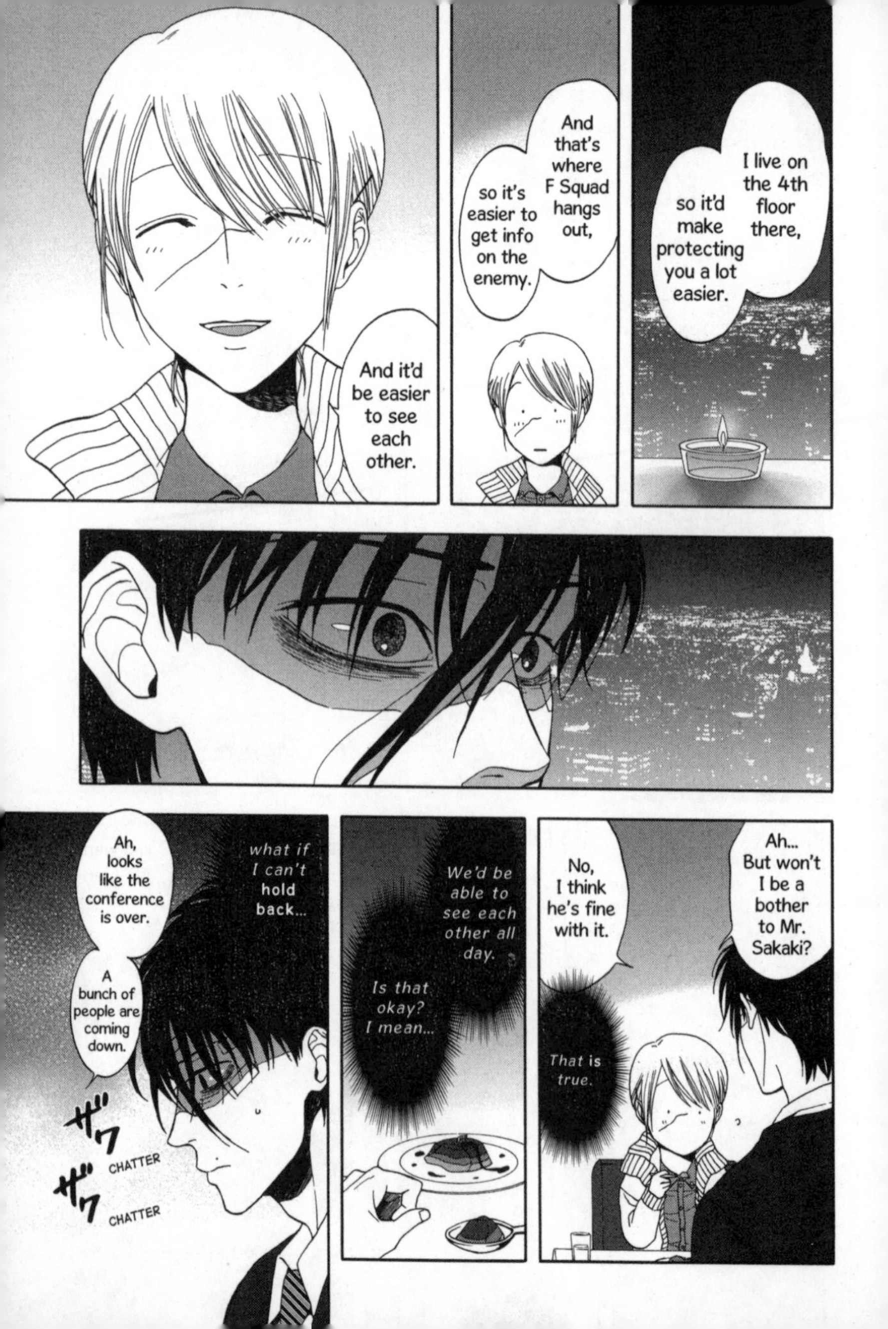
I live on the 4th floor there,
so it'd make protecting you a lot easier.
And that's where F Squad hangs out,
so it's easier to get info on the enemy.
And it'd be easier to see each other.
Ah... But won't I be a bother to Mr. Sakaki?
No, I think he's fine with it.
That is true.
We'd be able to see each other all day.
Is that okay? I mean...
what if I can't hold back...
Ah, looks like the conference is over.
A bunch of people are coming down.
ザワ
CHATTER
ザワ
CHATTER

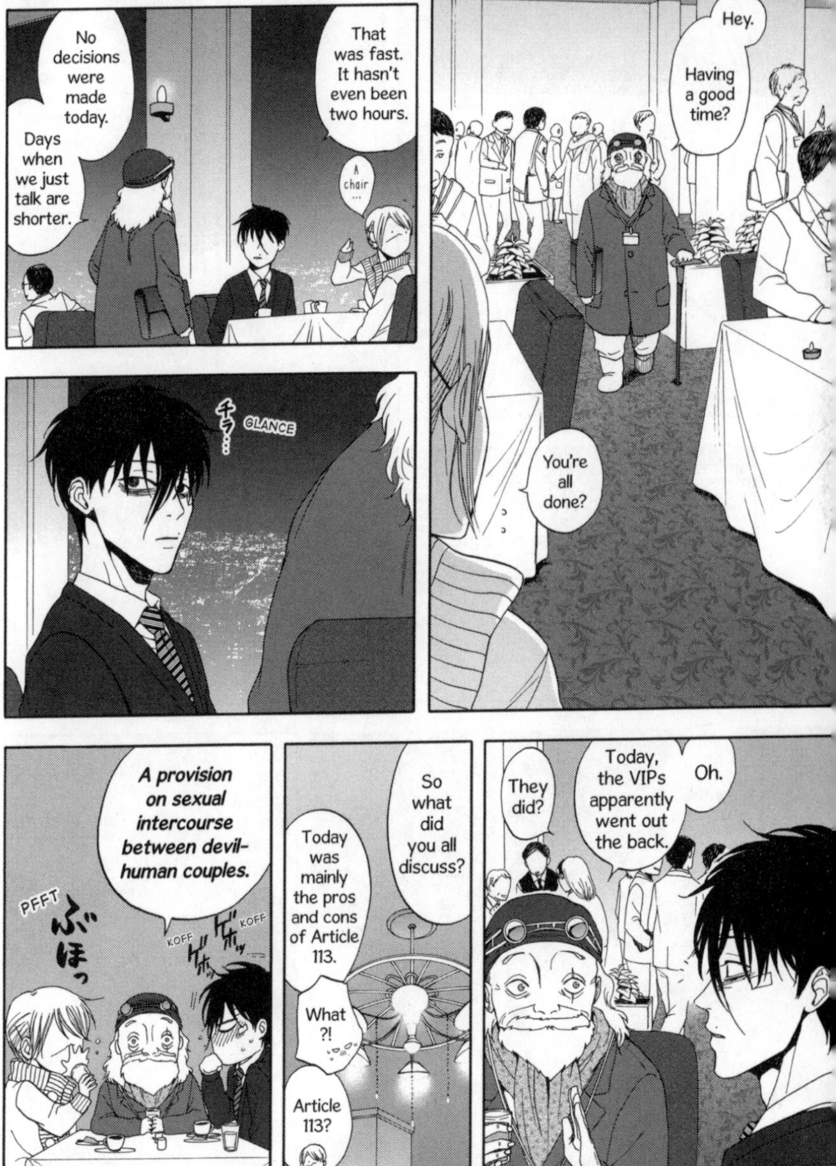
Hey.
Having a good time?
You're all done?
That was fast. It hasn't even been two hours.
No decisions were made today.
Days when we just talk are shorter.
A chair ...
チラ…
GLANCE
Oh.
Today, the VIPs apparently went out the back.
They did?
So what did you all discuss?
Today was mainly the pros and cons of Article 113.
What ?!
Article 113?
A provision on sexual intercourse between devil-human couples.
ゲホッ
KOFF
ゲホッ
KOFF
ぶほっ
PFFT

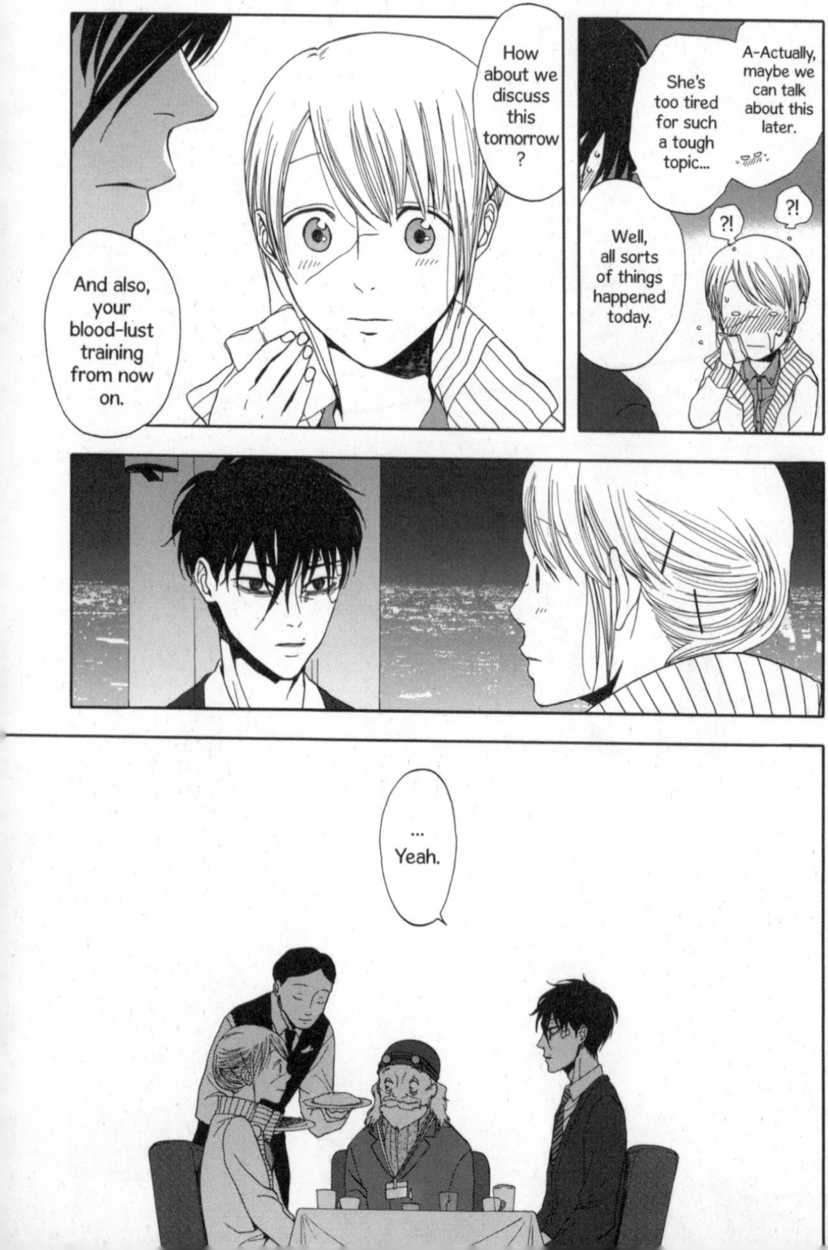
A-Actually, maybe we can talk about this later.
She's too tired for such a tough topic...
?!
?!
Well, all sorts of things happened today.
How about we discuss this tomorrow?
And also, your blood-lust training from now on.
... Yeah.

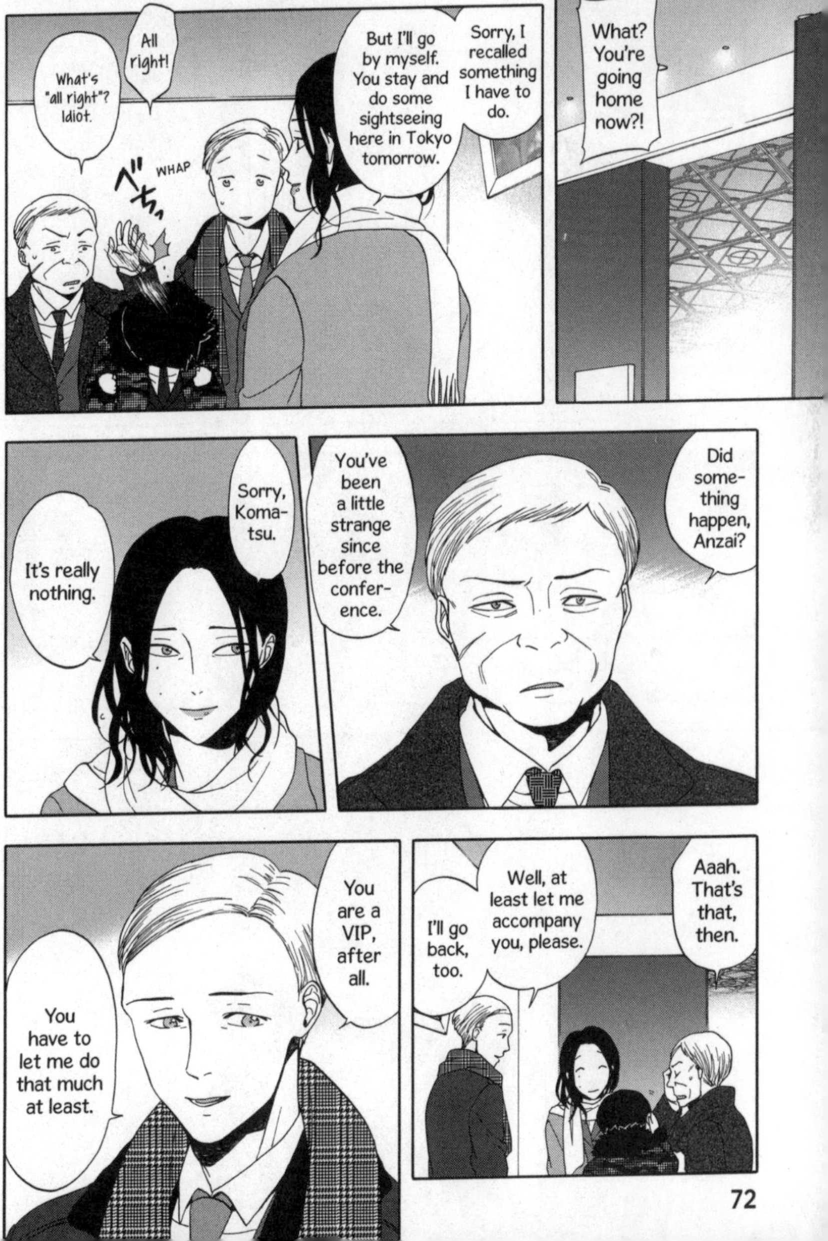
What? You're going home now?!
Sorry, I recalled something I have to do.
But I'll go by myself. You stay and do some sightseeing here in Tokyo tomorrow.
All right!
What's "all right"? Idiot.
WHAP
Did some-thing happen, Anzai?
You've been a little strange since before the confer-ence.
Sorry, Koma-tsu.
It's really nothing.
Aaah. That's that, then.
Well, at least let me accompany you, please.
I'll go back, too.
You are a VIP, after all.
You have to let me do that much at least.

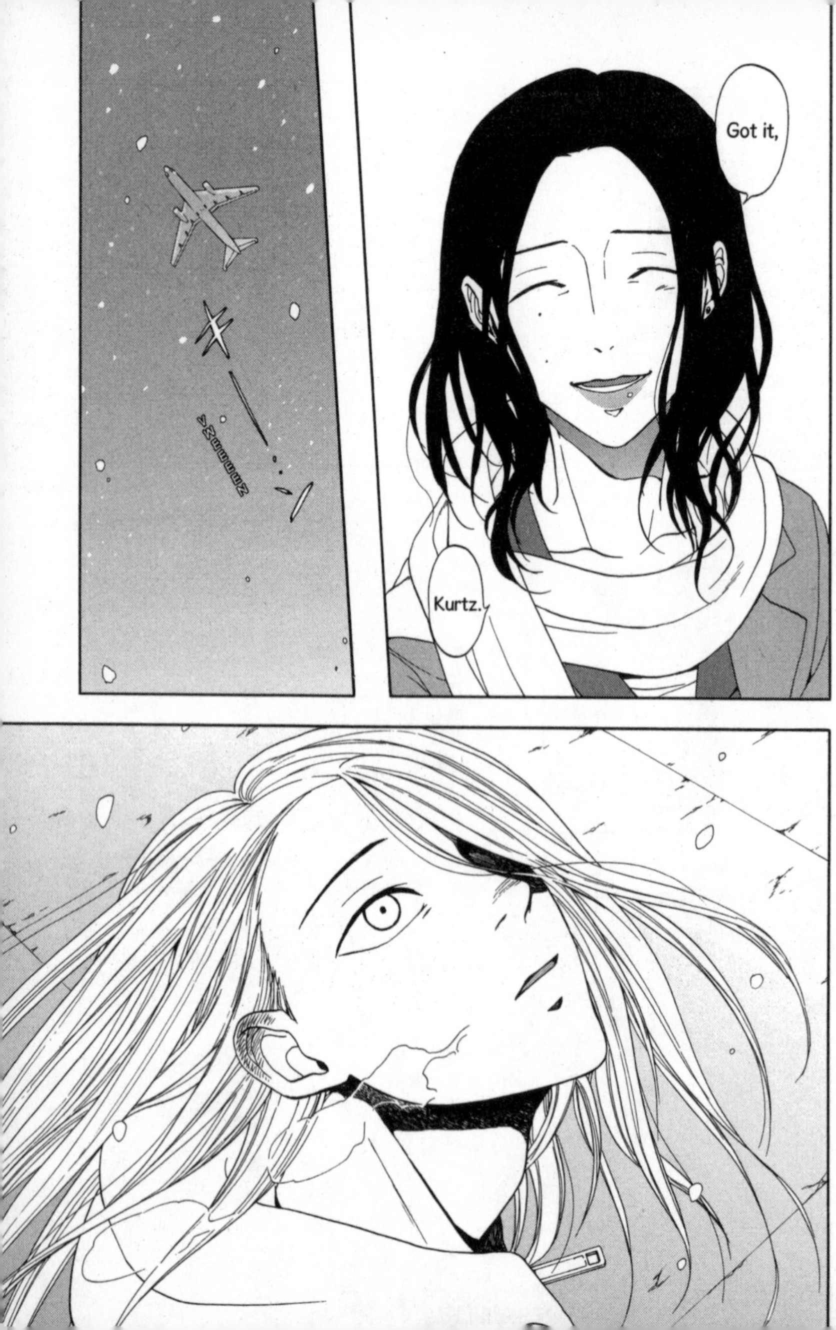
Got it,
Kurtz.

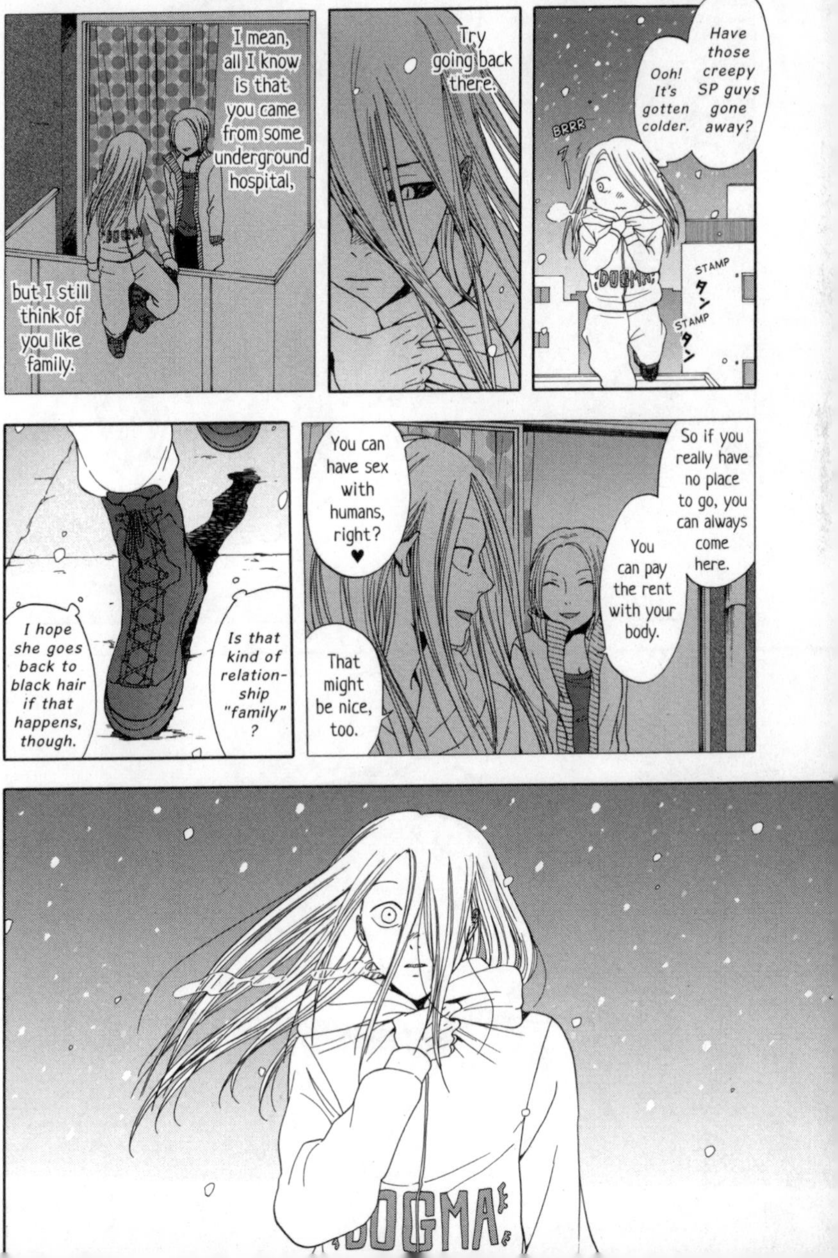
Have those creepy SP guys gone away?
Ooh! It's gotten colder.
BRRR
STAMP
タン
STAMP
タン
Try going back there.
I mean, all I know is that you came from some underground hospital,
but I still think of you like family.
So if you really have no place to go, you can always come here.
You can pay the rent with your body.
You can have sex with humans, right? ♥
That might be nice, too.
Is that kind of relationship "family"?
I hope she goes back to black hair if that happens, though.

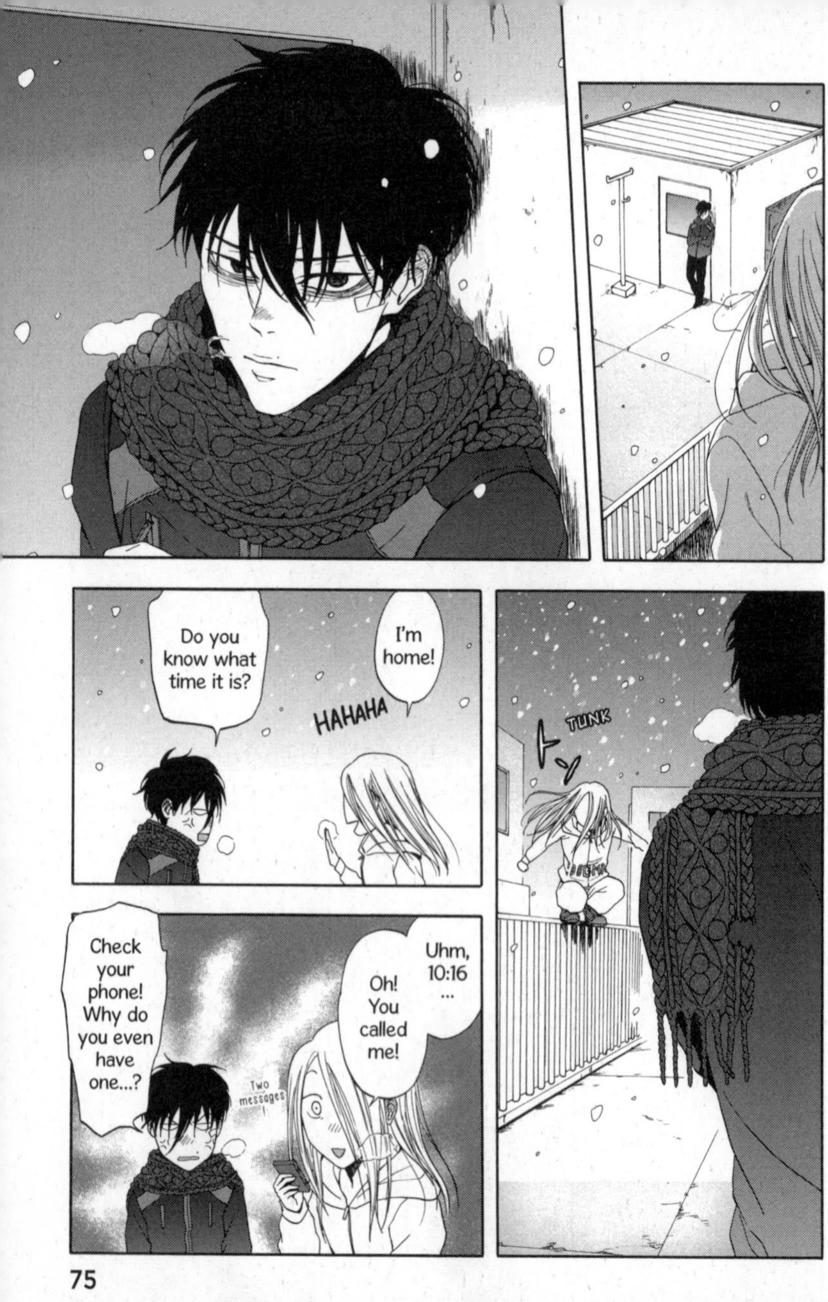
TUNK
I'm home!
HAHAHA
Do you know what time it is?
Uhm, 10:16 ...
Oh! You called me!
Two messages !
Check your phone! Why do you even have one...?

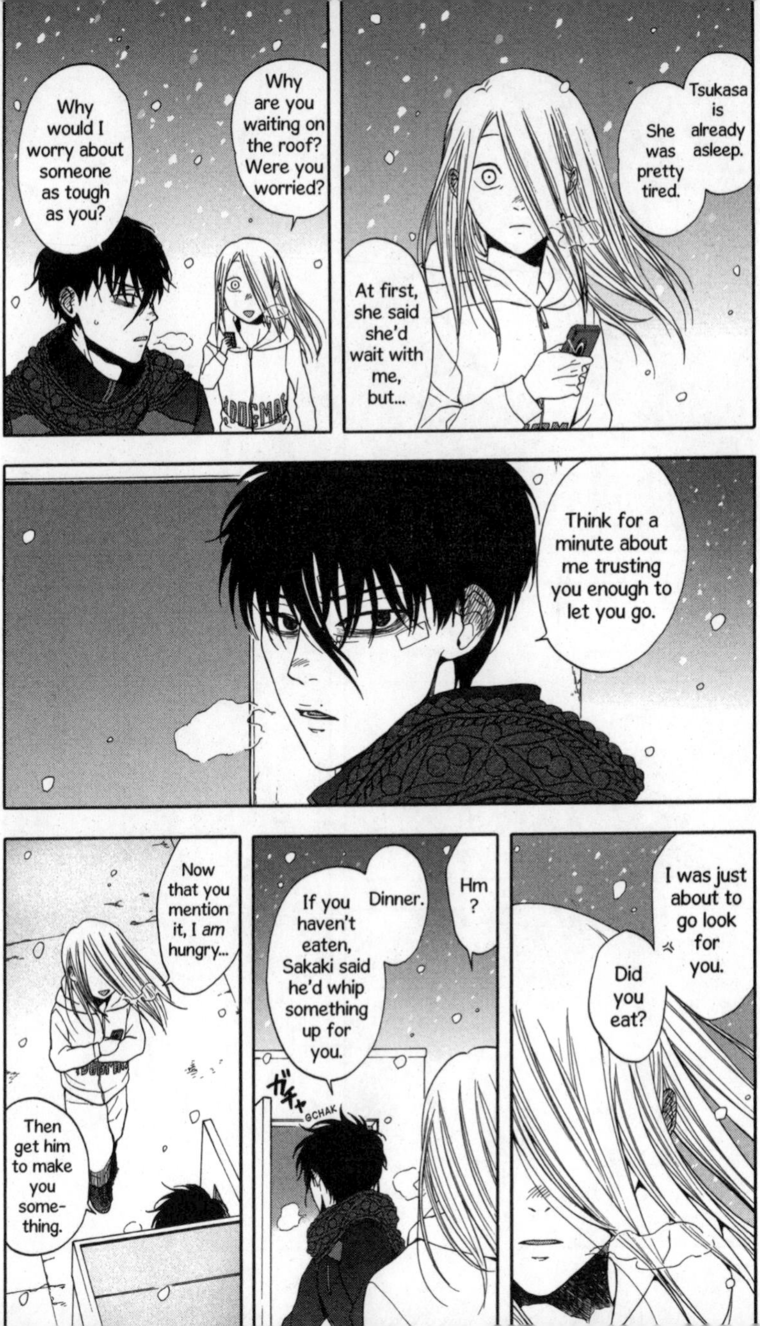
Tsukasa is already asleep.
She was pretty tired.
At first, she said she'd wait with me, but...
Why are you waiting on the roof? Were you worried?
Why would I worry about someone as tough as you?
Think for a minute about me trusting you enough to let you go.
I was just about to go look for you.
Did you eat?
Hm?
Dinner.
If you haven't eaten, Sakaki said he'd whip something up for you.
ガチャ
GCHAK
Now that you mention it, I *am* hungry...
Then get him to make you something.

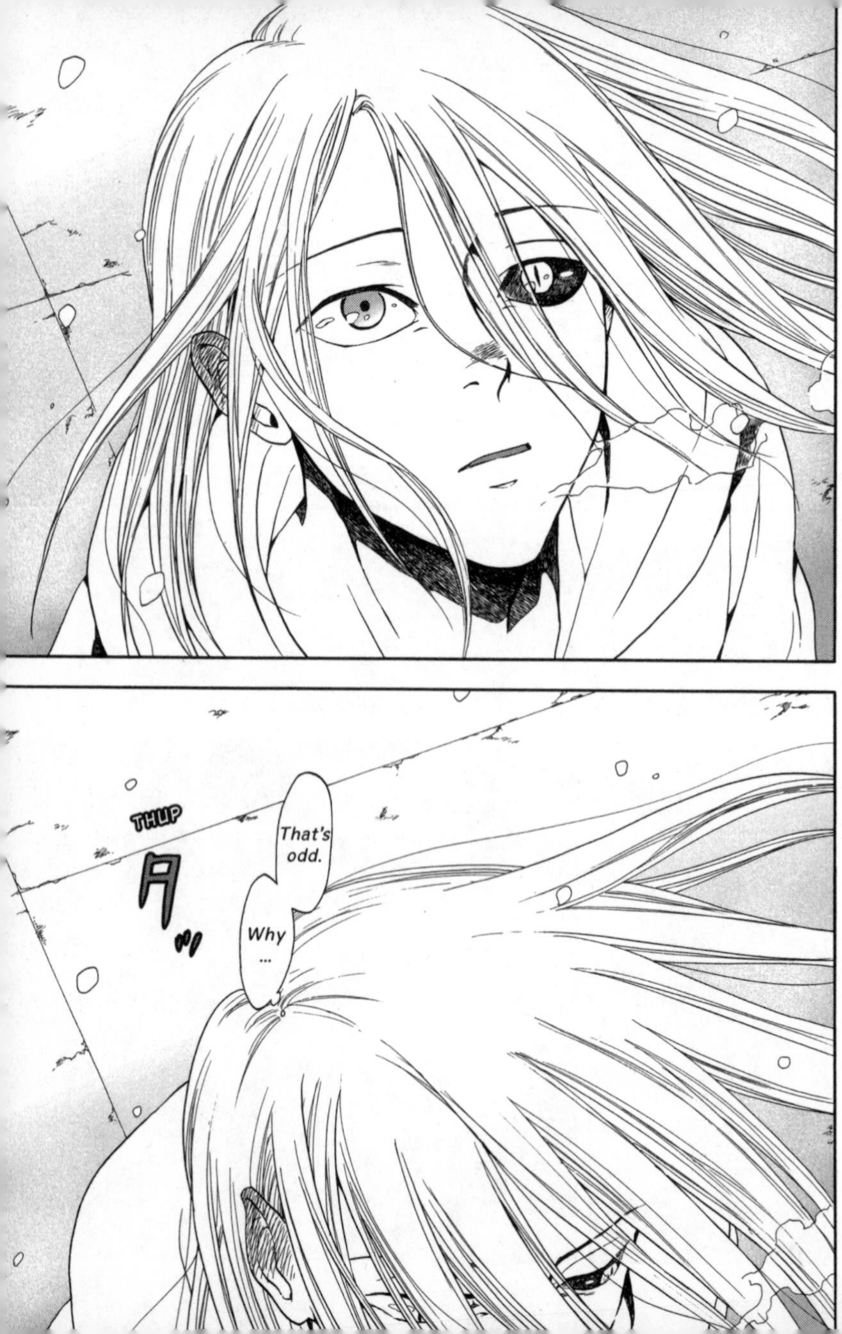
That's odd.
Why ...
THUP

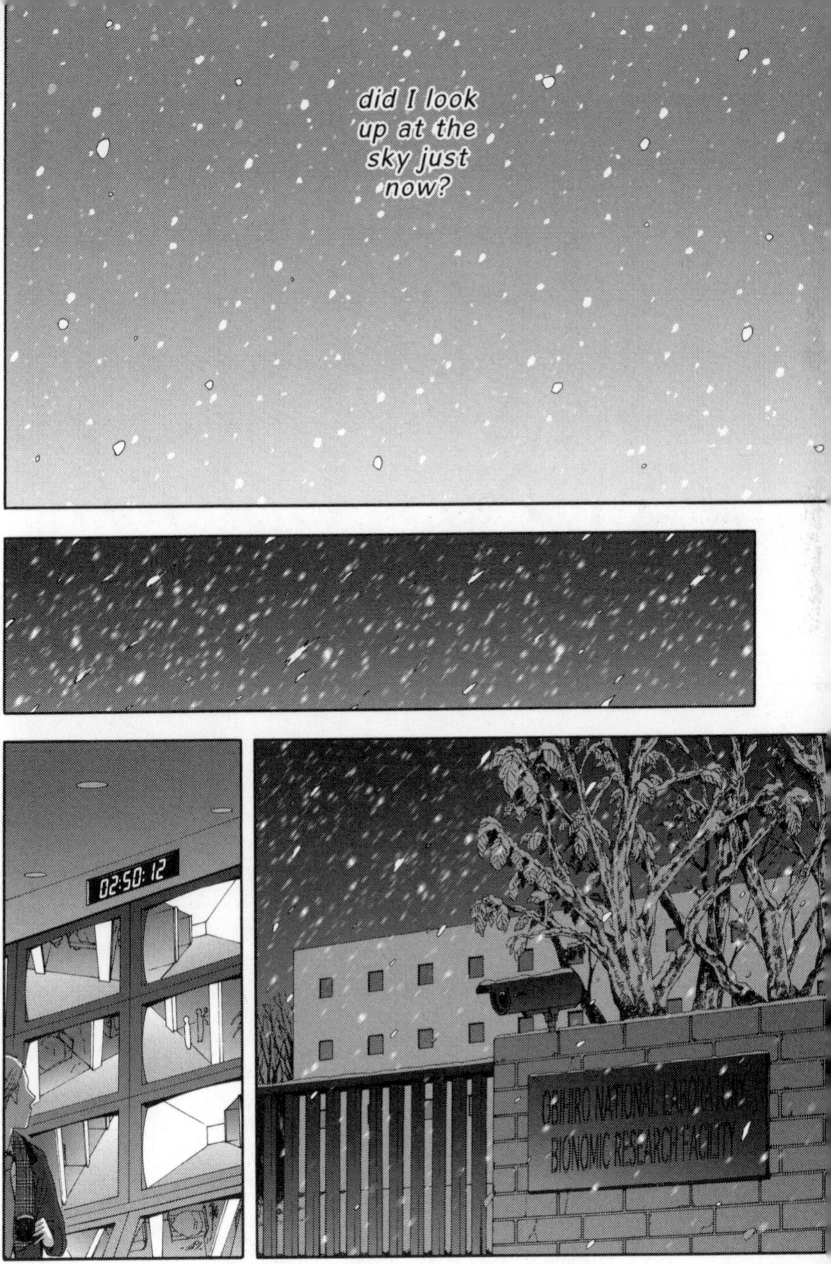
did I look up at the sky just now?
OBIHIRO NATIONAL
BIONOMIC RESEARCH FACILITY
02:50:12

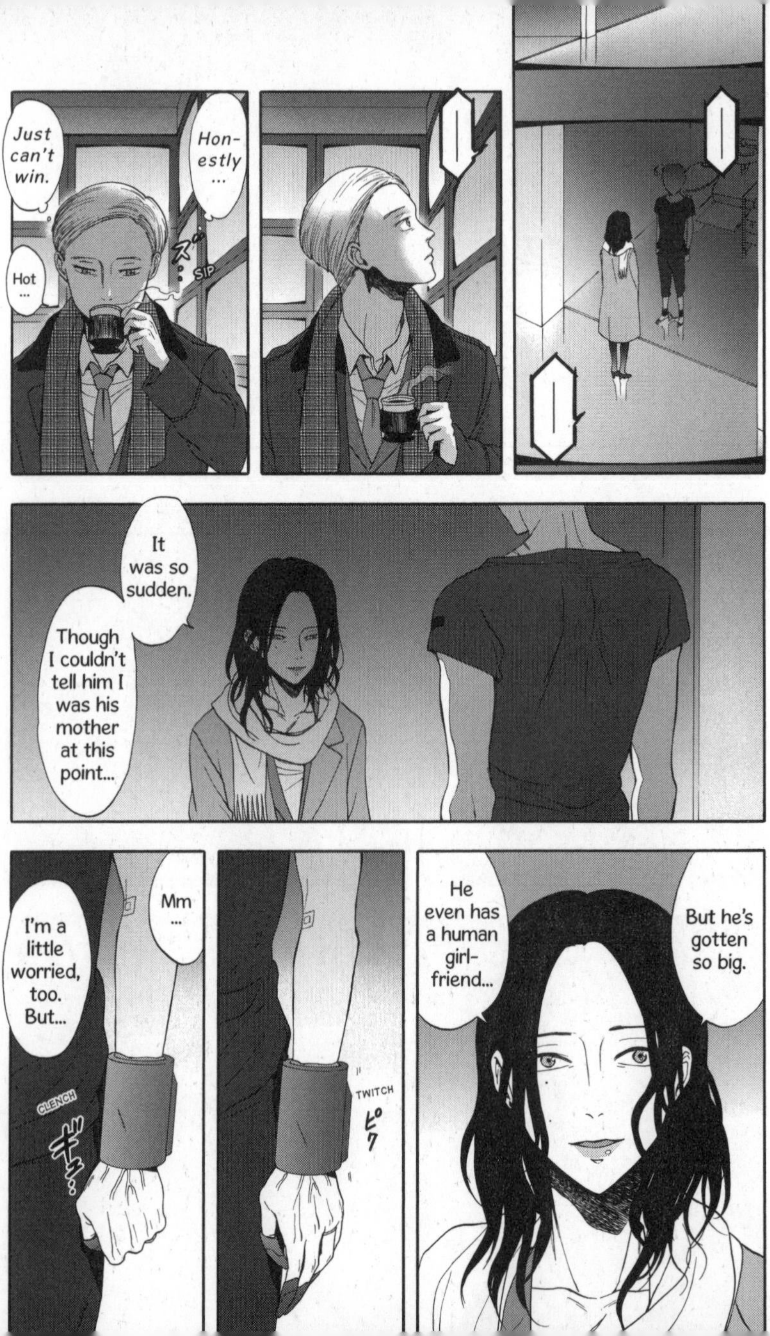
Hon-estly ...
Just can't win.
ズ
SIP
Hot ...
It was so sudden.
Though I couldn't tell him I was his mother at this point...
But he's gotten so big.
He even has a human girl-friend...
TWITCH
ピク
Mm ...
I'm a little worried, too. But...
CLENCH
ギュ

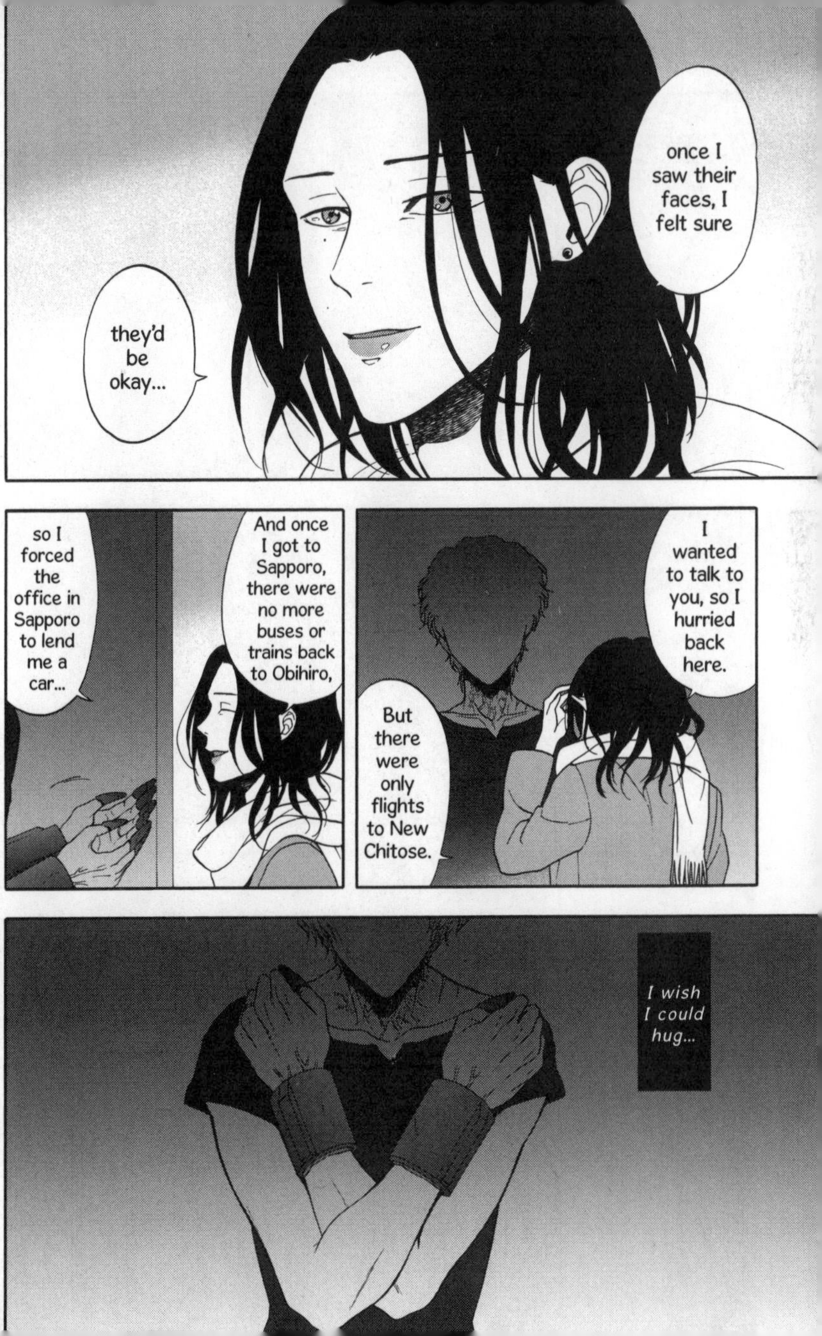
once I saw their faces, I felt sure
they'd be okay...
I wanted to talk to you, so I hurried back here.
But there were only flights to New Chitose.
And once I got to Sapporo, there were no more buses or trains back to Obihiro,
so I forced the office in Sapporo to lend me a car...
I wish I could hug...

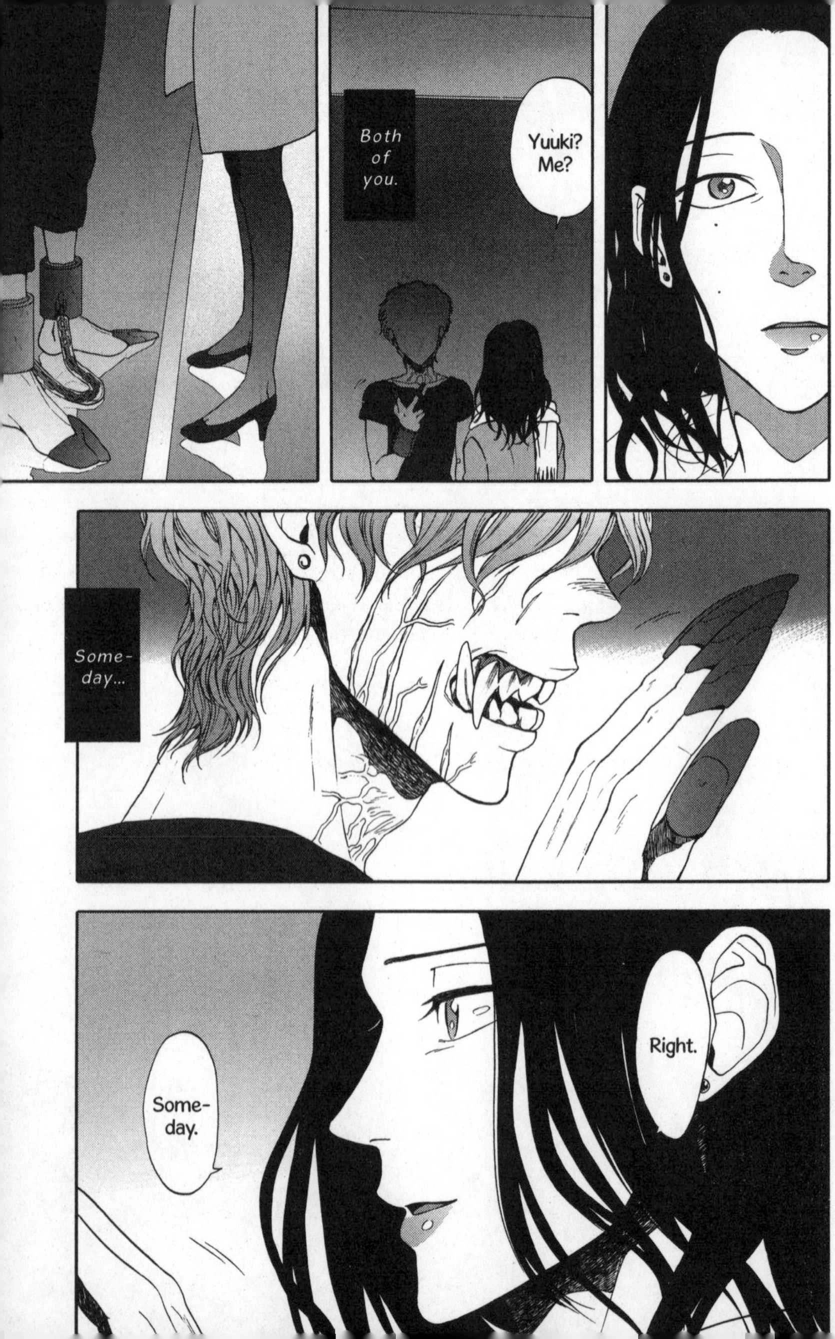
Yuuki? Me?
Both of you.
Some-day...
Right.
Some-day.

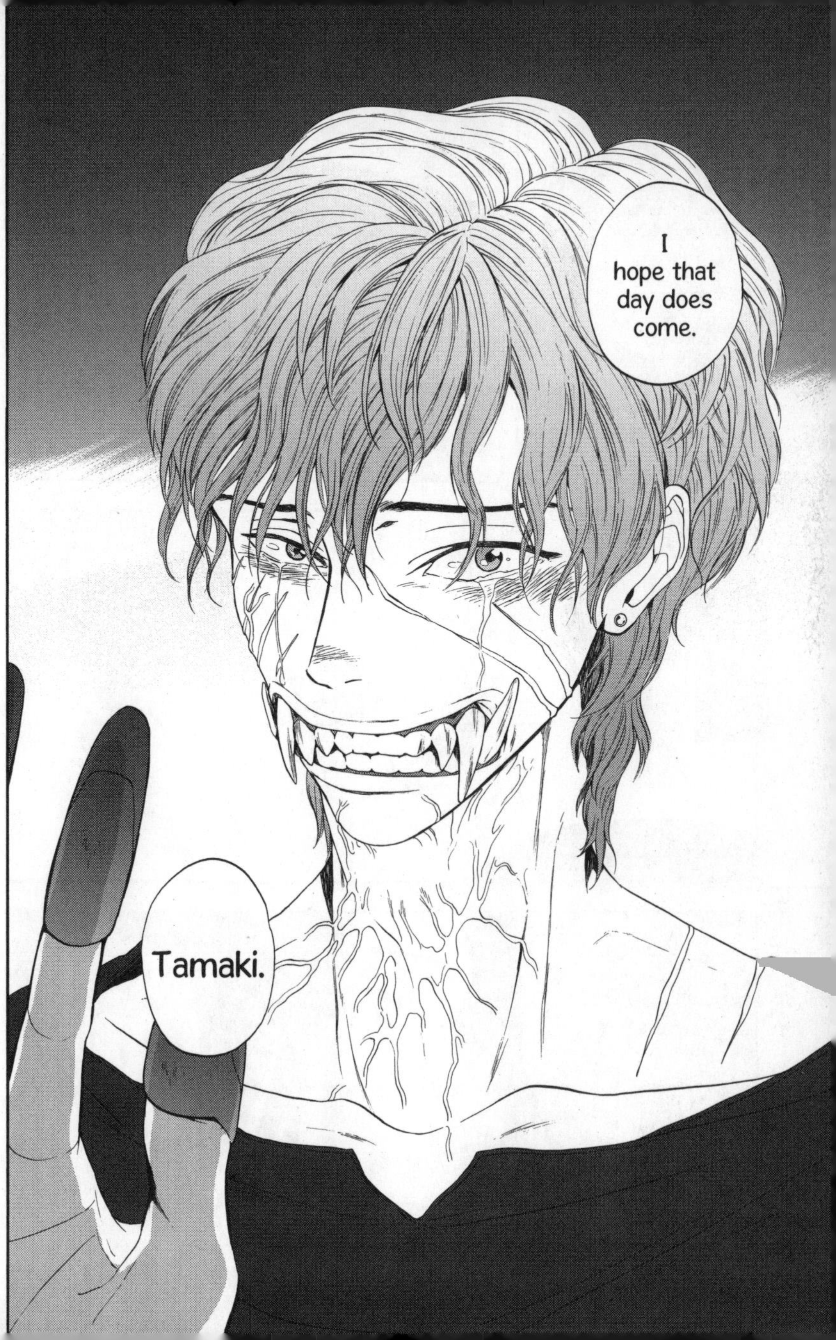
I hope that day does come.
Tamaki.

Dr. Feng Jing,
before she cut
and dyed her hair

(The shape of her chest
is lovely.)

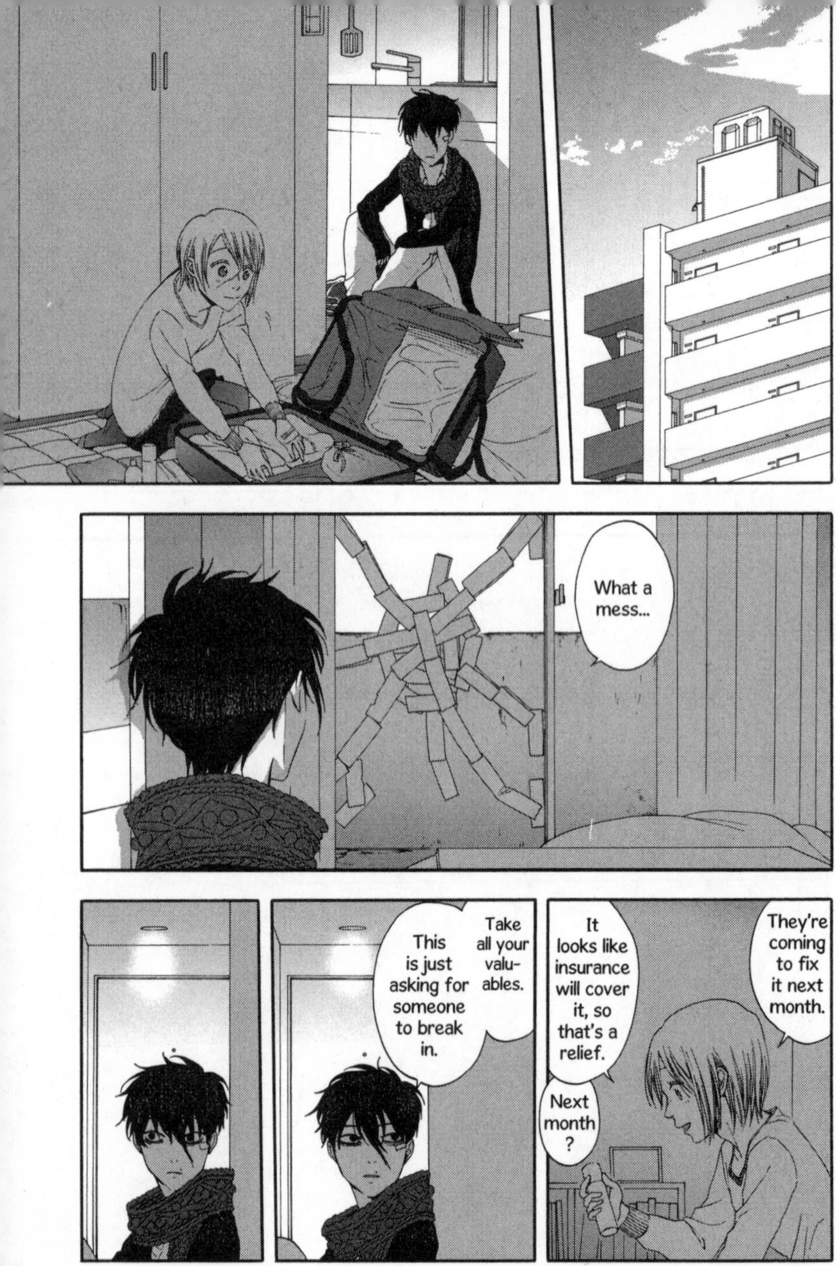
What a mess...
They're coming to fix it next month.
It looks like insurance will cover it, so that's a relief.
Next month?
Take all your valu-ables.
This is just asking for someone to break in.

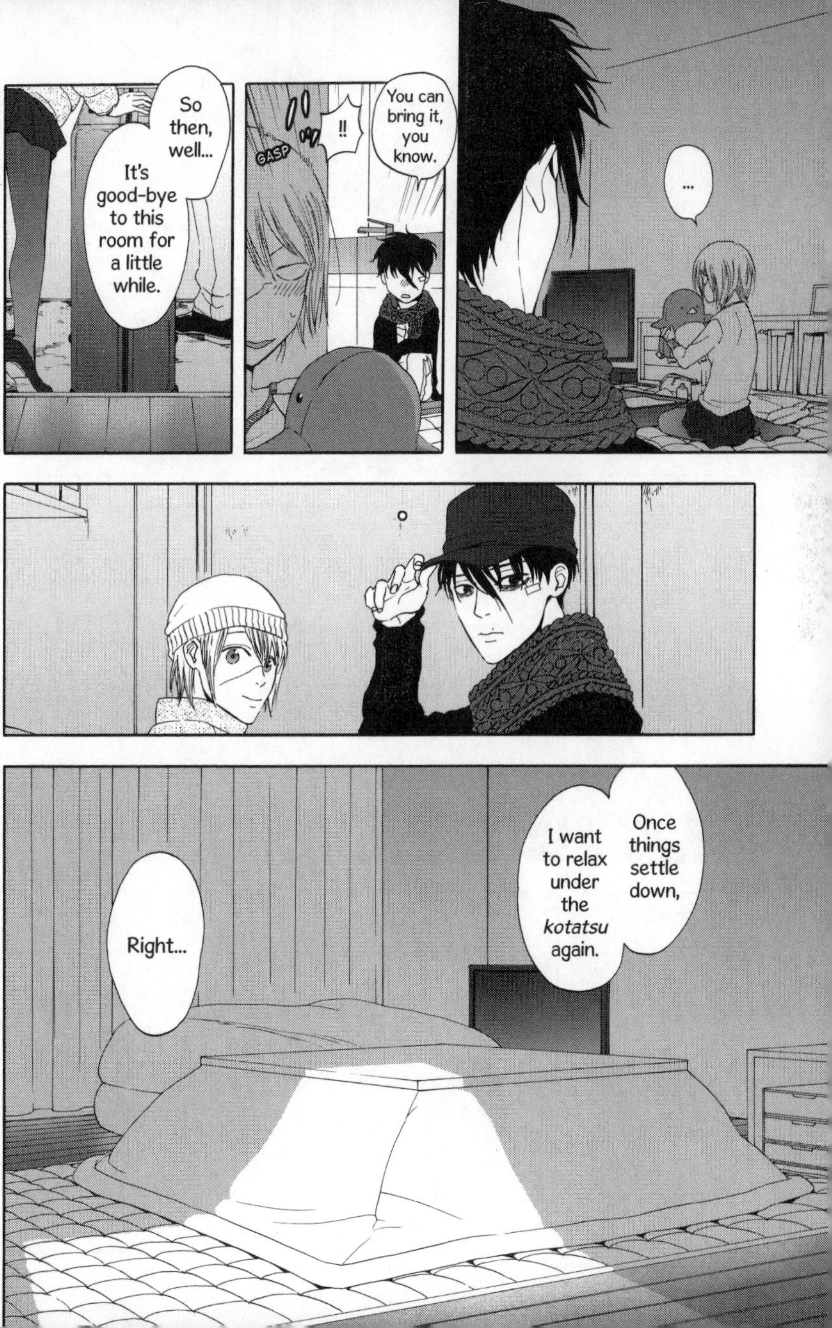
...
!!
GASP
You can bring it, you know.
So then, well...
It's good-bye to this room for a little while.
Once things settle down,
I want to relax under the *kotatsu* again.
Right...

Line 25
Offline

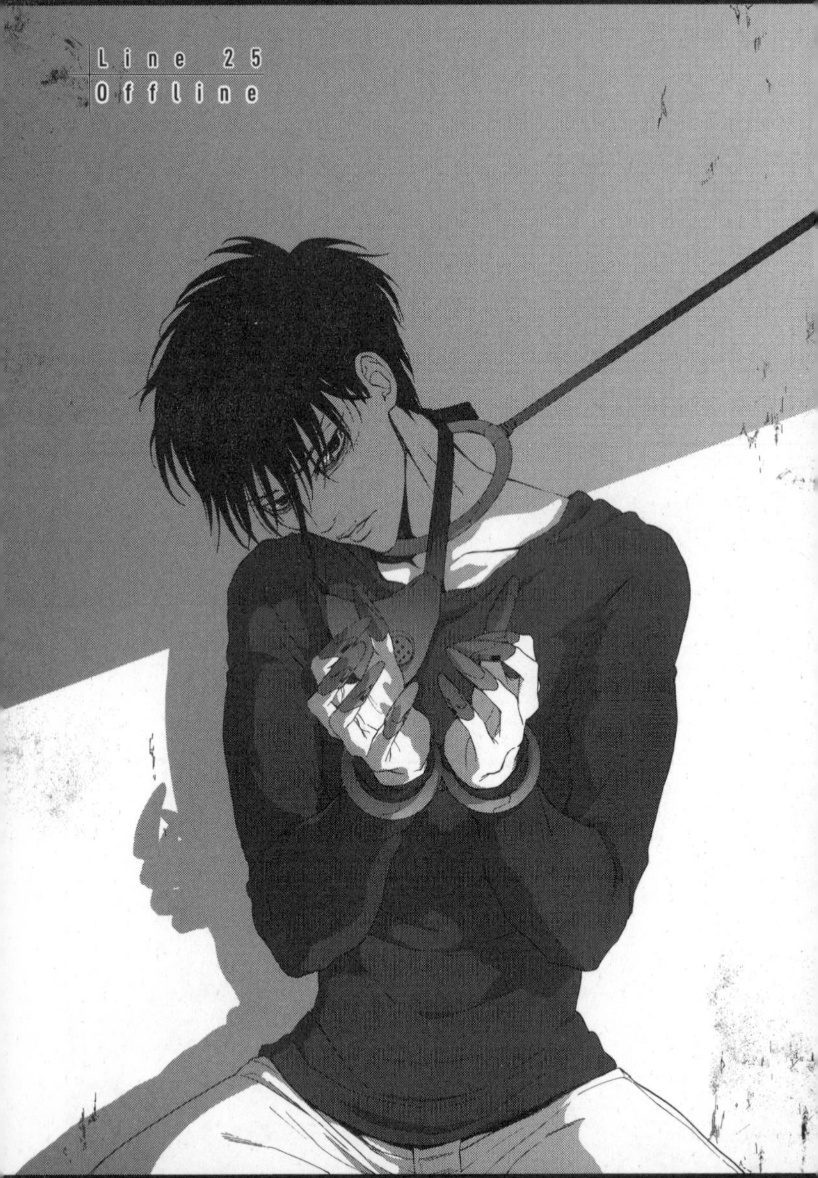

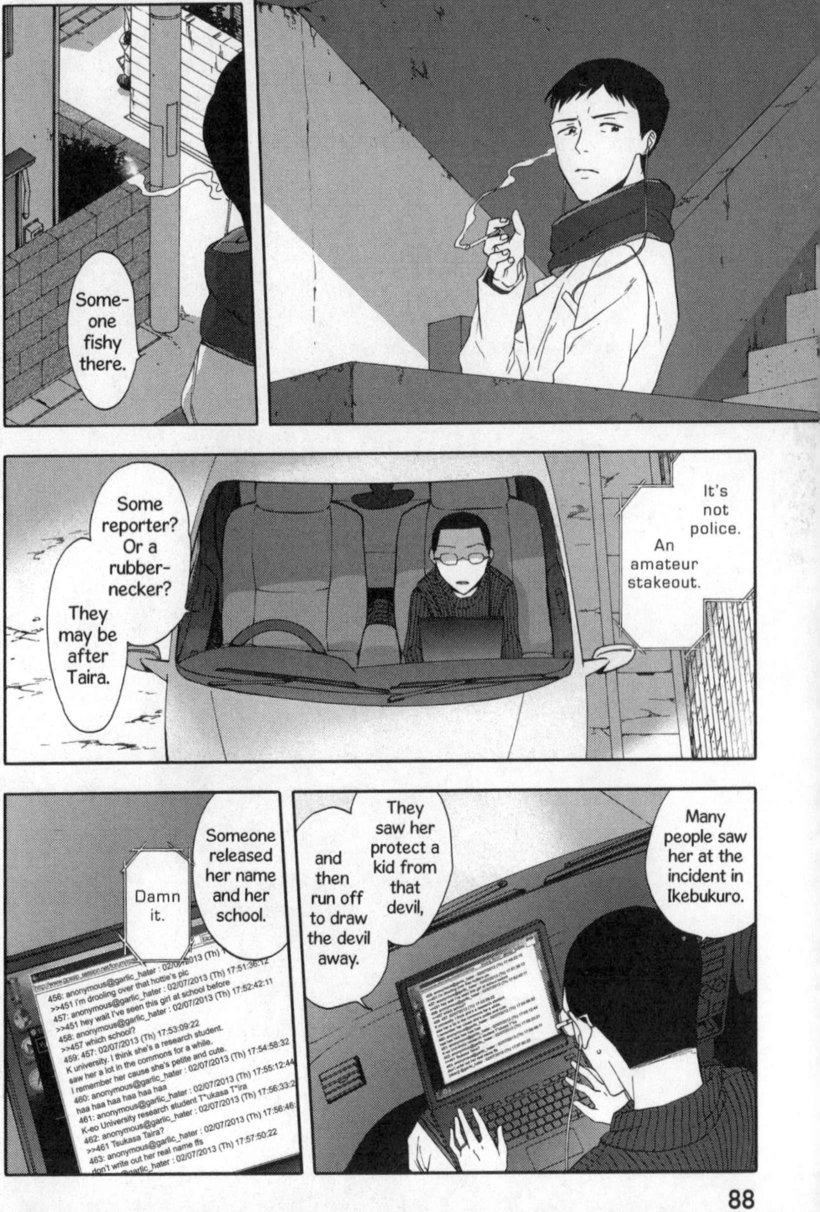
Some-one fishy there.
It's not police. An amateur stakeout.
Some reporter? Or a rubber-necker?
They may be after Taira.
Many people saw her at the incident in Ikebukuro.
They saw her protect a kid from that devil,
and then run off to draw the devil away.
Someone released her name and her school.
Damn it.
456: anonymous@garlic_hater :
>>451 I'm drooling over that hottie's pic
457: anonymous@garlic_hater : 02/07/2013 (Th) 17:51:36:12
>>451 hey wait I've seen this girl at school before
458: anonymous@garlic_hater : 02/07/2013 (Th) 17:52:42:11
>>457 which school?
459: 457: 02/07/2013 (Th) 17:53:09:22
K university. I think she's a research student.
saw her a lot in the commons for a while.
I remember her cause she's petite and cute.
460: anonymous@garlic_hater : 02/07/2013 (Th) 17:54:58:32
haa haa haa haa haa haa
461: anonymous@garlic_hater : 02/07/2013 (Th) 17:55:12:44
K-eo University research student T*ukasa T*ira
462: anonymous@garlic_hater : 02/07/2013 (Th) 17:56:33:2
>>461 Tsukasa Taira?
463: anonymous@garlic_hater : 02/07/2013 (Th) 17:56:46:
don't write out her real name ffs
@garlic_hater : 02/07/2013 (Th) 17:57:50:22

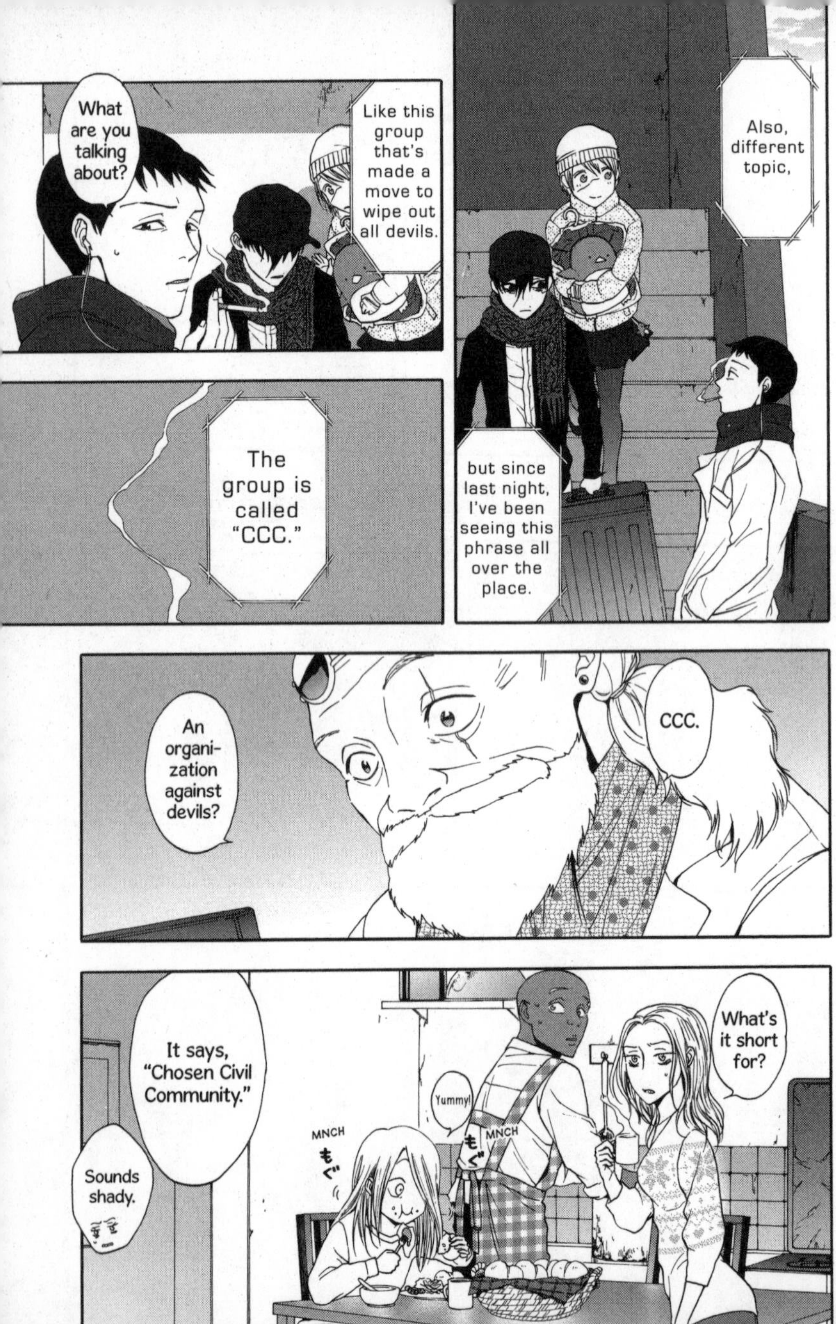

Also, different topic,
but since last night, I've been seeing this phrase all over the place.
Like this group that's made a move to wipe out all devils.
What are you talking about?
The group is called "CCC."
CCC.
An organization against devils?
What's it short for?
MNCH
もぐ
Yummy!
It says, "Chosen Civil Community."
MNCH
もぐ
Sounds shady.

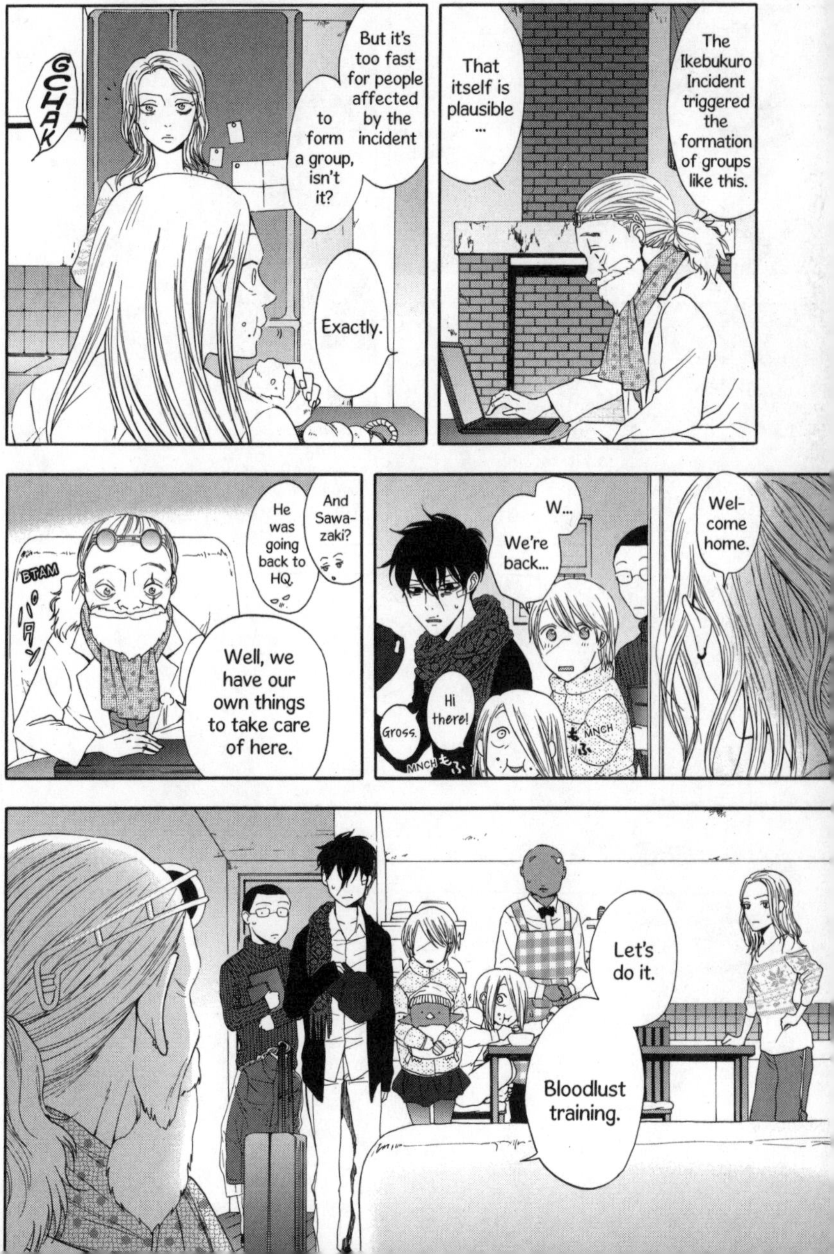

The Ikebukuro Incident triggered the formation of groups like this.
That itself is plausible ...
But it's too fast for people affected by the incident to form a group, isn't it?
GCHAK
Exactly.
Welcome home.
W... We're back...
Hi there!
Gross.
MNCH もふ
MNCH もふ
And Sawazaki?
He was going back to HQ.
BTAM
Well, we have our own things to take care of here.
Let's do it.
Bloodlust training.

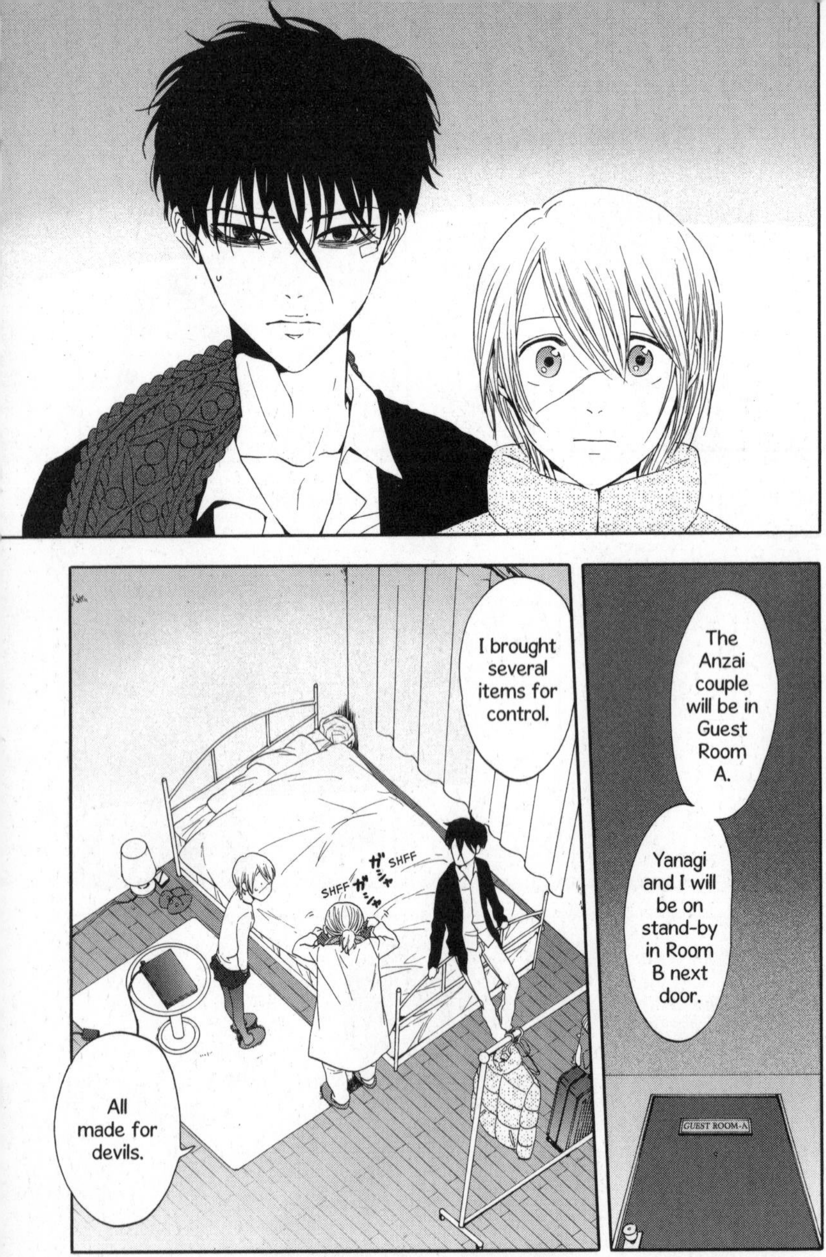
The Anzai couple will be in Guest Room A.
Yanagi and I will be on stand-by in Room B next door.
GUEST ROOM-A
I brought several items for control.
SHFF
ガシャ
SHFF
ガシャ
All made for devils.

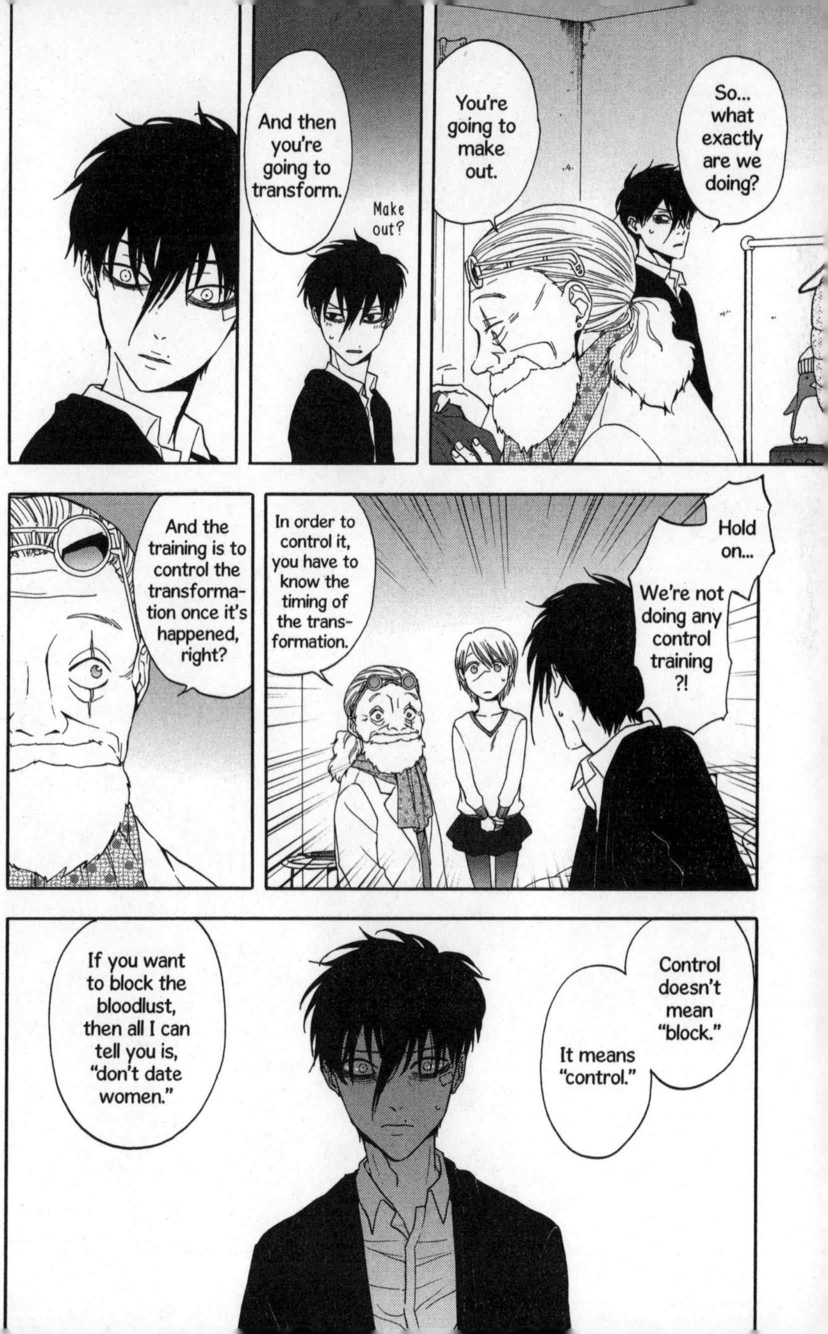
So... what exactly are we doing?
You're going to make out.
Make out?
And then you're going to transform.
Hold on...
We're not doing any control training?!
In order to control it, you have to know the timing of the trans-formation.
And the training is to control the transforma-tion once it's happened, right?
Control doesn't mean "block."
It means "control."
If you want to block the bloodlust, then all I can tell you is, "don't date women."

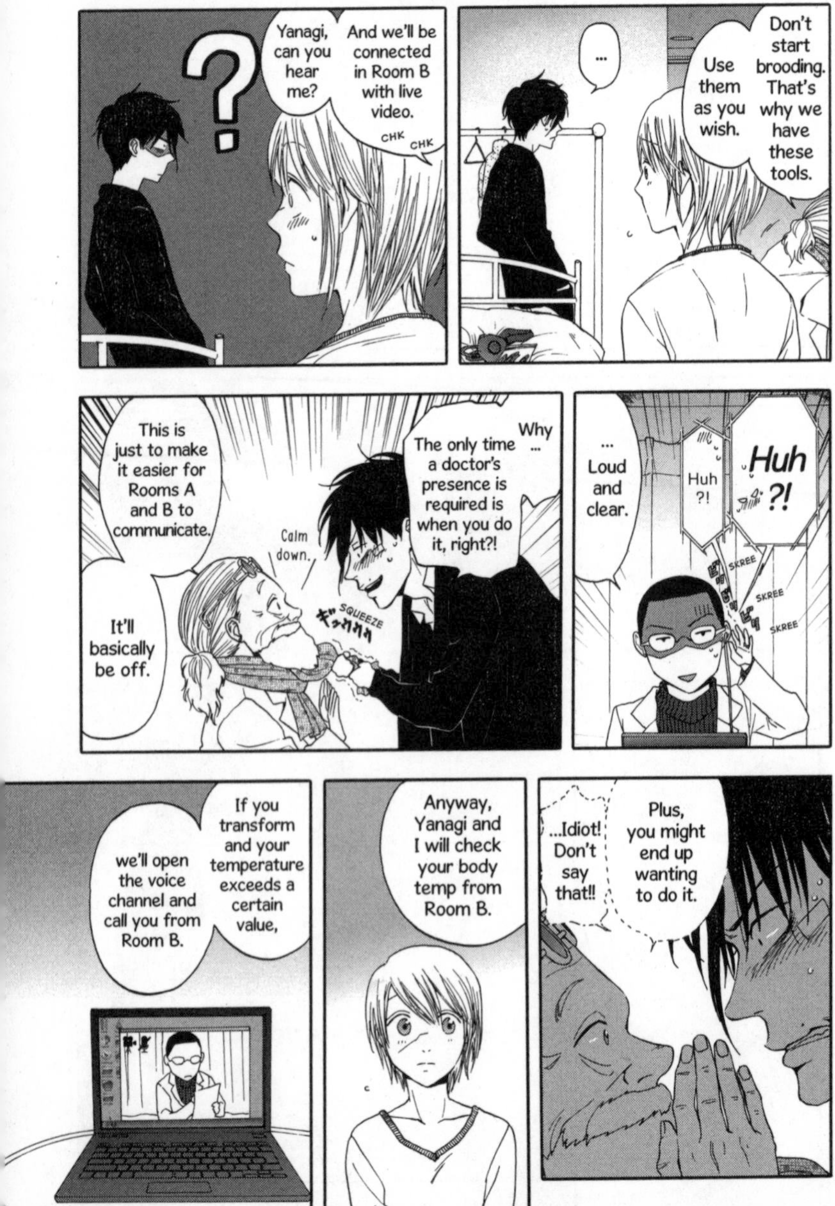
Don't start brooding. That's why we have these tools.
Use them as you wish.
...
And we'll be connected in Room B with live video.
Yanagi, can you hear me?
CHK
CHK
Huh ?!
Huh ?!
SKREE
SKREE
SKREE
... Loud and clear.
Why ...
The only time a doctor's presence is required is when you do it, right?!
SQUEEZE
This is just to make it easier for Rooms A and B to communicate.
Calm down.
It'll basically be off.
Plus, you might end up wanting to do it.
...Idiot! Don't say that!!
Anyway, Yanagi and I will check your body temp from Room B.
If you transform and your temperature exceeds a certain value,
we'll open the voice channel and call you from Room B.

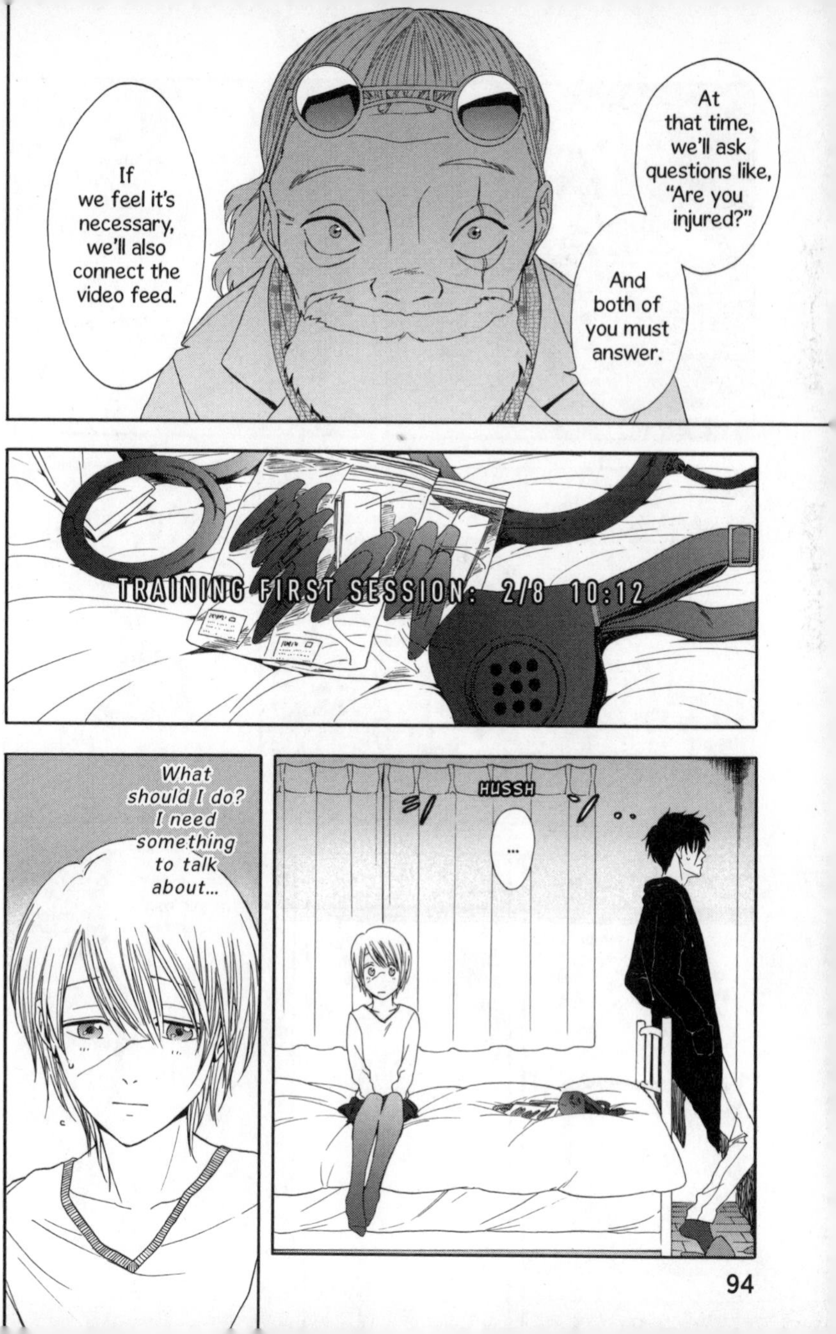
At that time, we'll ask questions like, "Are you injured?"
And both of you must answer.
If we feel it's necessary, we'll also connect the video feed.
TRAINING FIRST SESSION: 2/8 10:12
HUSSH
...
What should I do? I need something to talk about...

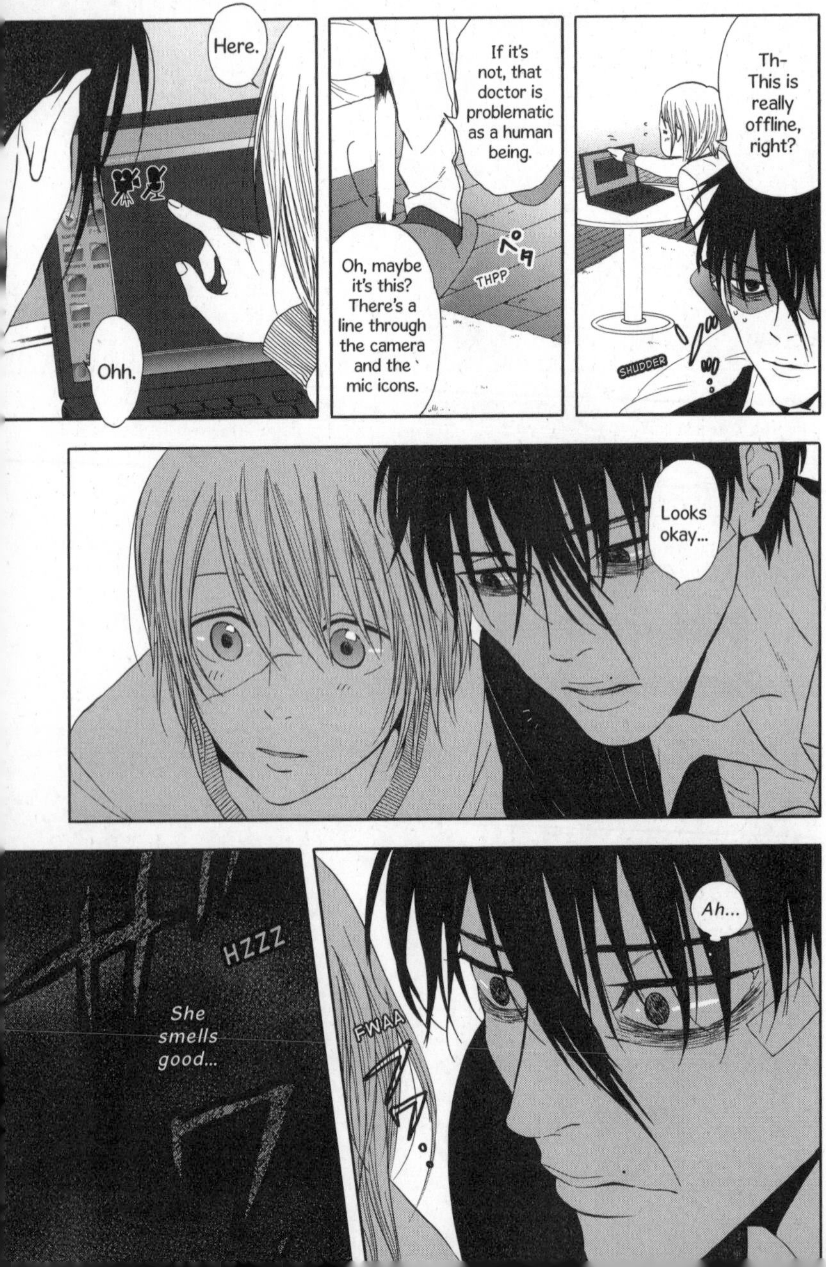
Th- This is really offline, right?
SHUDDER
If it's not, that doctor is problematic as a human being.
THPP
Oh, maybe it's this? There's a line through the camera and the mic icons.
Here.
Ohh.
Looks okay...
Ah...
FWAA
HZZZ
She smells good...

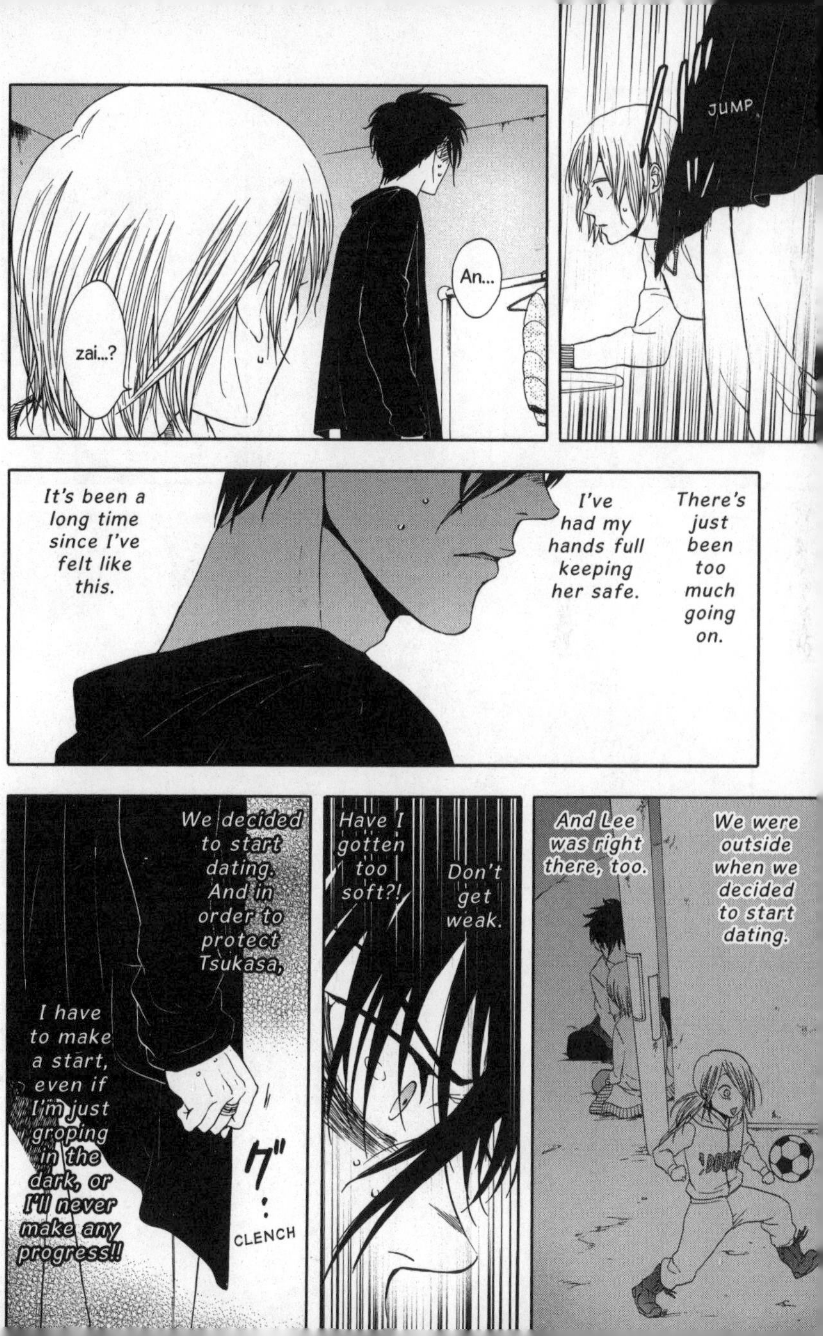
JUMP
An...
zai...?
There's just been too much going on.
I've had my hands full keeping her safe.
It's been a long time since I've felt like this.
We were outside when we decided to start dating.
And Lee was right there, too.
Don't get weak.
Have I gotten too soft?!
We decided to start dating. And in order to protect Tsukasa,
I have to make a start, even if I'm just groping in the dark, or I'll never make any progress!!
CLENCH

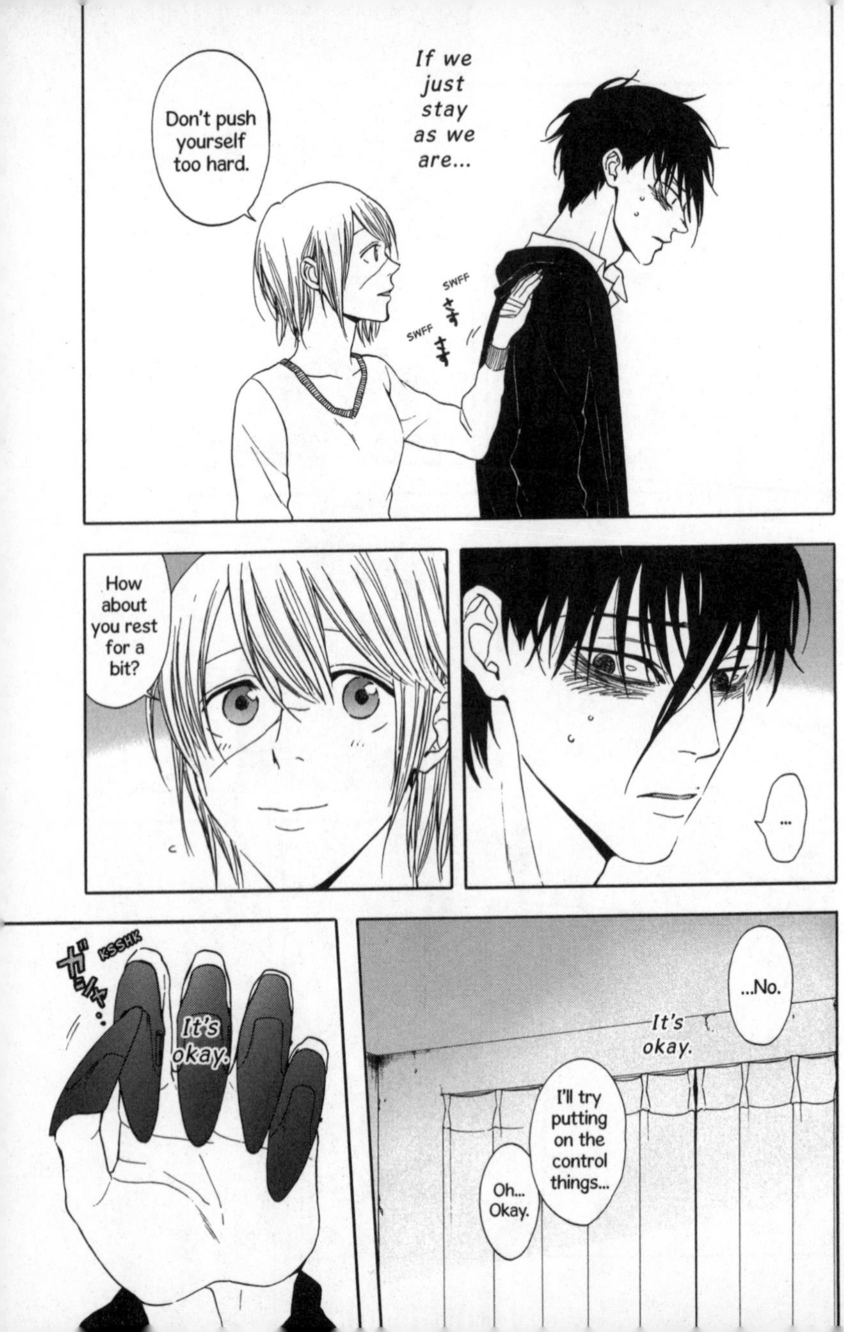
If we just stay as we are...
Don't push yourself too hard.
SWFF
さす
SWFF
さす
...
How about you rest for a bit?
...No.
It's okay.
I'll try putting on the control things...
Oh... Okay.
KSSHK
It's okay.

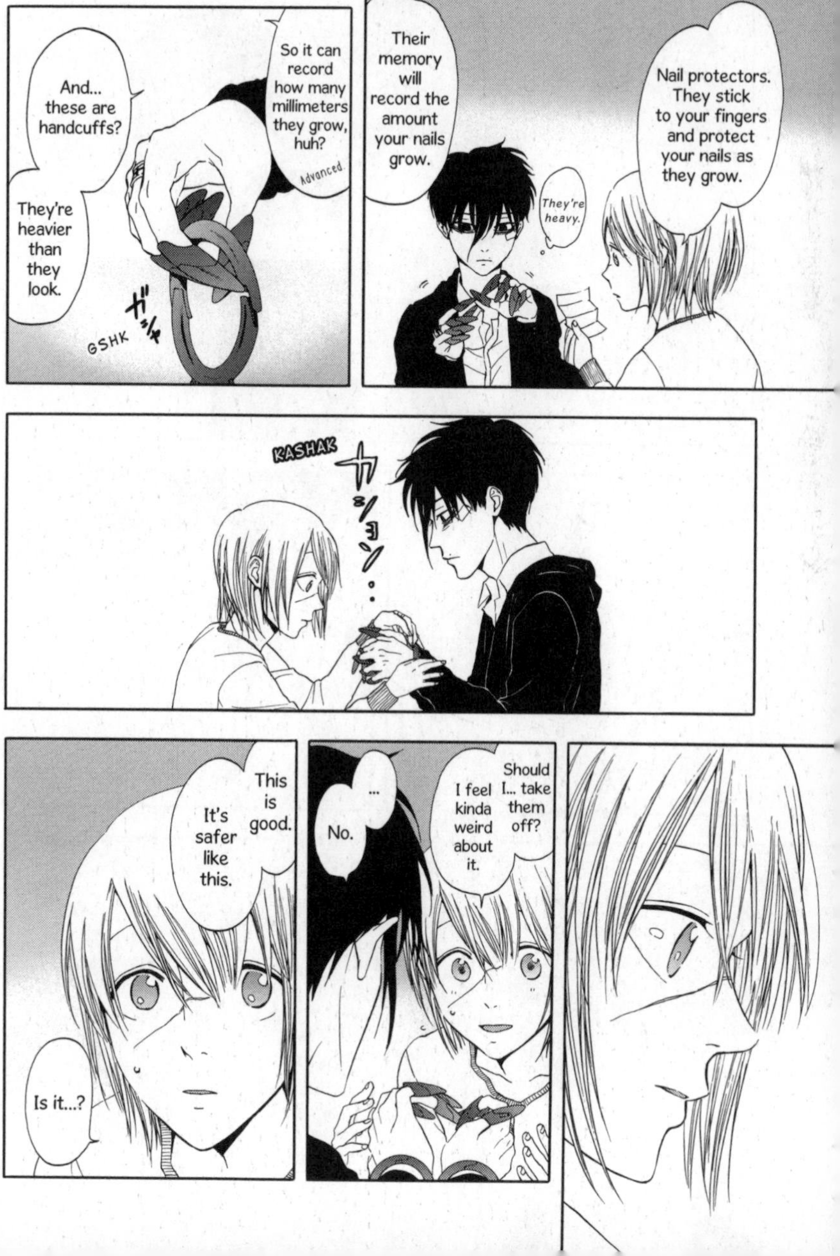
Nail protectors. They stick to your fingers and protect your nails as they grow.
They're heavy.
Their memory will record the amount your nails grow.
So it can record how many millimeters they grow, huh?
Advanced.
And... these are handcuffs?
They're heavier than they look.
GSHK
KASHAK
Should I... take them off?
I feel kinda weird about it.
...
No.
This is good.
It's safer like this.
Is it...?

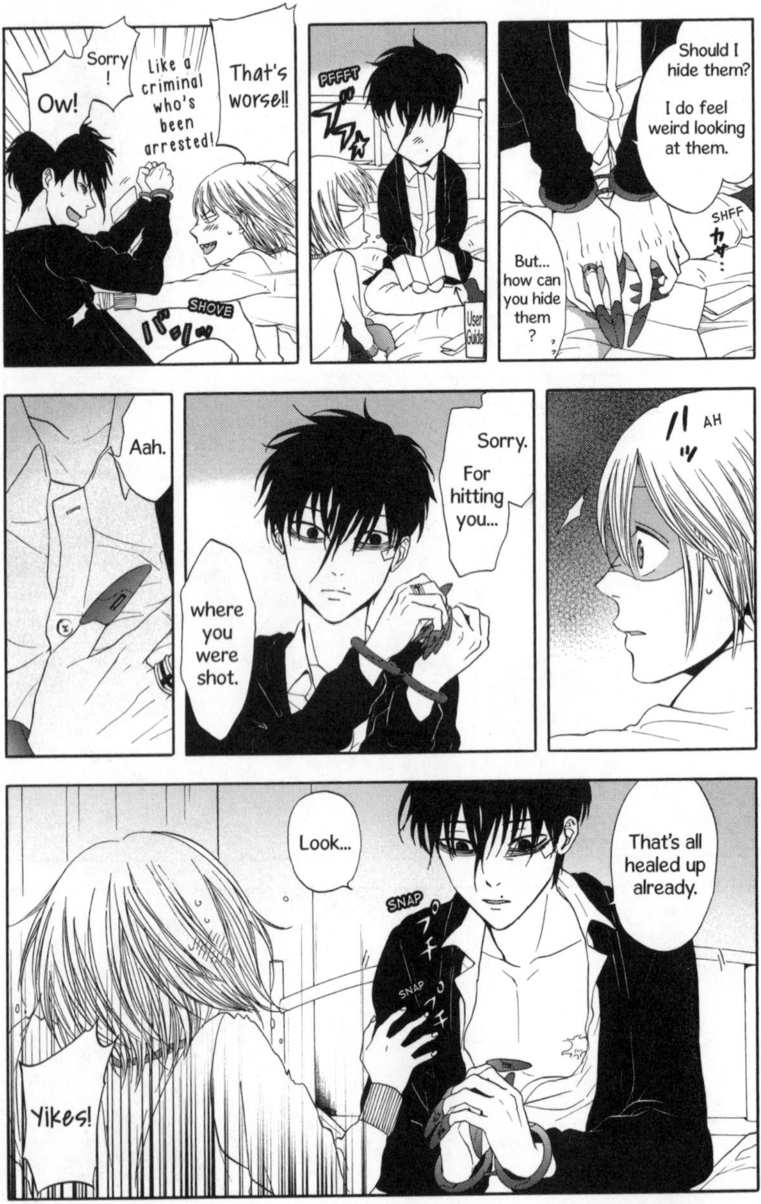
Should I hide them?
I do feel weird looking at them.
SHFF
カサ…
But... how can you hide them?
PFFFT
User Guide
That's worse!!
Like a criminal who's been arrested!
Sorry!
Ow!
SHOVE
AH
ハッ
Sorry.
For hitting you...
where you were shot.
Aah.
That's all healed up already.
Look...
SNAP
プチ
SNAP
プチ
Yikes!

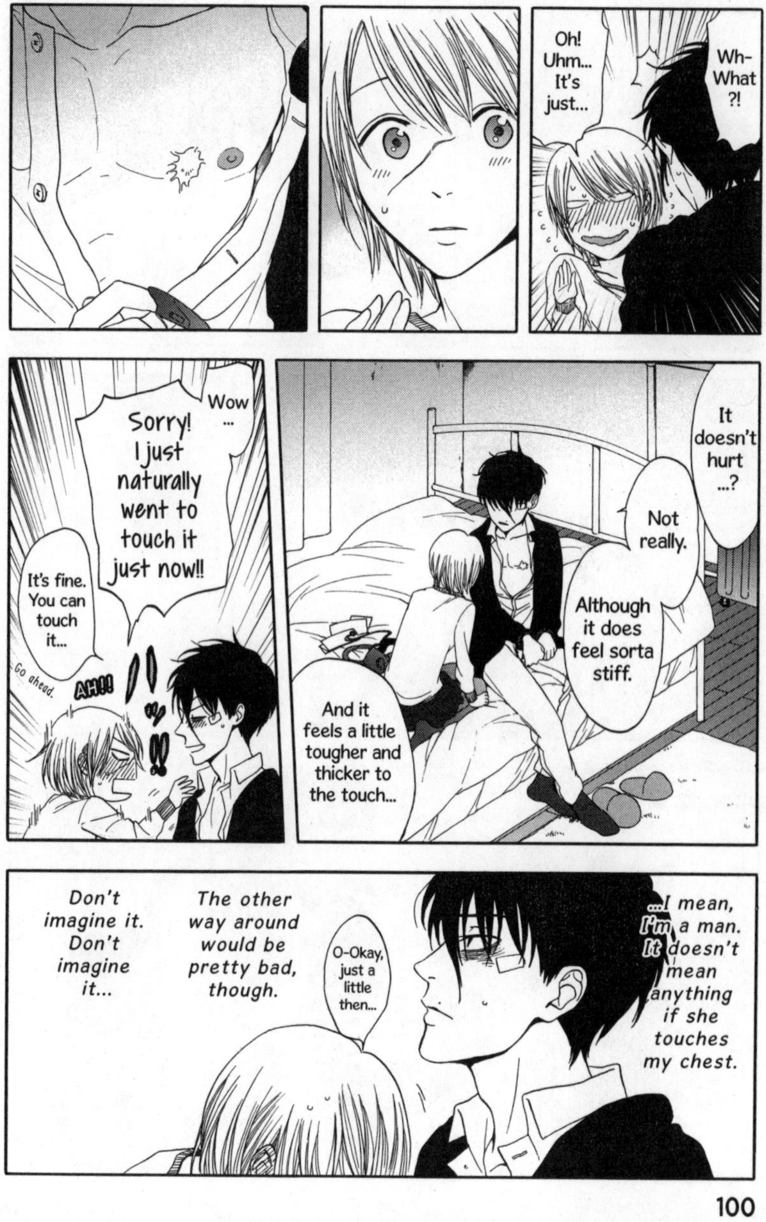
Wh- What ?!
Oh! Uhm... It's just...
It doesn't hurt ...?
Not really.
Although it does feel sorta stiff.
And it feels a little tougher and thicker to the touch...
Wow ...
Sorry! I just naturally went to touch it just now!!
It's fine. You can touch it...
Go ahead.
AH!!
...I mean, I'm a man. It doesn't mean anything if she touches my chest.
O-Okay, just a little then...
The other way around would be pretty bad, though.
Don't imagine it. Don't imagine it...

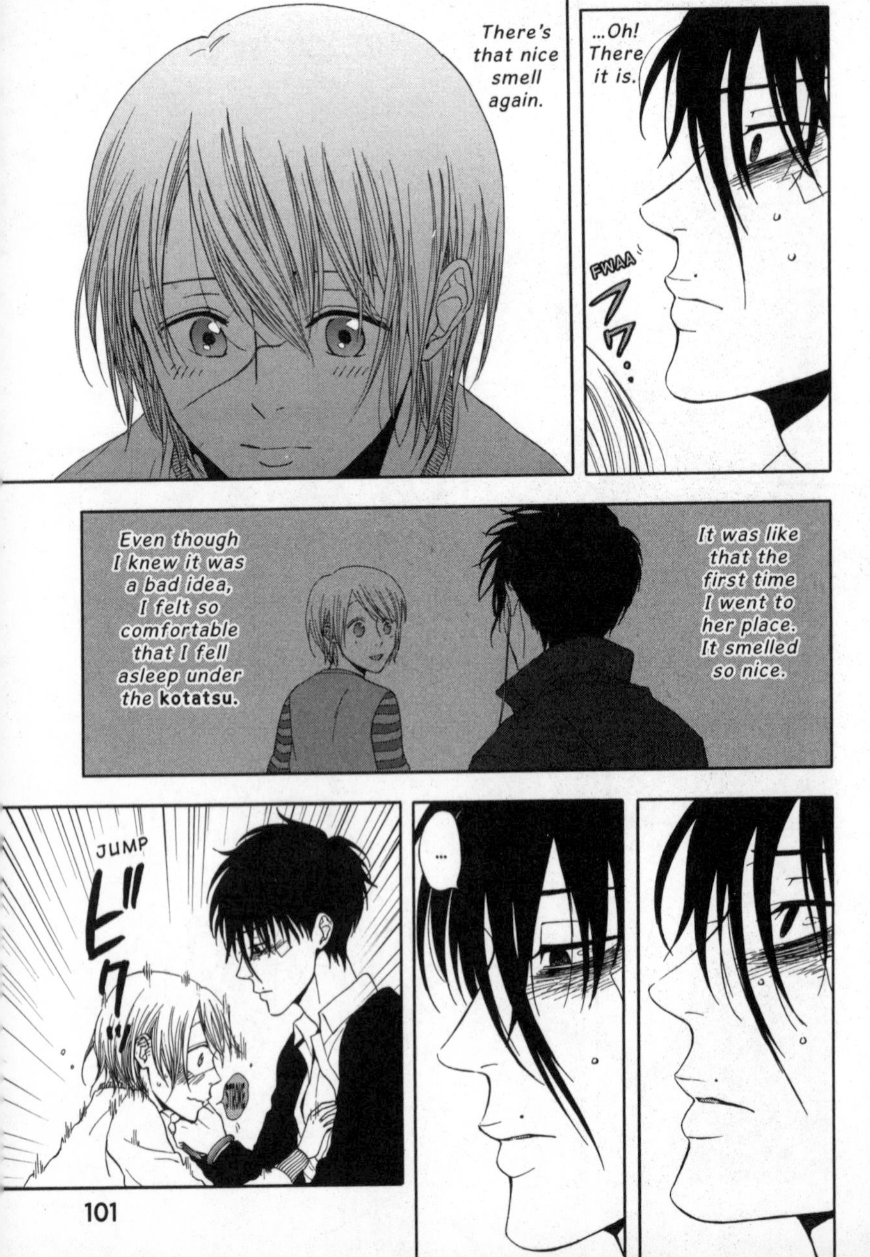
...Oh! There it is.
FWAA
There's that nice smell again.
It was like that the first time I went to her place. It smelled so nice.
Even though I knew it was a bad idea, I felt so comfortable that I fell asleep under the **kotatsu.**
...
JUMP

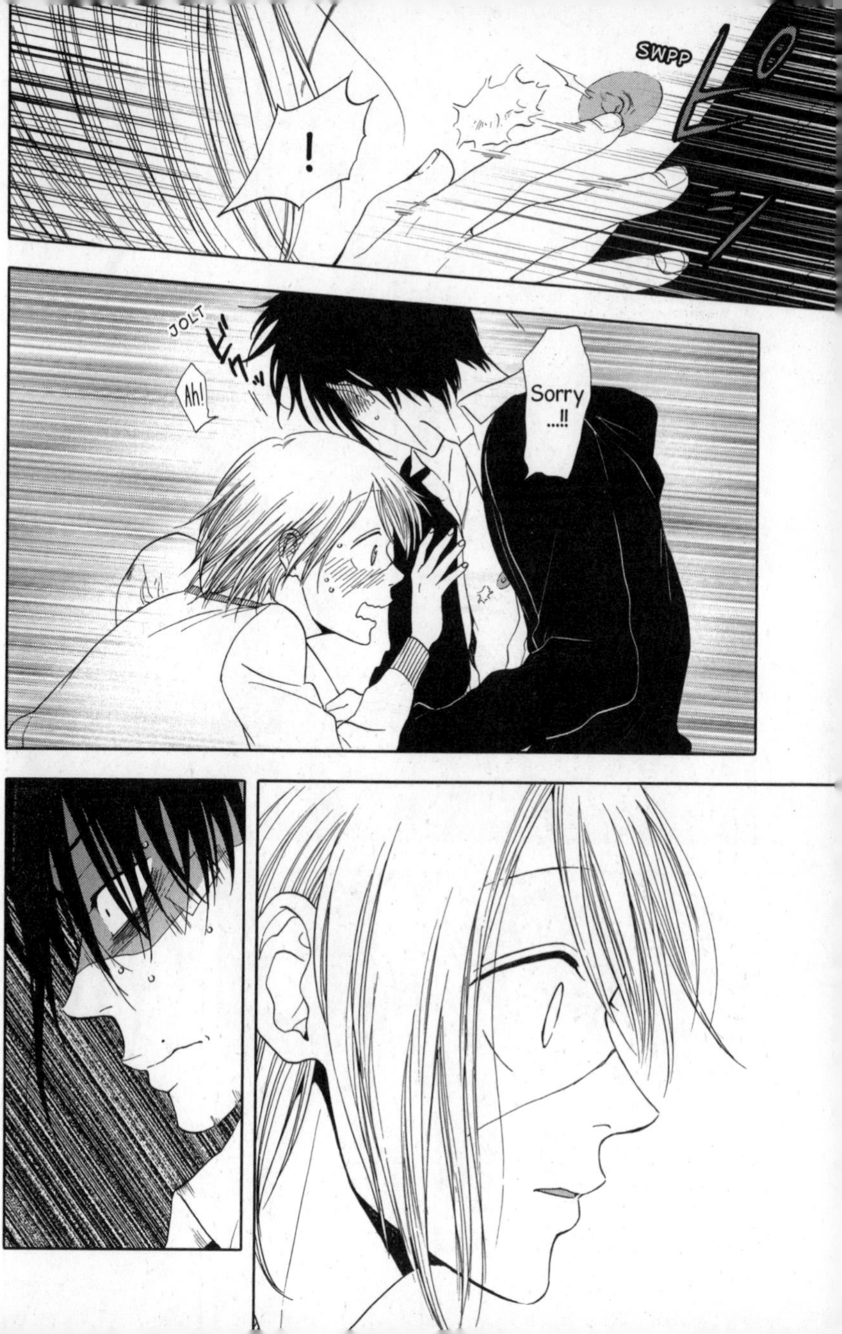
SWPP
!
Sorry ...!!
JOLT
Ah!

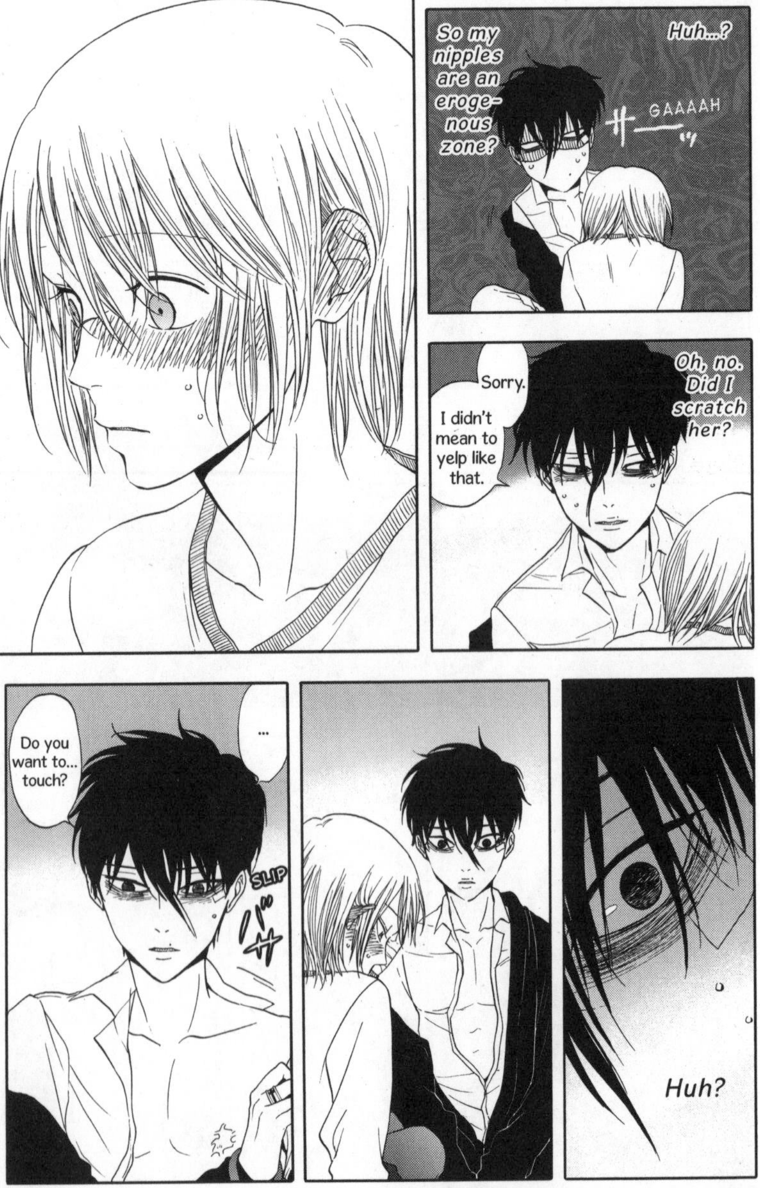
Huh...?
GAAAAH
So my nipples are an eroge-nous zone?
Oh, no. Did I scratch her?
Sorry.
I didn't mean to yelp like that.
Huh?
...
Do you want to... touch?
SLIP

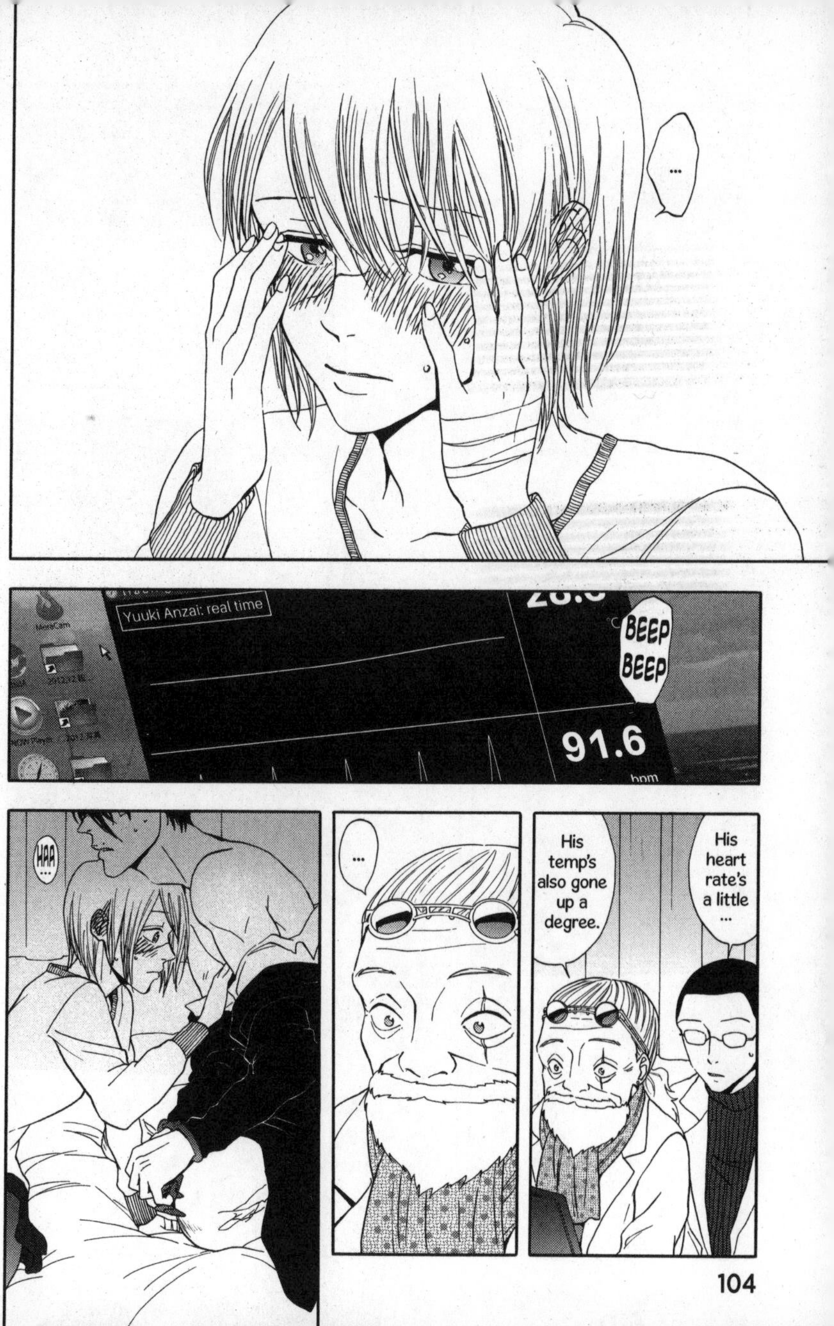
...
Yuuki Anzai: real time
BEEP BEEP
91.6
bpm
His heart rate's a little ...
His temp's also gone up a degree.
...
HAA ...

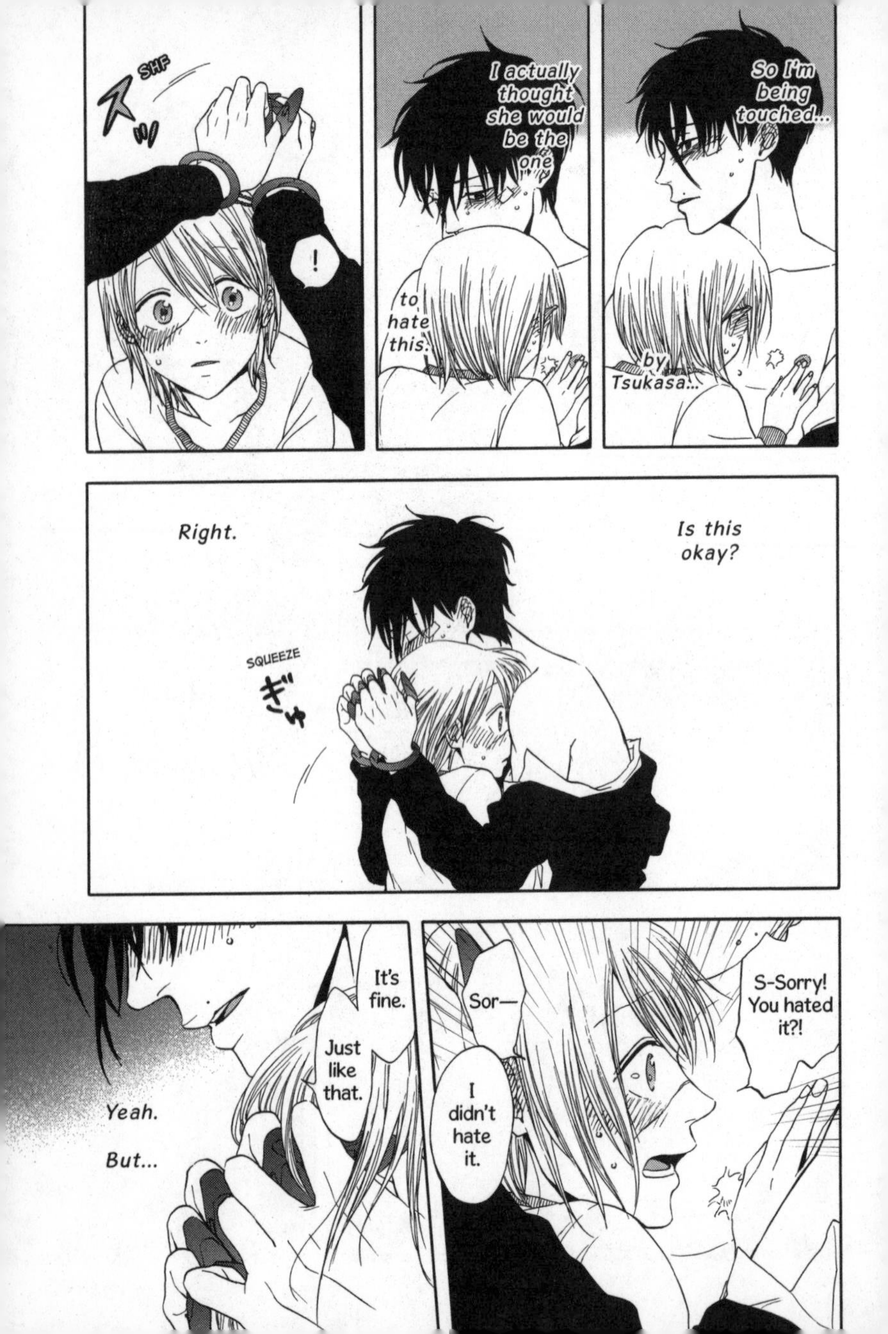
So I'm being touched...
by Tsukasa...
I actually thought she would be the one
to hate this.
SHF
ズッ
!
Is this okay?
Right.
SQUEEZE
ぎゅ
S-Sorry! You hated it?!
Sor—
I didn't hate it.
It's fine.
Just like that.
Yeah.
But...

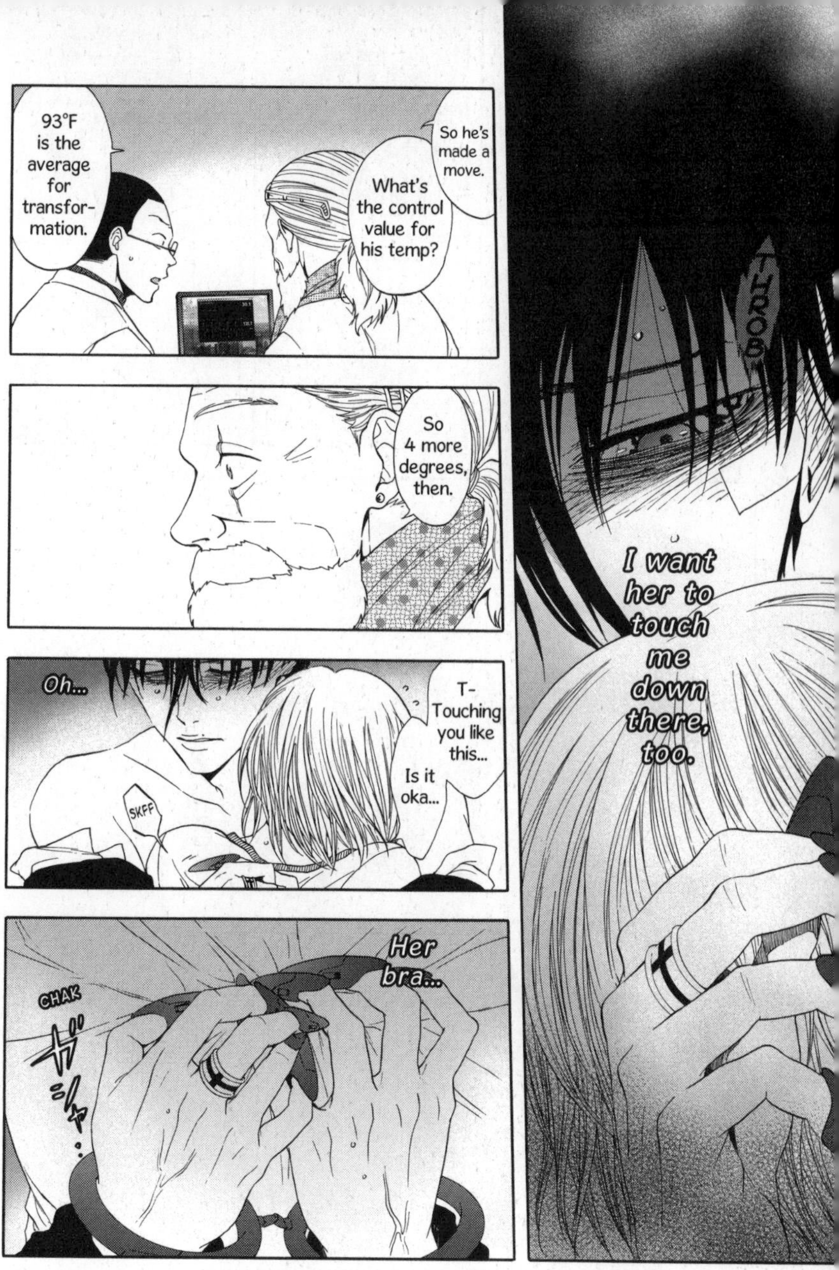
THROB
I want her to touch me down there, too.
So he's made a move.
What's the control value for his temp?
93°F is the average for transformation.
So 4 more degrees, then.
T- Touching you like this...
Is it oka...
SKFF
Oh...
Her bra...
CHAK
ガシャ

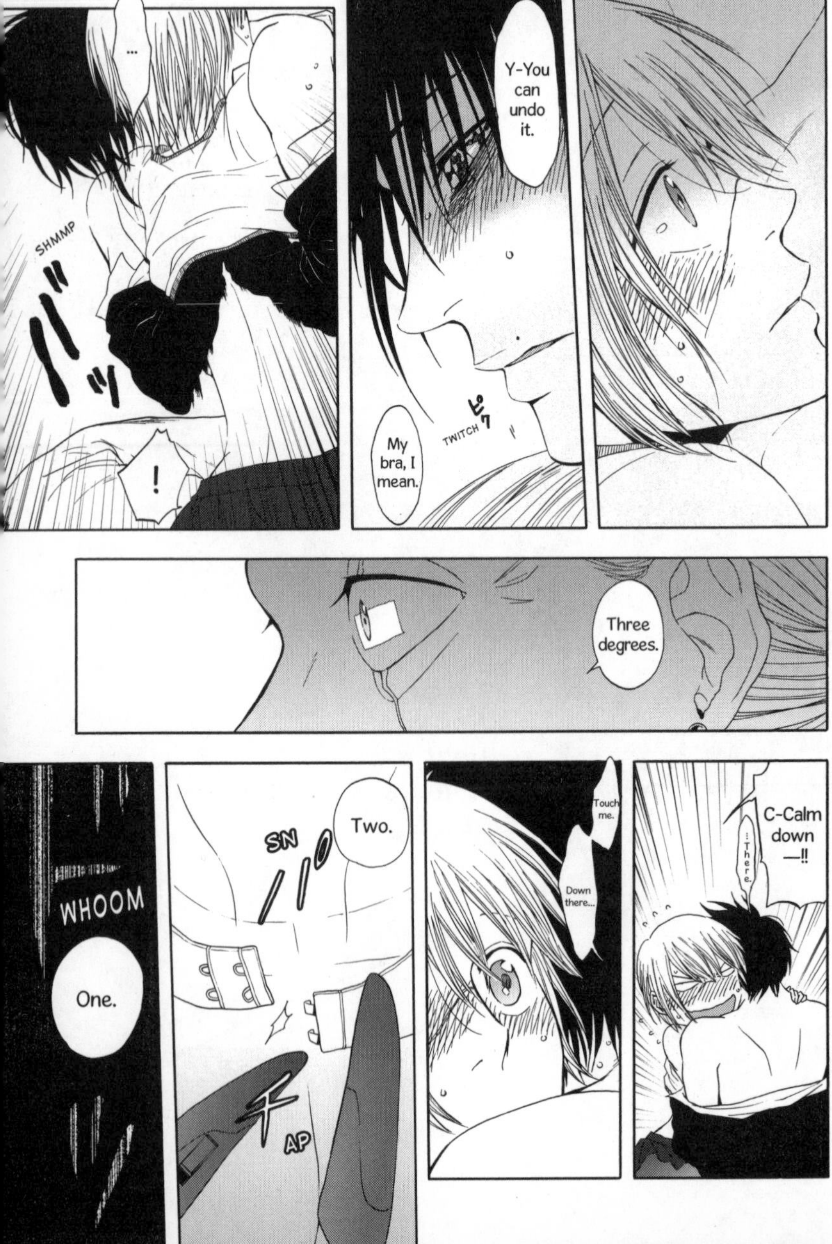

Y-You can undo it.
My bra, I mean.
TWITCH
ピク
...
SHMMP
バッ
!
Three degrees.
C-Calm down—!!
...There.
Touch me.
Down there...
Two.
SN
AP
WHOOM
One.

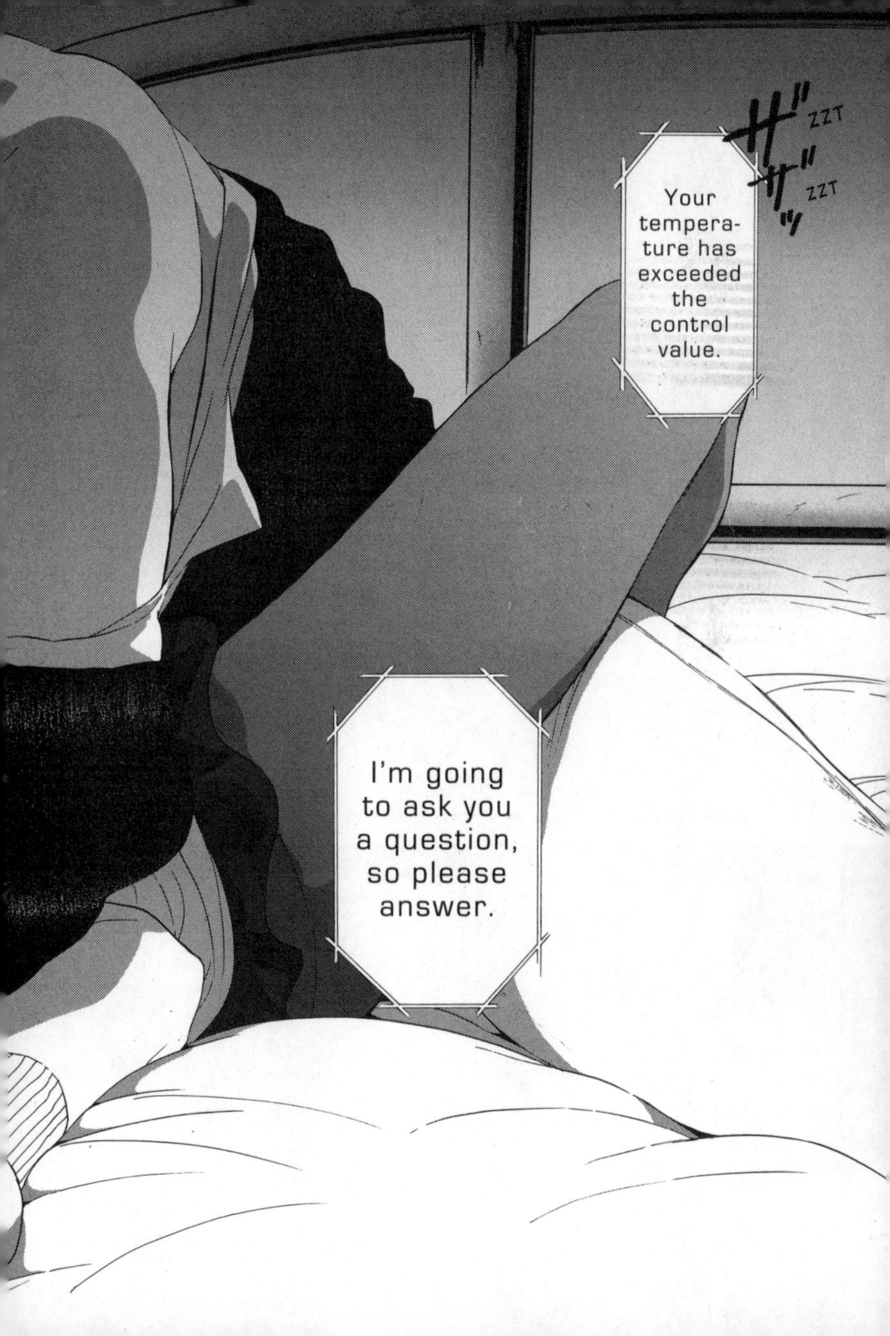
ZZT
ZZT
Your temperature has exceeded the control value.
I'm going to ask you a question, so please answer.

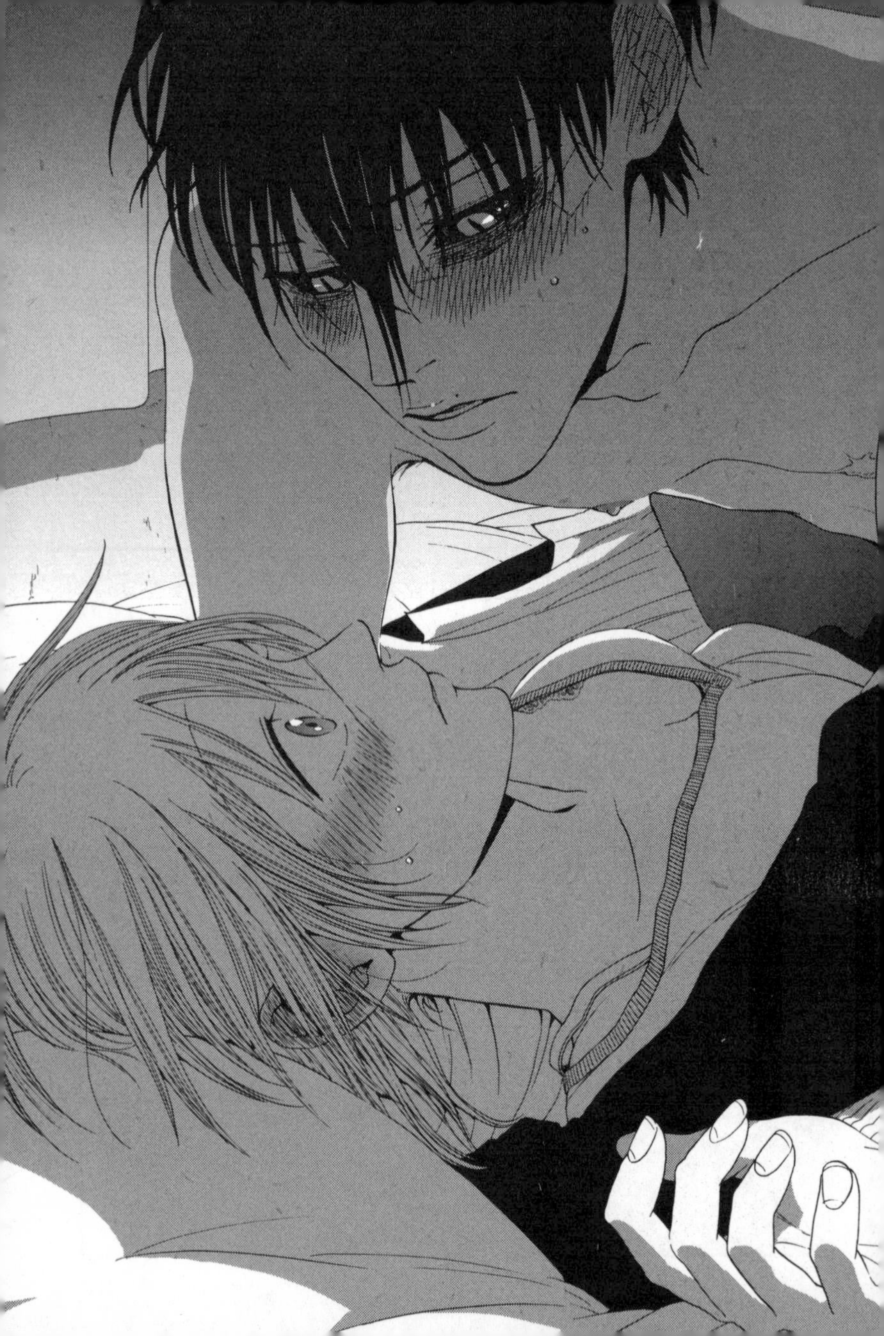

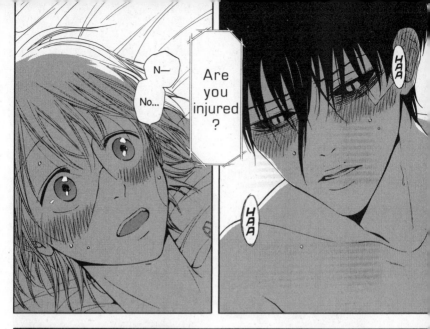

N—
No...

Are you injured?

HAA

HAA

?!

SLRP

If he doesn't answer quickly, the video will—

KISS

KISS

he didn't hear?!

Maybe...

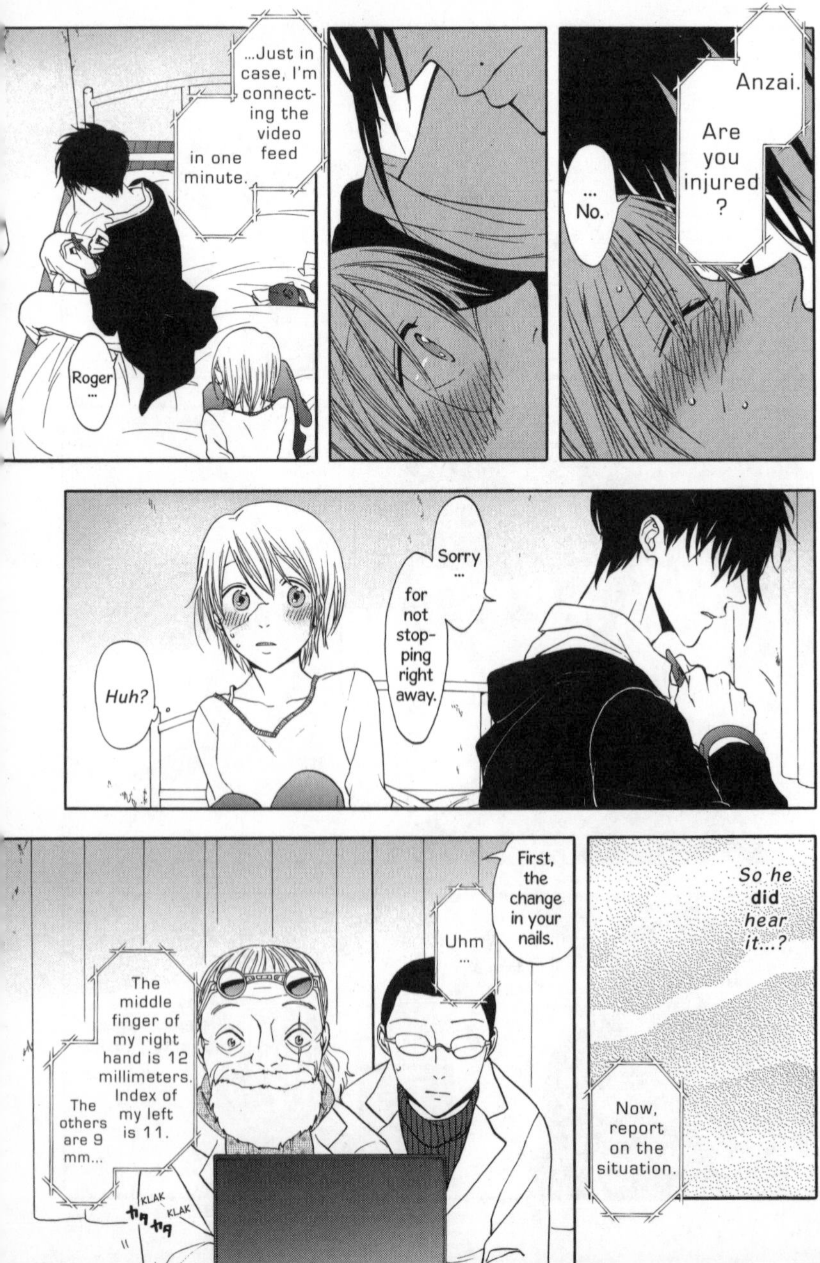
Anzai.
Are you injured?
...No.
...Just in case, I'm connecting the video feed
in one minute.
Roger...
Sorry... for not stopping right away.
Huh?
So he *did* hear it...?
Now, report on the situation.
First, the change in your nails.
Uhm...
The middle finger of my right hand is 12 millimeters. Index of my left is 11.
The others are 9 mm...
KLAK KLAK

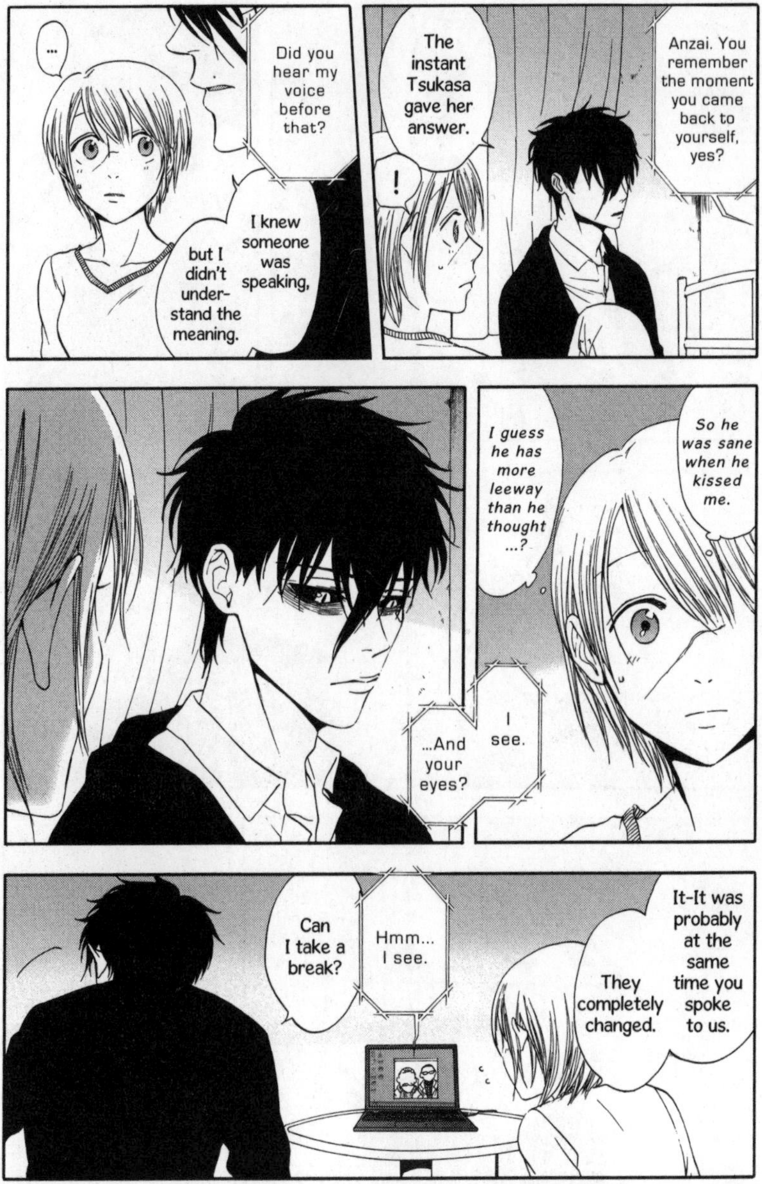
Anzai. You remember the moment you came back to yourself, yes?
The instant Tsukasa gave her answer.
!
Did you hear my voice before that?
...
I knew someone was speaking,
but I didn't under-stand the meaning.
So he was sane when he kissed me.
I guess he has more leeway than he thought ...?
I see.
...And your eyes?
It-It was probably at the same time you spoke to us.
They completely changed.
Hmm... I see.
Can I take a break?

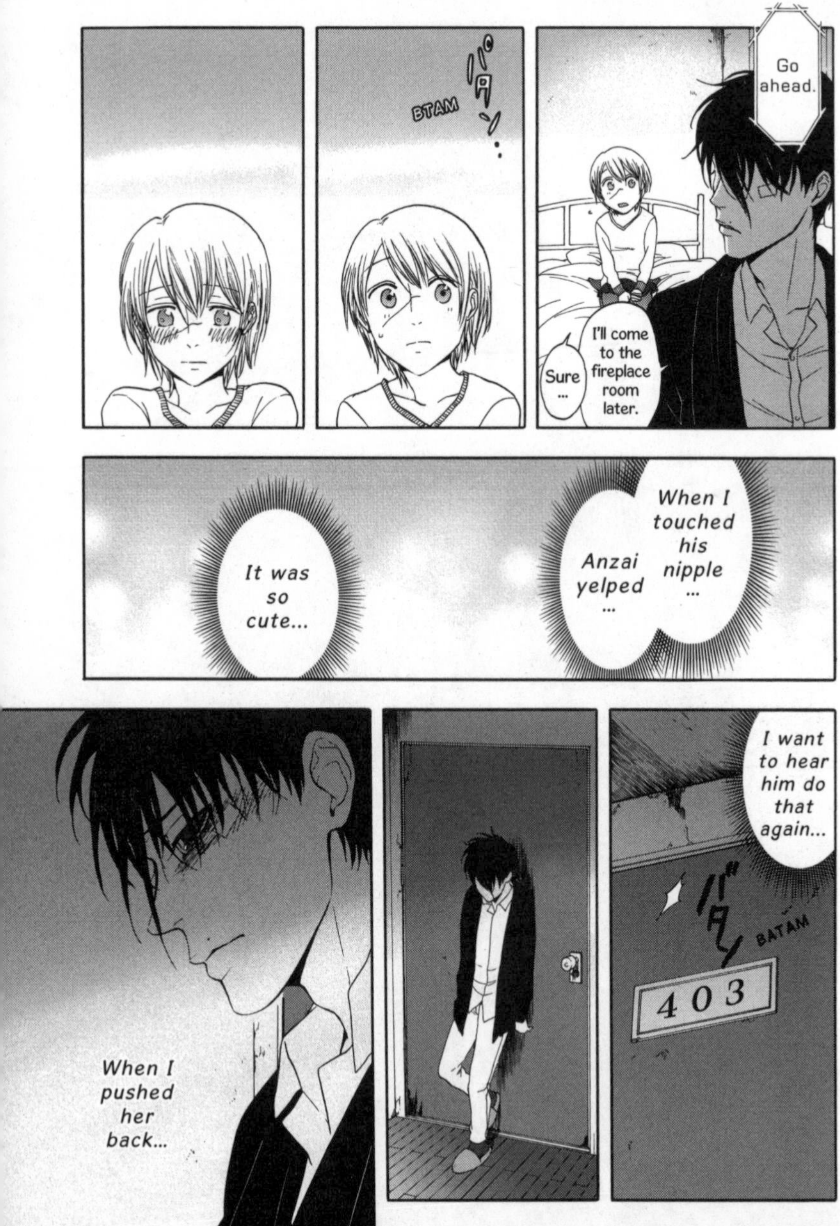
Go ahead.
I'll come to the fireplace room later.
Sure ...
BTAM
When I touched his nipple ...
Anzai yelped ...
It was so cute...
I want to hear him do that again...
BATAM
403
When I pushed her back...

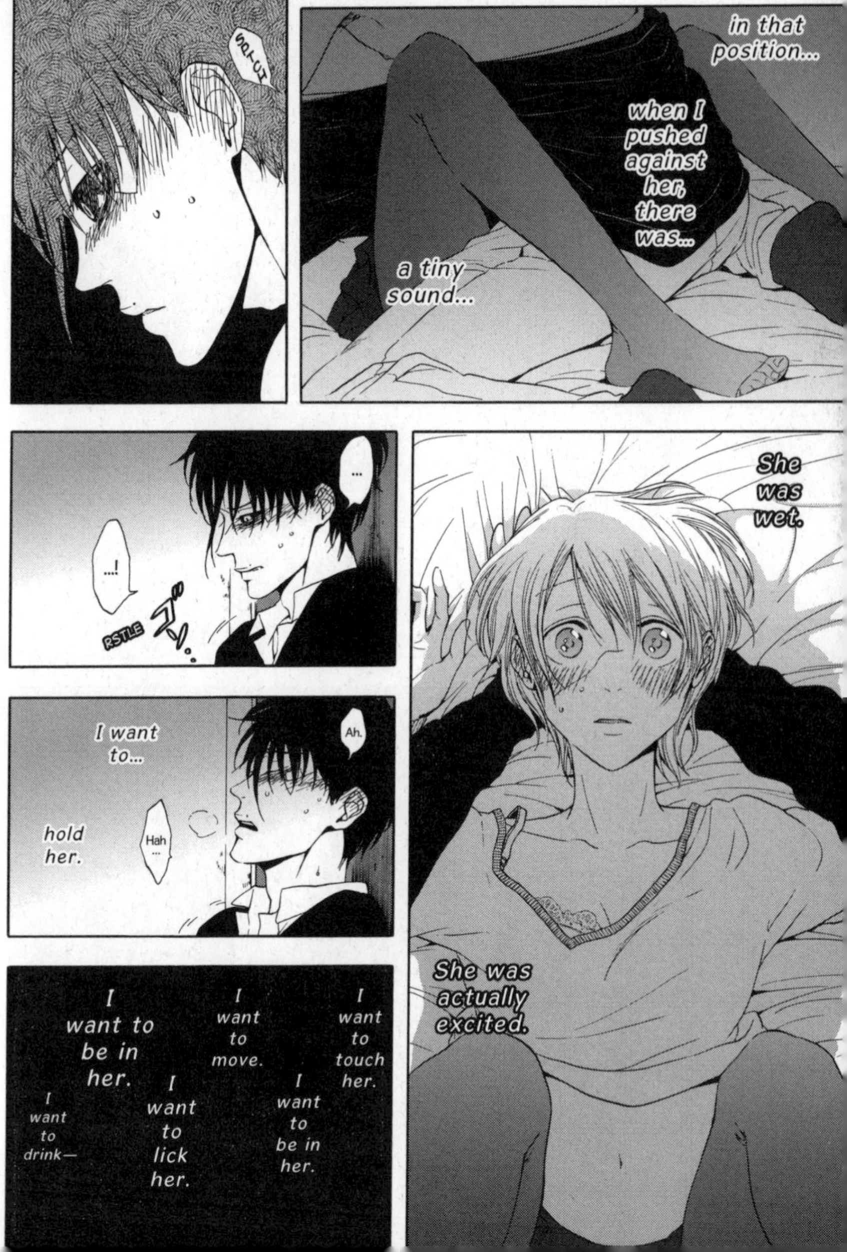
in that position...
when I pushed against her, there was...
a tiny sound...
She was wet.
She was actually excited.
...
...!
RSTLE
Ah.
I want to...
hold her.
Hah...
I want to be in her.
I want to move.
I want to touch her.
I want to be in her.
I want to lick her.
I want to drink—

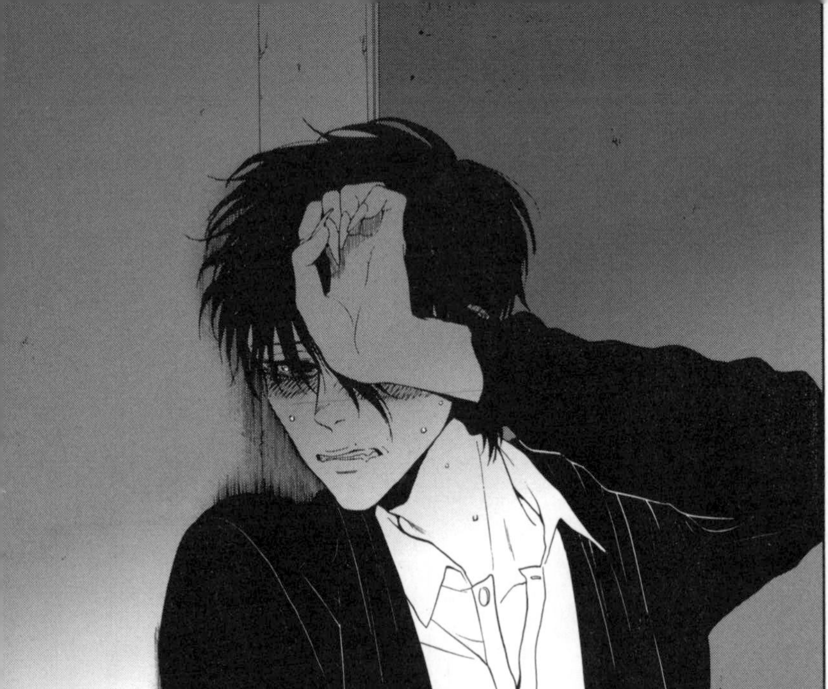

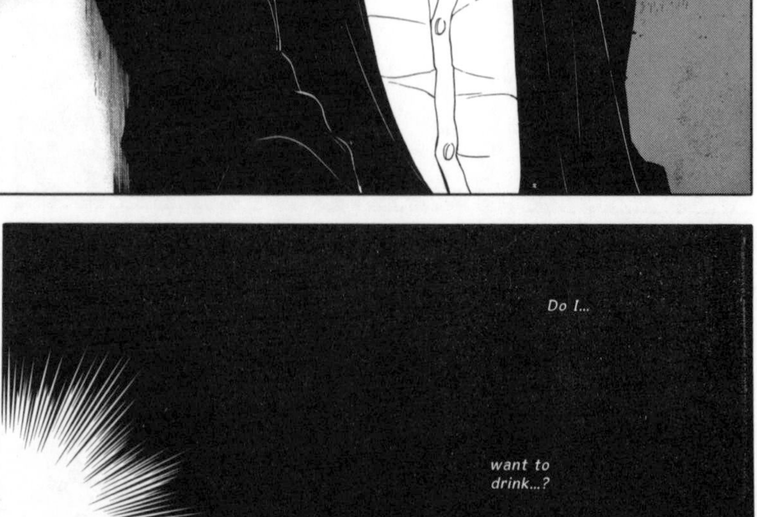
Do I...
want to drink...?

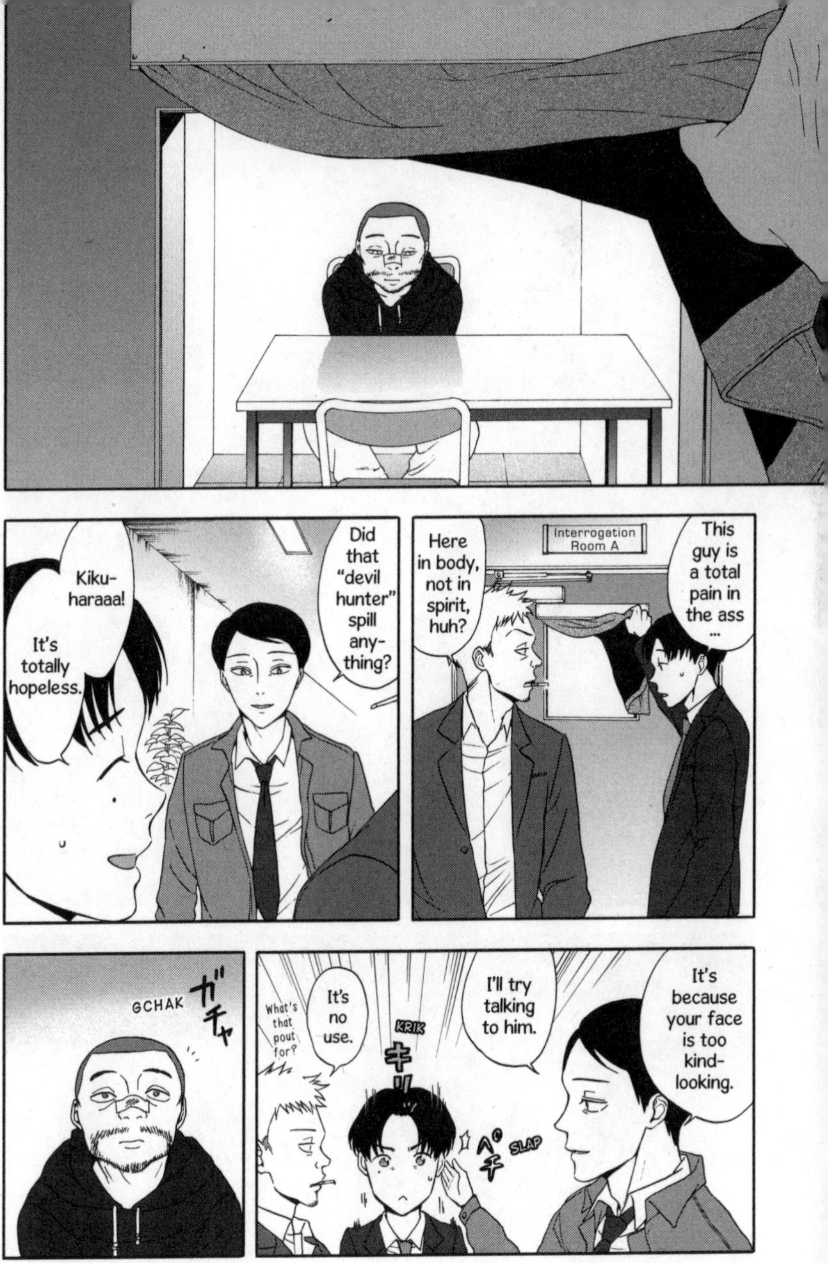
This guy is a total pain in the ass ...
Interrogation Room A
Here in body, not in spirit, huh?
Did that "devil hunter" spill anything?
Kiku-haraaa!
It's totally hopeless.
It's because your face is too kind-looking.
I'll try talking to him.
KRIK
SLAP
It's no use.
What's that pout for?
GCHAK
ガチャ

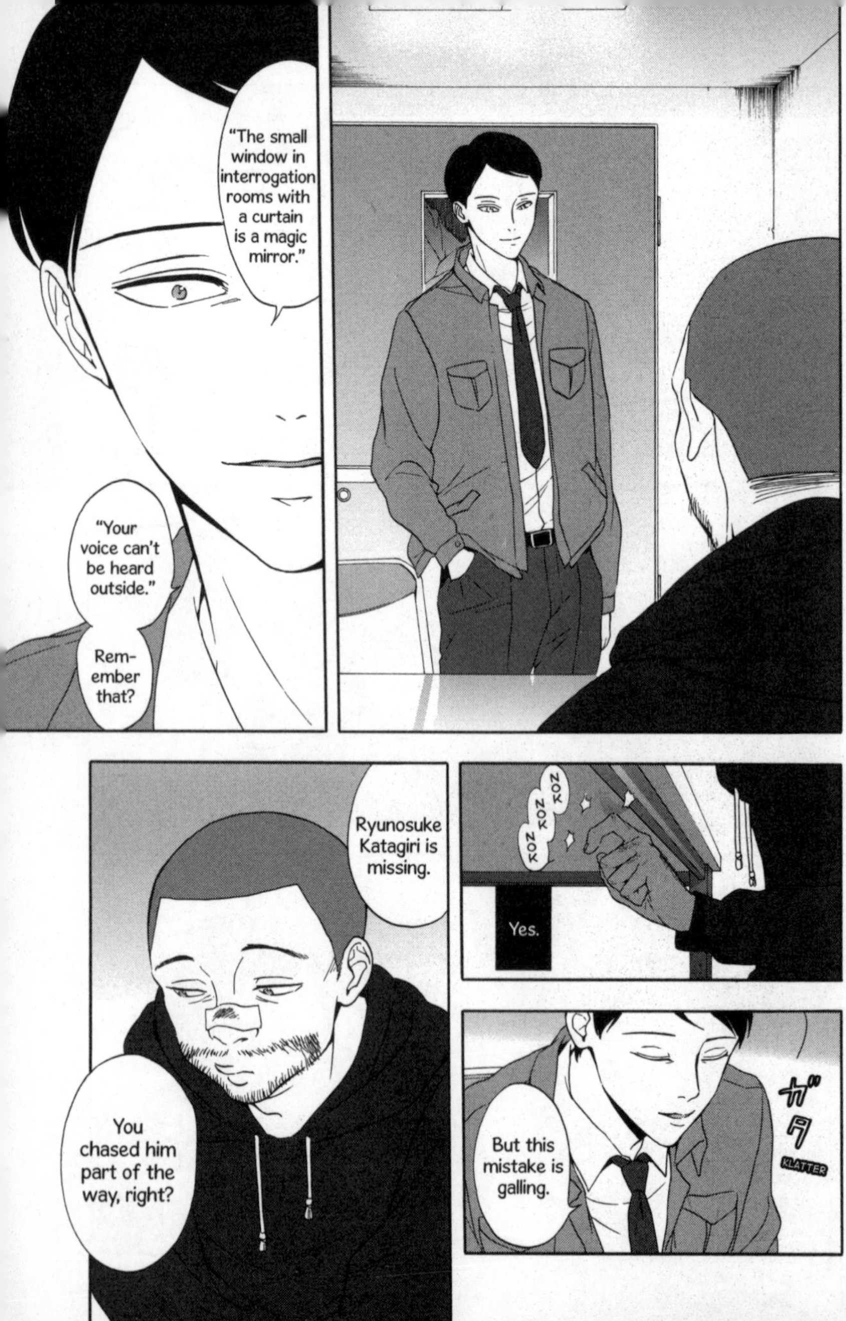
"The small window in interrogation rooms with a curtain is a magic mirror."
"Your voice can't be heard outside."
Remember that?
NOK NOK NOK
Yes.
ガタ
KLATTER
But this mistake is galling.
Ryunosuke Katagiri is missing.
You chased him part of the way, right?

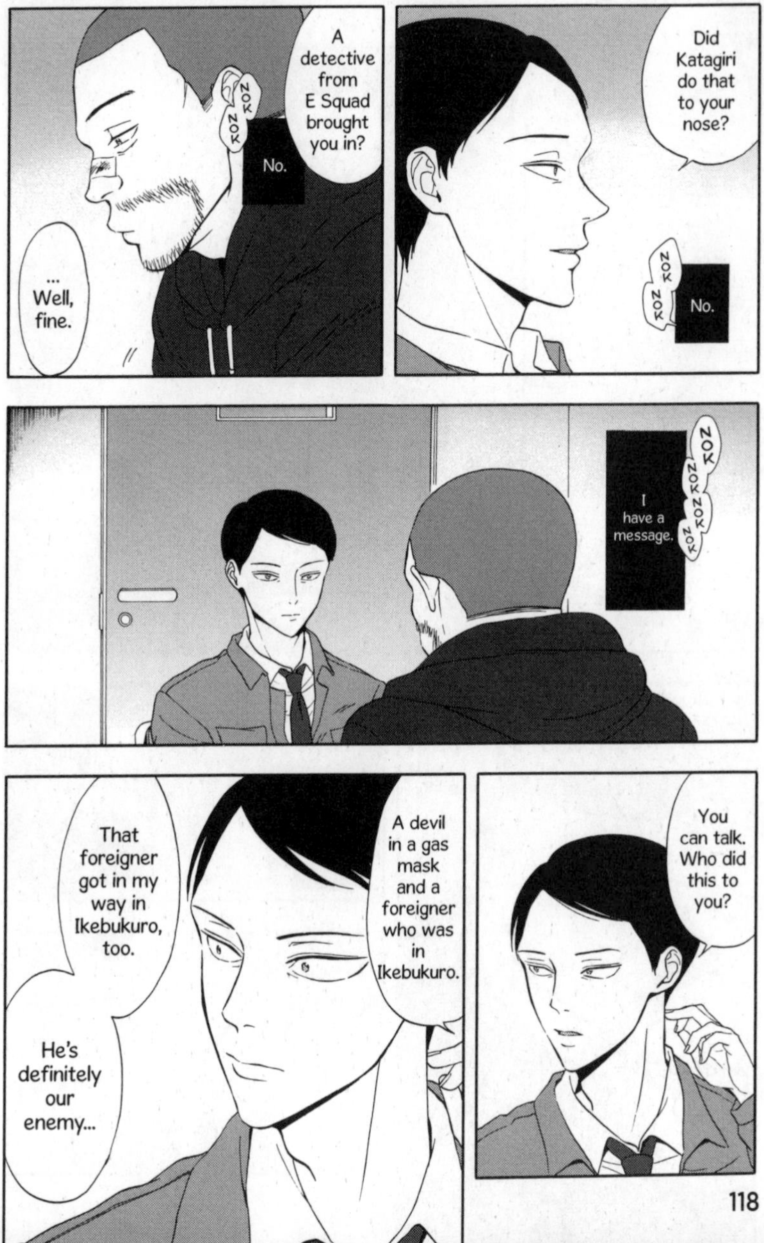
Did Katagiri do that to your nose?
NOK NOK
No.
A detective from E Squad brought you in?
NOK NOK
No.
... Well, fine.
NOK NOK NOK NOK
I have a message.
You can talk. Who did this to you?
A devil in a gas mask and a foreigner who was in Ikebukuro.
That foreigner got in my way in Ikebukuro, too.
He's definitely our enemy...

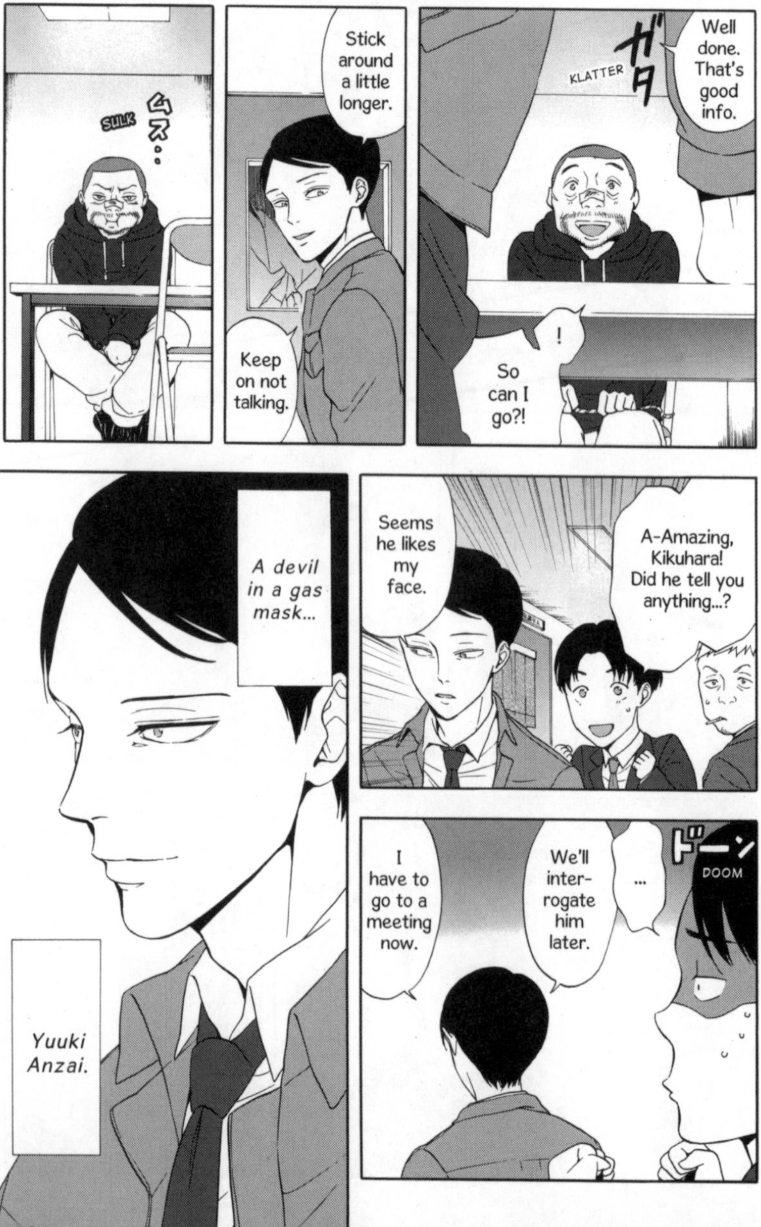
Well done. That's good info.
ガタ
KLATTER
!
So can I go?!
Stick around a little longer.
Keep on not talking.
ムス..
SULK
A-Amazing, Kikuhara! Did he tell you anything...?
Seems he likes my face.
ドーン
DOOM
...
We'll inter-rogate him later.
I have to go to a meeting now.
A devil in a gas mask...
Yuuki Anzai.

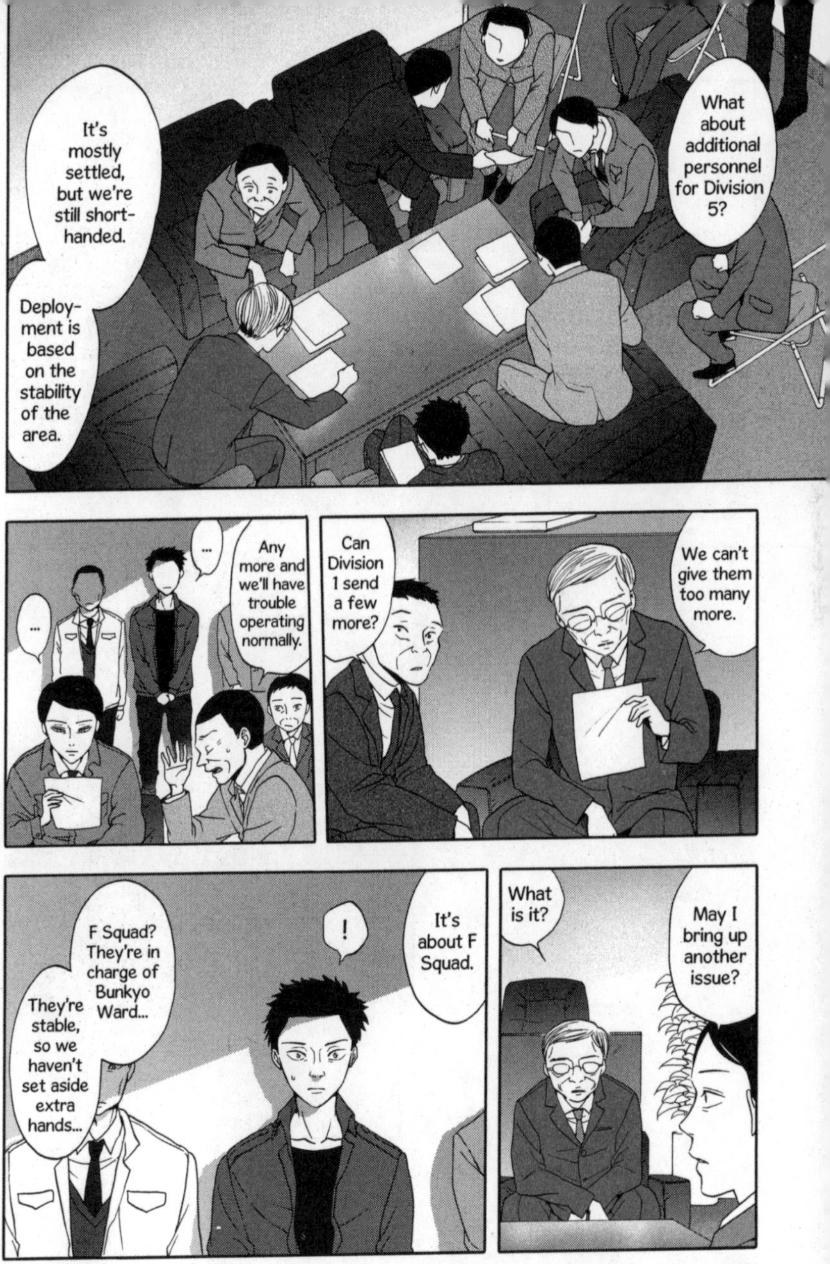
What about additional personnel for Division 5?
It's mostly settled, but we're still short-handed.
Deployment is based on the stability of the area.
We can't give them too many more.
Can Division 1 send a few more?
Any more and we'll have trouble operating normally.
...
...
May I bring up another issue?
What is it?
It's about F Squad.
!
F Squad? They're in charge of Bunkyo Ward...
They're stable, so we haven't set aside extra hands...

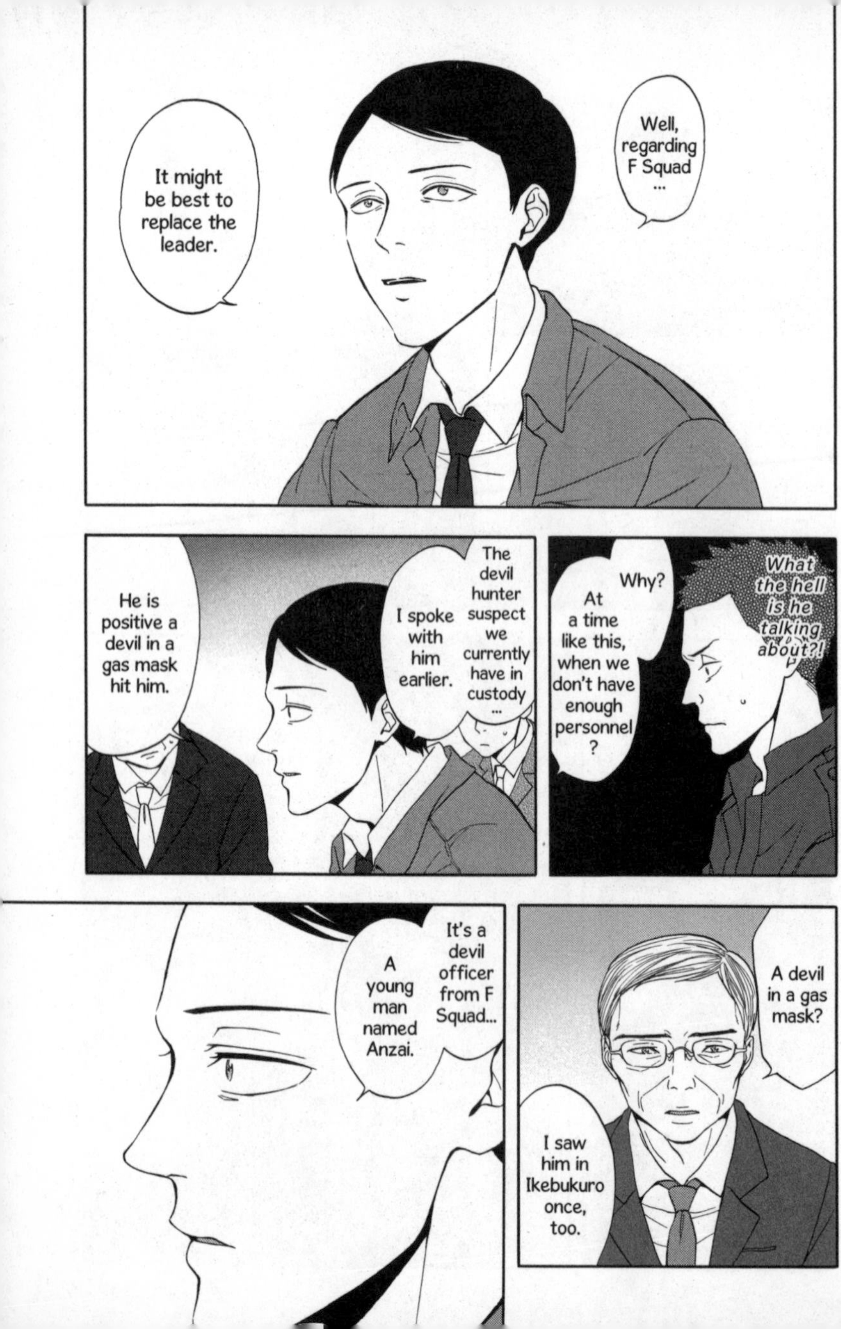
Well, regarding F Squad ...
It might be best to replace the leader.
What the hell is he talking about?!
Why?
At a time like this, when we don't have enough personnel ?
The devil hunter suspect we currently have in custody ...
I spoke with him earlier.
He is positive a devil in a gas mask hit him.
A devil in a gas mask?
I saw him in Ikebukuro once, too.
It's a devil officer from F Squad...
A young man named Anzai.

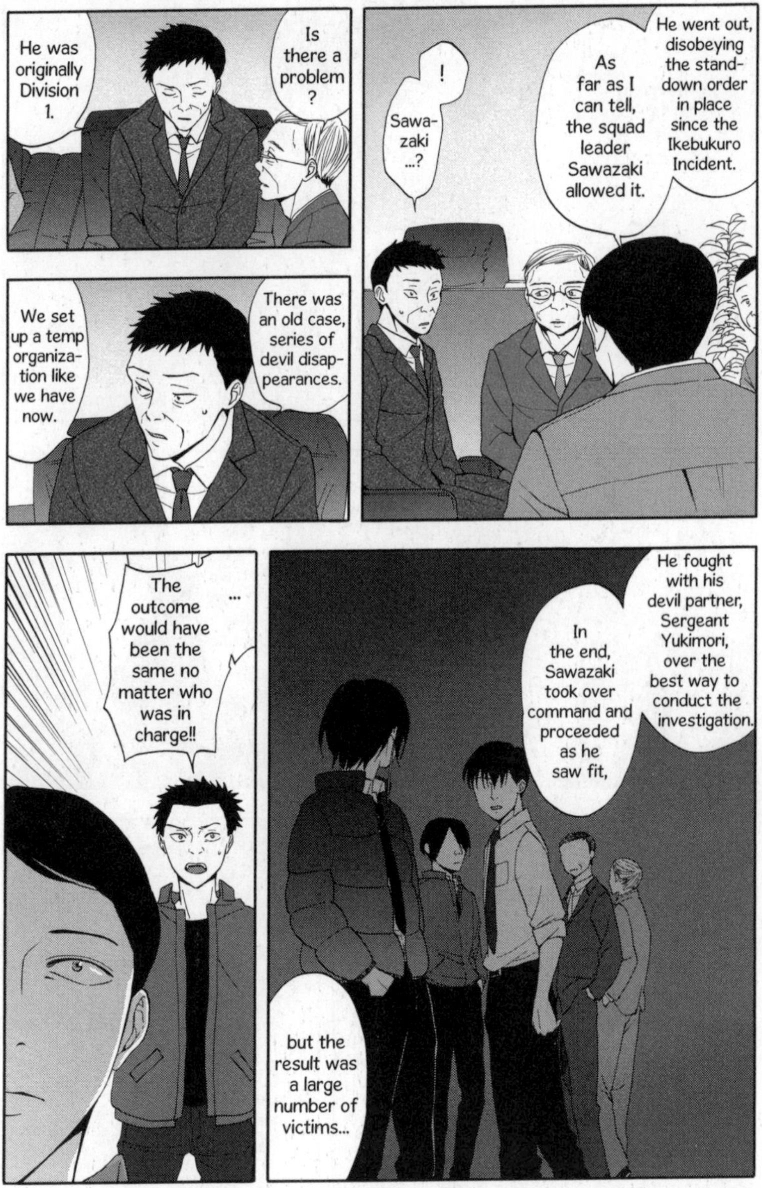
He went out, disobeying the stand-down order in place since the Ikebukuro Incident.
As far as I can tell, the squad leader Sawazaki allowed it.
!
Sawa-zaki ...?
Is there a problem ?
He was originally Division 1.
There was an old case, series of devil disap-pearances.
We set up a temp organiza-tion like we have now.
He fought with his devil partner, Sergeant Yukimori, over the best way to conduct the investigation.
In the end, Sawazaki took over command and proceeded as he saw fit,
but the result was a large number of victims...
...
The outcome would have been the same no matter who was in charge!!

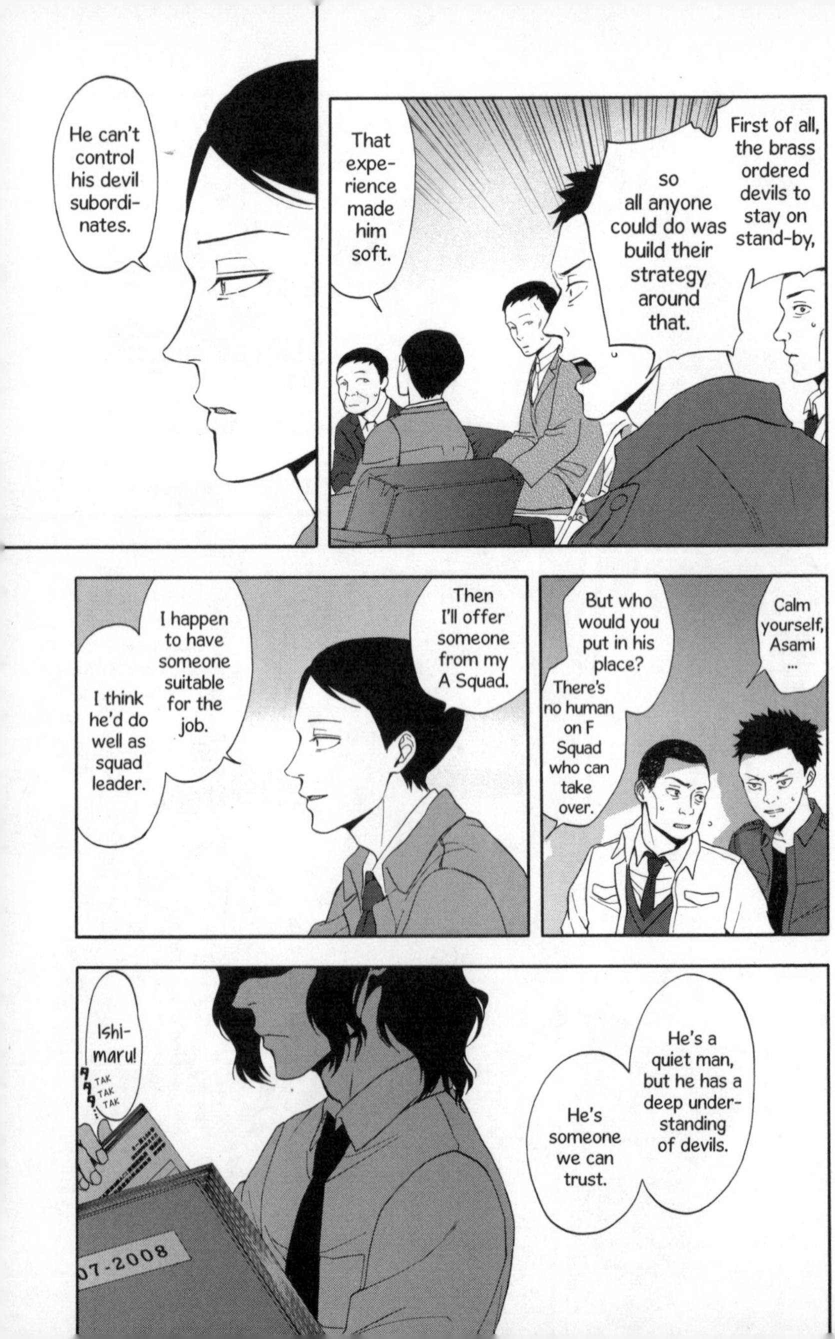
First of all, the brass ordered devils to stay on stand-by,
so all anyone could do was build their strategy around that.
That experience made him soft.
He can't control his devil subordinates.
Calm yourself, Asami ...
But who would you put in his place?
There's no human on F Squad who can take over.
Then I'll offer someone from my A Squad.
I happen to have someone suitable for the job.
I think he'd do well as squad leader.
He's a quiet man, but he has a deep understanding of devils.
He's someone we can trust.
Ishi-maru!
TAK TAK TAK
07-2008

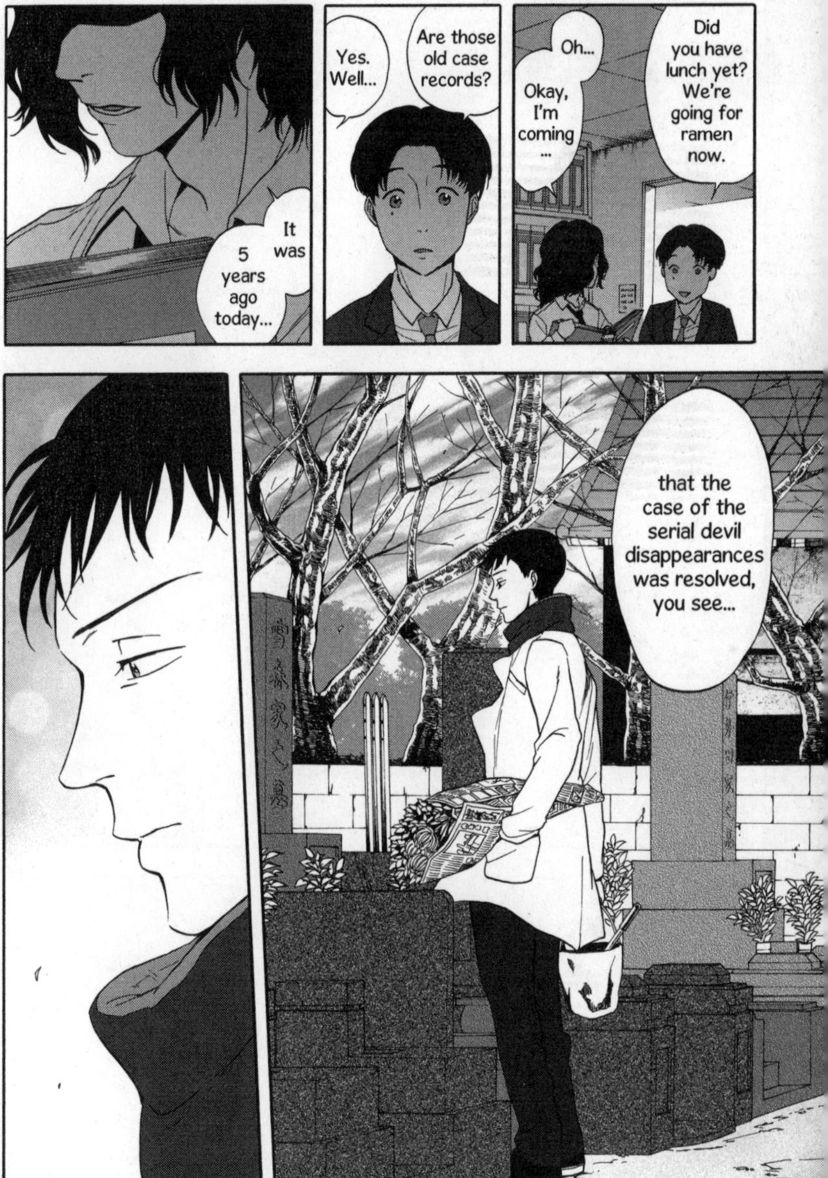
Did you have lunch yet? We're going for ramen now.
Oh...
Okay, I'm coming ...
Are those old case records?
Yes. Well...
It was 5 years ago today...
that the case of the serial devil disappearances was resolved, you see...

Mr. Penguin

A present to Tsukasa from her family when she left for college in Tokyo, "so you won't be lonely."

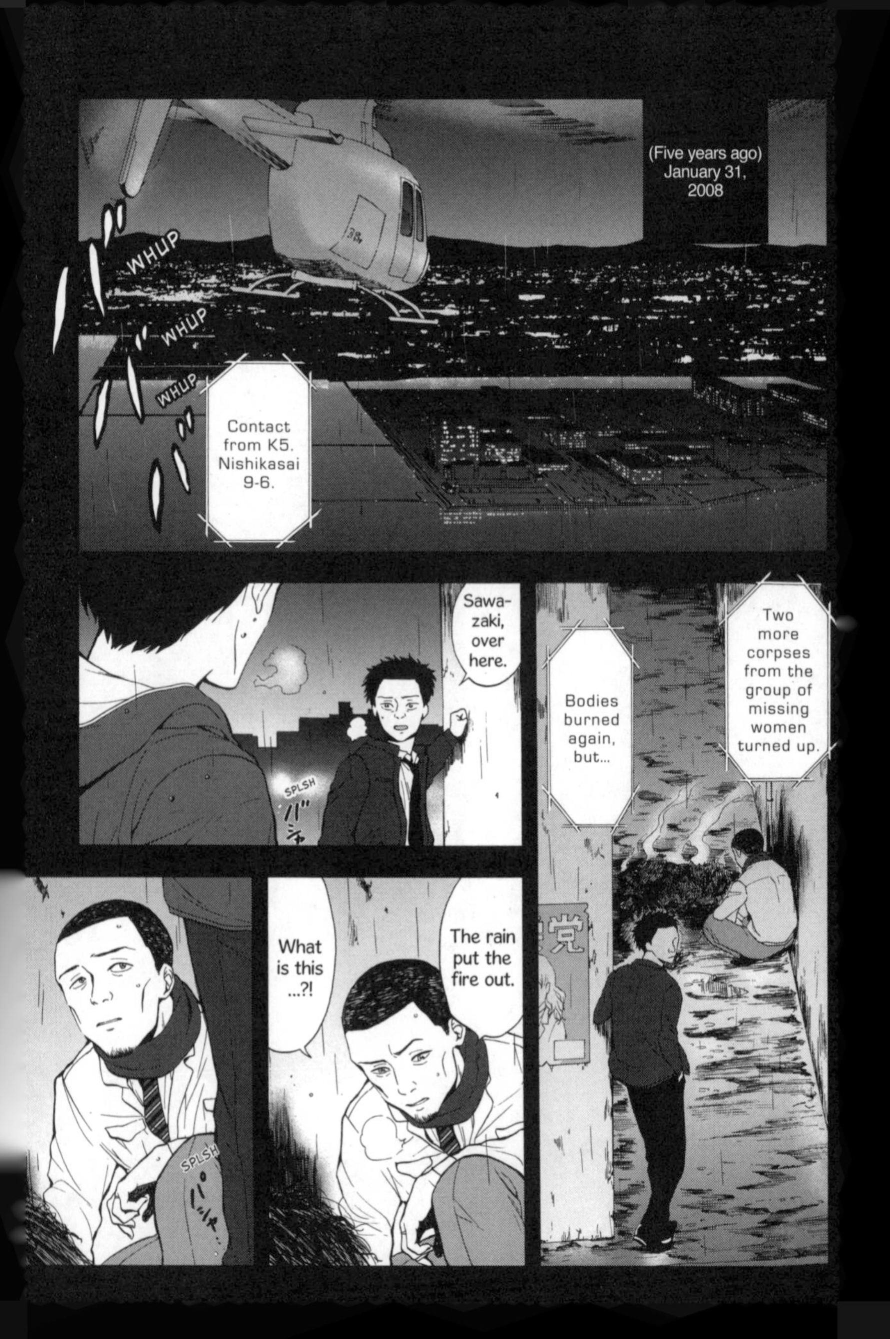
(Five years ago)
January 31,
2008
WHUP
WHUP
WHUP
Contact from K5. Nishikasai 9-6.
Two more corpses from the group of missing women turned up.
Bodies burned again, but...
Sawa-zaki, over here.
SPLSH
バシャ
The rain put the fire out.
What is this ...?!
SPLSH
パシャ...

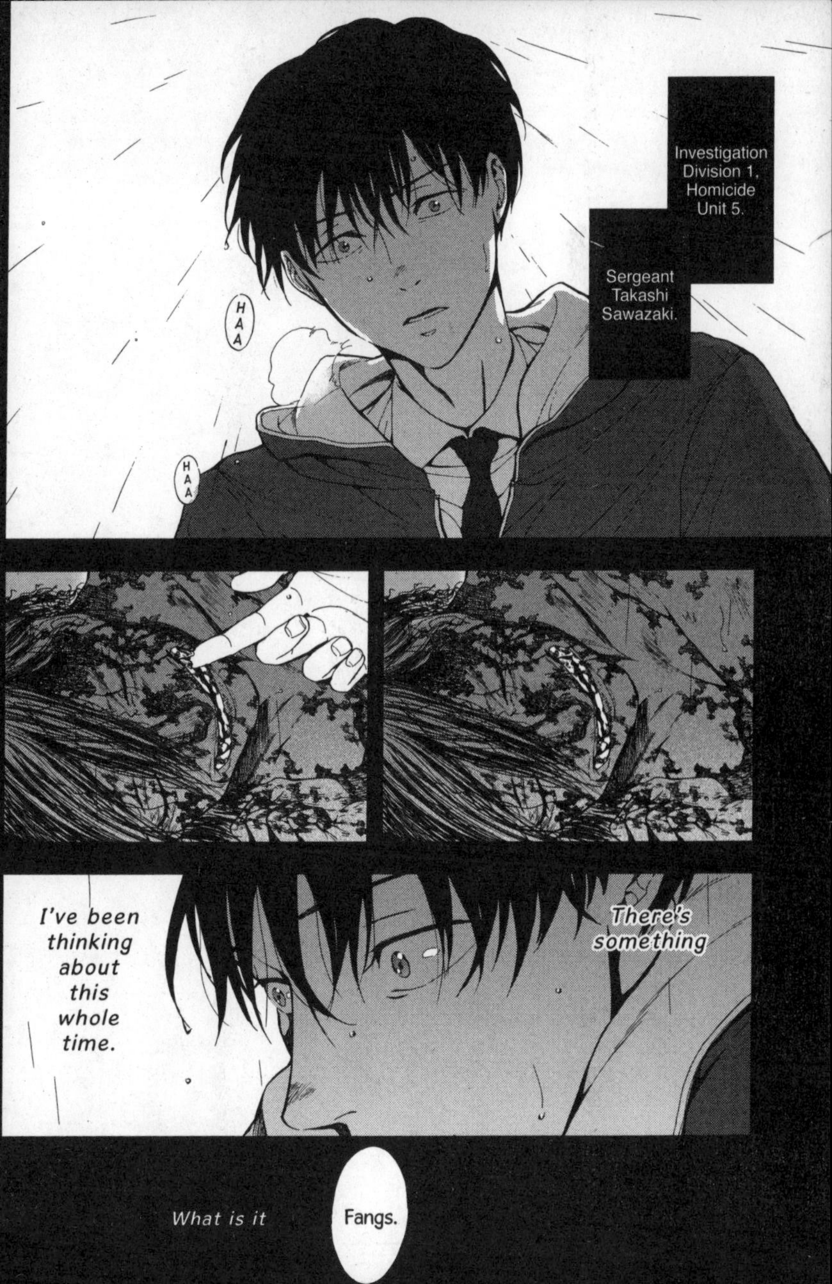
Investigation Division 1, Homicide Unit 5.
Sergeant Takashi Sawazaki.
HAA
HAA
There's something
I've been thinking about this whole time.
Fangs.
What is it

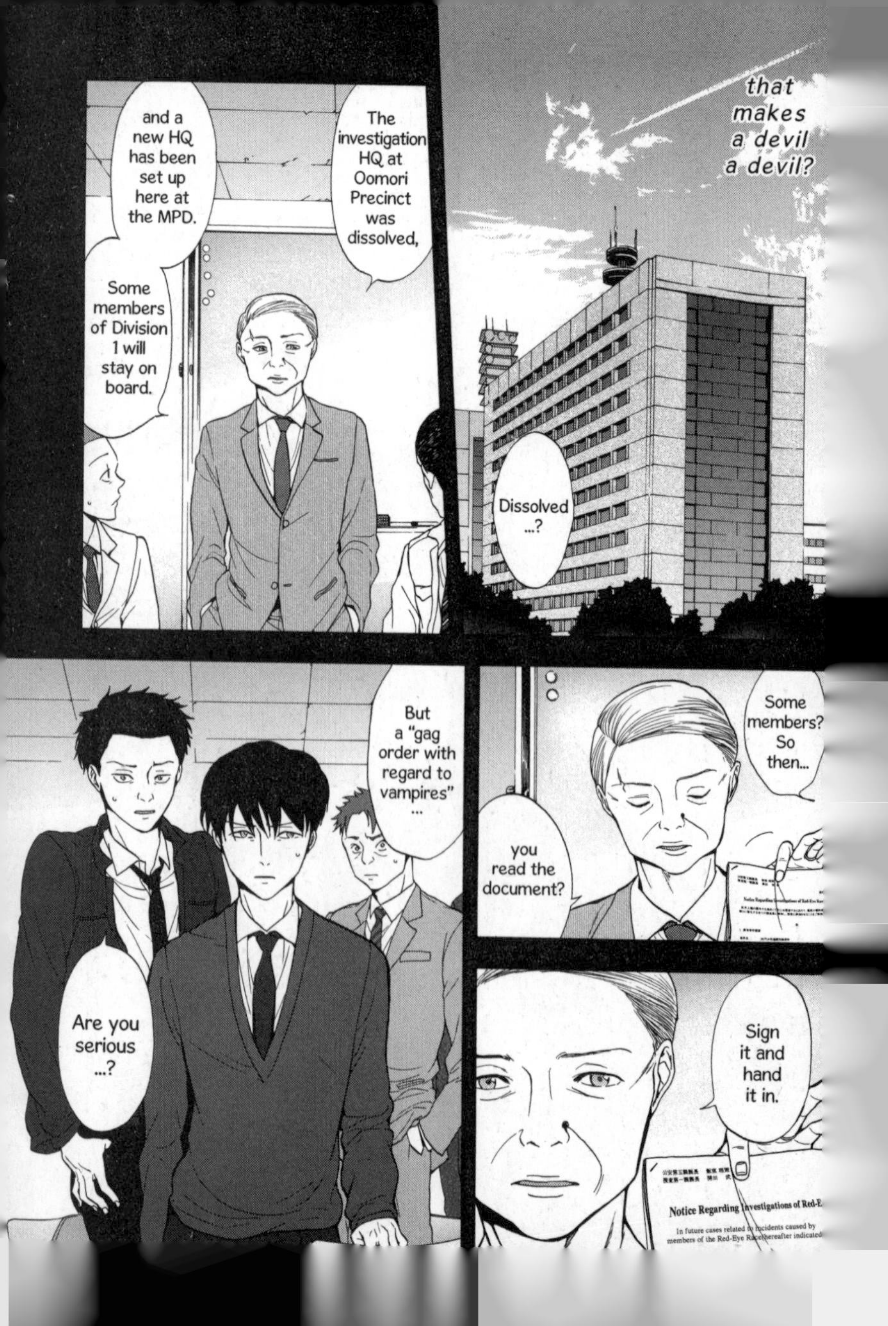
that makes a devil a devil?
Dissolved ...?
The investigation HQ at Oomori Precinct was dissolved,
and a new HQ has been set up here at the MPD.
Some members of Division 1 will stay on board.
Some members? So then...
you read the document?
Sign it and hand it in.
Notice Regarding Investigations of Red-E
In future cases related to incidents caused by members of the Red-Eye Race hereafter indicated
But a "gag order with regard to vampires" ...
Are you serious ...?

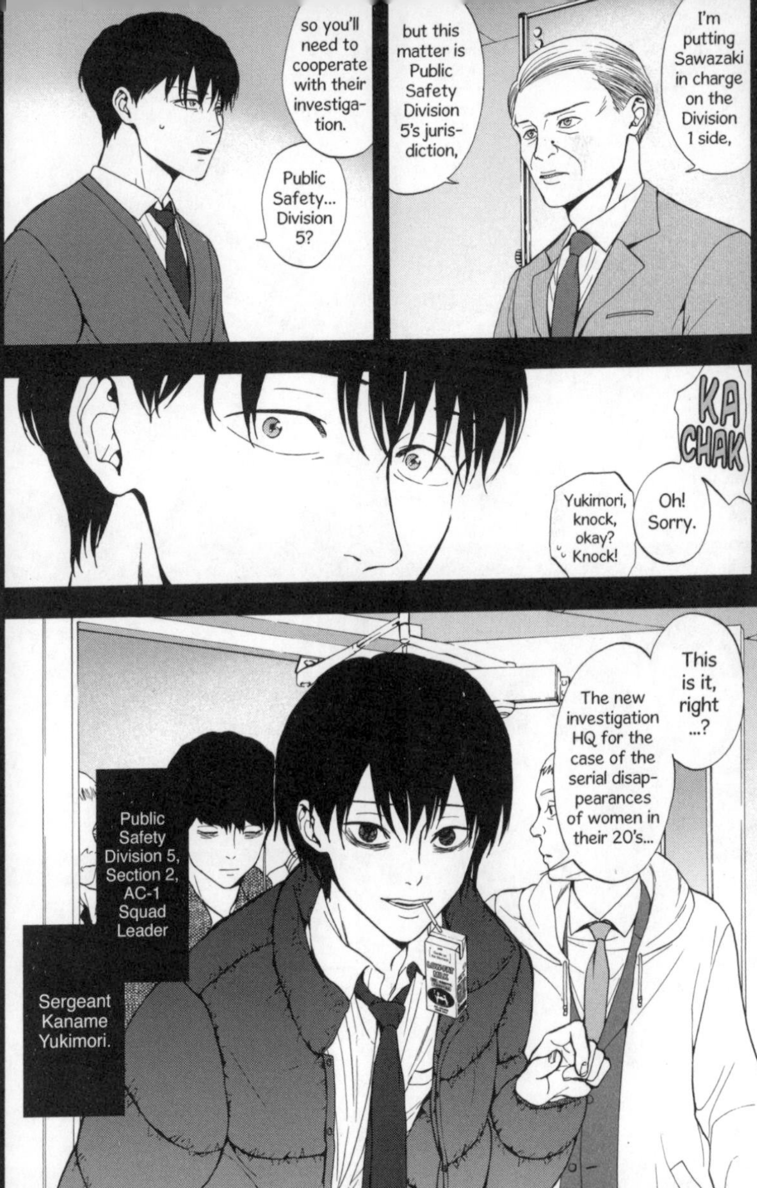
I'm putting Sawazaki in charge on the Division 1 side,
but this matter is Public Safety Division 5's jurisdiction,
so you'll need to cooperate with their investiga-tion.
Public Safety... Division 5?
KA CHAK
Oh! Sorry.
Yukimori, knock, okay? Knock!
This is it, right ...?
The new investigation HQ for the case of the serial disap-pearances of women in their 20's...
Public Safety Division 5, Section 2, AC-1 Squad Leader
Sergeant Kaname Yukimori.

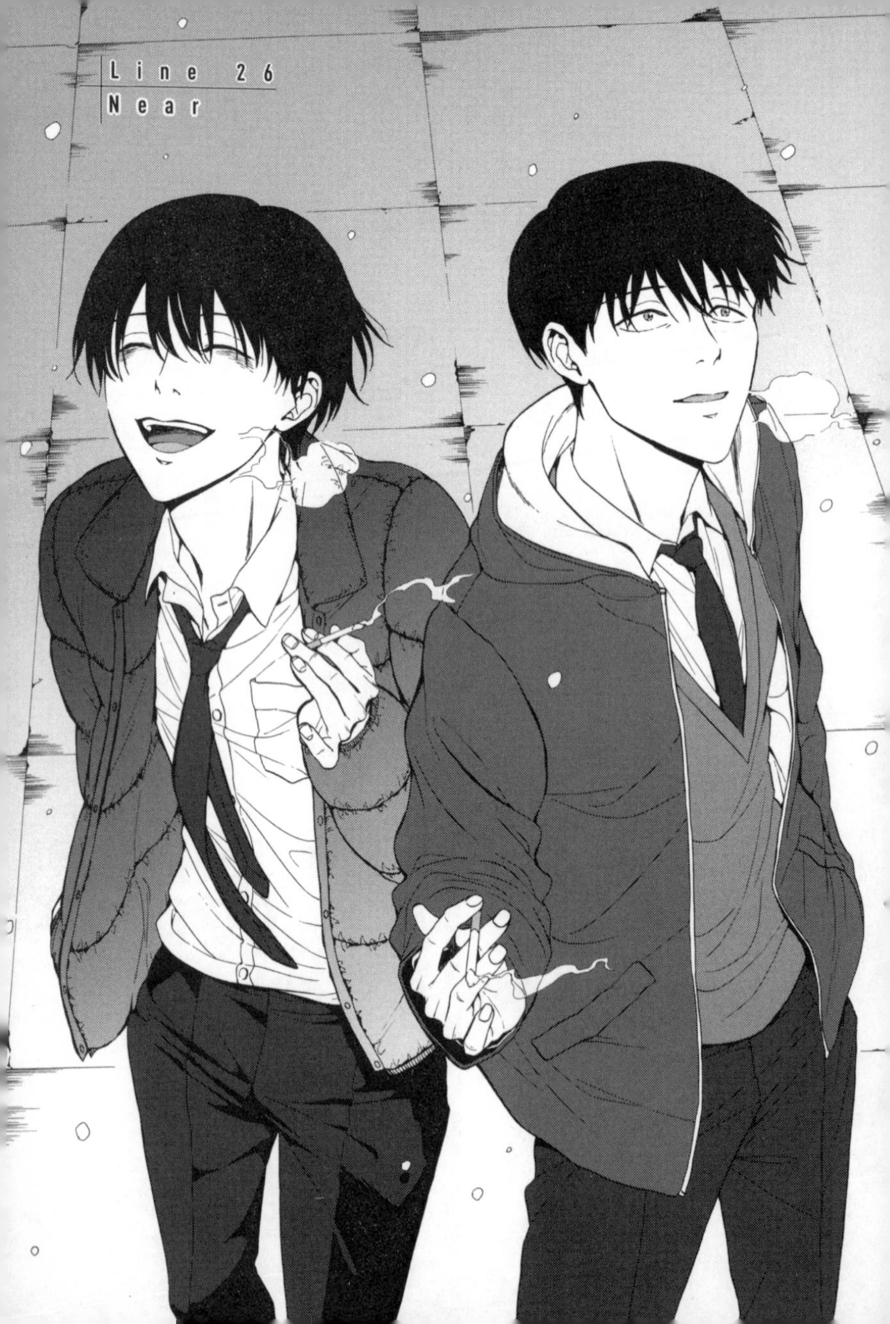
Line 26
Near

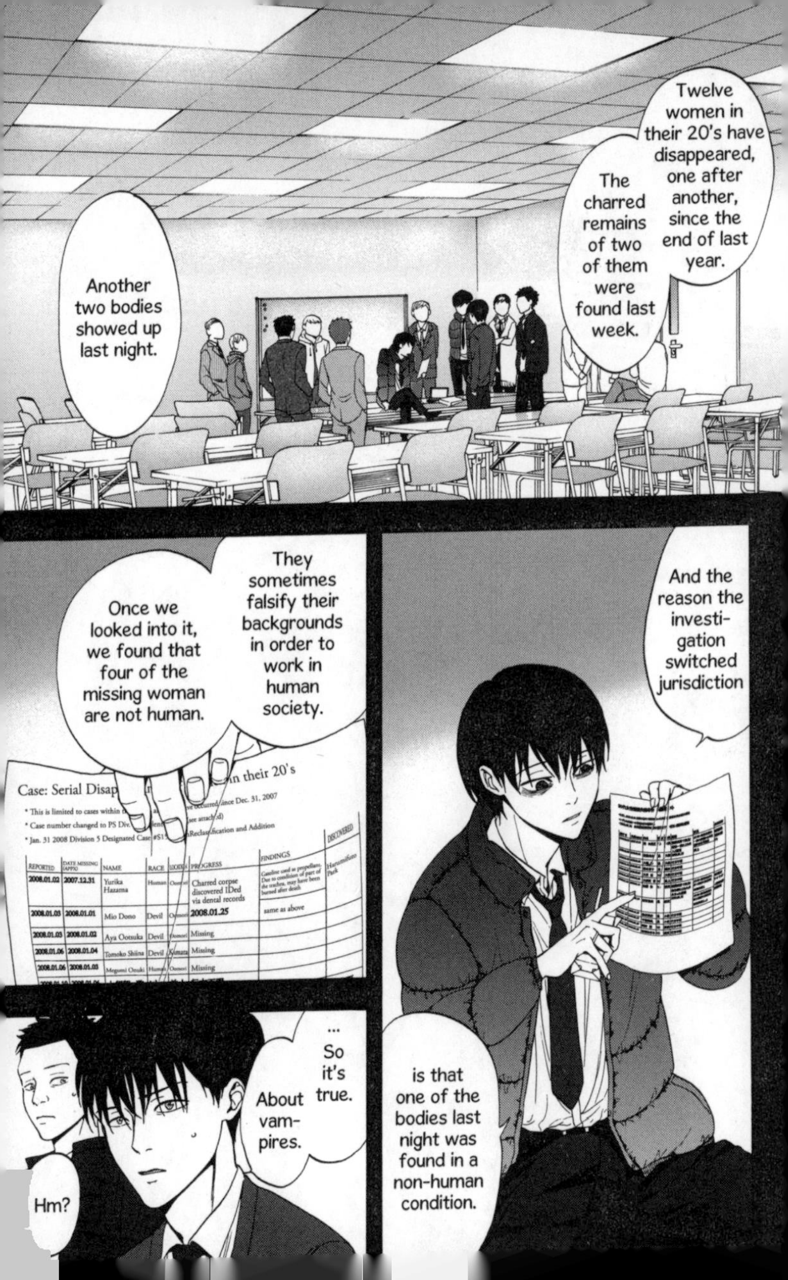
Twelve women in their 20's have disappeared, one after another, since the end of last year.
The charred remains of two of them were found last week.
Another two bodies showed up last night.
And the reason the investigation switched jurisdiction
is that one of the bodies last night was found in a non-human condition.
Once we looked into it, we found that four of the missing woman are not human.
They sometimes falsify their backgrounds in order to work in human society.
Case: Serial Disap
in their 20's
* This is limited to cases within
since Dec. 31, 2007
* Case number changed to PS Div.
* Jan. 31 2008 Division 5 Designated Case
Reclassification and Addition
REPORTED
DATE MISSING (APPX)
NAME
RACE
PROGRESS
FINDINGS
DISCOVERED
2008.01.02
2007.12.31
Yurika Hazama
Human
Charred corpse discovered IDed via dental records
Harumifuto Park
2008.01.03
2008.01.01
Mio Dono
Devil
2008.01.25
same as above
2008.01.03
2008.01.02
Aya Ootsuka
Devil
Missing
2008.01.06
2008.01.04
Tomoko Shiina
Devil
Kamata
Missing
2008.01.06
2008.01.03
Megumi Onuki
Human
Omori
Missing
... So it's true.
About vampires.
Hm?

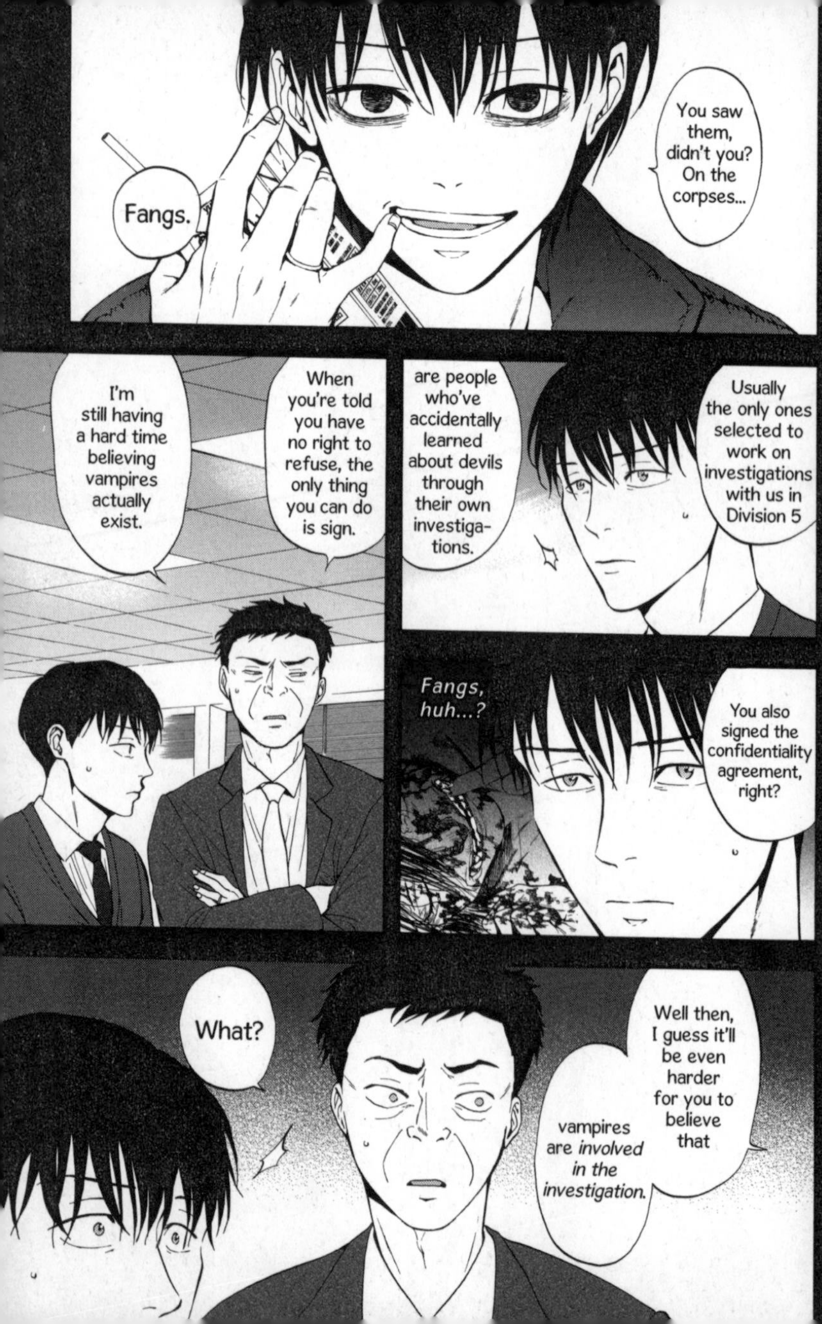
You saw them, didn't you? On the corpses...
Fangs.
Usually the only ones selected to work on investigations with us in Division 5
are people who've accidentally learned about devils through their own investigations.
You also signed the confidentiality agreement, right?
Fangs, huh...?
When you're told you have no right to refuse, the only thing you can do is sign.
I'm still having a hard time believing vampires actually exist.
Well then, I guess it'll be even harder for you to believe that
vampires are *involved in the investigation.*
What?

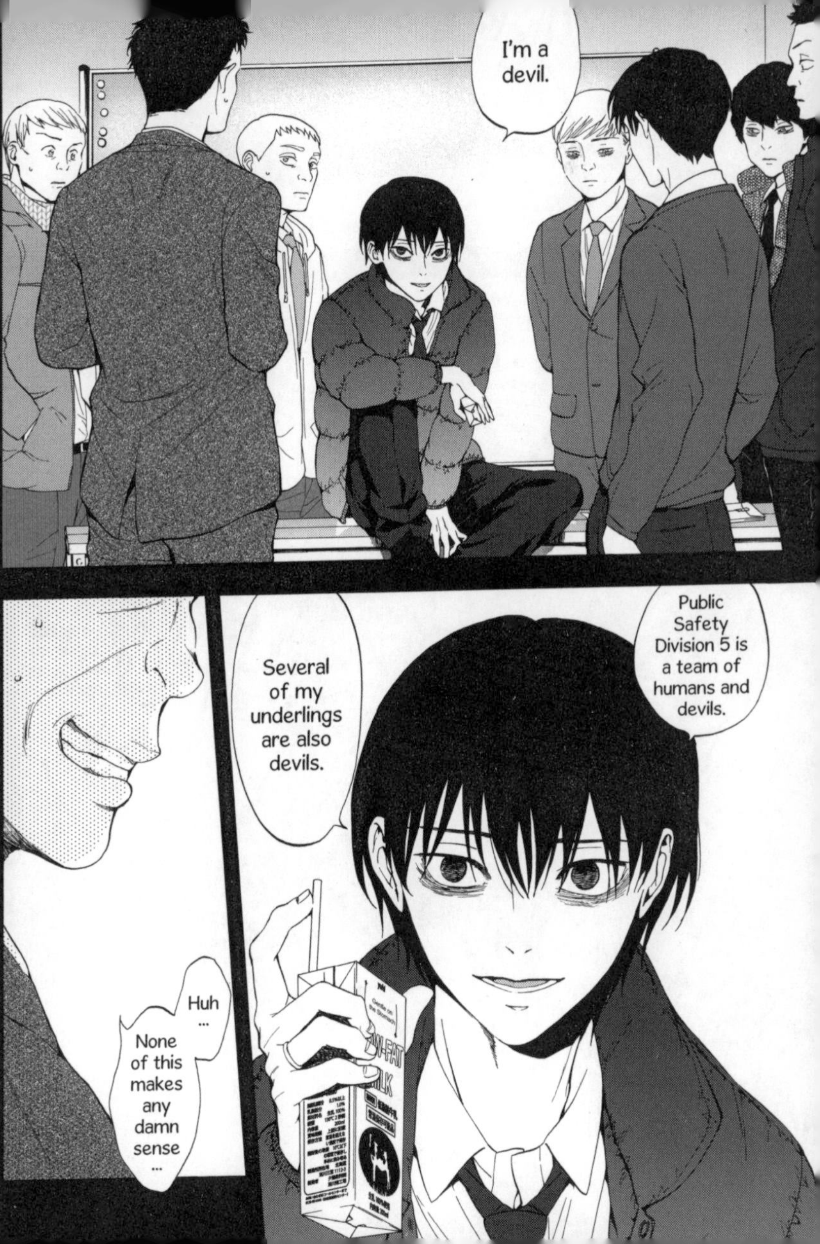
I'm a devil.
Public Safety Division 5 is a team of humans and devils.
Several of my underlings are also devils.
Huh ...
None of this makes any damn sense ...

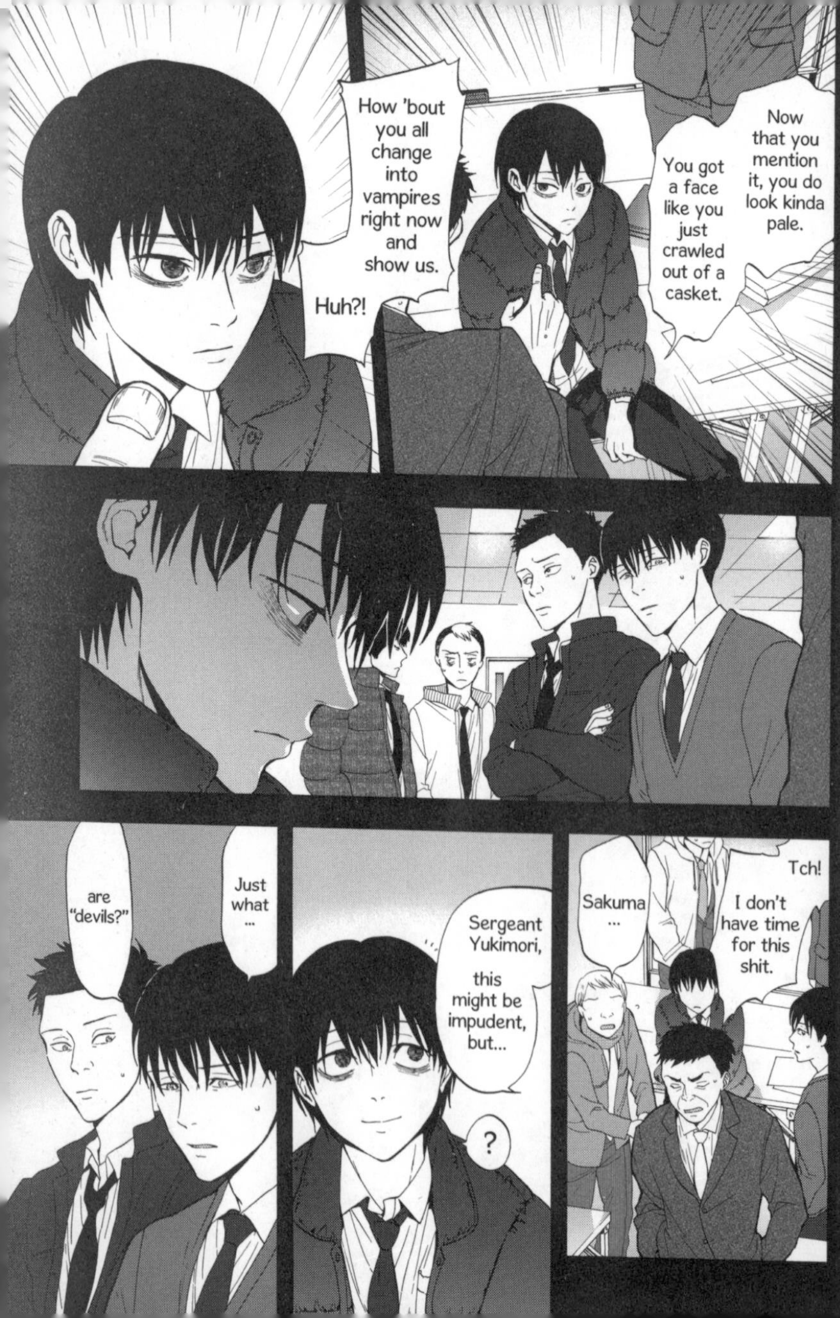
Now that you mention it, you do look kinda pale.
You got a face like you just crawled out of a casket.
How 'bout you all change into vampires right now and show us.
Huh?!
Tch!
I don't have time for this shit.
Sakuma ...
Sergeant Yukimori,
this might be impudent, but...
?
Just what ...
are "devils?"

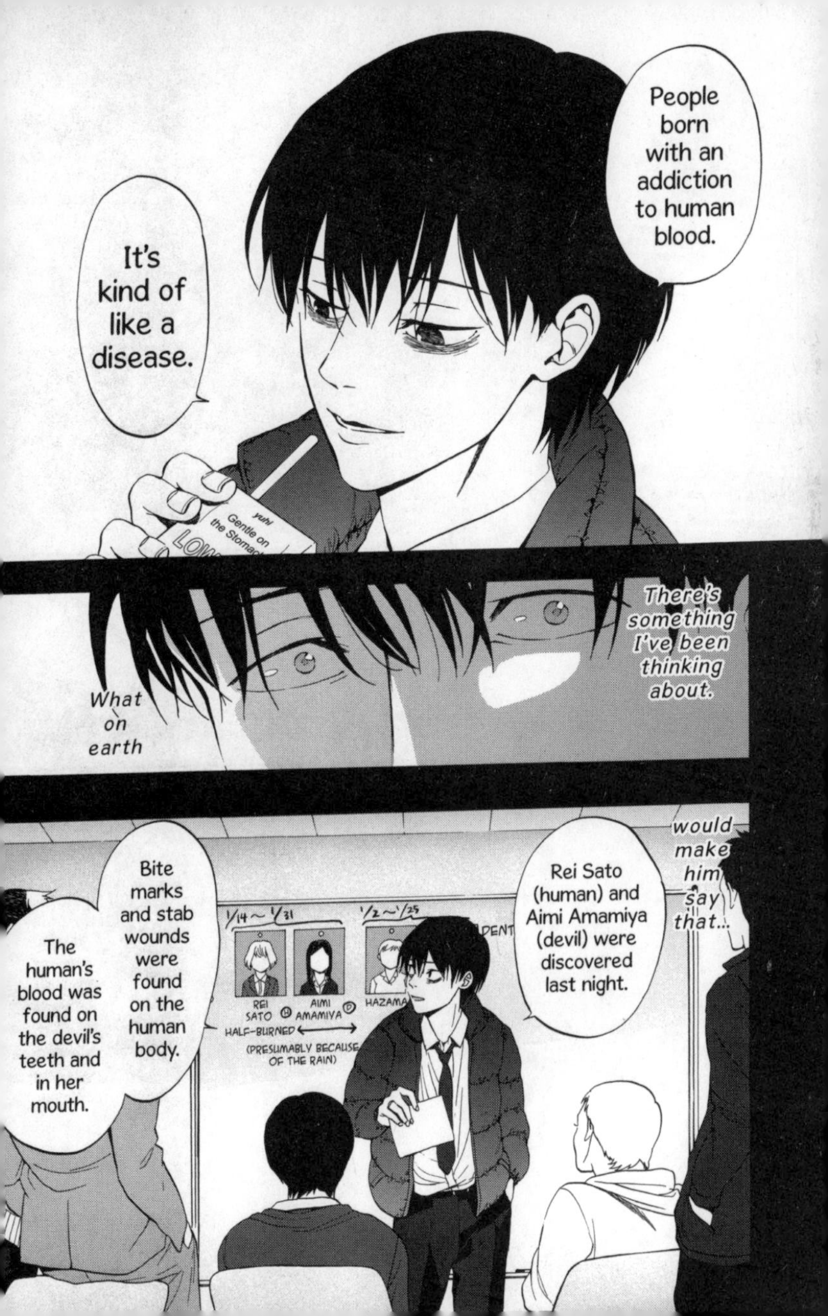
People born with an addiction to human blood.
It's kind of like a disease.
yuhi
Gentle on the Stomach
There's something I've been thinking about.
What on earth
would make him say that...
Rei Sato (human) and Aimi Amamiya (devil) were discovered last night.
1/14 ~ 1/31
1/2 ~ 1/25
REI SATO (H)
AIMI AMAMIYA (D)
HAZAMA
HALF-BURNED
(PRESUMABLY BECAUSE OF THE RAIN)
Bite marks and stab wounds were found on the human body.
The human's blood was found on the devil's teeth and in her mouth.

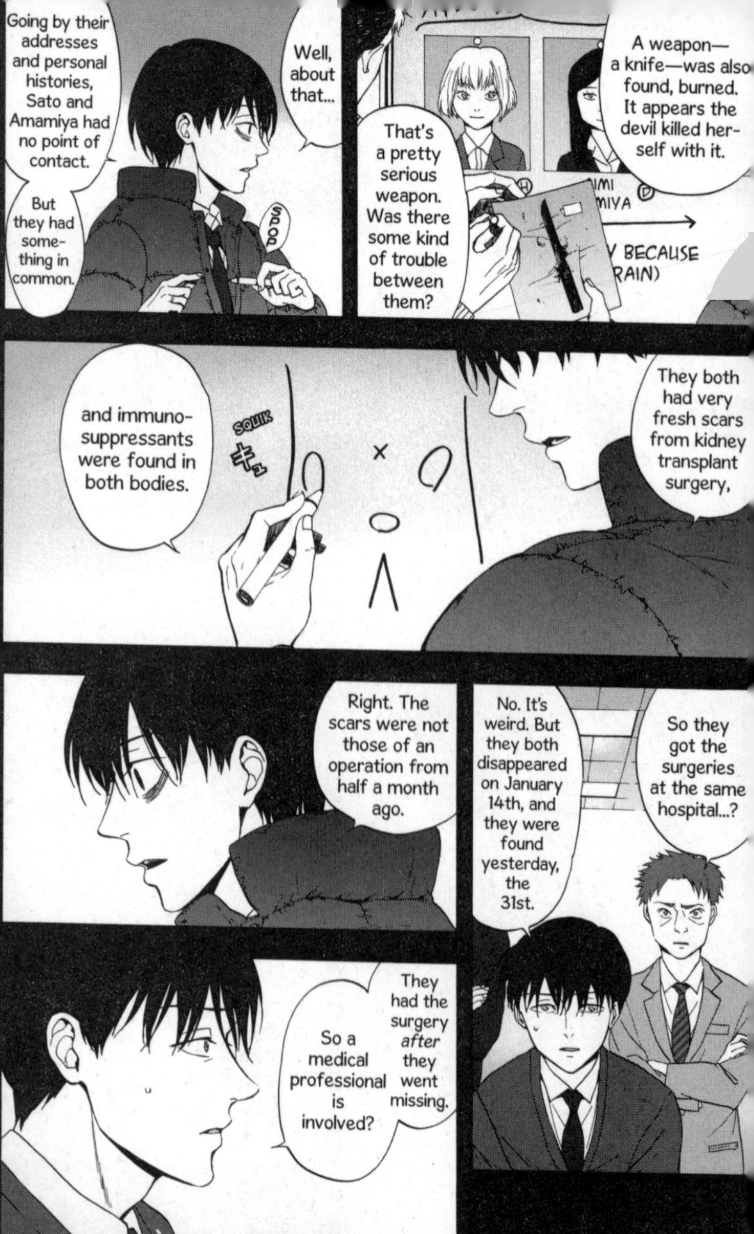
A weapon—a knife—was also found, burned. It appears the devil killed herself with it.
That's a pretty serious weapon. Was there some kind of trouble between them?
Well, about that...
Going by their addresses and personal histories, Sato and Amamiya had no point of contact.
SPOP
But they had something in common.
They both had very fresh scars from kidney transplant surgery,
SQUIK
キュ
and immuno-suppressants were found in both bodies.
So they got the surgeries at the same hospital...?
No. It's weird. But they both disappeared on January 14th, and they were found yesterday, the 31st.
Right. The scars were not those of an operation from half a month ago.
They had the surgery *after* they went missing.
So a medical professional is involved?

Are these the photos of the bodies?

Geez, so damn touchy...

RSTLE

Yeah.

Please don't show the human's photos to the devil officers. There's a ton of blood.

...

The autopsy shows they each had both kidneys removed

and each had *two new kidneys transplanted into them.*

REI SATO (H)

01/31　18：33に発見された死体　恒心会の死
部冤菜会の遺体の遺体について

Y

N

IMPLANT SCAR

(略1)

1）移植点
　移植　砂（ヒト）の部位は上腹部、肝び背心
　（私）は右腹部、腎びの状況・免疫等心的関係は
　免炎に接された心に認められる。
　前区の借も、複製で並記された心物の複製
　気まれかせて追込みて、力すで口分を報した心腎
　作がある。(内臓・ぢ(内)

2）形成点
　いずれも腹部に肝臓状の拡張が認められる。な
　お感染世界状が必要な素の心や前、自身の肝
　臓けたまおアーの腎臓を下腹部に移植
　する。

AIMI AMAMIYA (D)

N

REMOVAL SCAR

2-1）
　移植一前区ともに左腕の肝臓を摘出されてい
　る。

2-2）
　移植一前区ともに、下腹部に腎臓を移植され
　ている。

2-3）
　移植一前区ともに予移植の大きさは比較的に、
　また、腎の腎臓心力合は心予動時暗し近い心思と
　み。
　新腹要とも橡添される

3）
　移植一前区ともに肝内から免疫抑制剤（第3
　作）が投与されている。

Organ swapping.

Between a human and a devil...

Normally, for a kidney transplant, the donor retains one of their own kidneys...

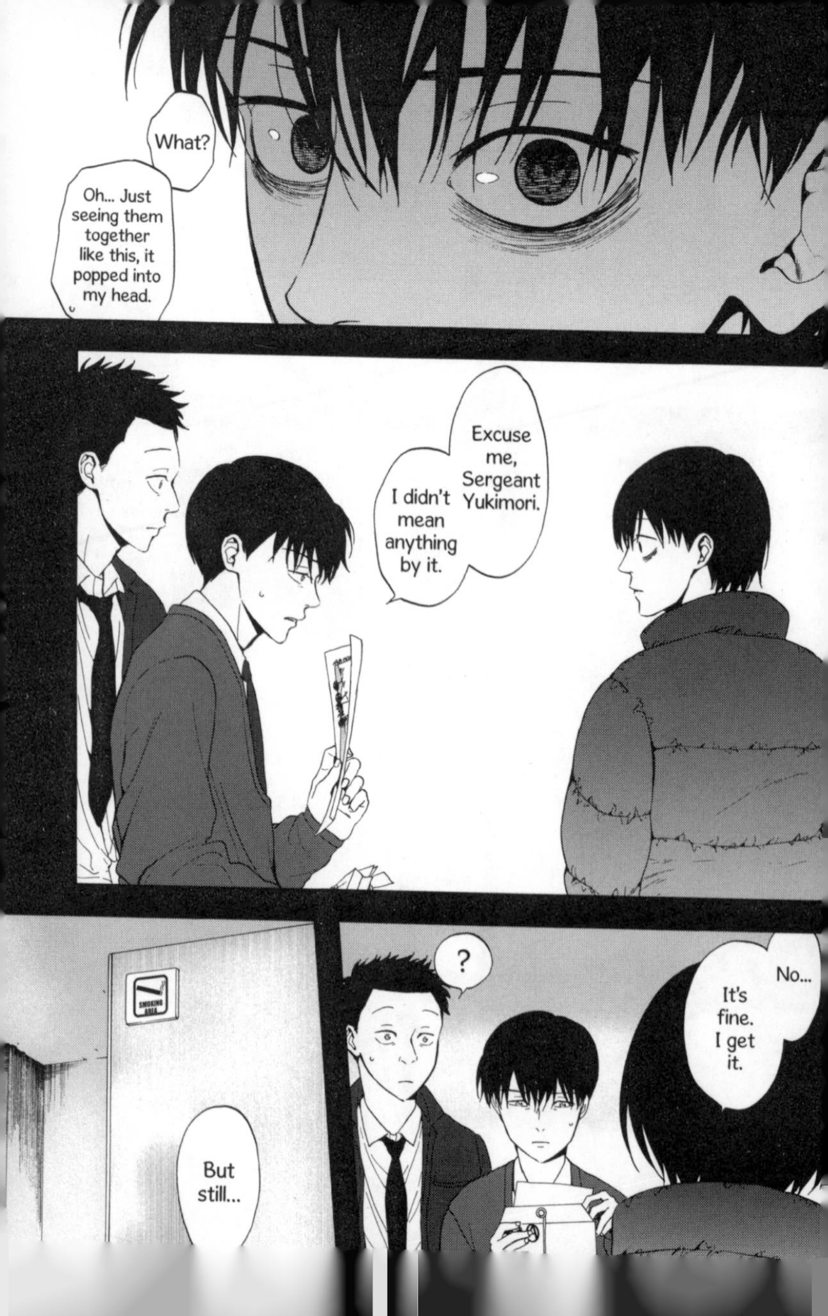
What?
Oh... Just seeing them together like this, it popped into my head.
Excuse me, Sergeant Yukimori.
I didn't mean anything by it.
No... It's fine. I get it.
?
SMOKING AREA
But still...

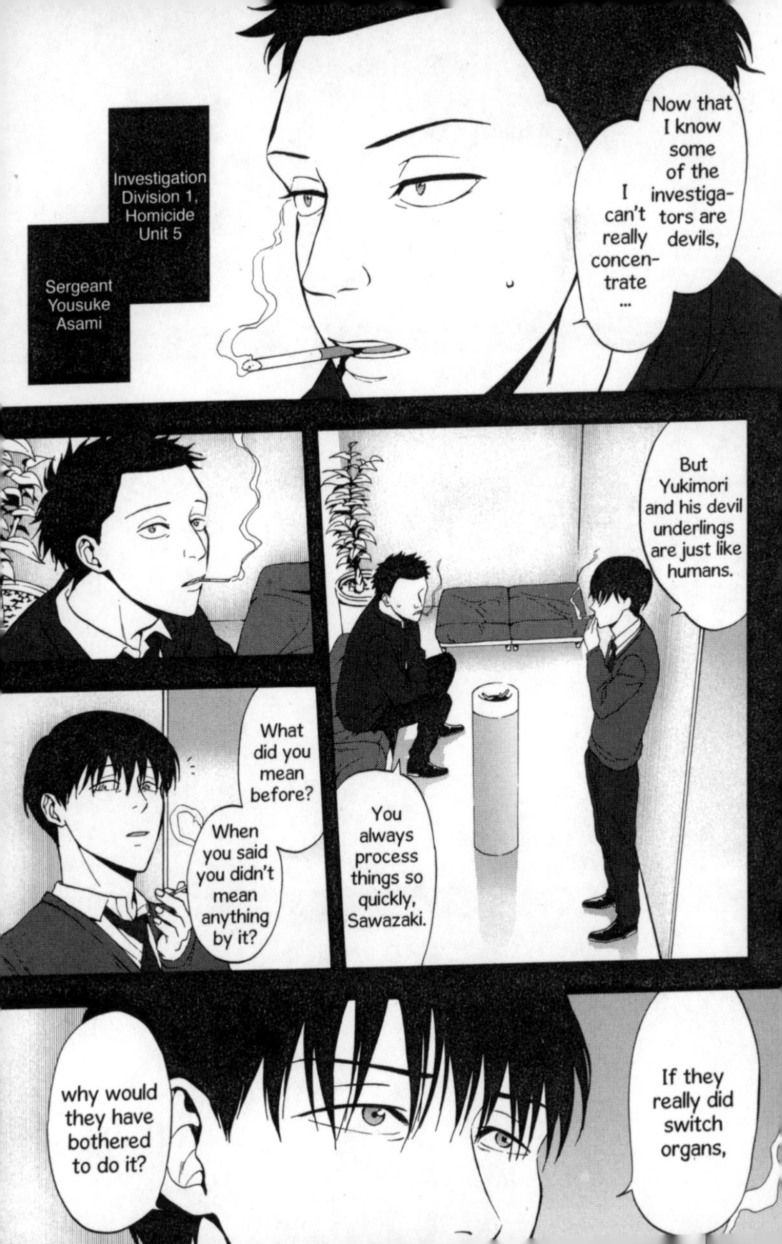
Now that I know some of the investigators are devils,
I can't really concentrate...
Investigation Division 1, Homicide Unit 5
Sergeant Yousuke Asami
But Yukimori and his devil underlings are just like humans.
You always process things so quickly, Sawazaki.
What did you mean before?
When you said you didn't mean anything by it?
If they really did switch organs,
why would they have bothered to do it?

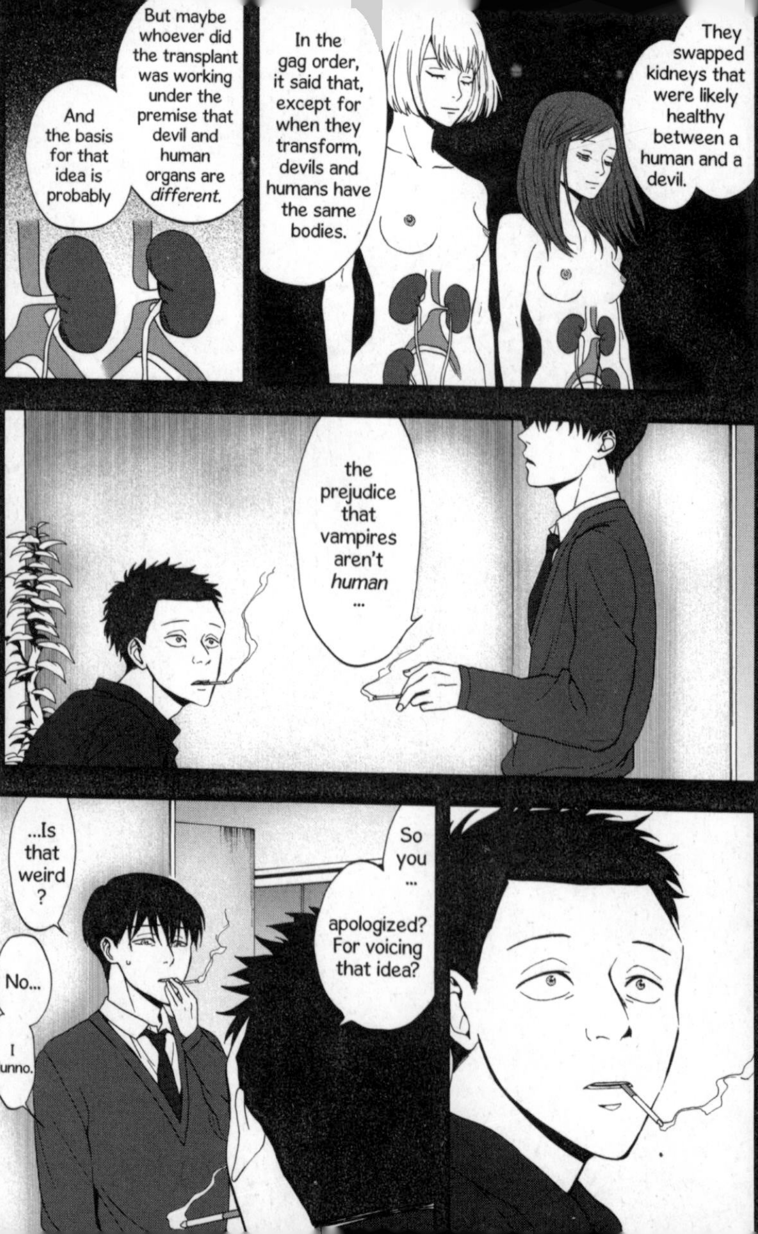
They swapped kidneys that were likely healthy between a human and a devil.
In the gag order, it said that, except for when they transform, devils and humans have the same bodies.
But maybe whoever did the transplant was working under the premise that devil and human organs are *different*.
And the basis for that idea is probably
the prejudice that vampires aren't *human* ...
So you ... apologized? For voicing that idea?
...Is that weird?
No...
I dunno.

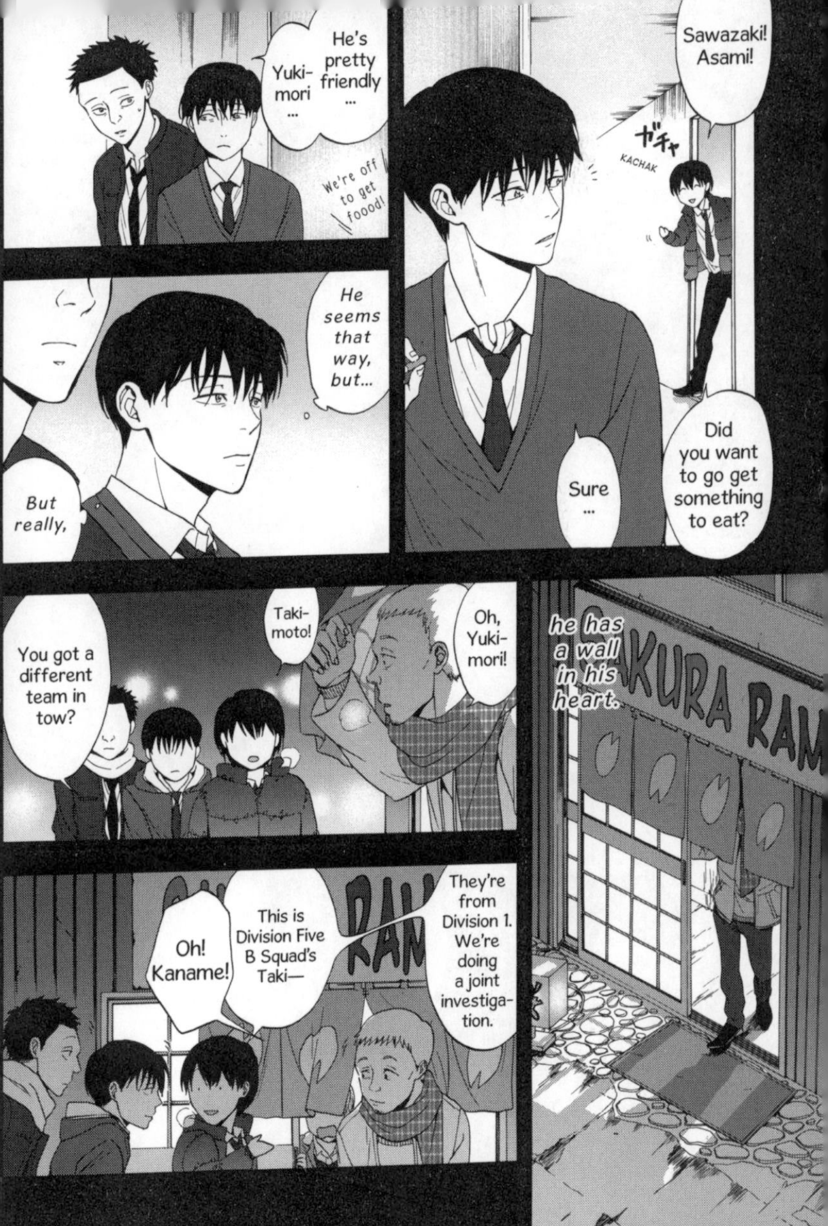
Sawazaki! Asami!
ガチャ
KACHAK
Did you want to go get something to eat?
Sure...
He's pretty friendly...
Yuki-mori...
We're off to get foood!
He seems that way, but...
But really,
he has a wall in his heart.
SAKURA RAM
Oh, Yuki-mori!
Taki-moto!
You got a different team in tow?
They're from Division 1. We're doing a joint investiga-tion.
This is Division Five B Squad's Taki—
Oh! Kaname!

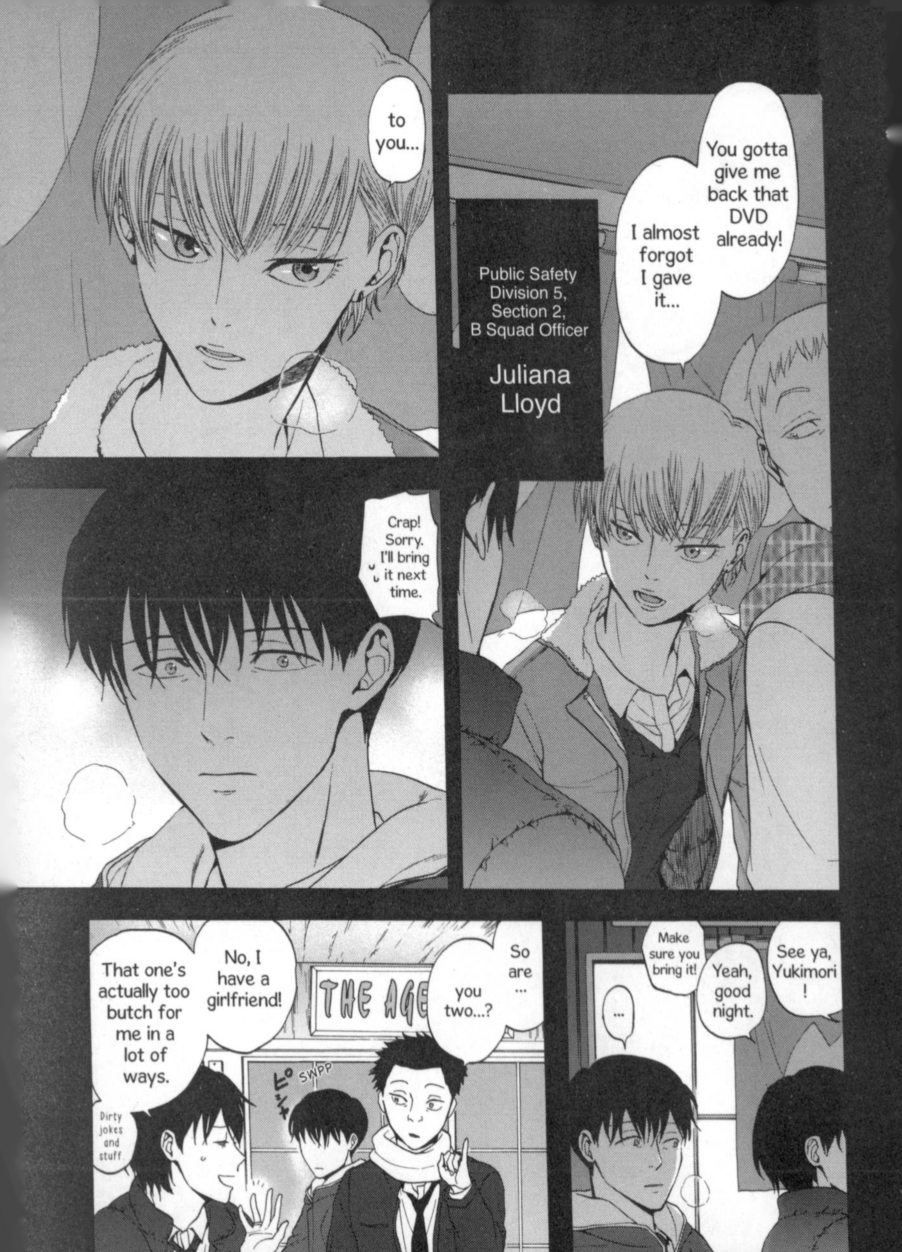
to you...
You gotta give me back that DVD already!
I almost forgot I gave it...
Public Safety Division 5, Section 2, B Squad Officer
Juliana Lloyd
Crap! Sorry. I'll bring it next time.
See ya, Yukimori!
Make sure you bring it!
Yeah, good night.
...
So are ... you two...?
No, I have a girlfriend!
That one's actually too butch for me in a lot of ways.
Dirty jokes and stuff.
THE AGE
SWPP

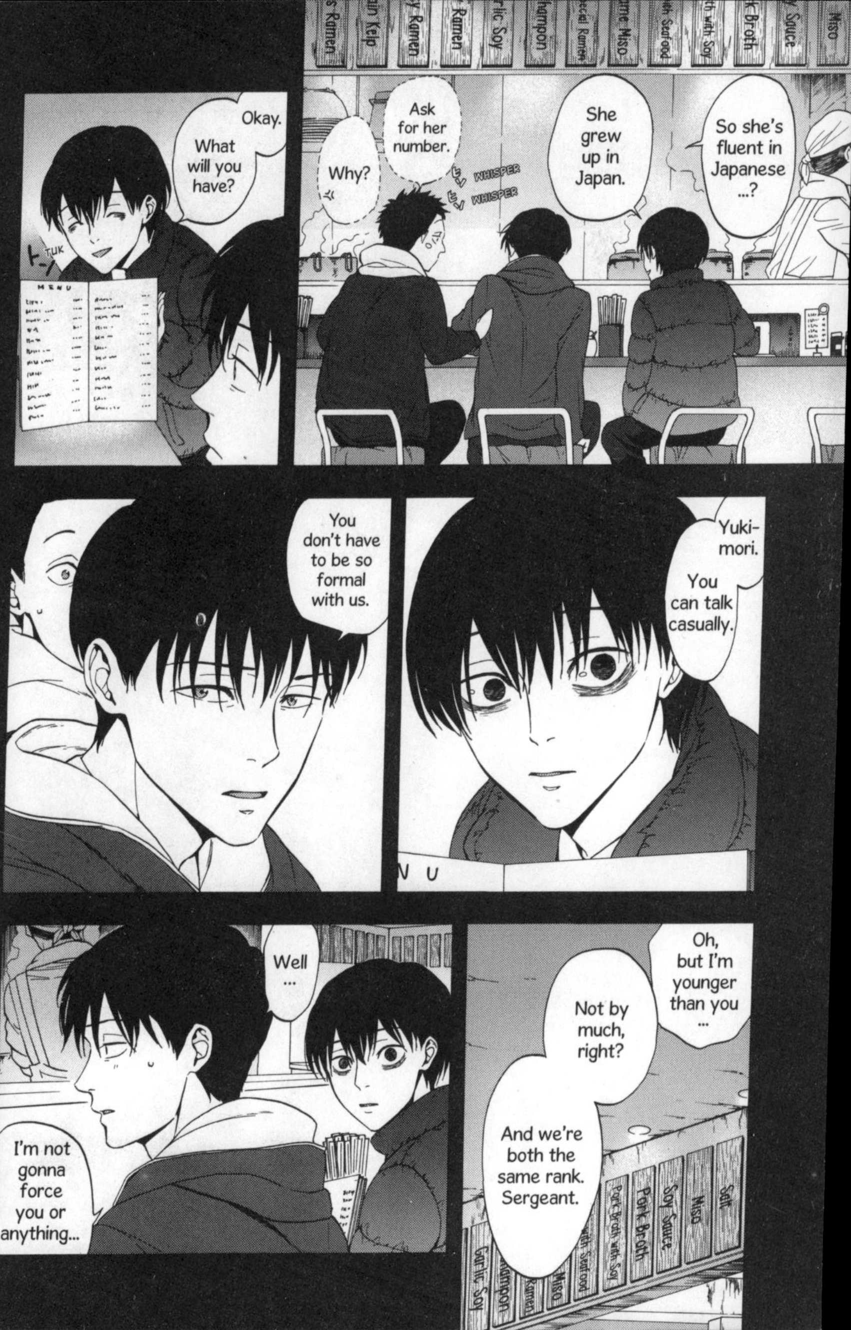
Miso
So she's fluent in Japanese ...?
She grew up in Japan.
WHISPER
WHISPER
Ask for her number.
Why?
Okay.
What will you have?
TUK
MENU
Yuki-mori.
You can talk casually.
You don't have to be so formal with us.
Oh, but I'm younger than you ...
Not by much, right?
And we're both the same rank. Sergeant.
Salt
Miso
Soy Sauce
Pork Broth
Pork Broth with Soy
with Seafood
Miso
Garlic Soy
Well ...
I'm not gonna force you or anything...

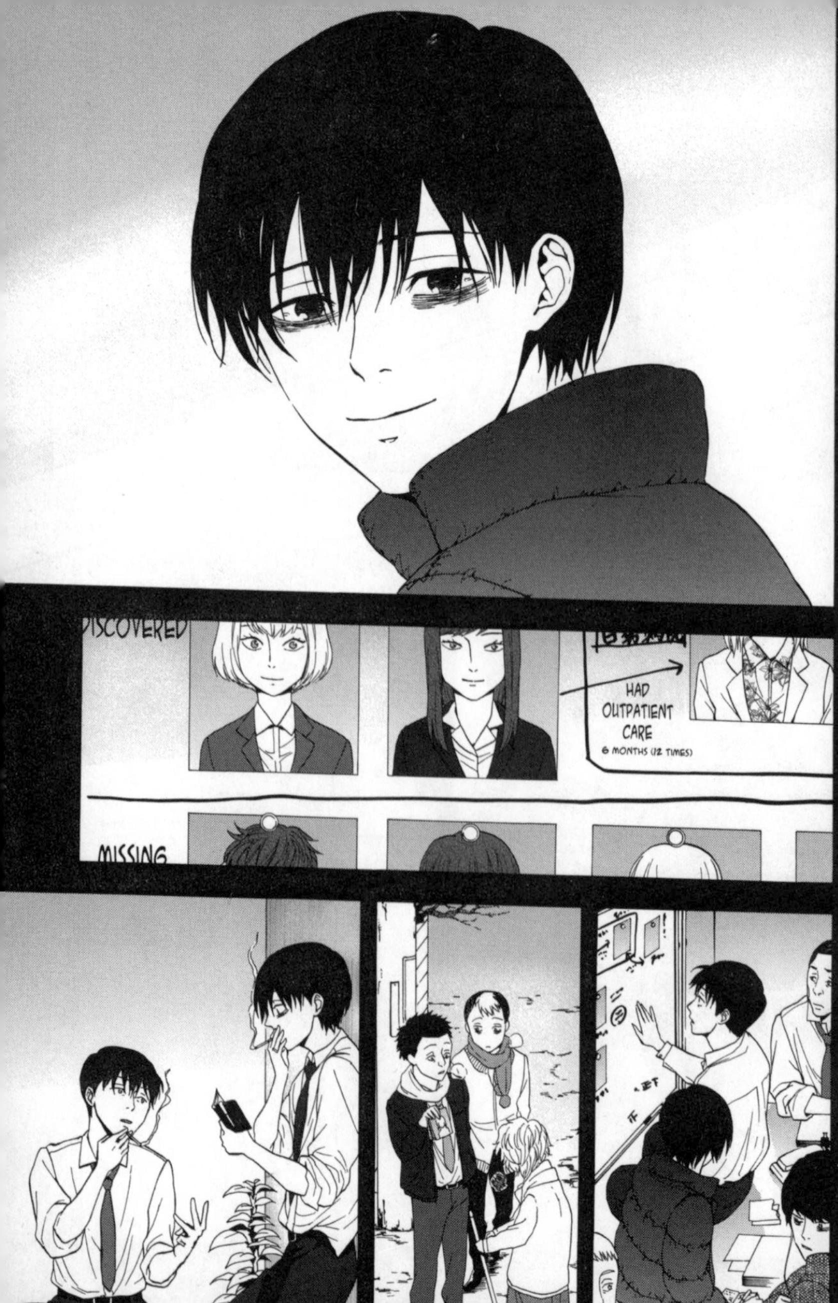
DISCOVERED
HAD OUTPATIENT CARE
6 MONTHS (12 TIMES)
MISSING

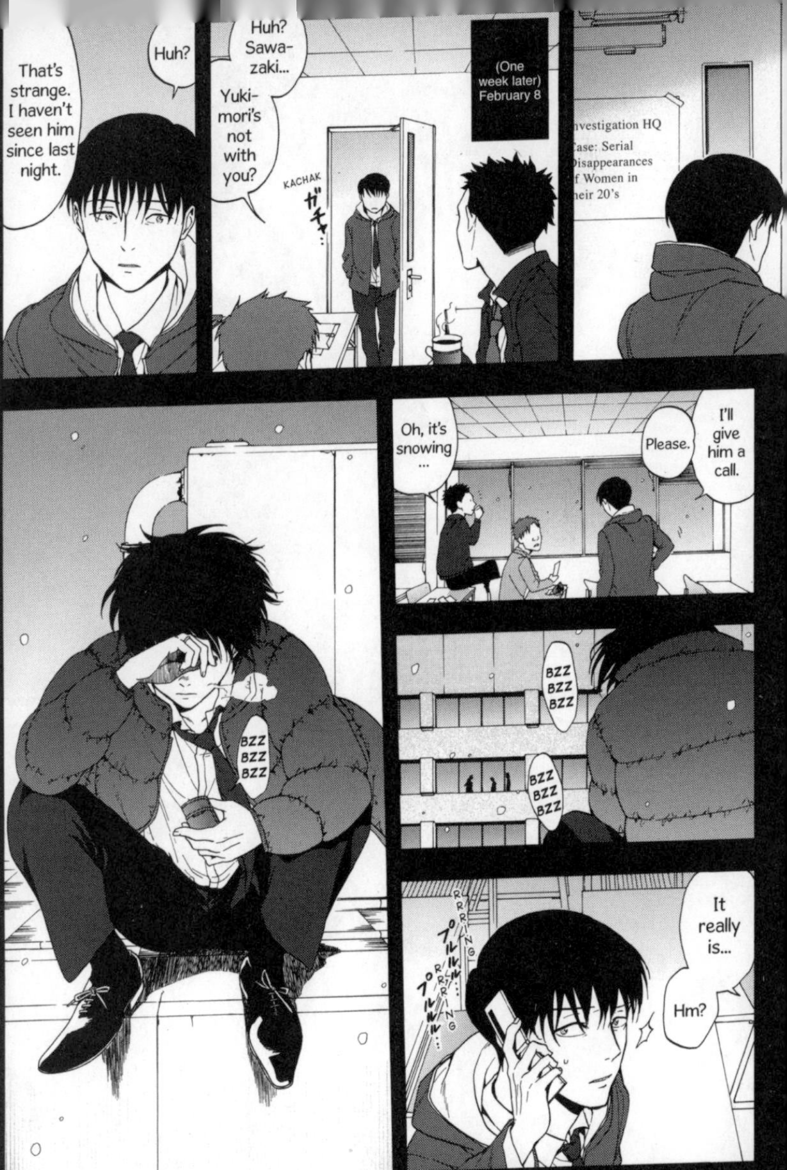
nvestigation HQ
ase: Serial
isappearances
f Women in
heir 20's
(One week later) February 8
Huh? Sawazaki...
Yukimori's not with you?
KACHAK
ガチャ…
Huh?
That's strange. I haven't seen him since last night.
I'll give him a call.
Please.
Oh, it's snowing...
BZZ BZZ BZZ
BZZ BZZ BZZ
RRRING
プルルル…
RRRING
プルルル…
It really is...
Hm?
BZZ BZZ BZZ

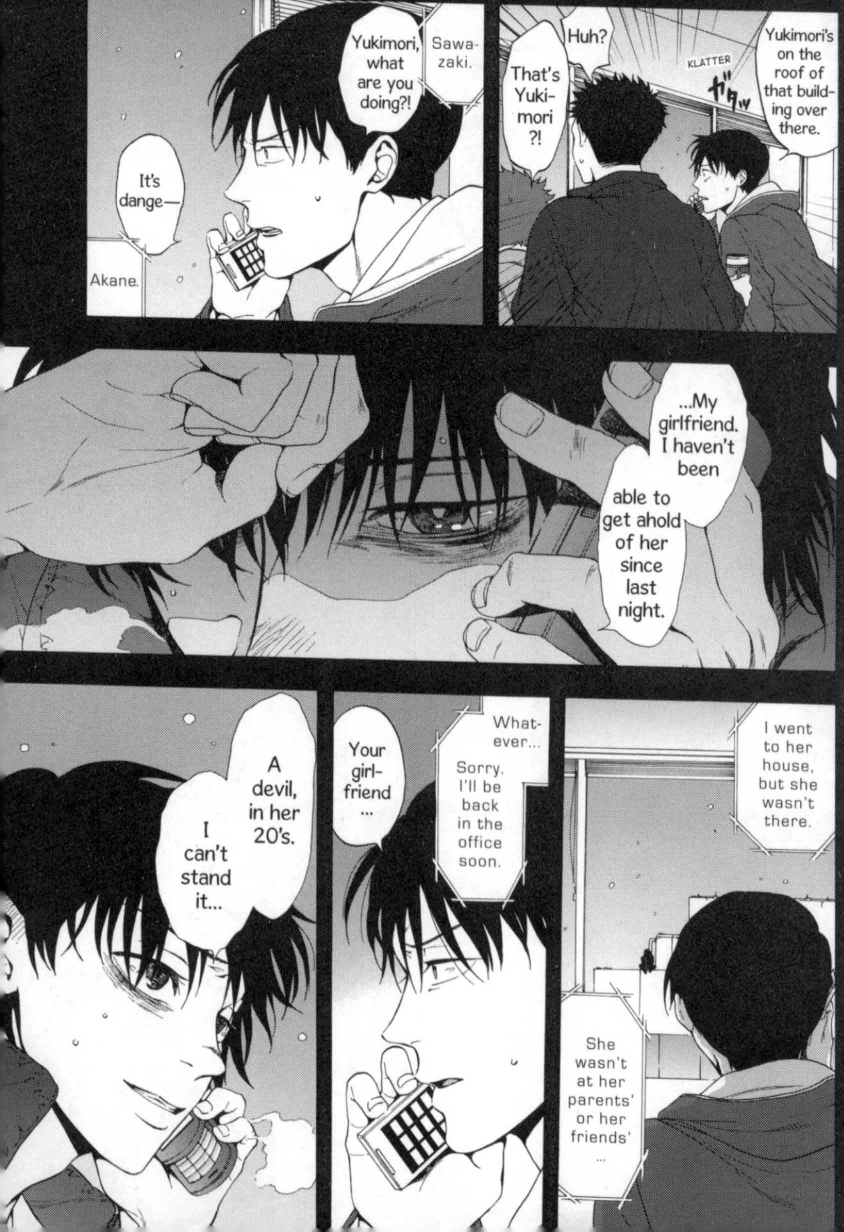
Yukimori's on the roof of that building over there.
KLATTER
ガタッ
Huh?
That's Yukimori ?!
Sawazaki.
Yukimori, what are you doing?!
It's dange—
Akane.
...My girlfriend. I haven't been able to get ahold of her since last night.
I went to her house, but she wasn't there.
She wasn't at her parents' or her friends' ...
Whatever...
Sorry. I'll be back in the office soon.
Your girlfriend ...
A devil, in her 20's.
I can't stand it...

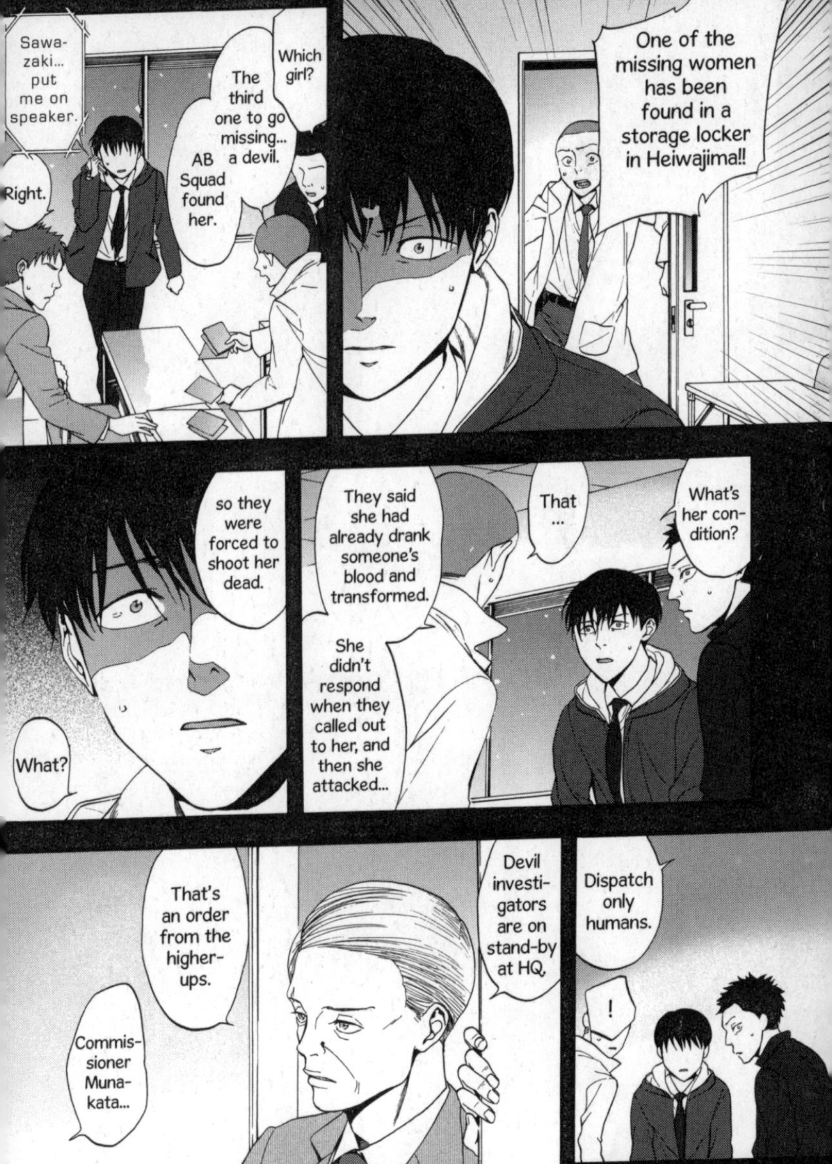
One of the missing women has been found in a storage locker in Heiwajima!!
Which girl?
The third one to go missing... a devil. AB Squad found her.
Sawa-zaki... put me on speaker.
Right.
What's her con-dition?
That ...
They said she had already drank someone's blood and transformed.
She didn't respond when they called out to her, and then she attacked...
so they were forced to shoot her dead.
What?
Dispatch only humans.
!
Devil investi-gators are on stand-by at HQ.
That's an order from the higher-ups.
Commis-sioner Muna-kata...

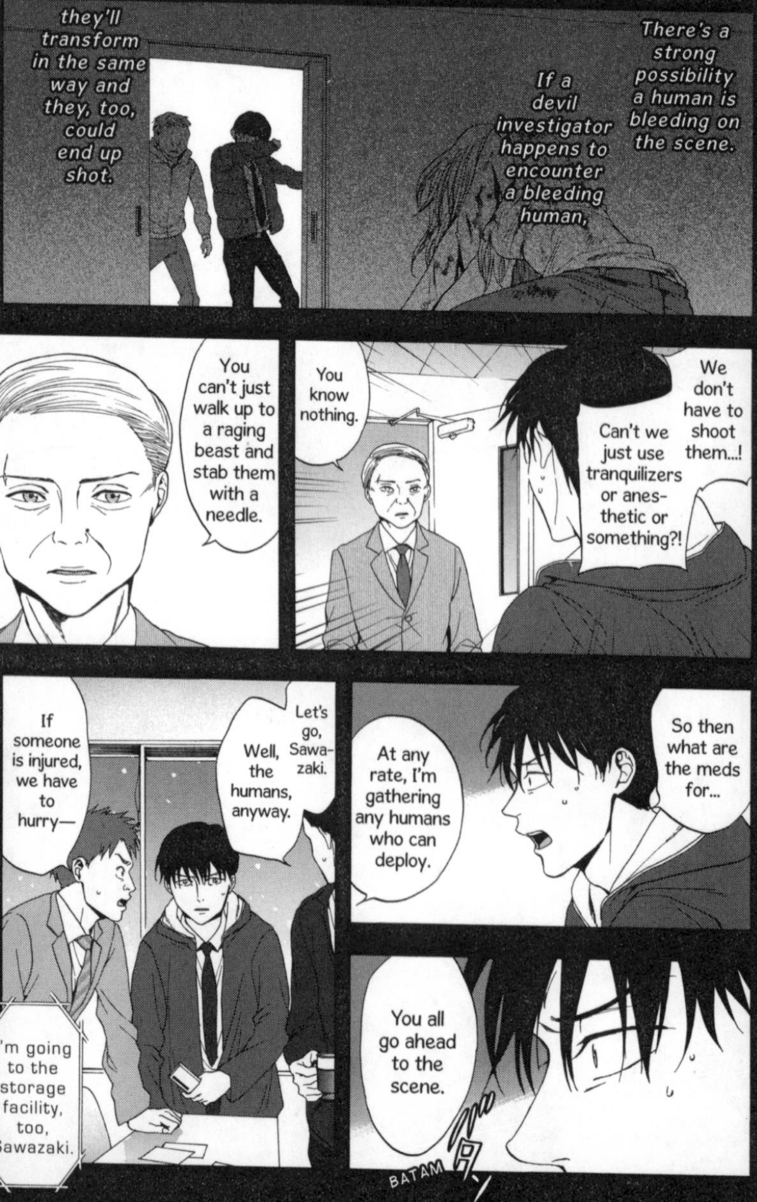
There's a strong possibility a human is bleeding on the scene.
If a devil investigator happens to encounter a bleeding human,
they'll transform in the same way and they, too, could end up shot.
We don't have to shoot them...!
Can't we just use tranquilizers or anes-thetic or something?!
You know nothing.
You can't just walk up to a raging beast and stab them with a needle.
So then what are the meds for...
At any rate, I'm gathering any humans who can deploy.
You all go ahead to the scene.
BATAM
Let's go, Sawa-zaki.
Well, the humans, anyway.
If someone is injured, we have to hurry—
I'm going to the storage facility, too, Sawazaki.

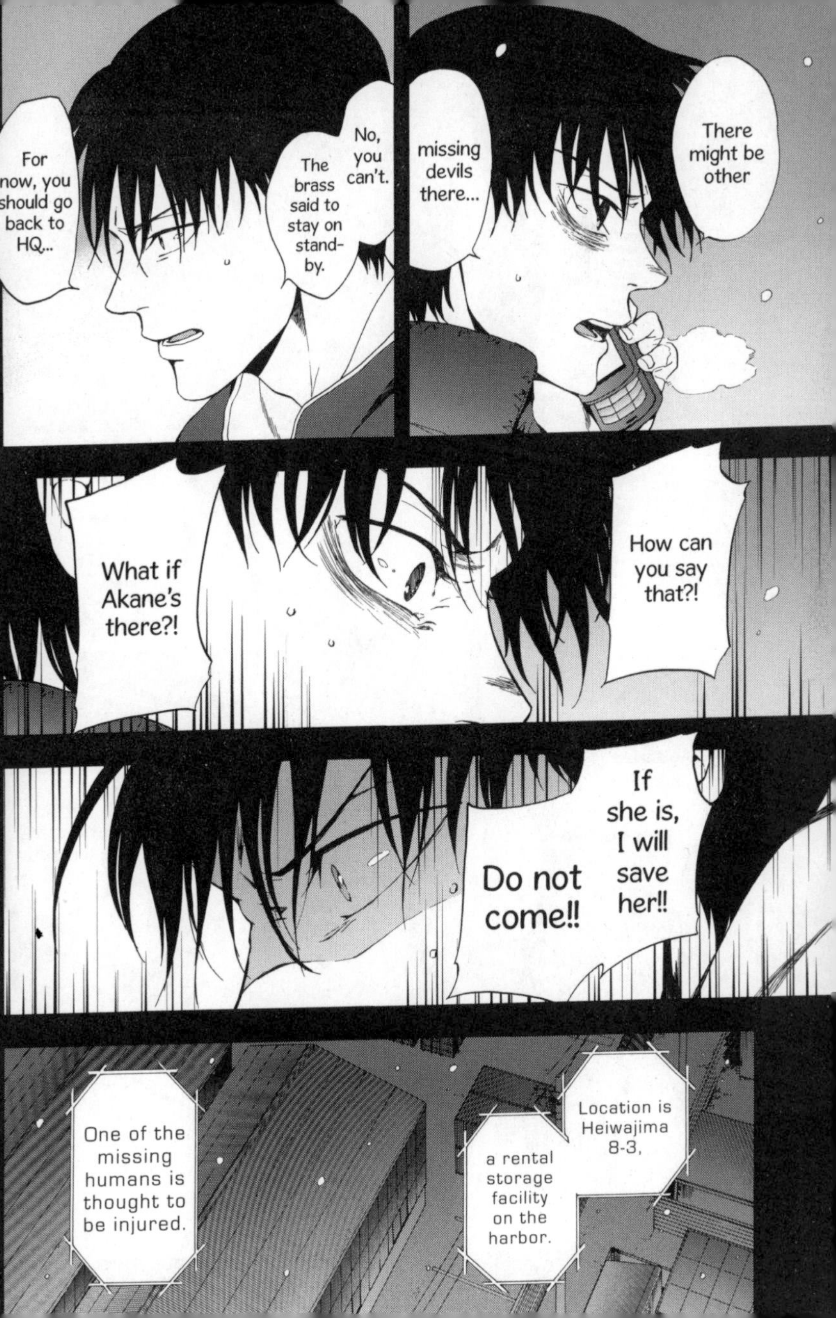
There might be other
missing devils there...
No, you can't.
The brass said to stay on stand-by.
For now, you should go back to HQ...
How can you say that?!
What if Akane's there?!
If she is, I will save her!!
Do not come!!
Location is Heiwajima 8-3,
a rental storage facility on the harbor.
One of the missing humans is thought to be injured.

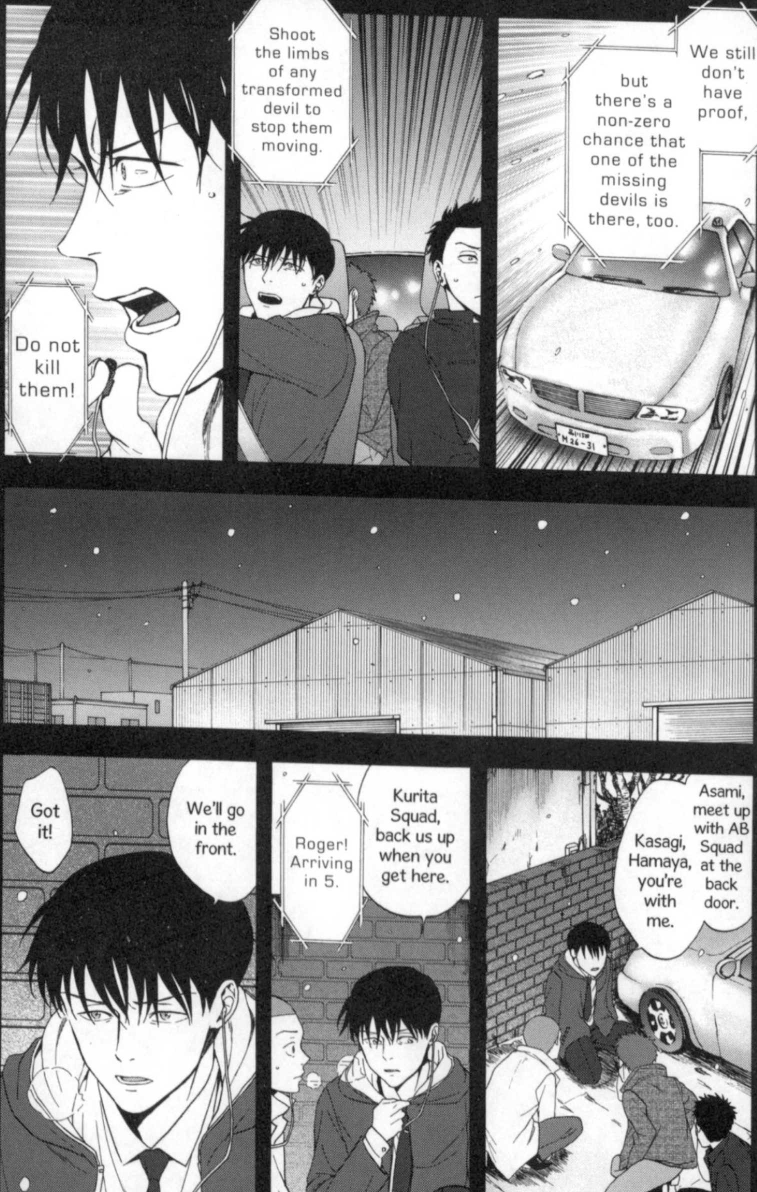
We still don't have proof,
but there's a non-zero chance that one of the missing devils is there, too.
Shoot the limbs of any transformed devil to stop them moving.
Do not kill them!
Asami, meet up with AB Squad at the back door.
Kasagi, Hamaya, you're with me.
Kurita Squad, back us up when you get here.
Roger! Arriving in 5.
We'll go in the front.
Got it!

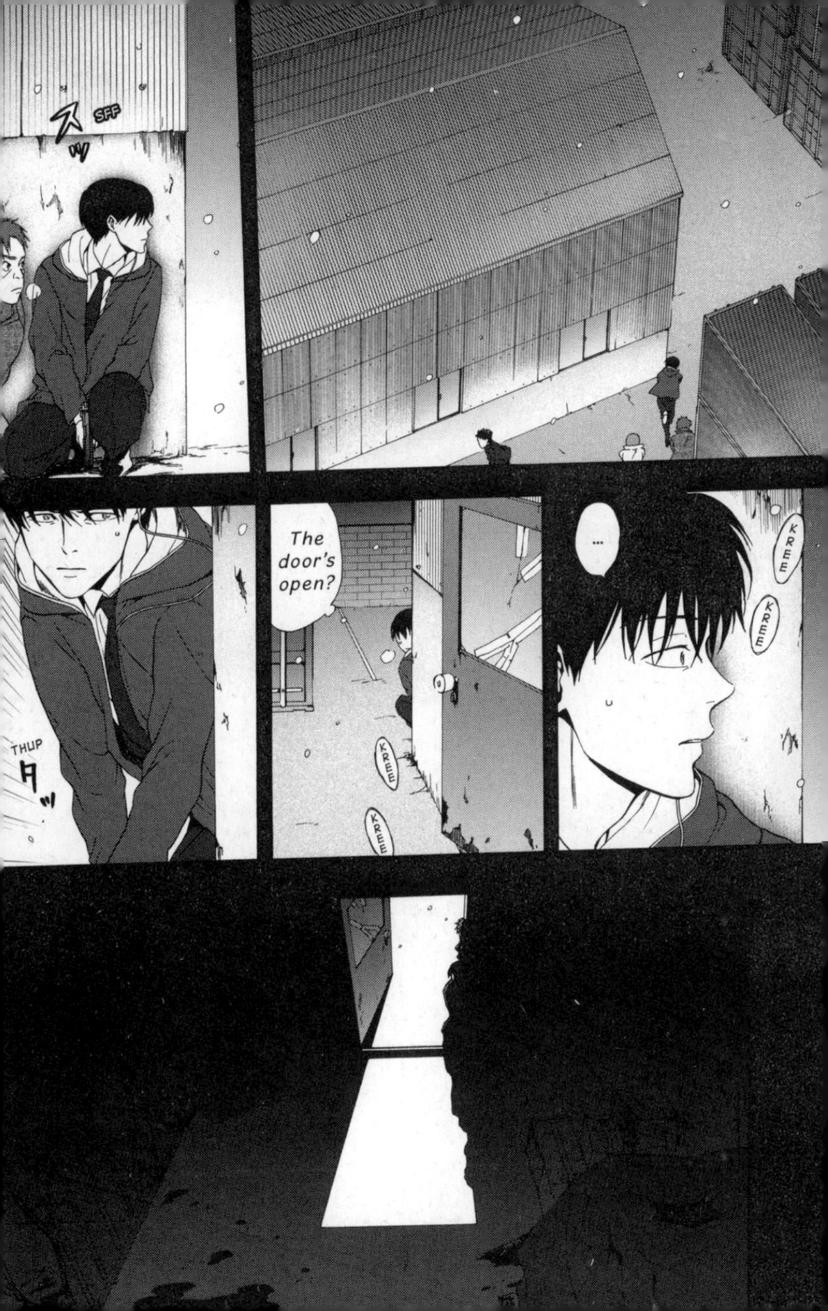
SFF
スッ
...
KREE
KREE
The door's open?
KREE
KREE
THUP
タッ

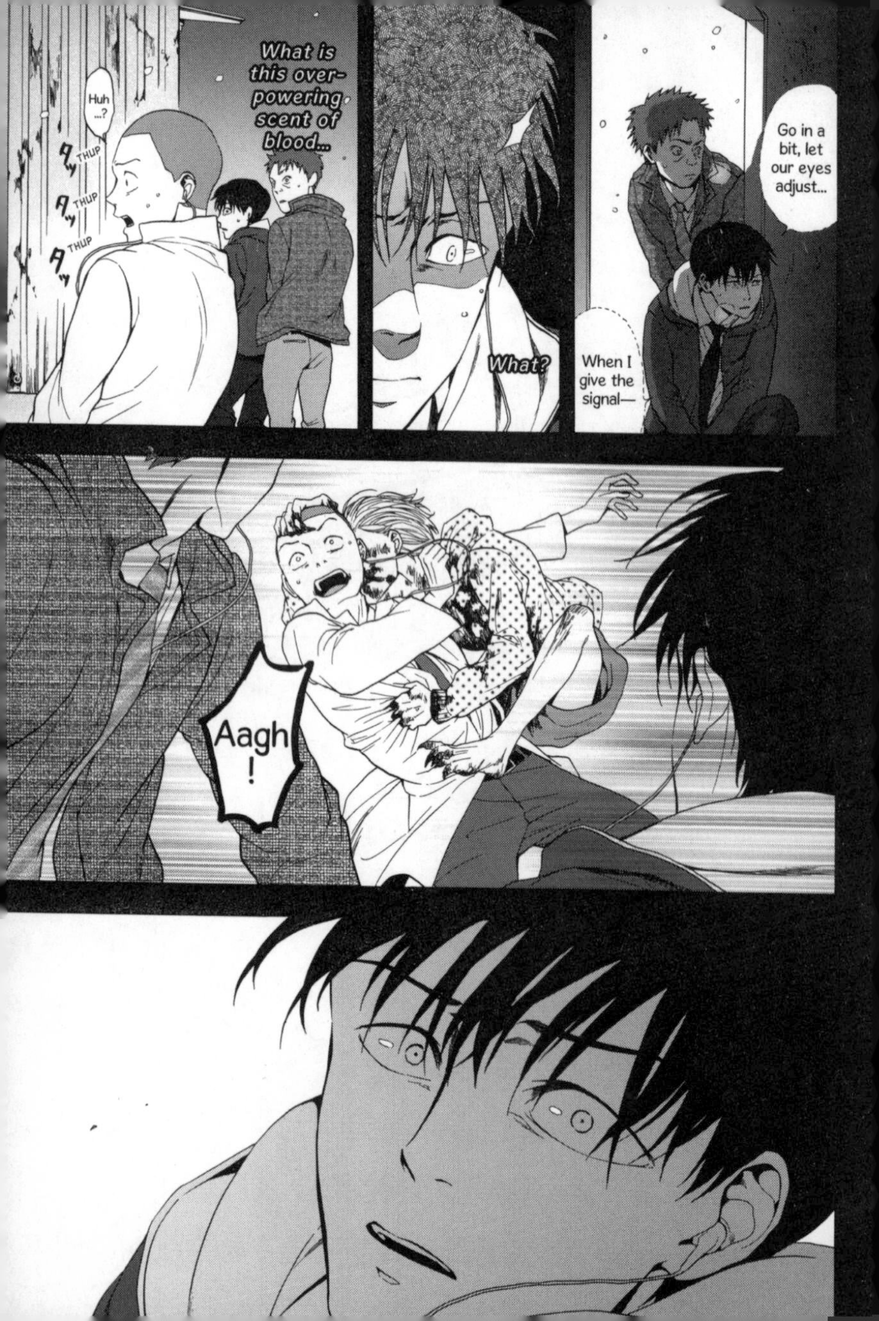
Go in a bit, let our eyes adjust...
When I give the signal—
What?
What is this over-powering scent of blood...
Huh ...?
THUP
THUP
THUP
Aagh !

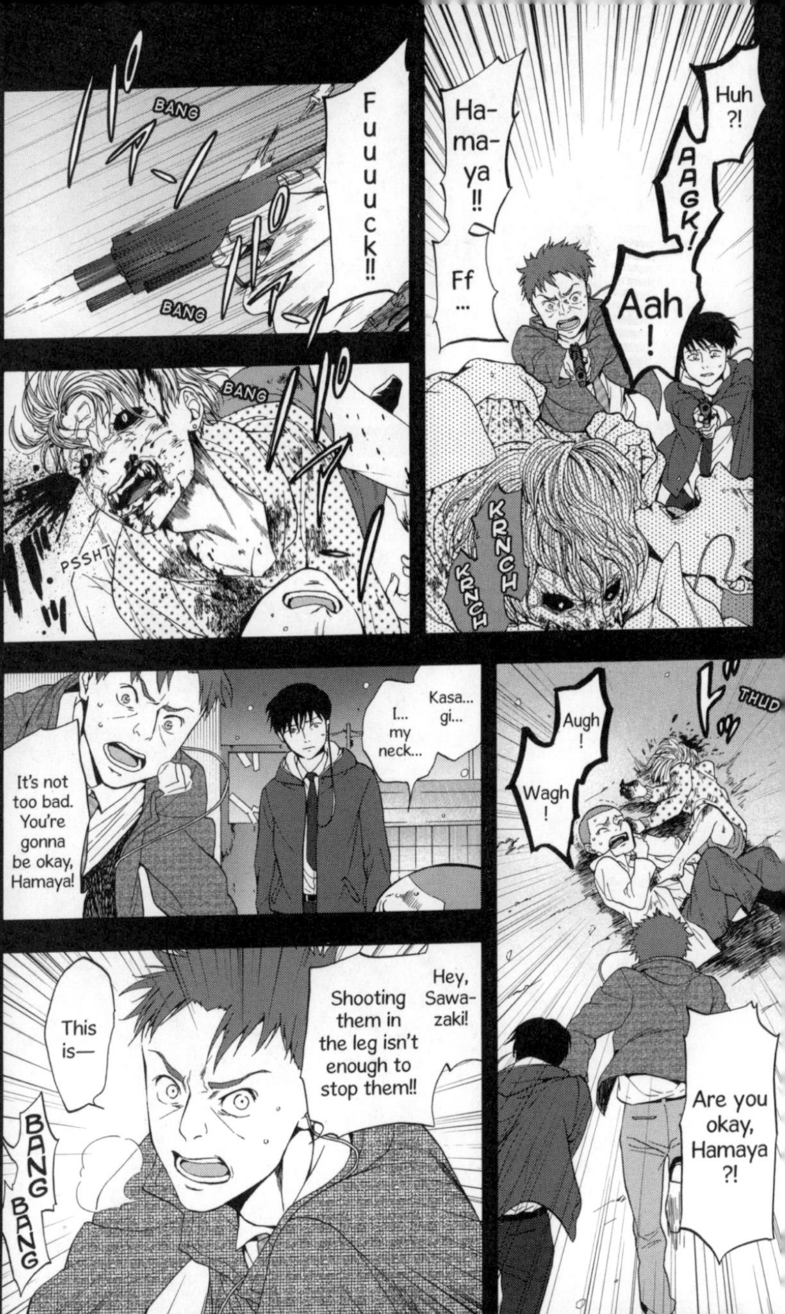
Huh ?!
AAGK!
Aah !
Ha-ma-ya !!
Ff ...
KRNCH
KRNCH
Fuuuuck!!
BANG
BANG
BANG
PSSHT
THUD
Augh !
Wagh !
Are you okay, Hamaya ?!
Kasa... gi...
I... my neck...
It's not too bad. You're gonna be okay, Hamaya!
Hey, Sawa-zaki!
Shooting them in the leg isn't enough to stop them!!
This is—
BANG
BANG

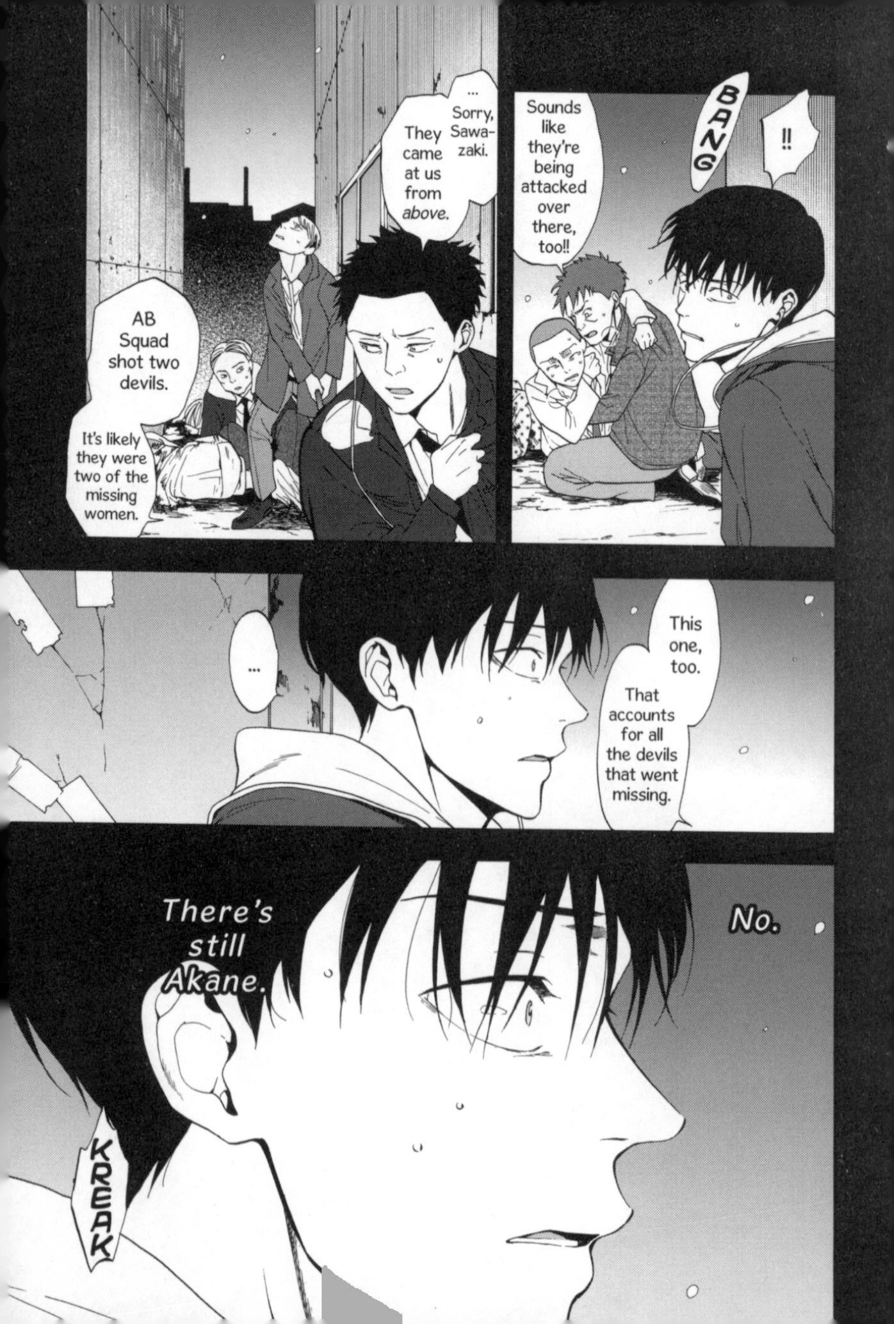
BANG
!!
Sounds like they're being attacked over there, too!!
... Sorry, Sawa-zaki.
They came at us from *above*.
AB Squad shot two devils.
It's likely they were two of the missing women.
This one, too.
That accounts for all the devils that went missing.
...
No.
There's still Akane.
KREAK

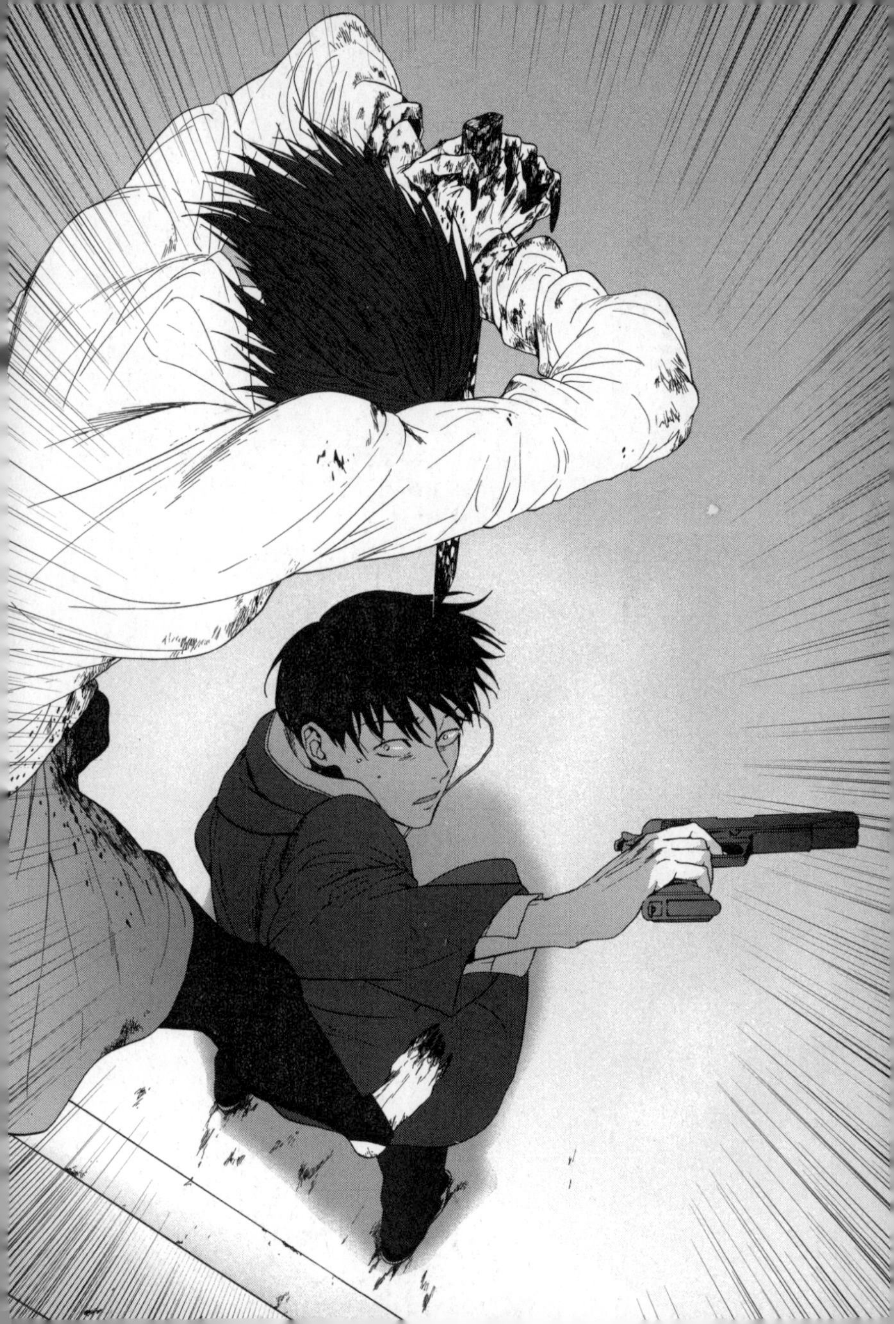

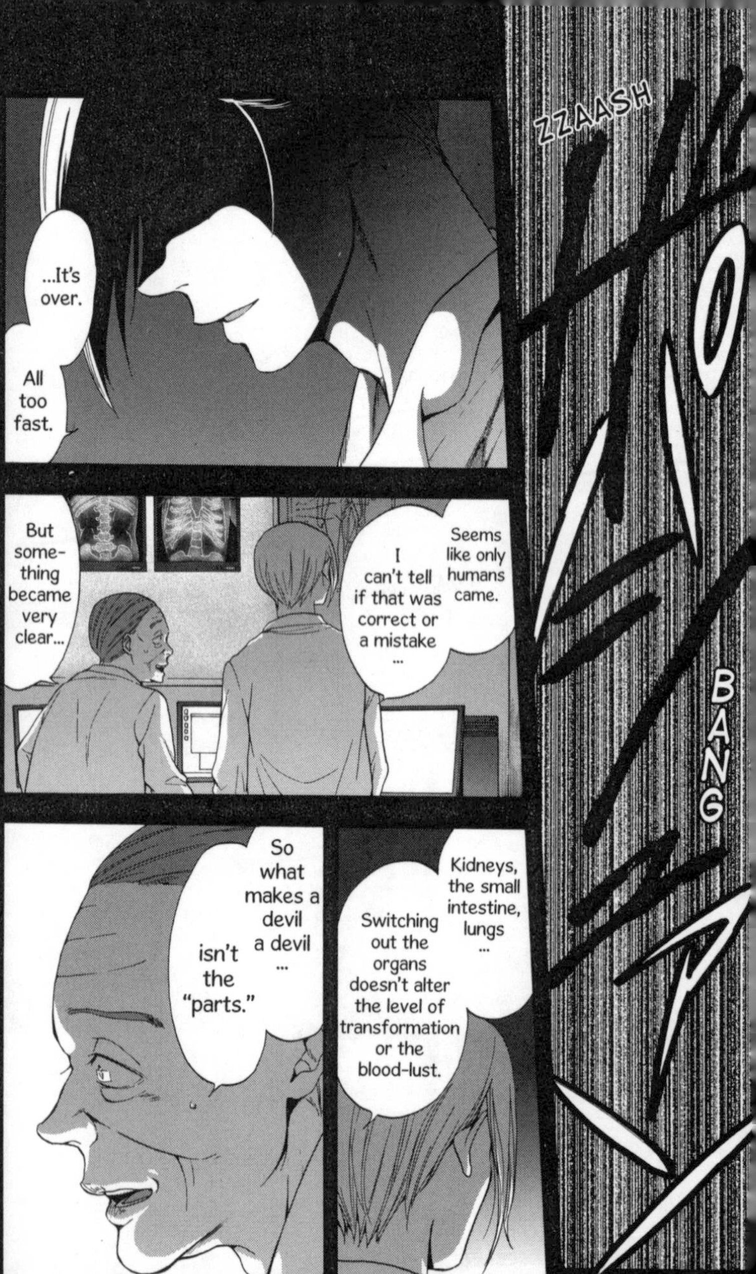

ZZAASH
BANG
...It's over.
All too fast.
Seems like only humans came.
I can't tell if that was correct or a mistake ...
But something became very clear...
Kidneys, the small intestine, lungs ...
Switching out the organs doesn't alter the level of transformation or the blood-lust.
So what makes a devil a devil ...
isn't the "parts."

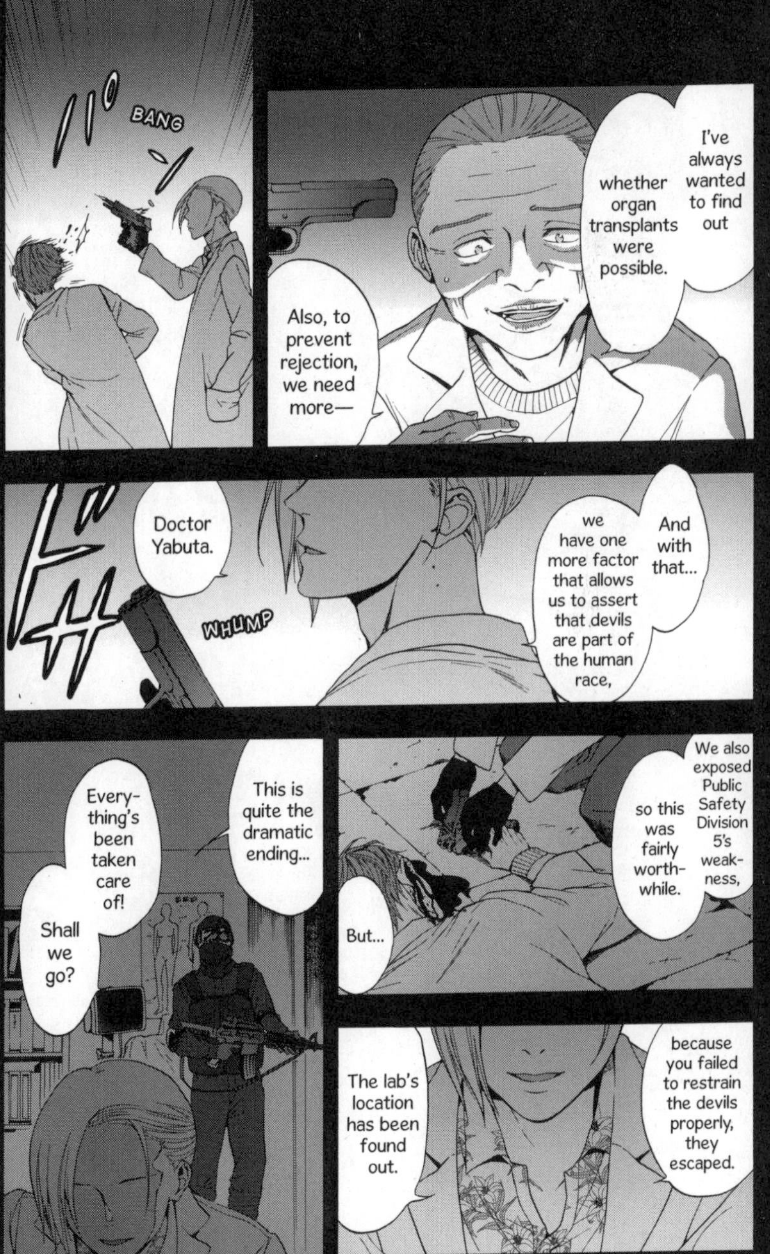
I've always wanted to find out
whether organ transplants were possible.
Also, to prevent rejection, we need more—
BANG
And with that...
we have one more factor that allows us to assert that devils are part of the human race,
Doctor Yabuta.
WHUMP
We also exposed Public Safety Division 5's weak-ness,
so this was fairly worth-while.
But...
because you failed to restrain the devils properly, they escaped.
The lab's location has been found out.
This is quite the dramatic ending...
Every-thing's been taken care of!
Shall we go?

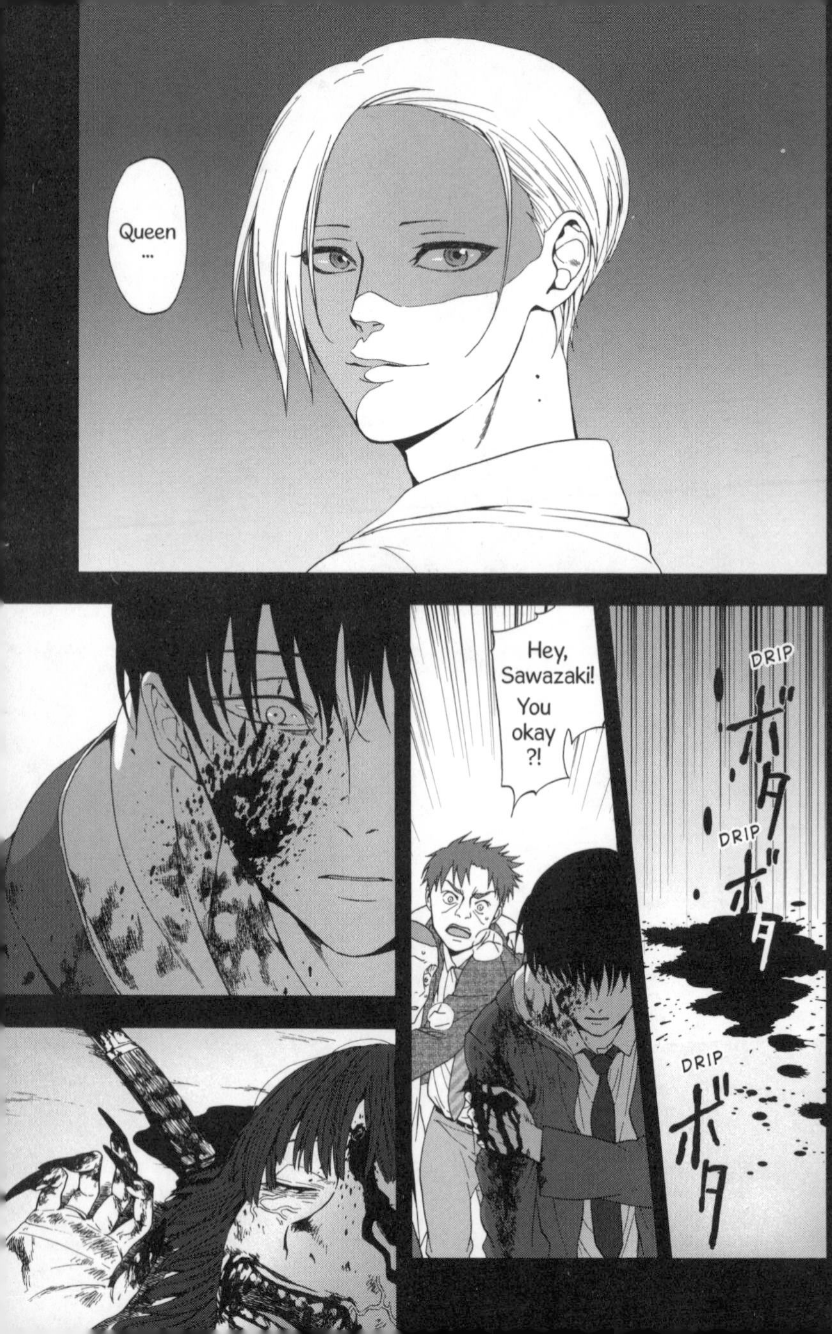
Queen ...
DRIP
ボタ
DRIP
ボタ
DRIP
ボタ
Hey, Sawazaki! You okay?!

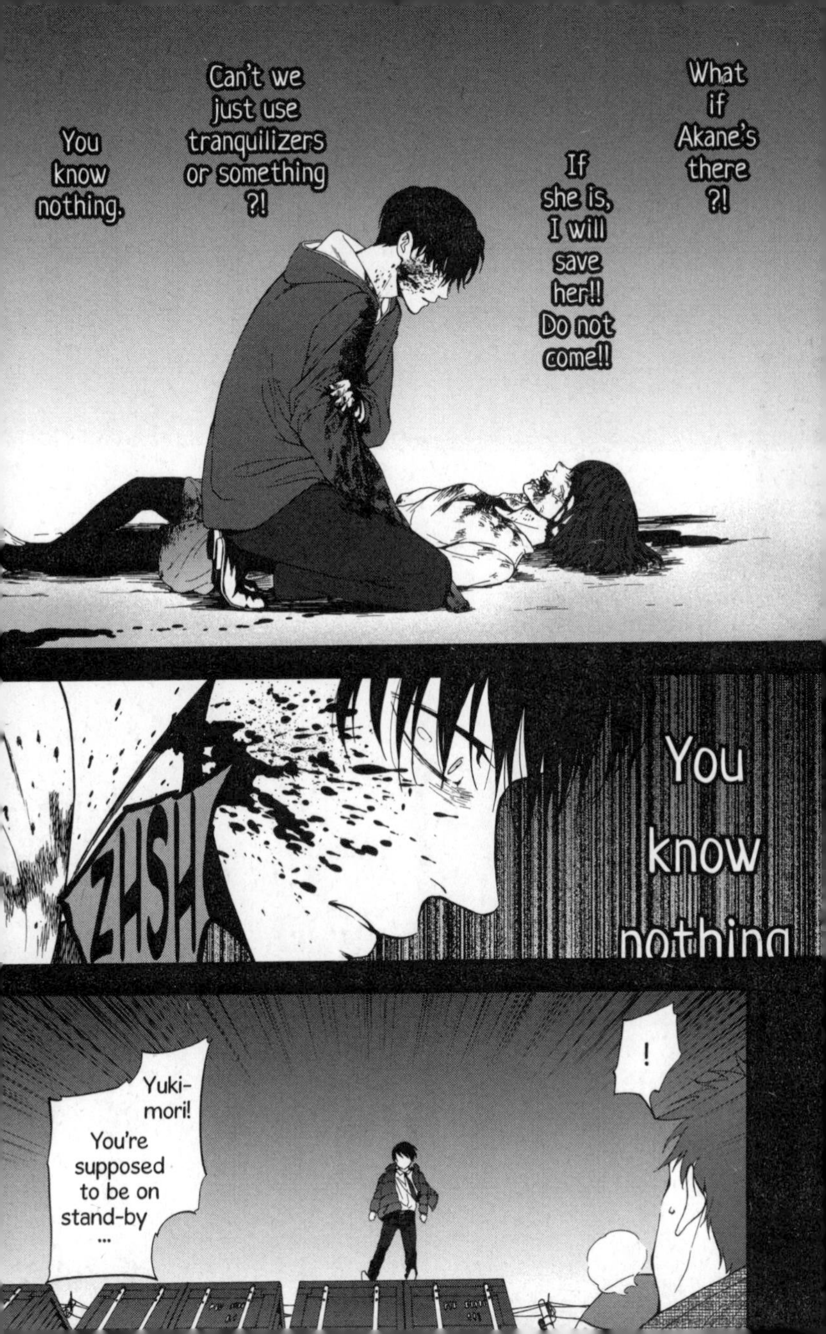
What if Akane's there ?!
If she is, I will save her!! Do not come!!
Can't we just use tranquilizers or something ?!
You know nothing.
You know nothing
ZHSH
!
Yuki-mori! You're supposed to be on stand-by ...

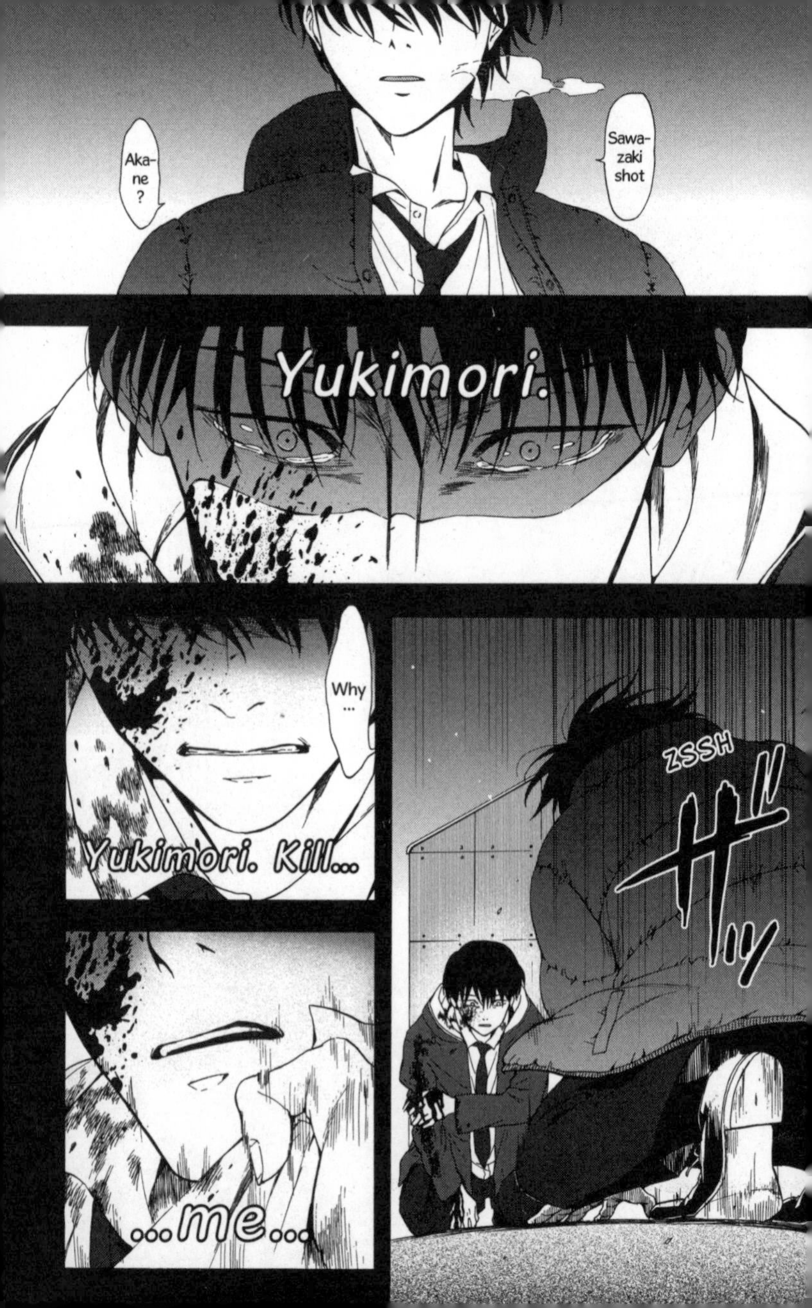
Sawa-zaki shot
Aka-ne?
Yukimori.
ZSSH
Why...
Yukimori. Kill...
...me...

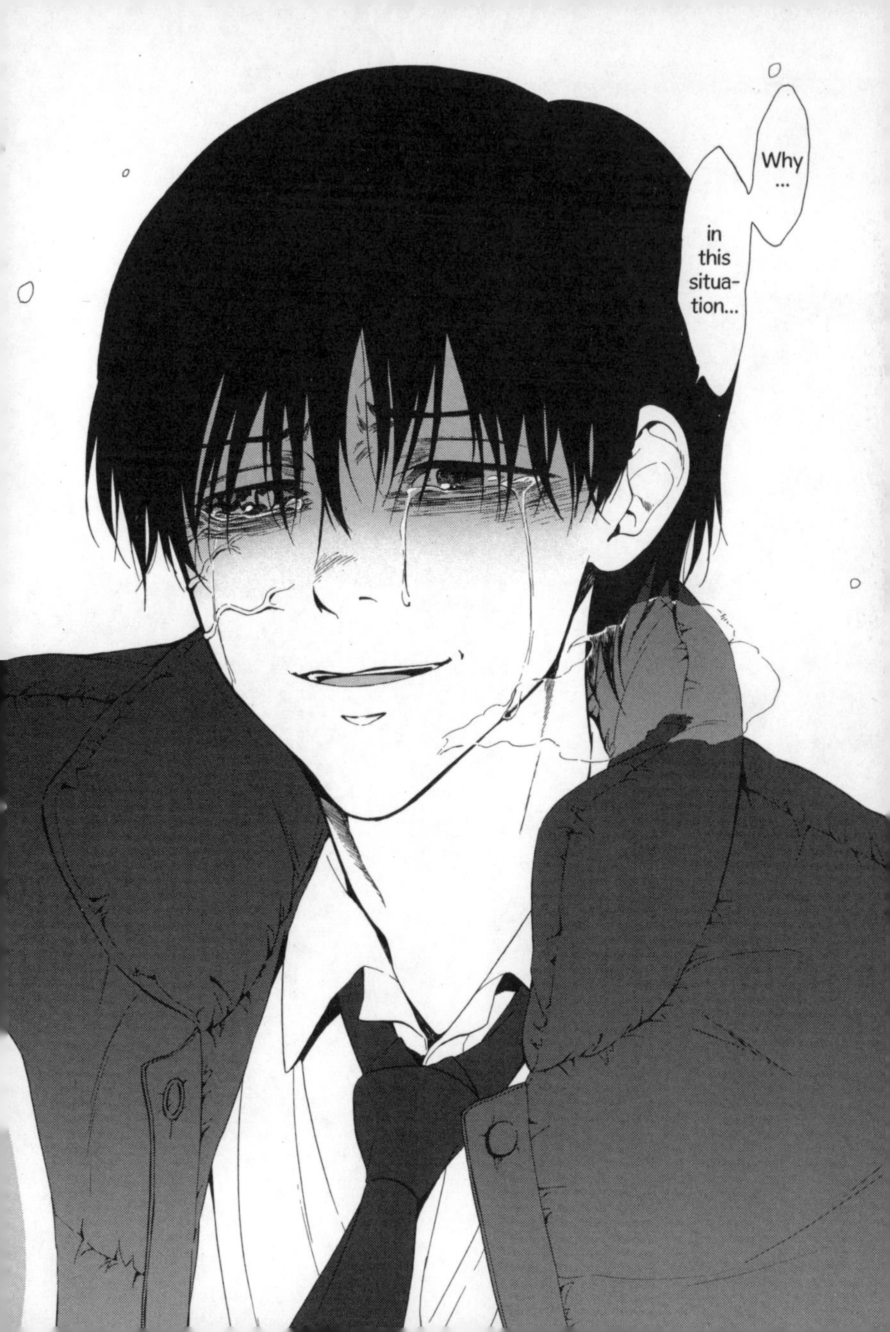
Why...
in this situation...

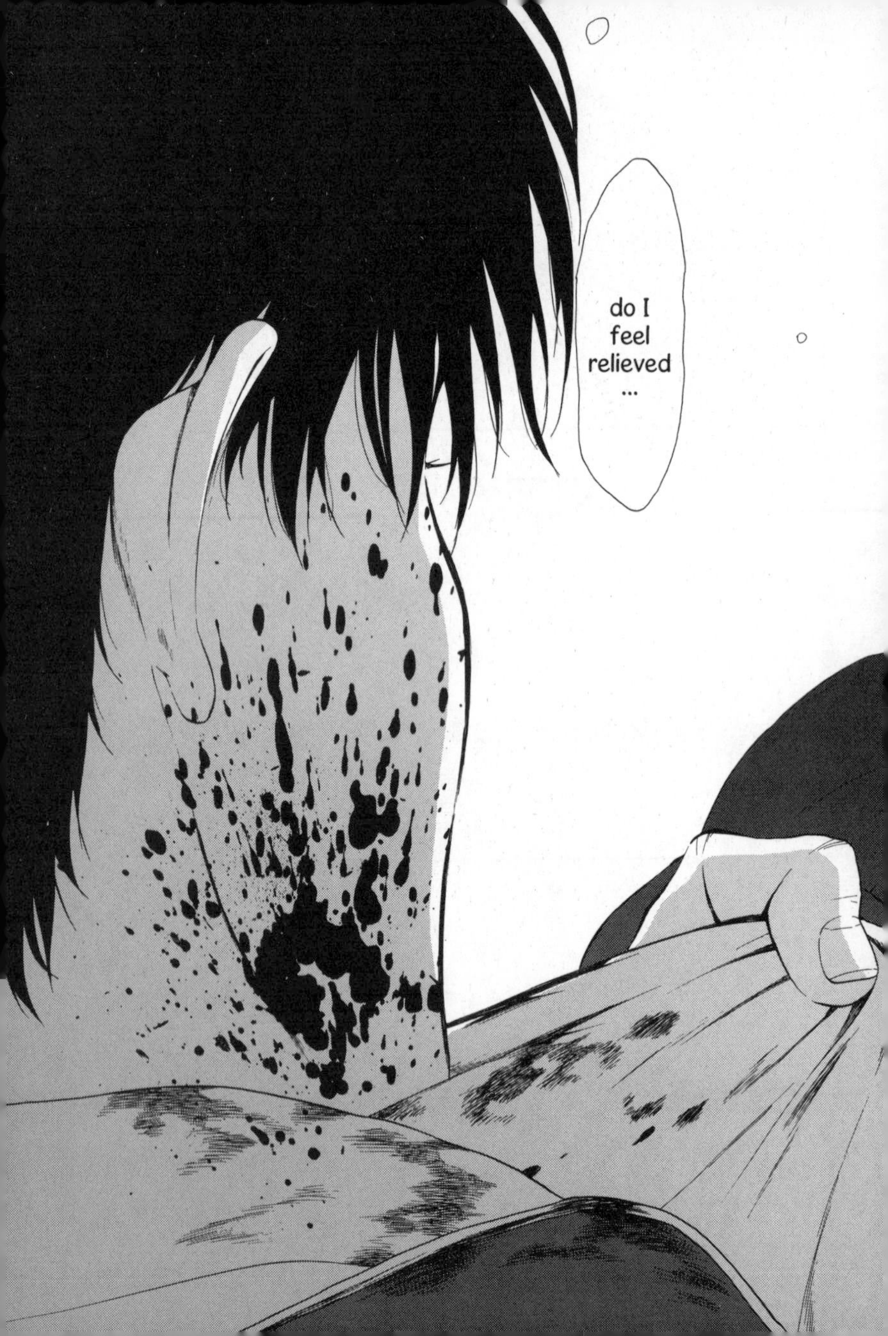
do I feel relieved ...

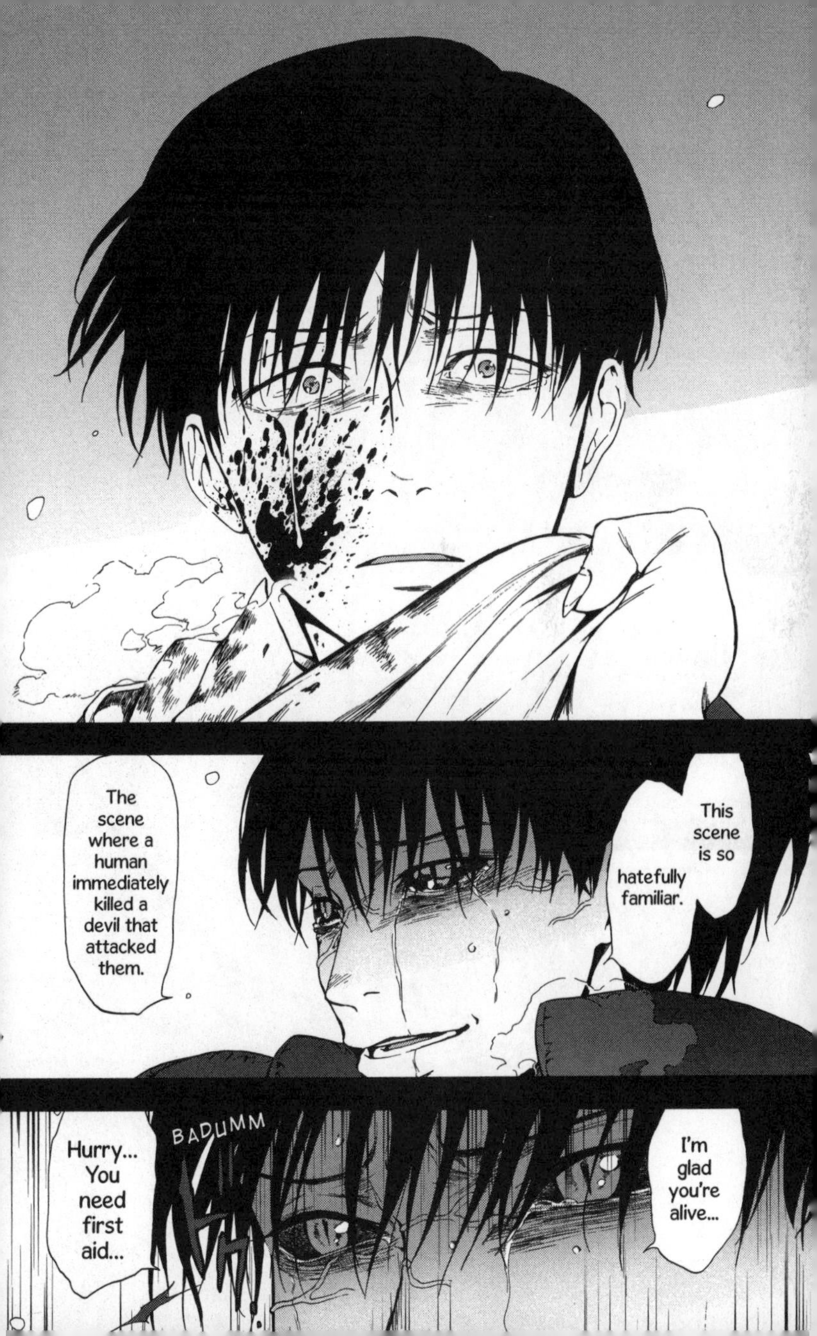
This scene is so hatefully familiar.
The scene where a human immediately killed a devil that attacked them.
I'm glad you're alive...
BADUMM
Hurry... You need first aid...

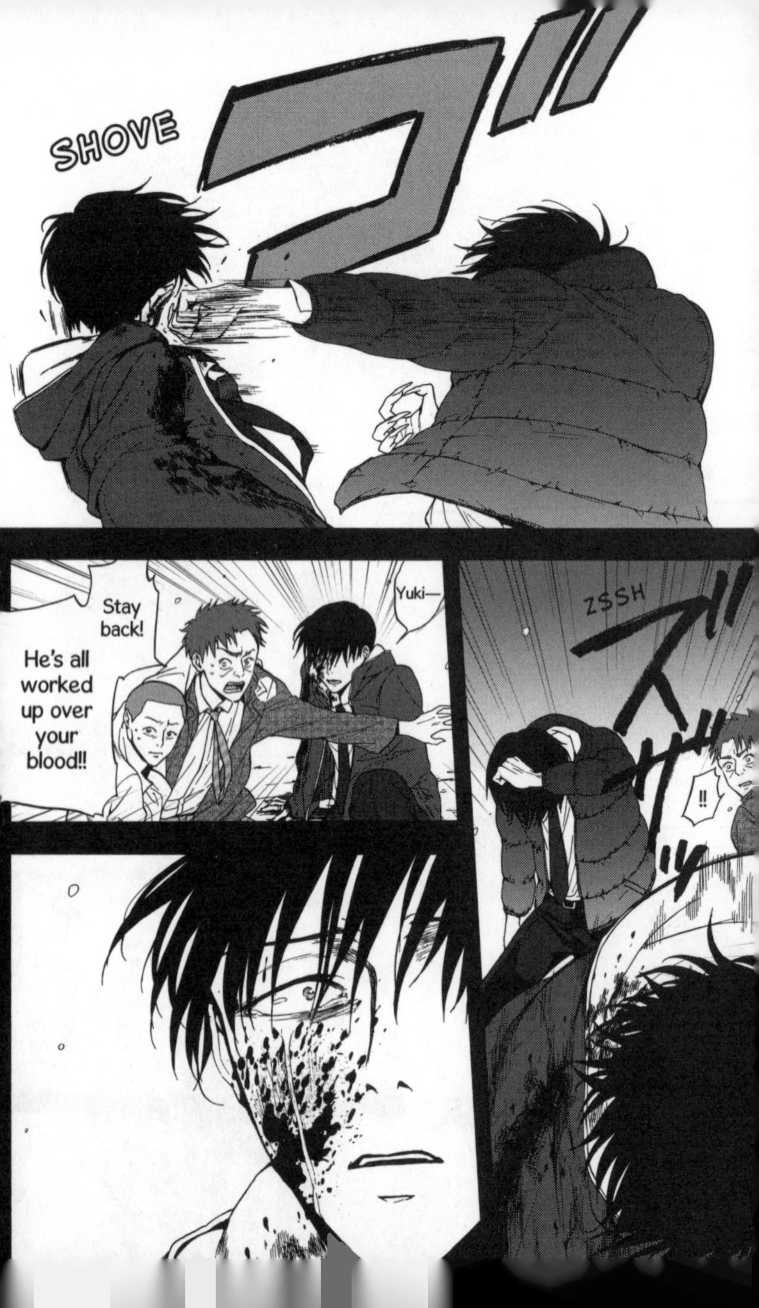
SHOVE
ゴ
ZSSH
!!
Yuki—
Stay back!
He's all worked up over your blood!!

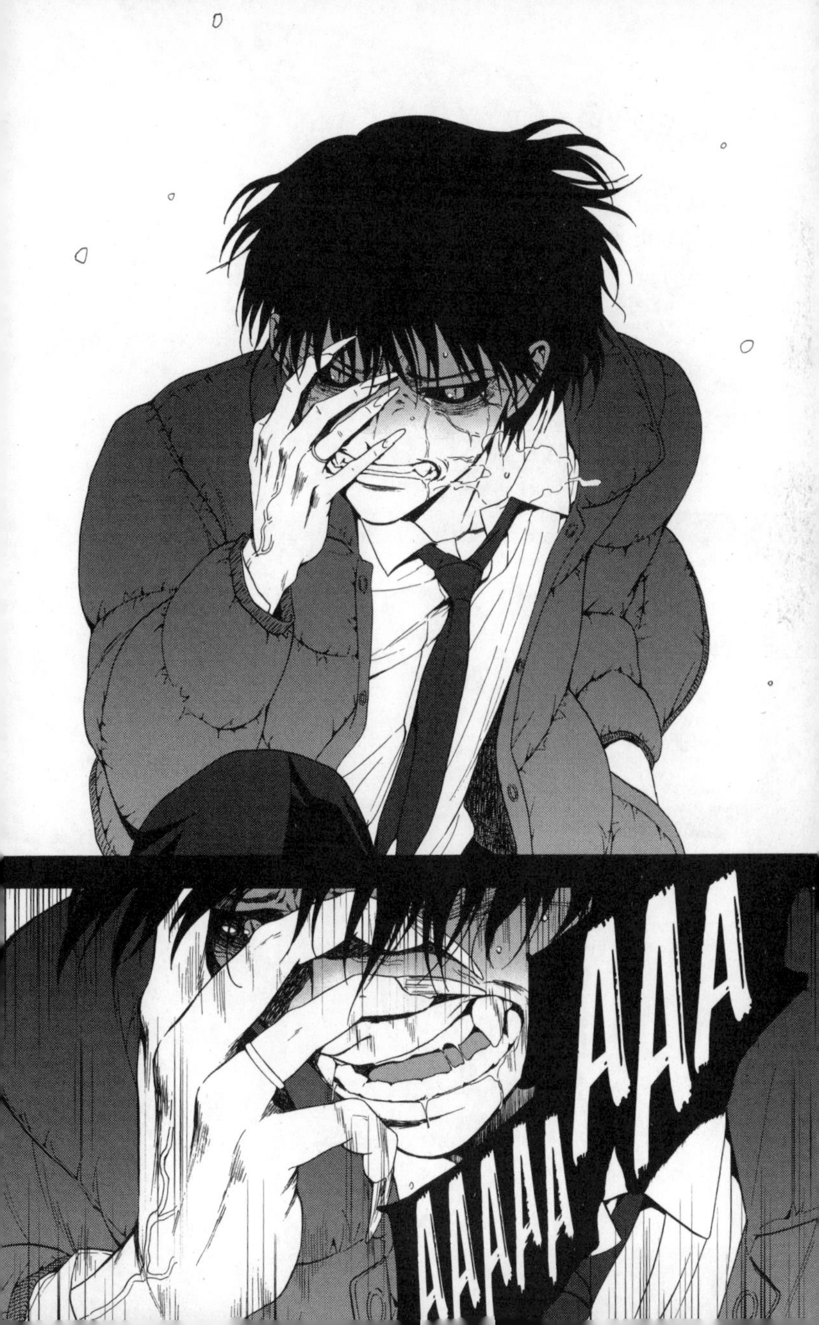
AAAAAAAA

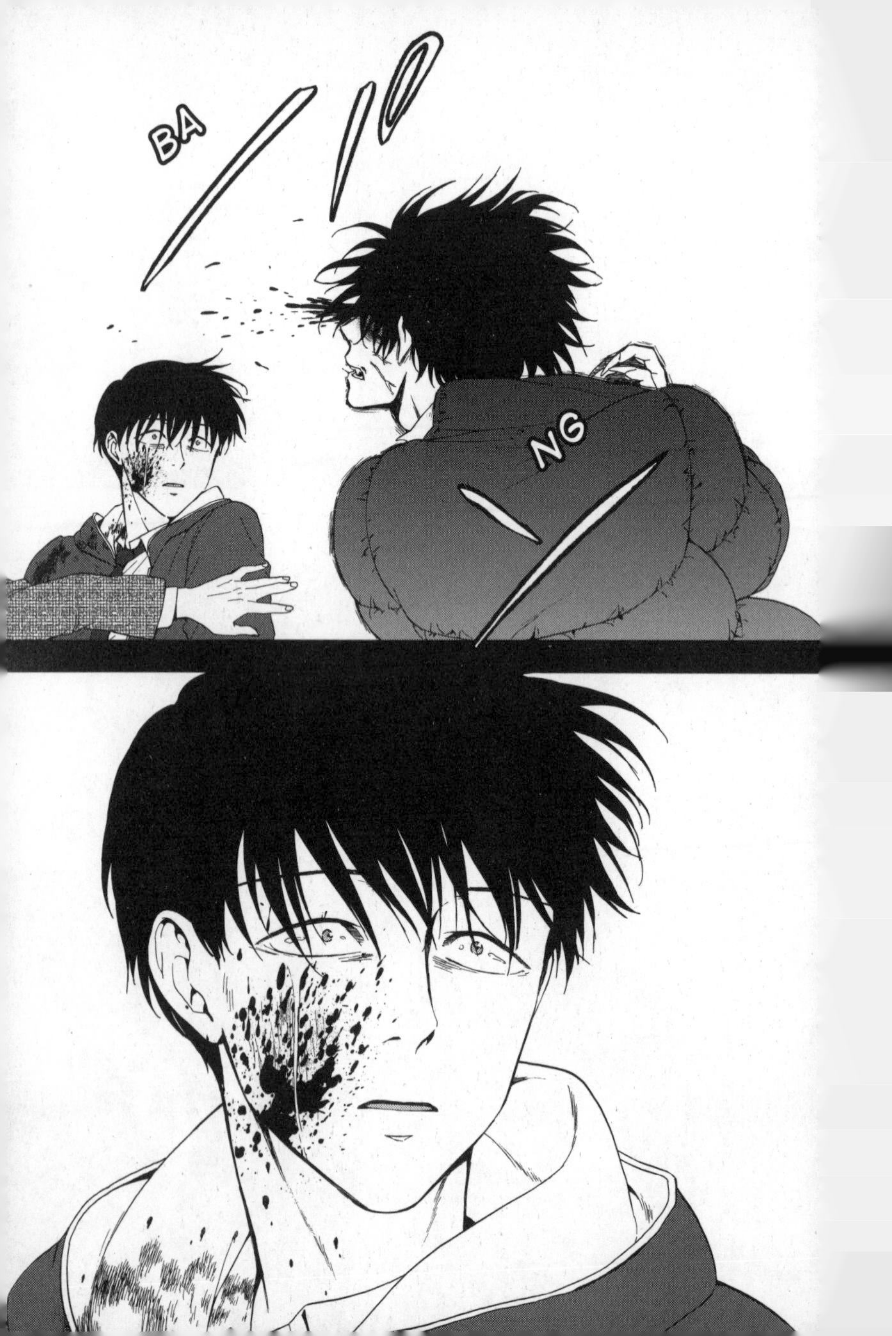
BA
NG

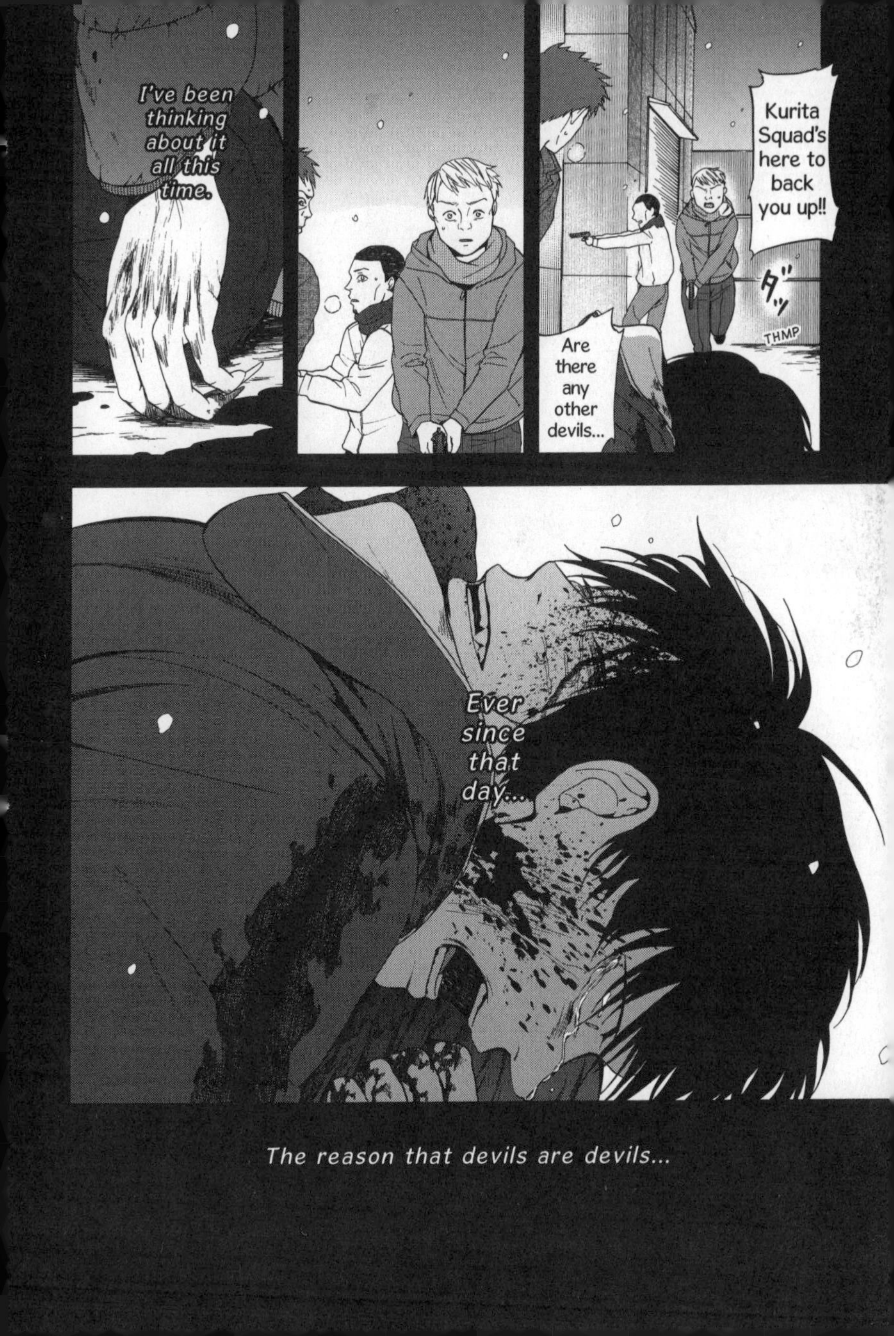
Kurita Squad's here to back you up!!
ダッ
THMP
Are there any other devils...
I've been thinking about it all this time.
Ever since that day...
The reason that devils are devils...

Gentle on the Stomach
LOW-FAT MILK
Low-fat Milk
年間成分平均値
echthros
-light-

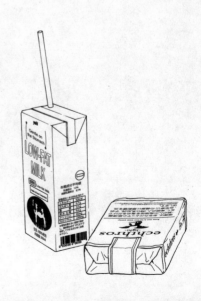

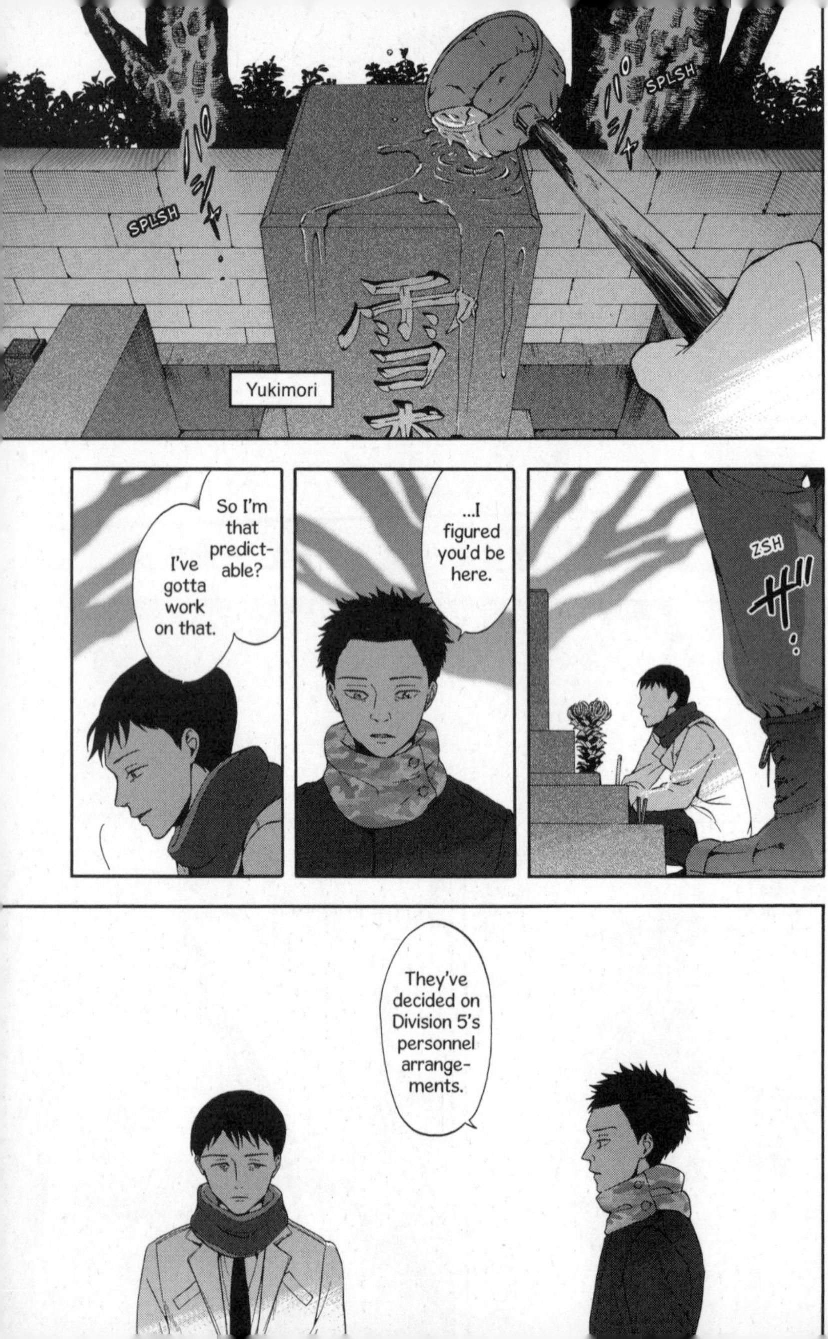
SPLSH
SPLSH
Yukimori
ZSH
...I figured you'd be here.
So I'm that predictable?
I've gotta work on that.
They've decided on Division 5's personnel arrangements.

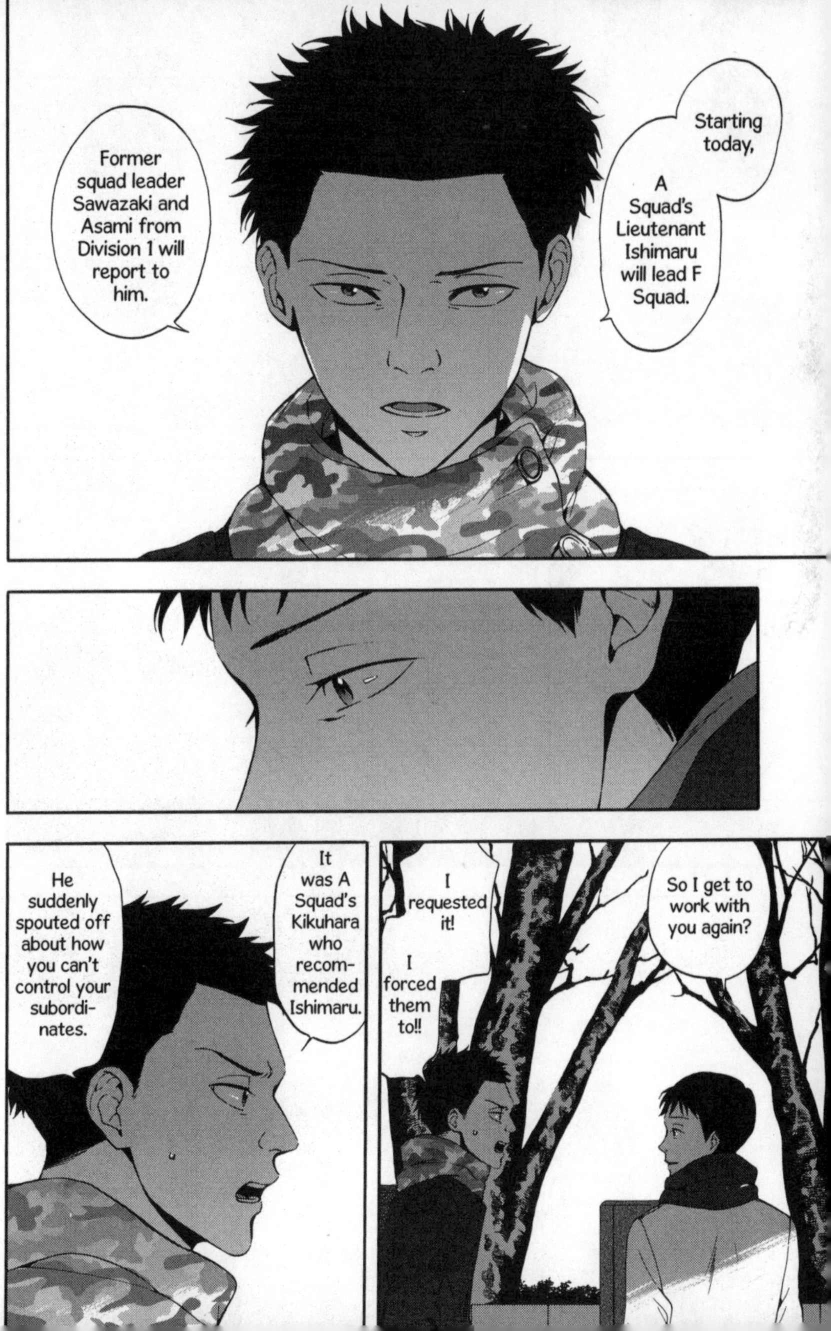
Starting today,
A Squad's Lieutenant Ishimaru will lead F Squad.
Former squad leader Sawazaki and Asami from Division 1 will report to him.
So I get to work with you again?
I requested it!
I forced them to!!
It was A Squad's Kikuhara who recom-mended Ishimaru.
He suddenly spouted off about how you can't control your subordi-nates.

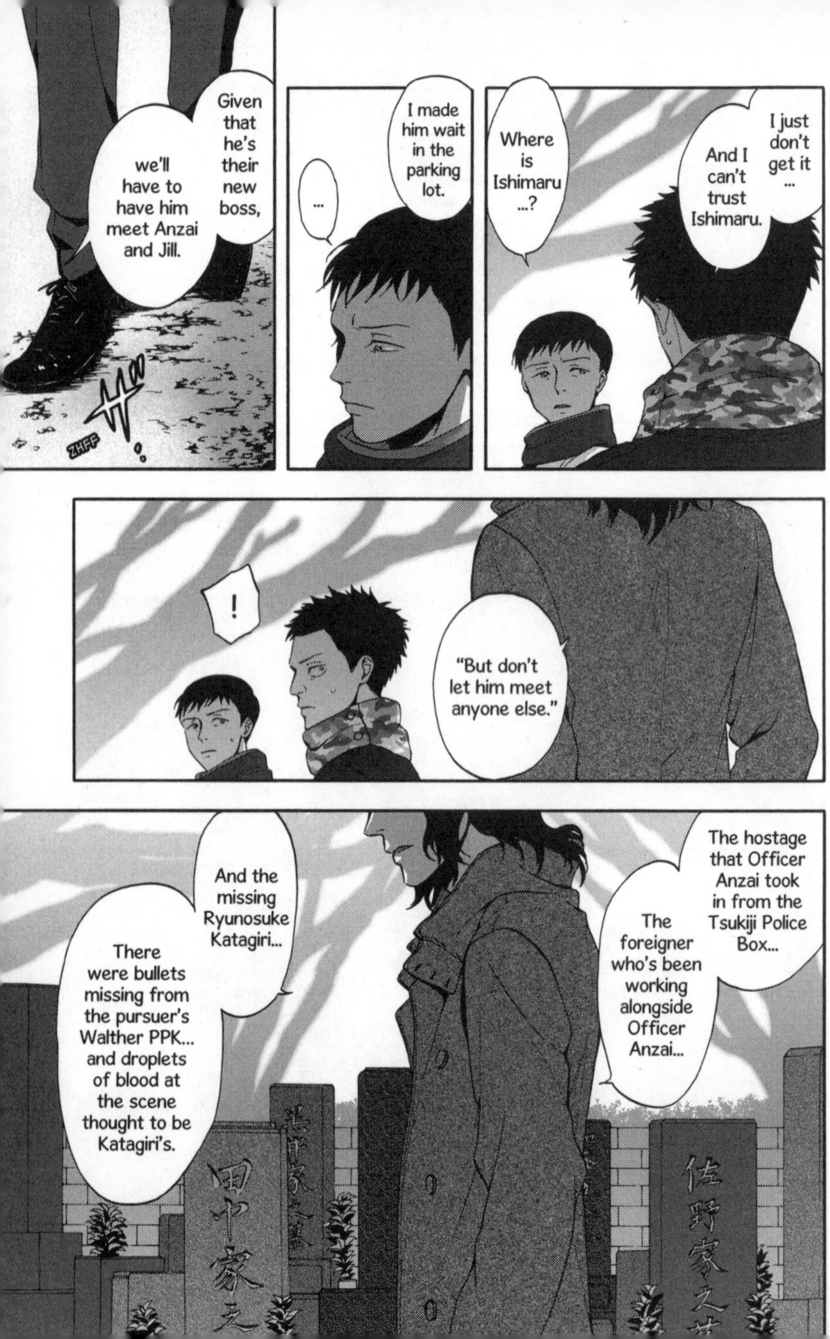
I just don't get it ...
And I can't trust Ishimaru.
Where is Ishimaru ...?
I made him wait in the parking lot.
...
Given that he's their new boss,
we'll have to have him meet Anzai and Jill.
ZHFF
"But don't let him meet anyone else."
!
The hostage that Officer Anzai took in from the Tsukiji Police Box...
The foreigner who's been working alongside Officer Anzai...
And the missing Ryunosuke Katagiri...
There were bullets missing from the pursuer's Walther PPK... and droplets of blood at the scene thought to be Katagiri's.

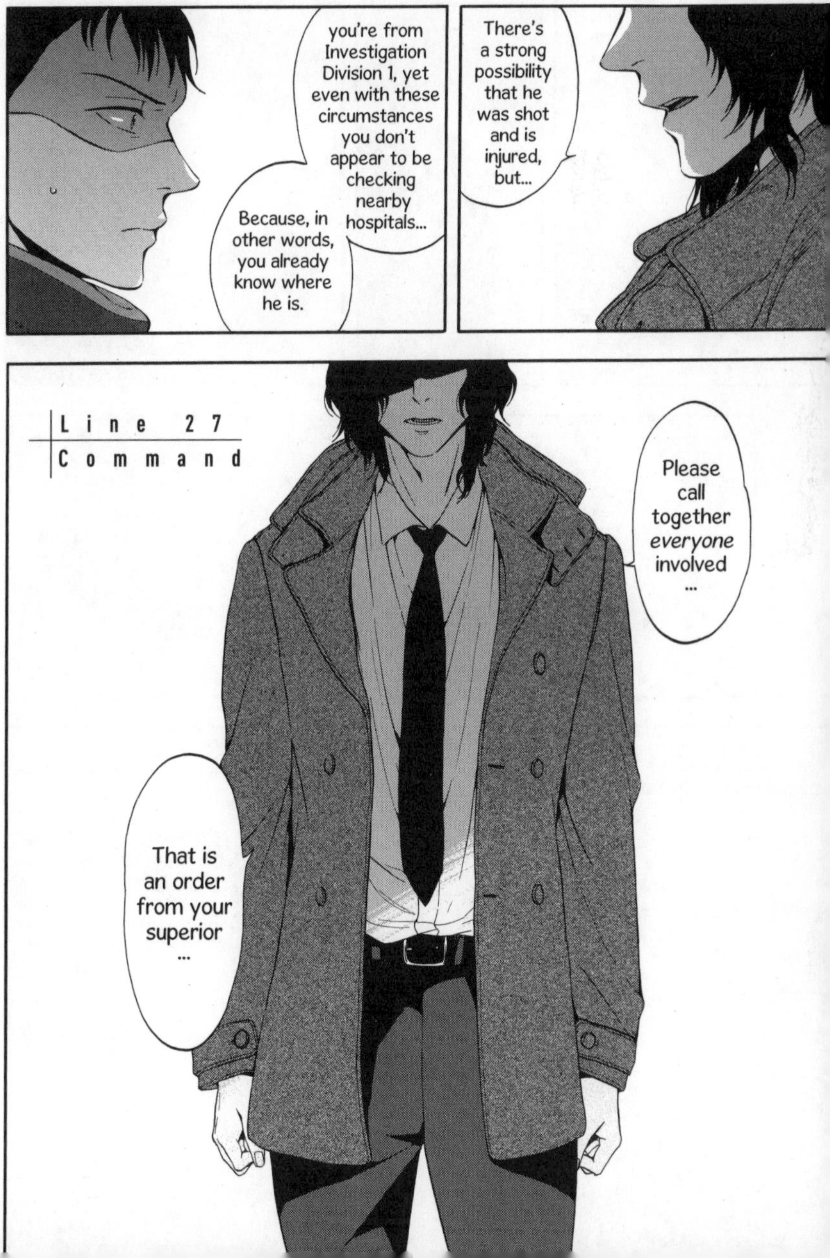
There's a strong possibility that he was shot and is injured, but...
you're from Investigation Division 1, yet even with these circumstances you don't appear to be checking nearby hospitals...
Because, in other words, you already know where he is.
Line 27
Command
Please call together *everyone* involved ...
That is an order from your superior ...

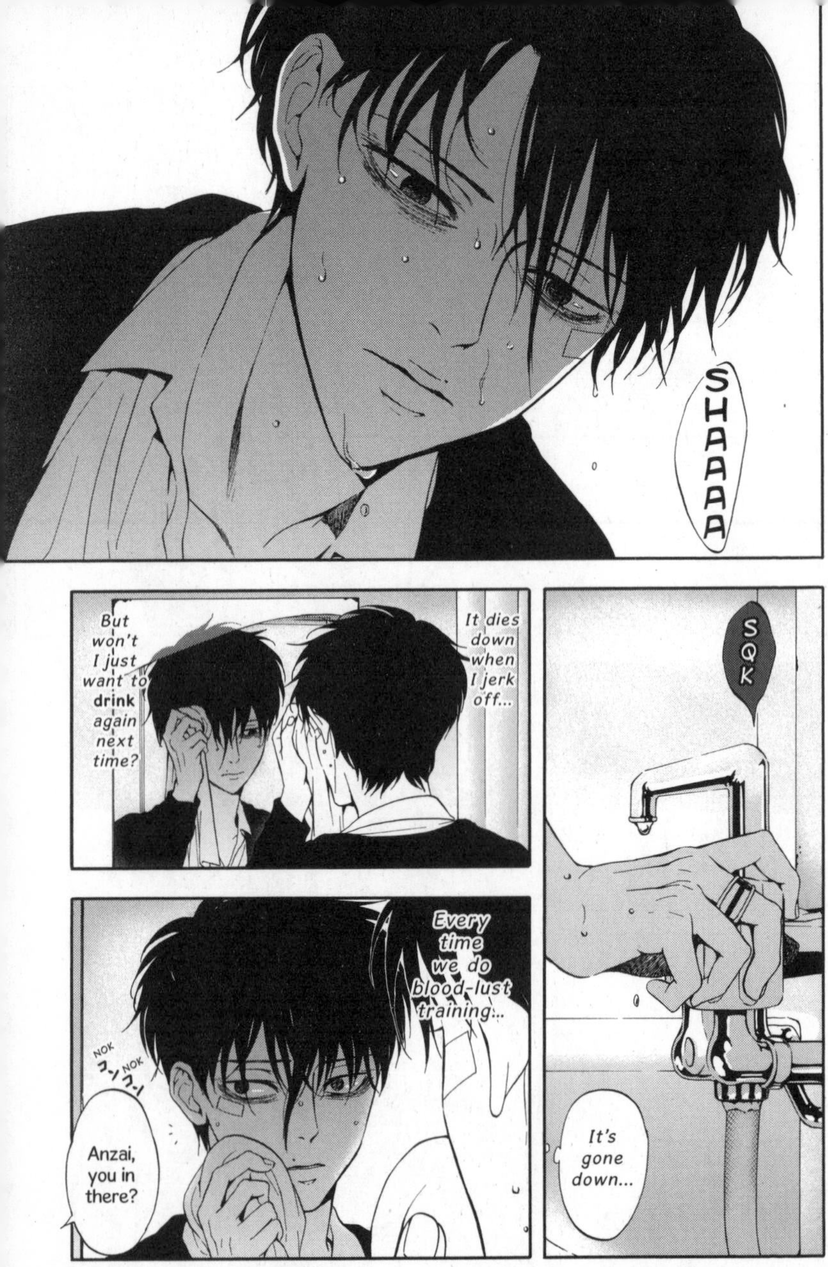
SHAAAA
SQK
It's gone down...
It dies down when I jerk off...
But won't I just want to drink again next time?
Every time we do blood-lust training...
NOK NOK
Anzai, you in there?

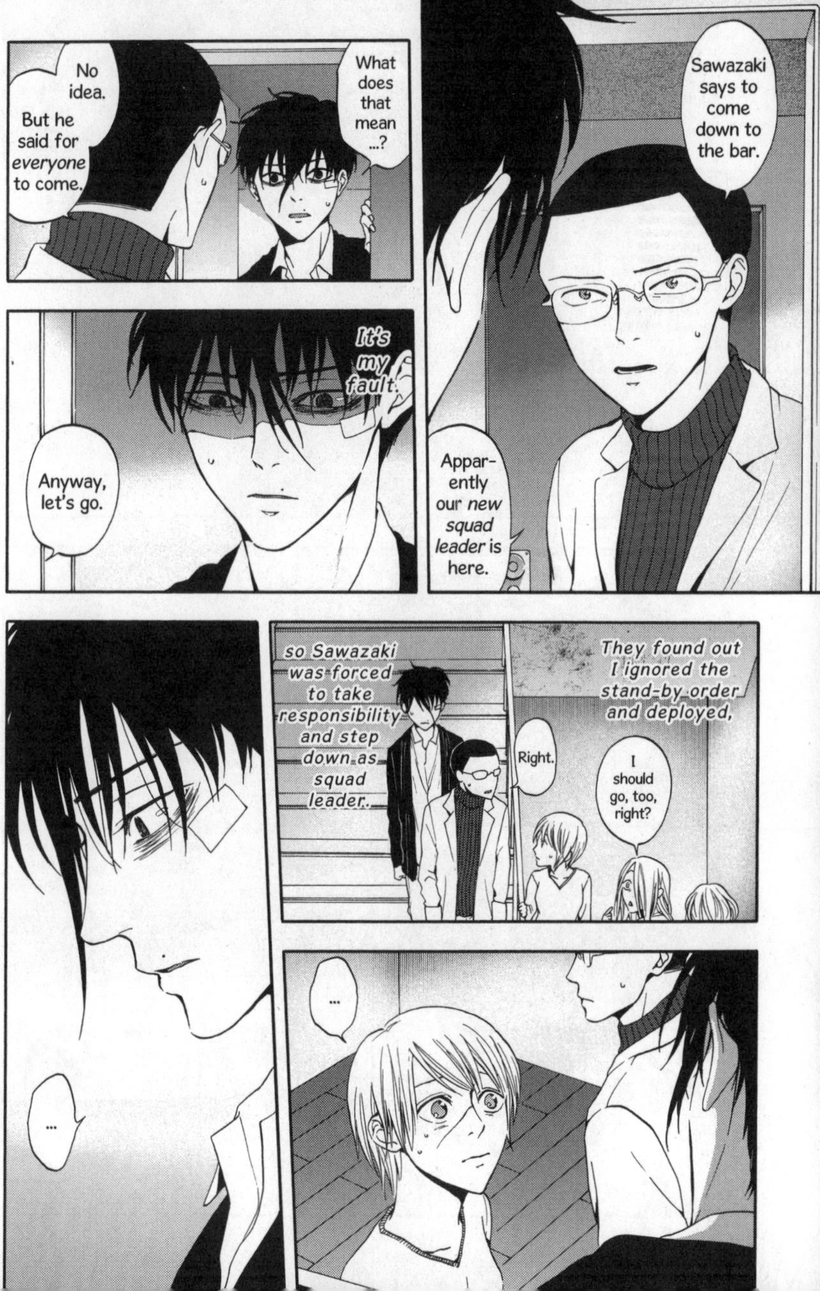
Sawazaki says to come down to the bar.
Apparently our *new squad leader* is here.
What does that mean ...?
No idea.
But he said for *everyone* to come.
It's my fault.
Anyway, let's go.
They found out I ignored the stand-by order and deployed,
I should go, too, right?
Right.
so Sawazaki was forced to take responsibility and step down as squad leader.
...
...

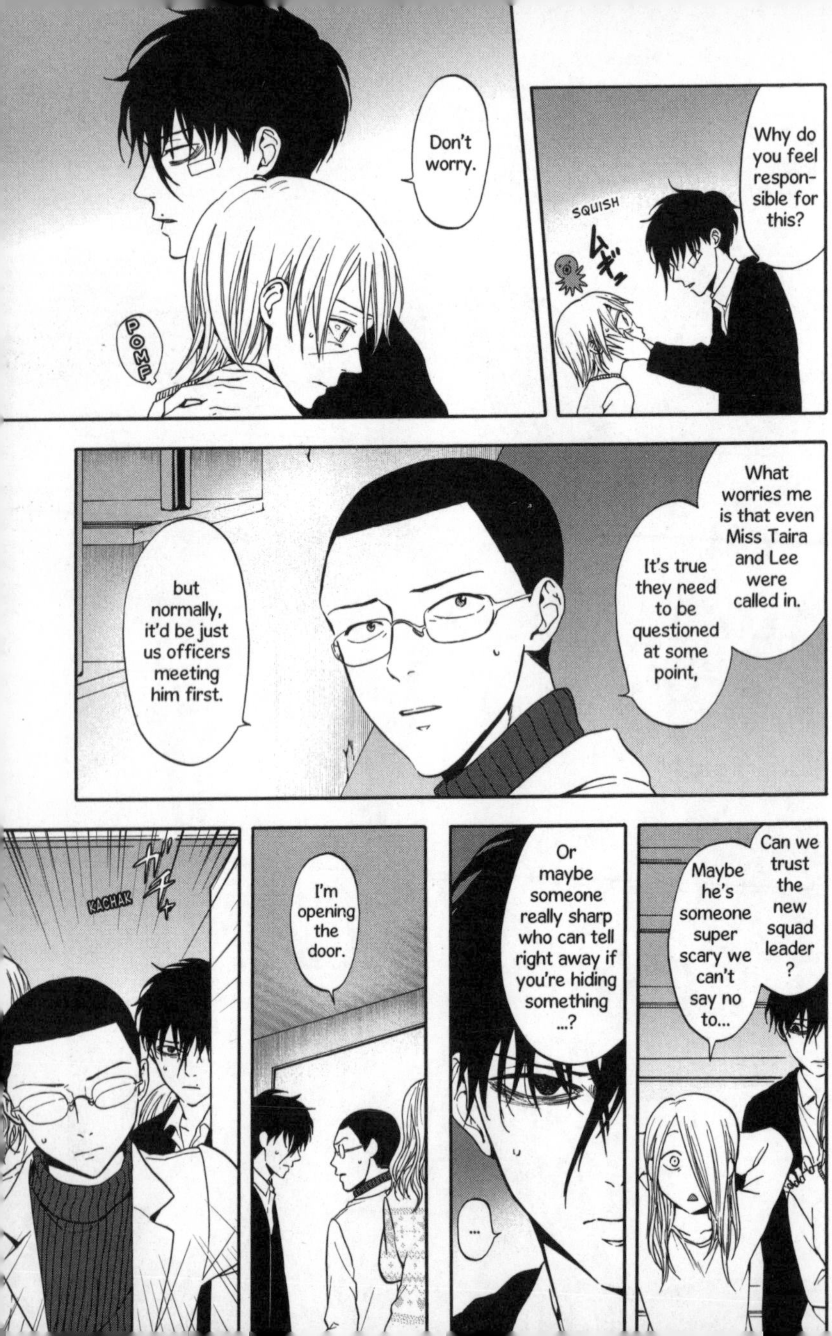
Why do you feel responsible for this?
SQUISH
Don't worry.
POMF
What worries me is that even Miss Taira and Lee were called in.
It's true they need to be questioned at some point,
but normally, it'd be just us officers meeting him first.
Can we trust the new squad leader?
Maybe he's someone super scary we can't say no to...
Or maybe someone really sharp who can tell right away if you're hiding something ...?
...
I'm opening the door.
KACHAK

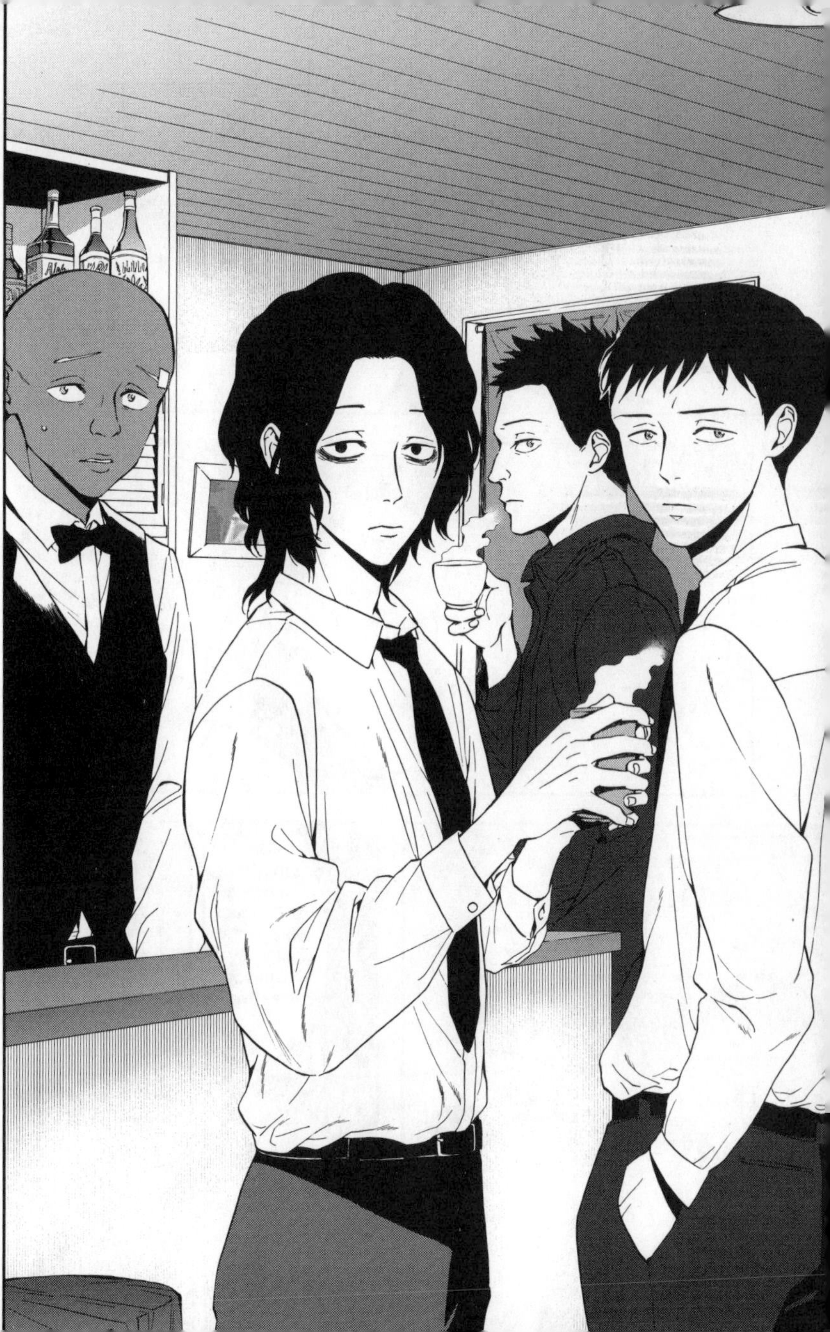

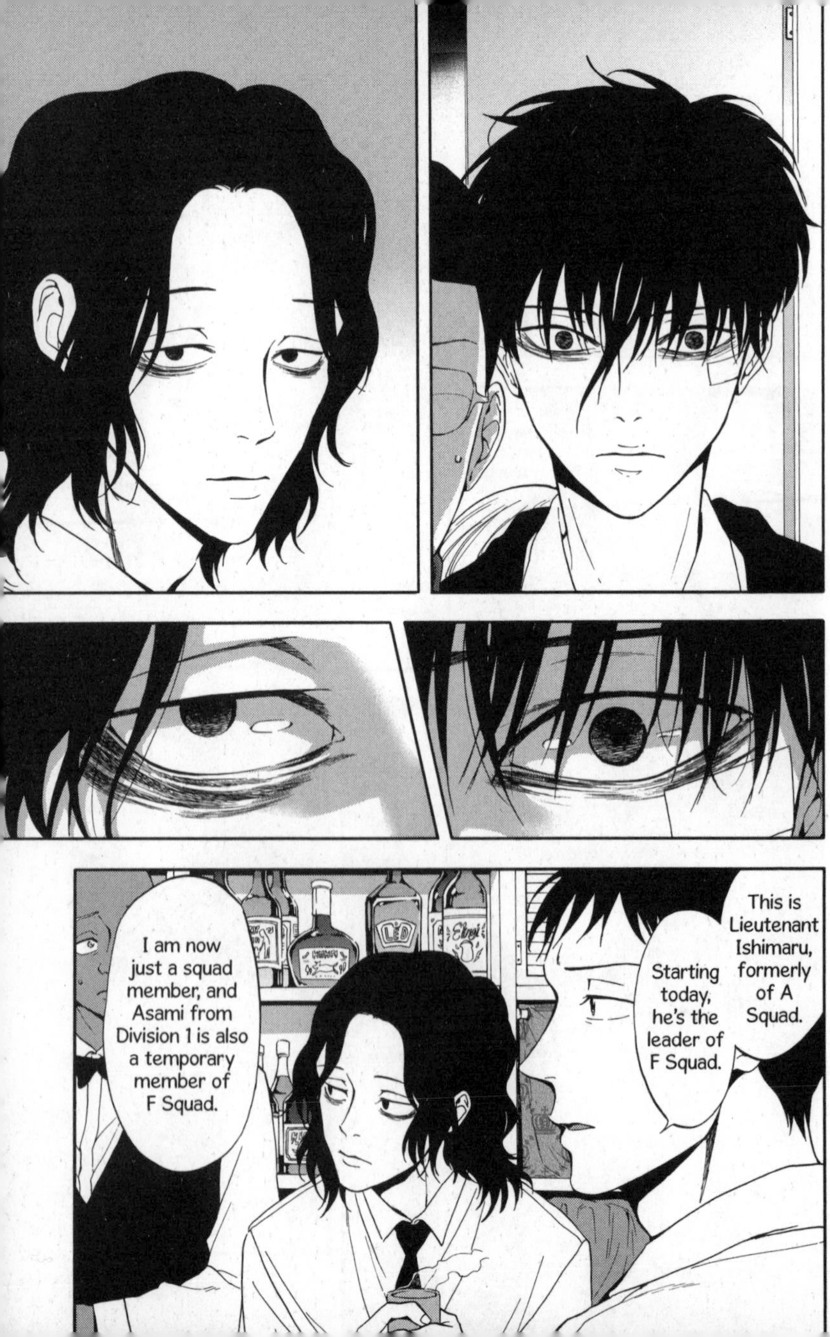
This is Lieutenant Ishimaru, formerly of A Squad.
Starting today, he's the leader of F Squad.
I am now just a squad member, and Asami from Division 1 is also a temporary member of F Squad.

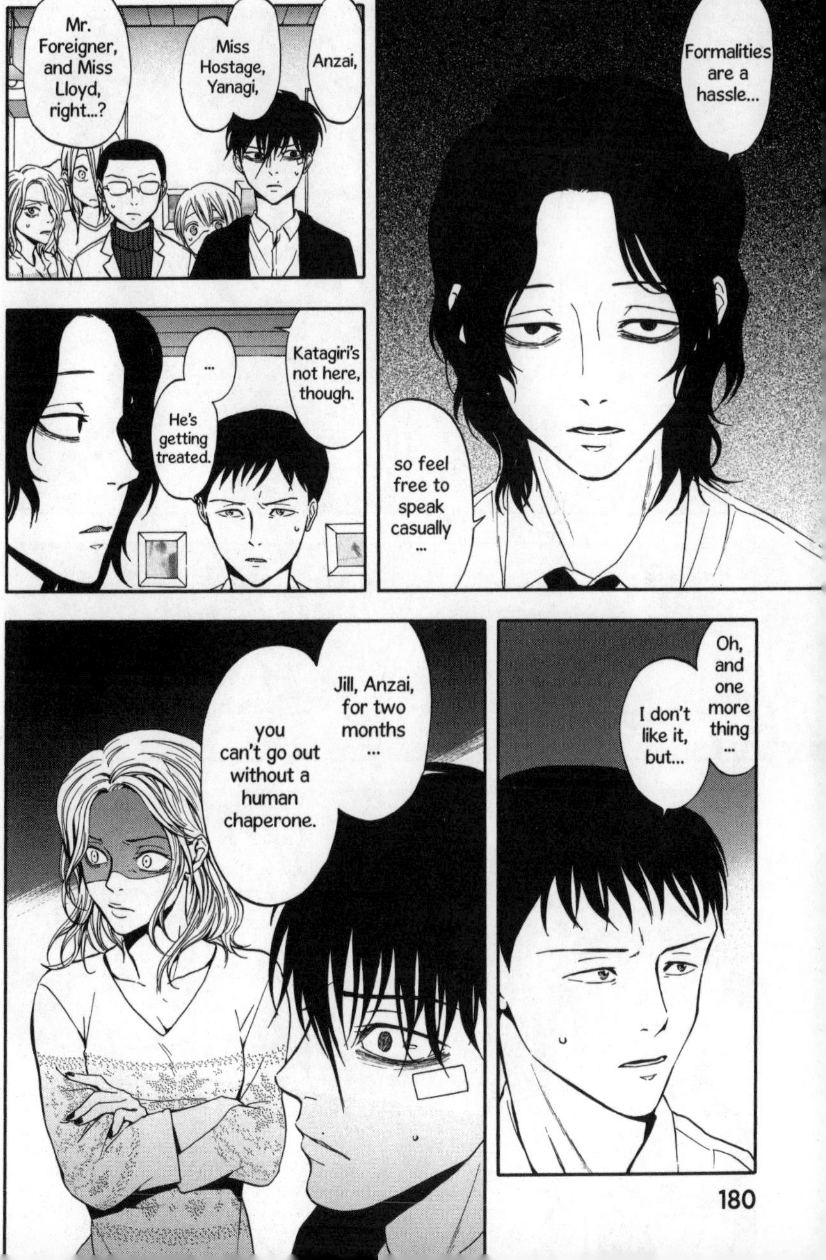
Formalities are a hassle...
so feel free to speak casually ...
Anzai,
Miss Hostage, Yanagi,
Mr. Foreigner, and Miss Lloyd, right...?
Katagiri's not here, though.
...
He's getting treated.
Oh, and one more thing ...
I don't like it, but...
Jill, Anzai, for two months ...
you can't go out without a human chaperone.

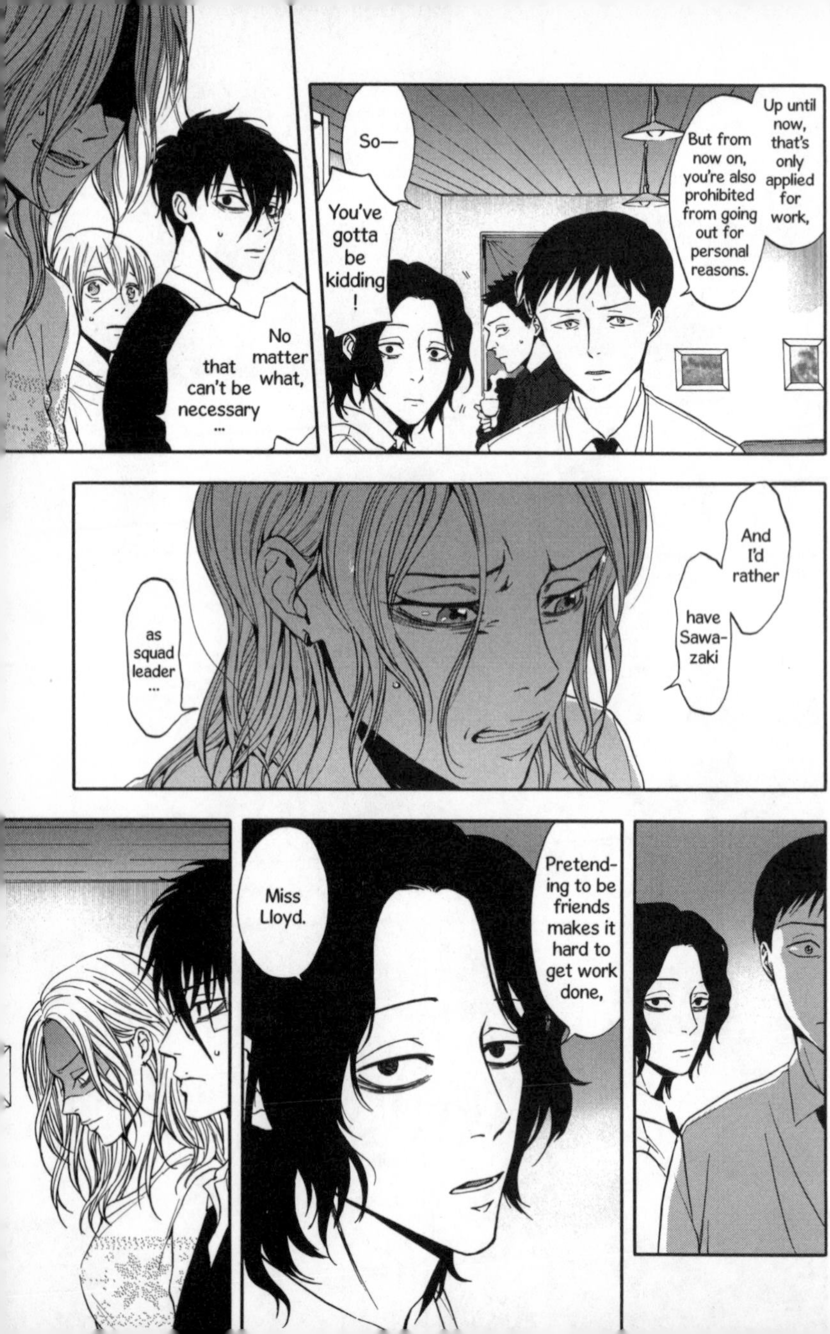
Up until now, that's only applied for work,
But from now on, you're also prohibited from going out for personal reasons.
So—
You've gotta be kidding!
No matter what, that can't be necessary...
And I'd rather have Sawazaki
as squad leader...
Pretending to be friends makes it hard to get work done,
Miss Lloyd.

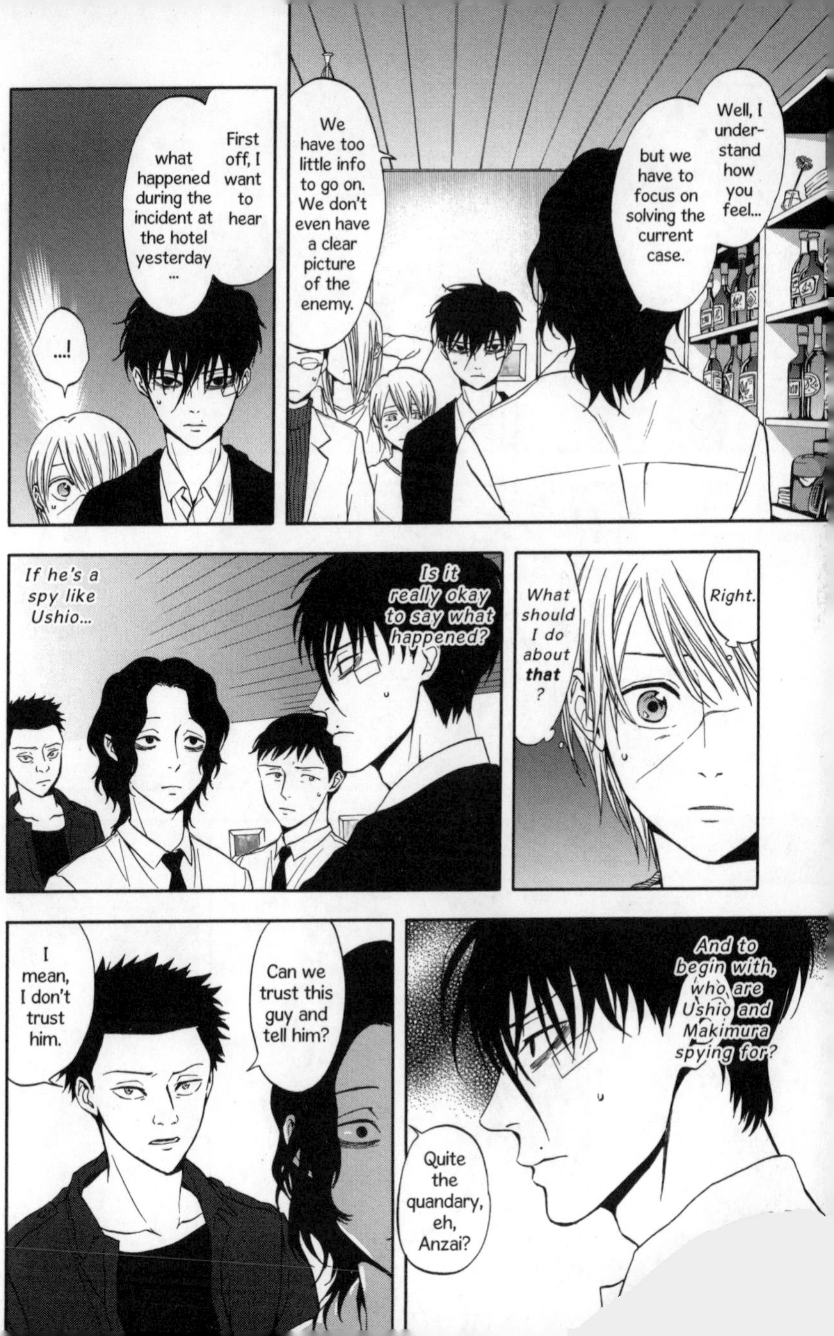
Well, I understand how you feel...
but we have to focus on solving the current case.
We have too little info to go on. We don't even have a clear picture of the enemy.
First off, I want to hear what happened during the incident at the hotel yesterday ...
...!
Right.
What should I do about that?
Is it really okay to say what happened?
If he's a spy like Ushio...
And to begin with, who are Ushio and Makimura spying for?
Quite the quandary, eh, Anzai?
Can we trust this guy and tell him?
I mean, I don't trust him.

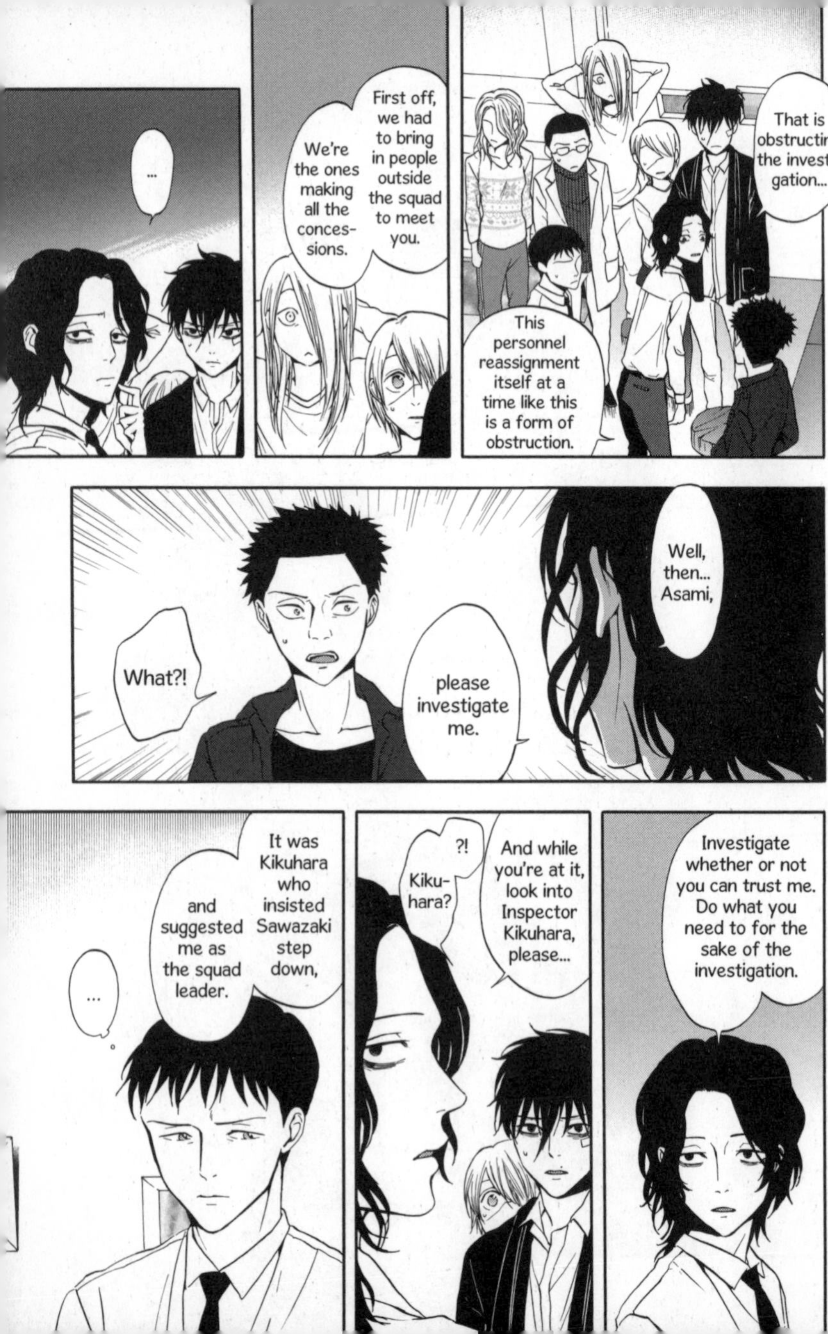
That is obstructing the investi-gation...
This personnel reassignment itself at a time like this is a form of obstruction.
First off, we had to bring in people outside the squad to meet you.
We're the ones making all the conces-sions.
...
Well, then... Asami,
please investigate me.
What?!
Investigate whether or not you can trust me. Do what you need to for the sake of the investigation.
And while you're at it, look into Inspector Kikuhara, please...
?!
Kiku-hara?
It was Kikuhara who insisted Sawazaki step down,
and suggested me as the squad leader.
...

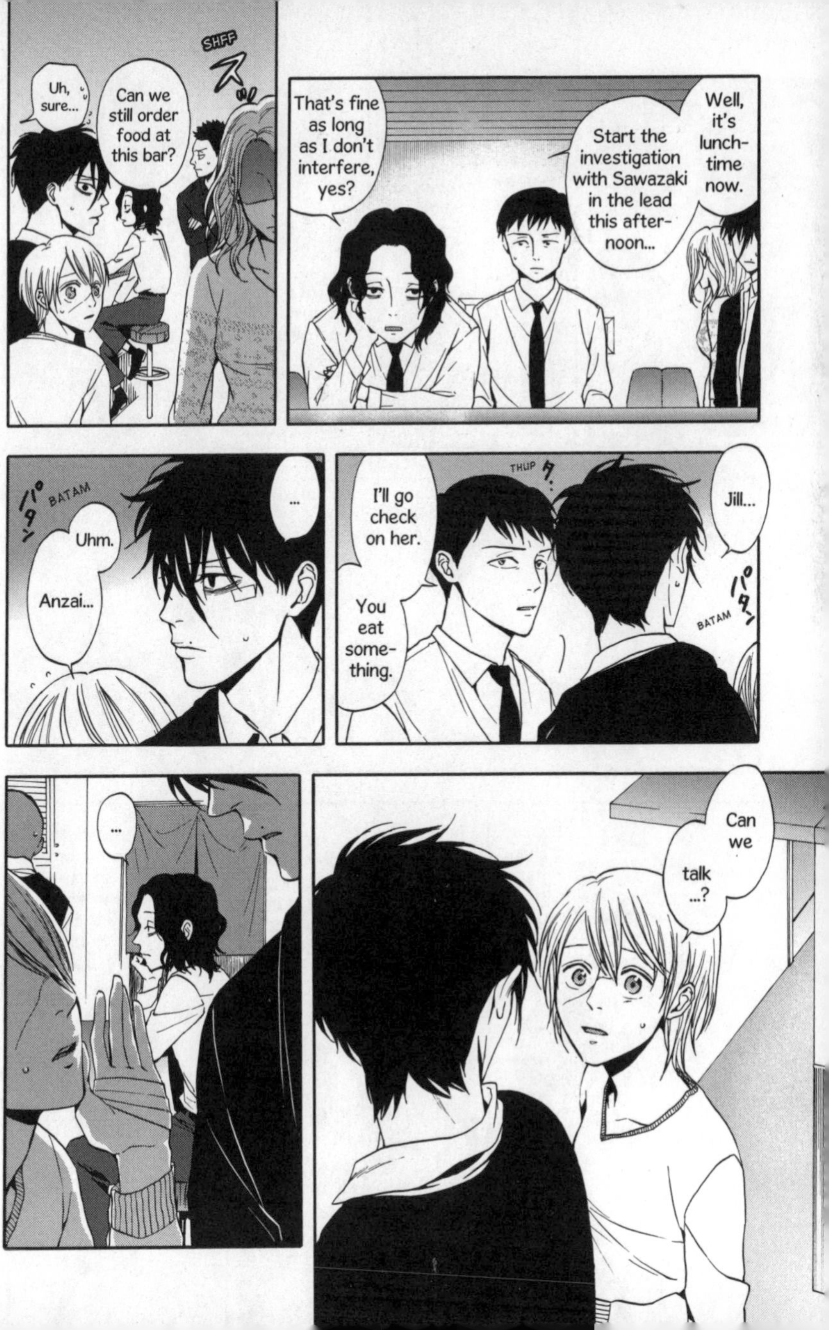
Well, it's lunch-time now.
Start the investigation with Sawazaki in the lead this afternoon...
That's fine as long as I don't interfere, yes?
SHFF
Can we still order food at this bar?
Uh, sure...
Jill...
BATAM
THUP
I'll go check on her.
You eat something.
...
BATAM
Uhm.
Anzai...
Can we talk ...?
...

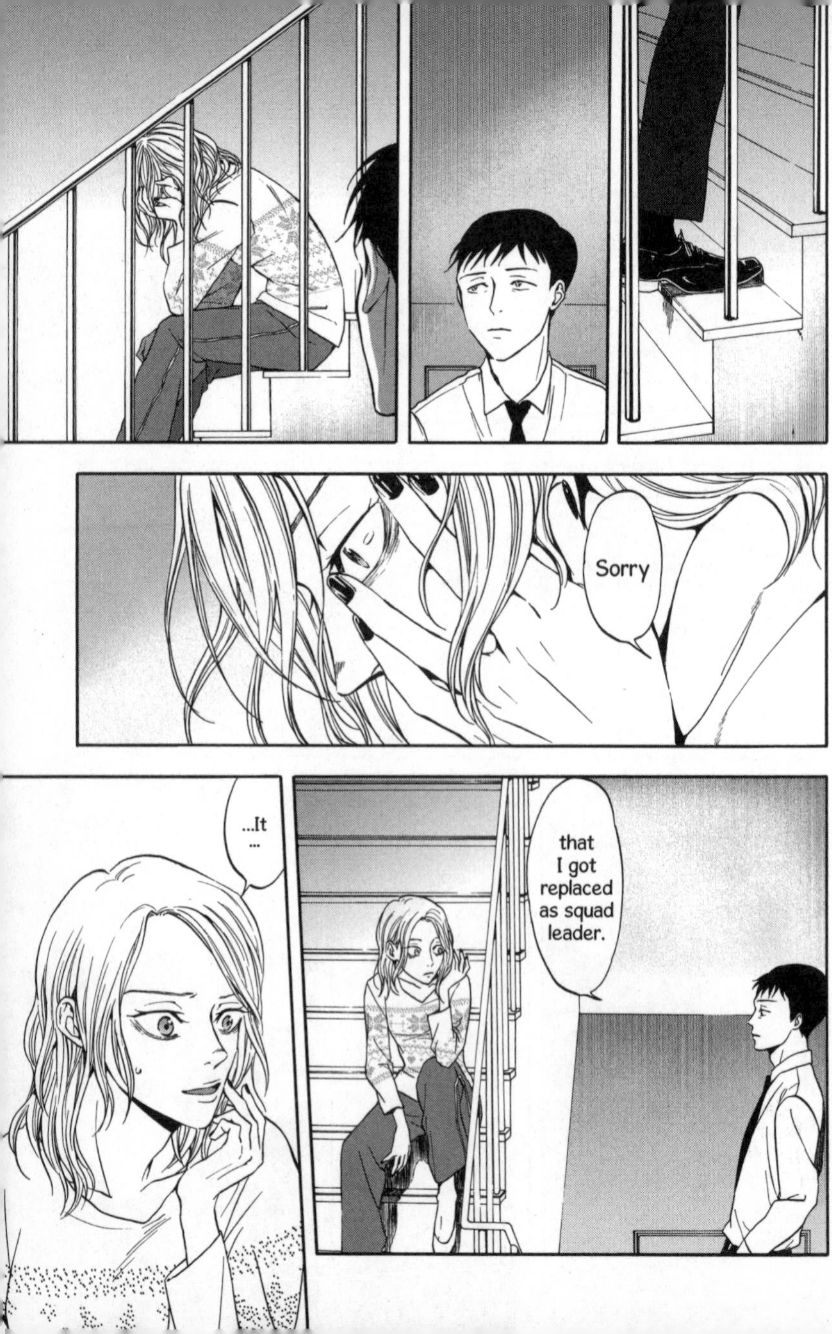
Sorry
that I got replaced as squad leader.
...It ...

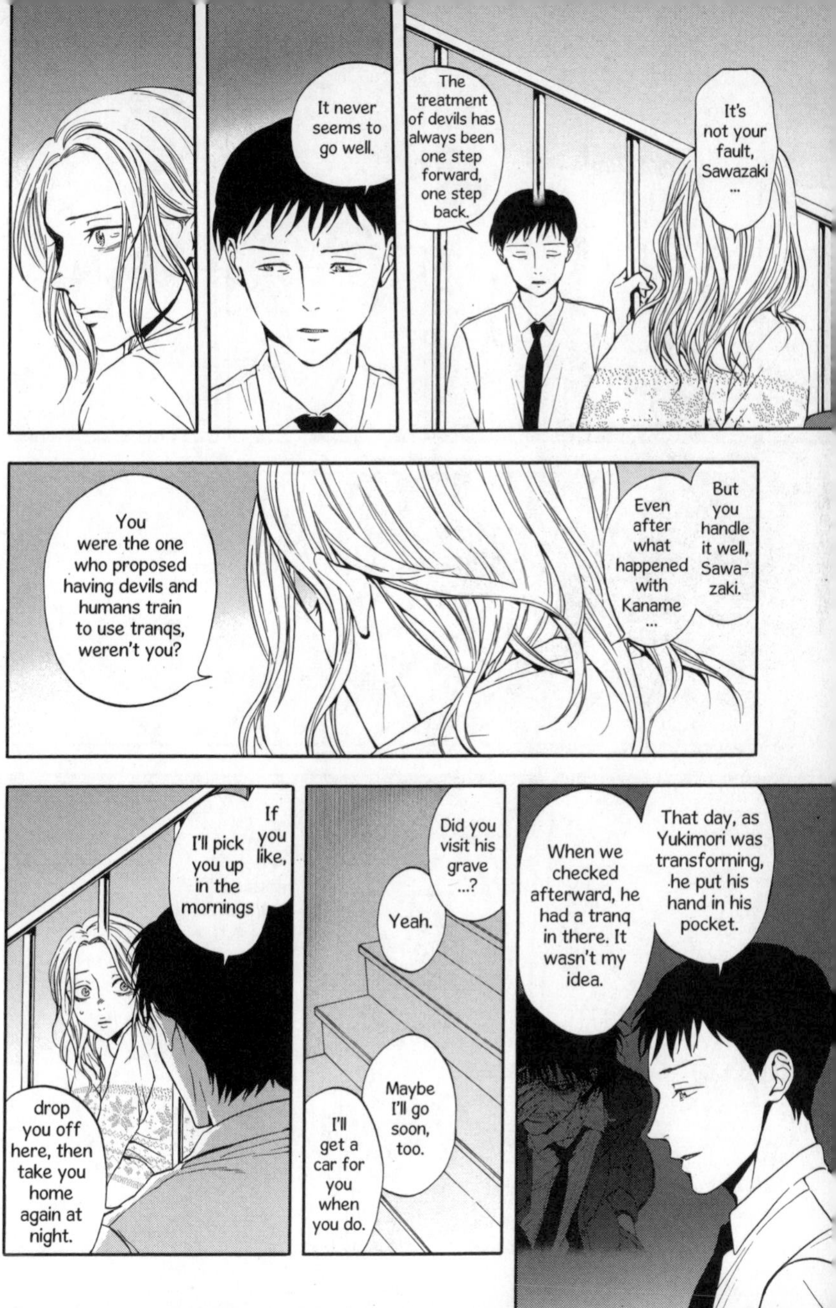
It's not your fault, Sawazaki...
The treatment of devils has always been one step forward, one step back.
It never seems to go well.
But you handle it well, Sawazaki.
Even after what happened with Kaname...
You were the one who proposed having devils and humans train to use tranqs, weren't you?
That day, as Yukimori was transforming, he put his hand in his pocket.
When we checked afterward, he had a tranq in there. It wasn't my idea.
Did you visit his grave...?
Yeah.
Maybe I'll go soon, too.
I'll get a car for you when you do.
If you like,
I'll pick you up in the mornings
drop you off here, then take you home again at night.

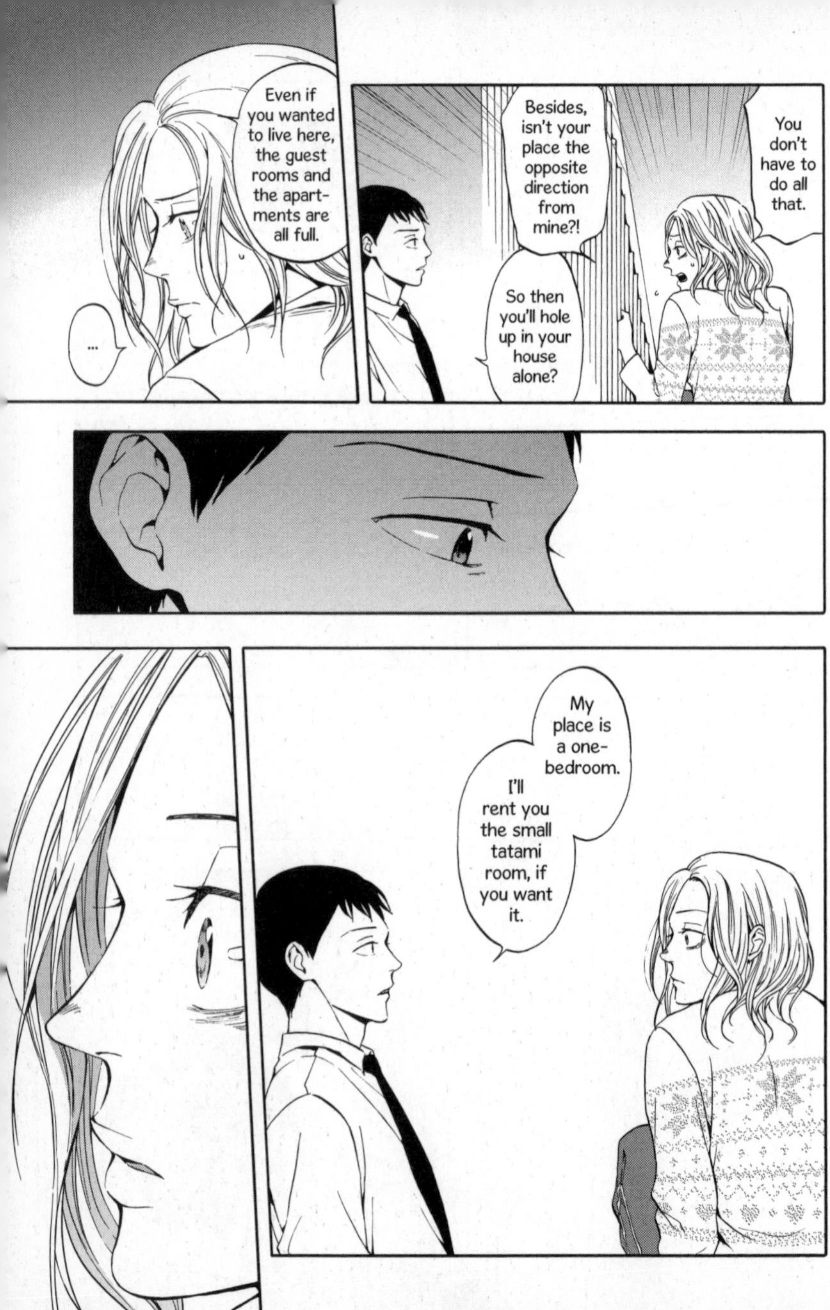
You don't have to do all that.
Besides, isn't your place the opposite direction from mine?!
So then you'll hole up in your house alone?
Even if you wanted to live here, the guest rooms and the apartments are all full.
...
My place is a one-bedroom.
I'll rent you the small tatami room, if you want it.

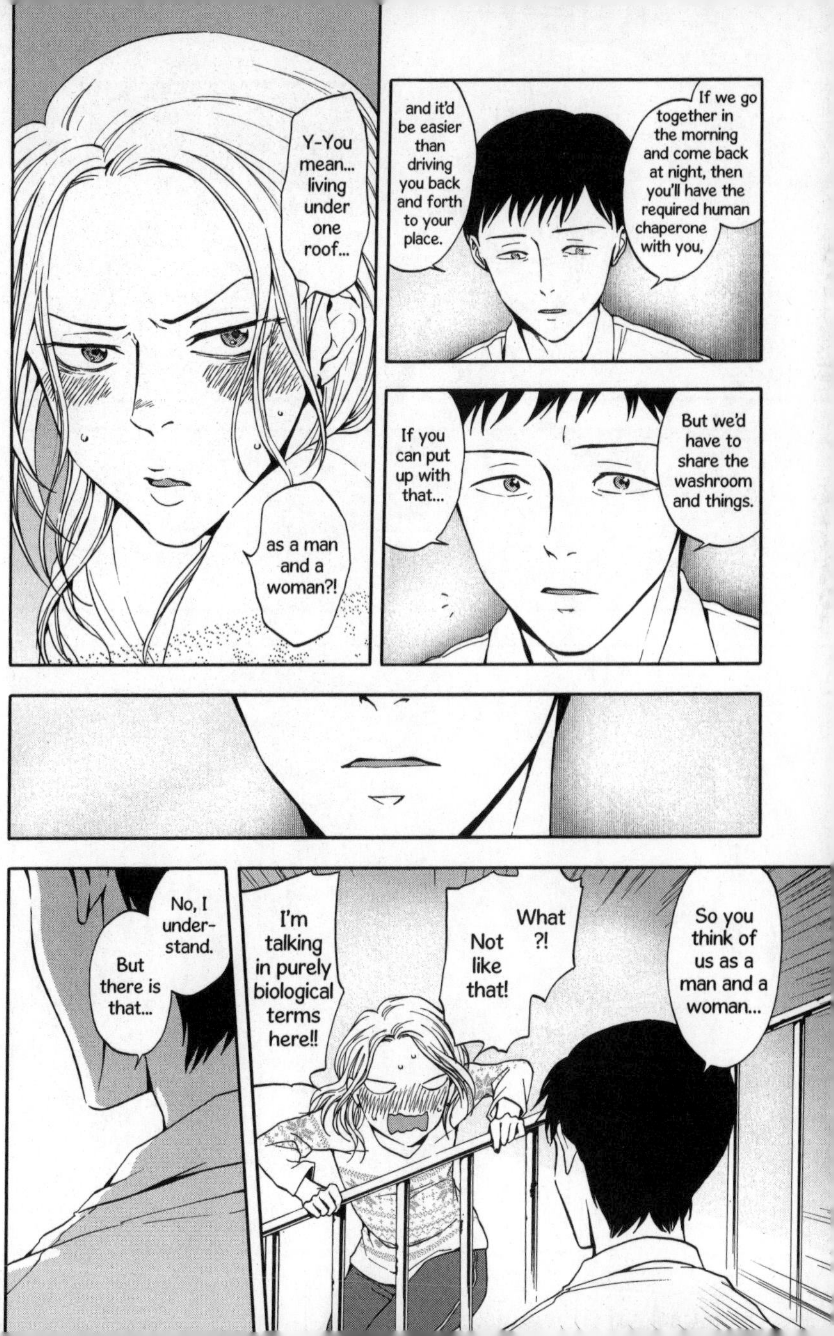
If we go together in the morning and come back at night, then you'll have the required human chaperone with you,
and it'd be easier than driving you back and forth to your place.
But we'd have to share the washroom and things.
If you can put up with that...
Y-You mean... living under one roof...
as a man and a woman?!
So you think of us as a man and a woman...
What ?!
Not like that!
I'm talking in purely biological terms here!!
No, I understand.
But there is that...

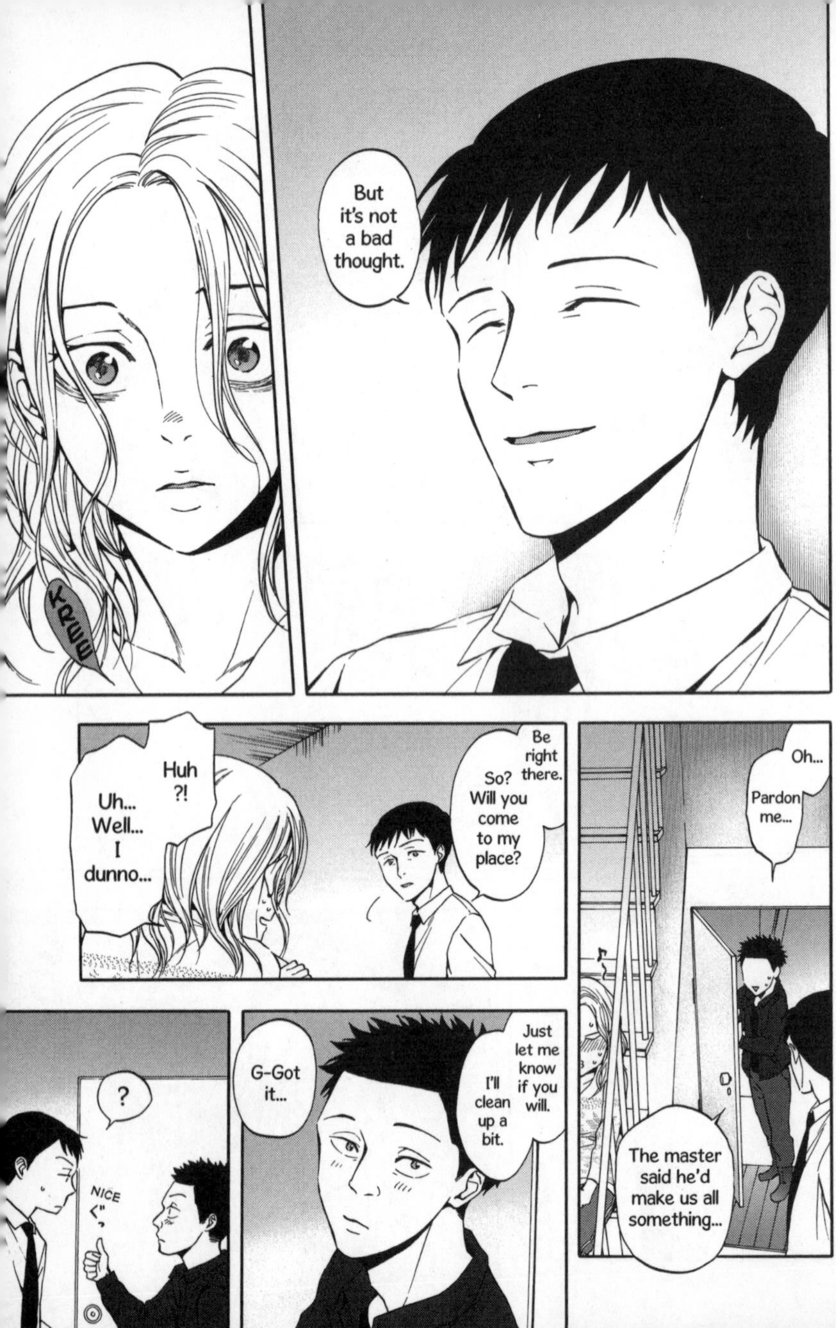

But it's not a bad thought.
KREE
Oh...
Pardon me...
The master said he'd make us all something...
Be right there.
So? Will you come to my place?
Huh?!
Uh... Well... I dunno...
Just let me know if you will.
I'll clean up a bit.
G-Got it...
?
NICE

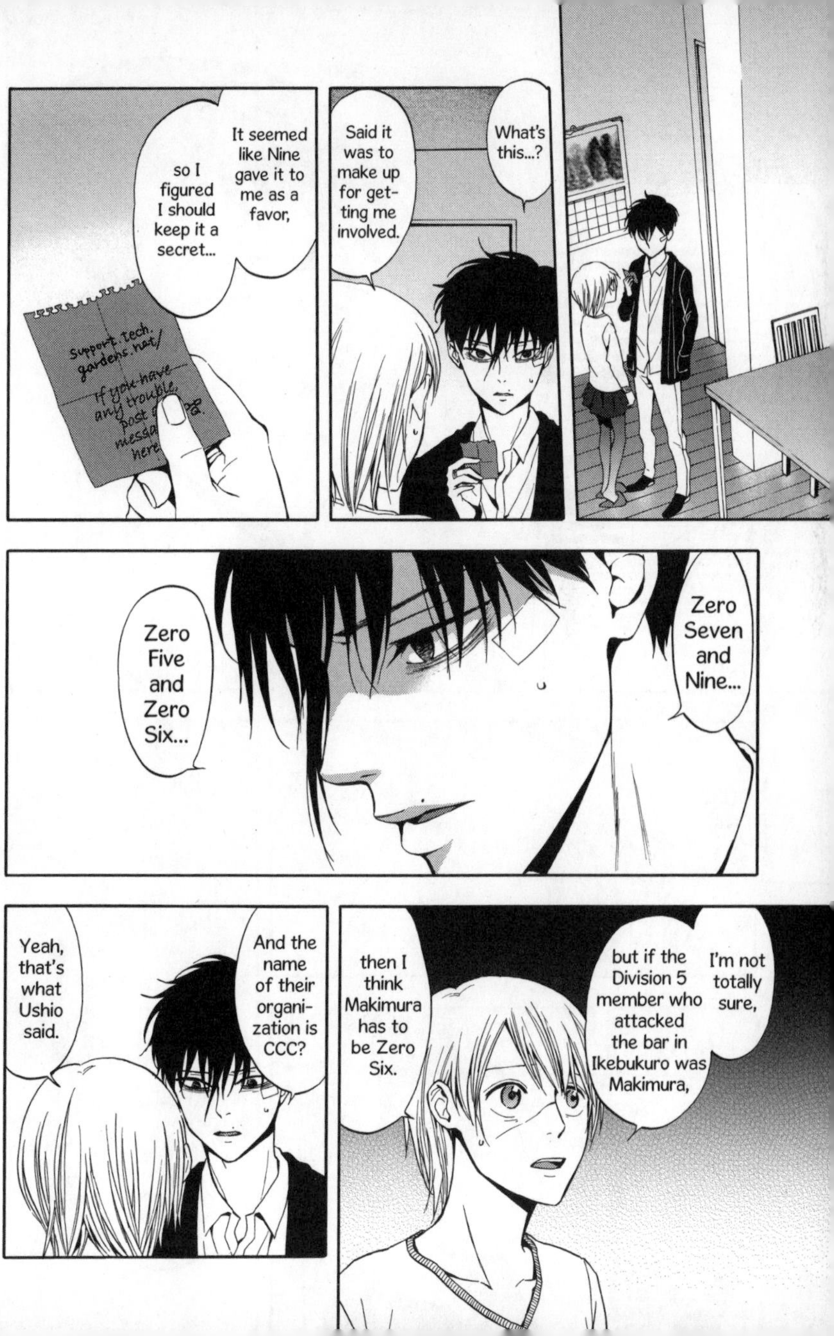
What's this...?
Said it was to make up for getting me involved.
It seemed like Nine gave it to me as a favor,
so I figured I should keep it a secret...
Support.tech. gardens.nat/
If you have any trouble, post
Zero Seven and Nine...
Zero Five and Zero Six...
I'm not totally sure,
but if the Division 5 member who attacked the bar in Ikebukuro was Makimura,
then I think Makimura has to be Zero Six.
And the name of their organization is CCC?
Yeah, that's what Ushio said.

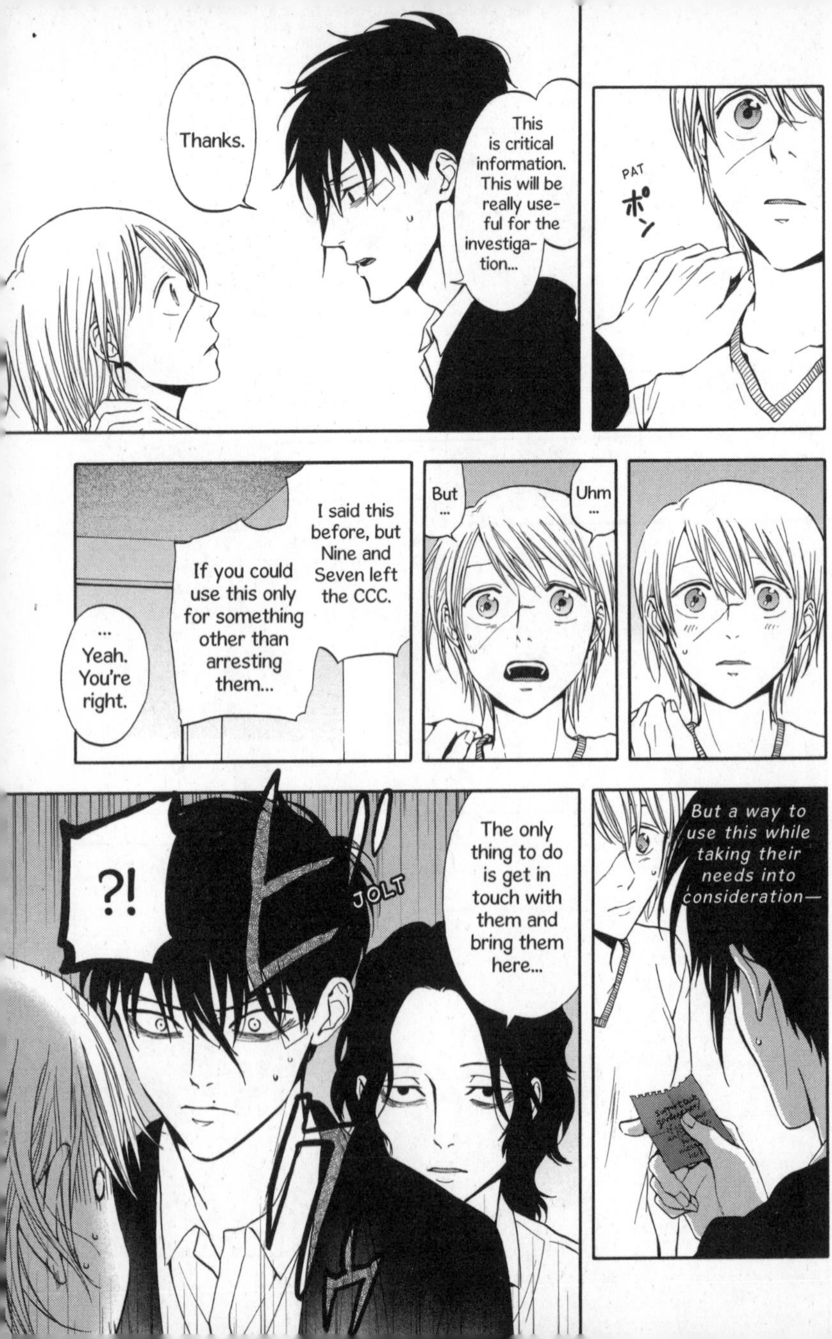
PAT
ポン
This is critical information. This will be really useful for the investigation...
Thanks.
Uhm ...
But ...
I said this before, but Nine and Seven left the CCC.
If you could use this only for something other than arresting them...
... Yeah. You're right.
But a way to use this while taking their needs into consideration—
The only thing to do is get in touch with them and bring them here...
JOLT
?!

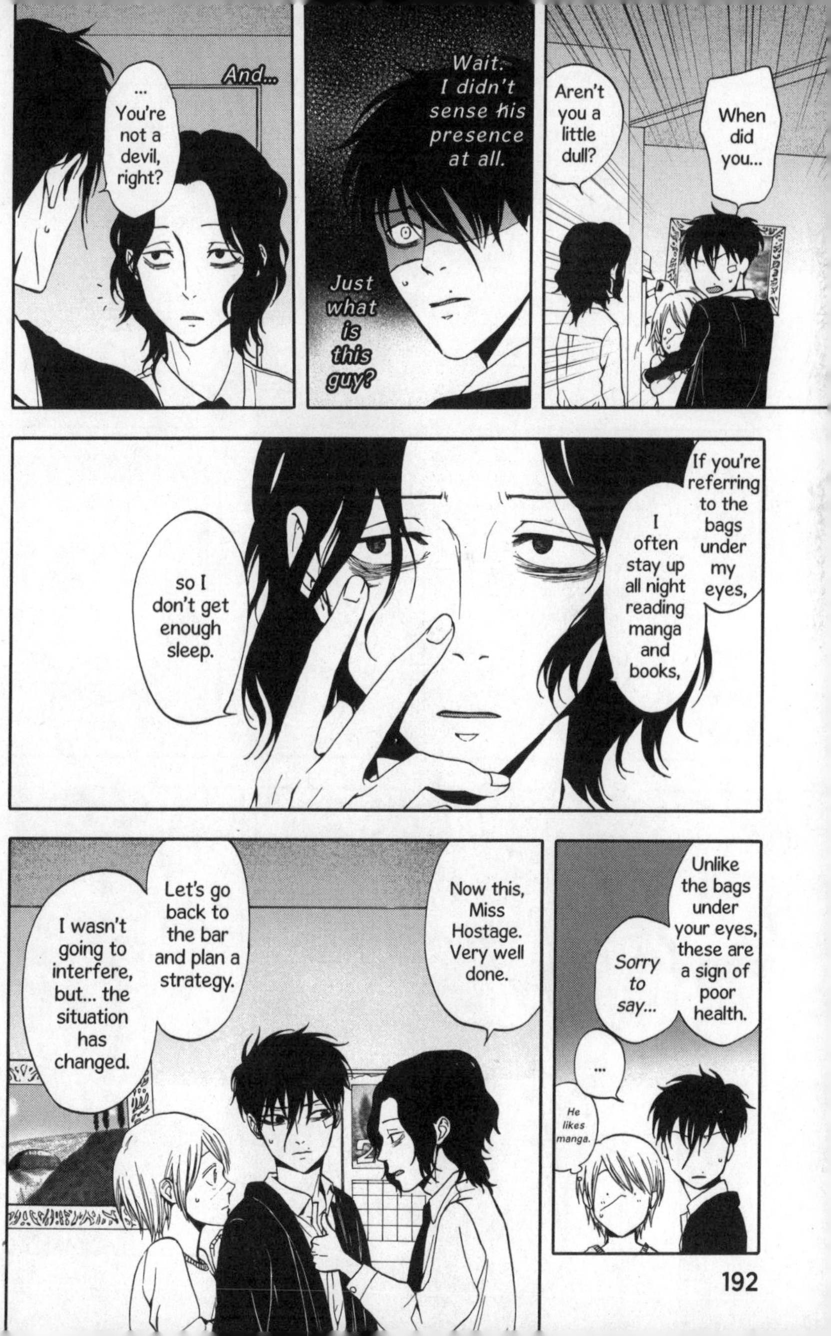
When did you...
Aren't you a little dull?
Wait. I didn't sense his presence at all.
Just what is this guy?
And...
... You're not a devil, right?
If you're referring to the bags under my eyes,
I often stay up all night reading manga and books,
so I don't get enough sleep.
Unlike the bags under your eyes, these are a sign of poor health.
Sorry to say...
...
He likes manga.
Now this, Miss Hostage. Very well done.
Let's go back to the bar and plan a strategy.
I wasn't going to interfere, but... the situation has changed.

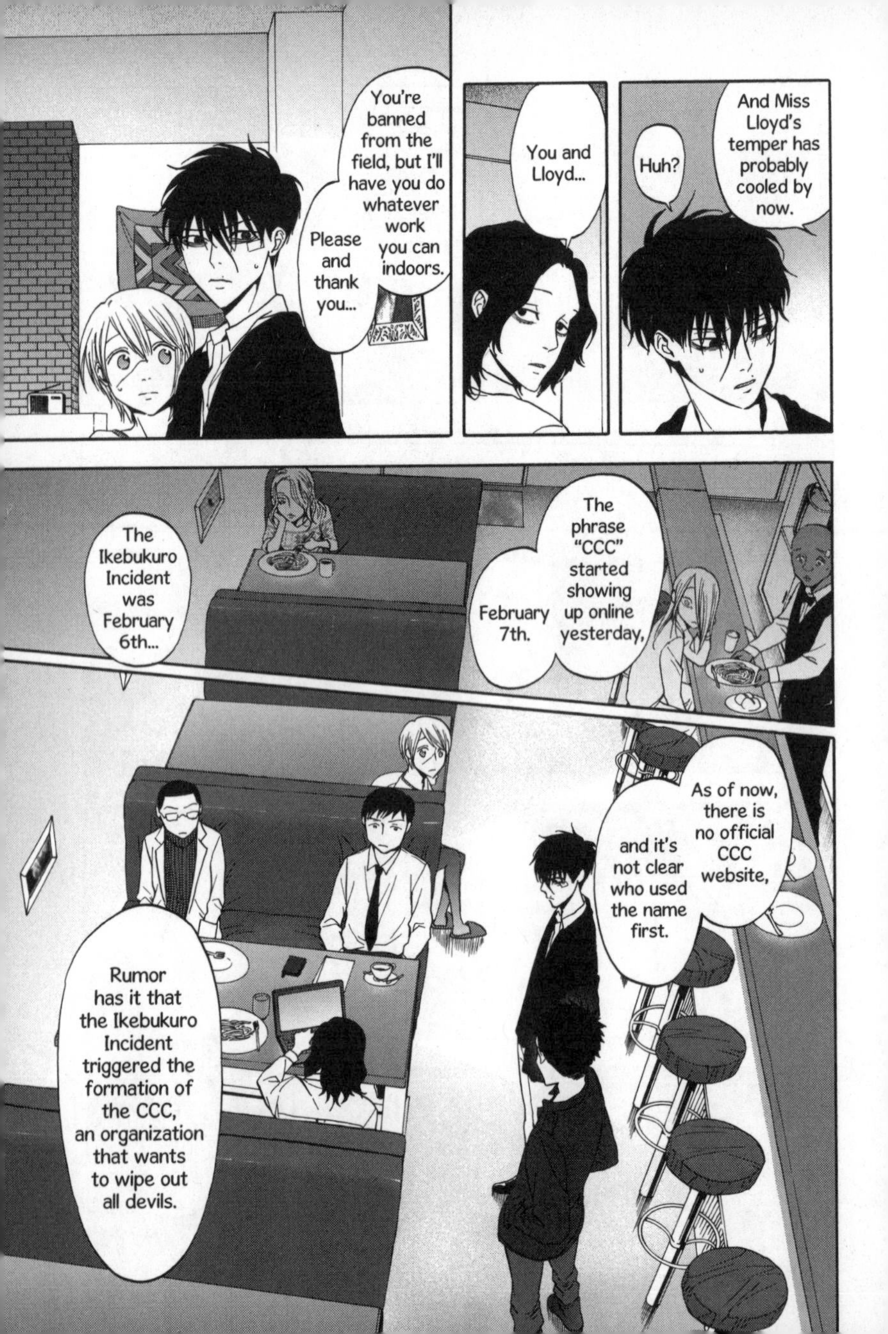
And Miss Lloyd's temper has probably cooled by now.
Huh?
You and Lloyd...
You're banned from the field, but I'll have you do whatever work you can indoors.
Please and thank you...
The phrase "CCC" started showing up online yesterday,
February 7th.
The Ikebukuro Incident was February 6th...
As of now, there is no official CCC website,
and it's not clear who used the name first.
Rumor has it that the Ikebukuro Incident triggered the formation of the CCC, an organization that wants to wipe out all devils.

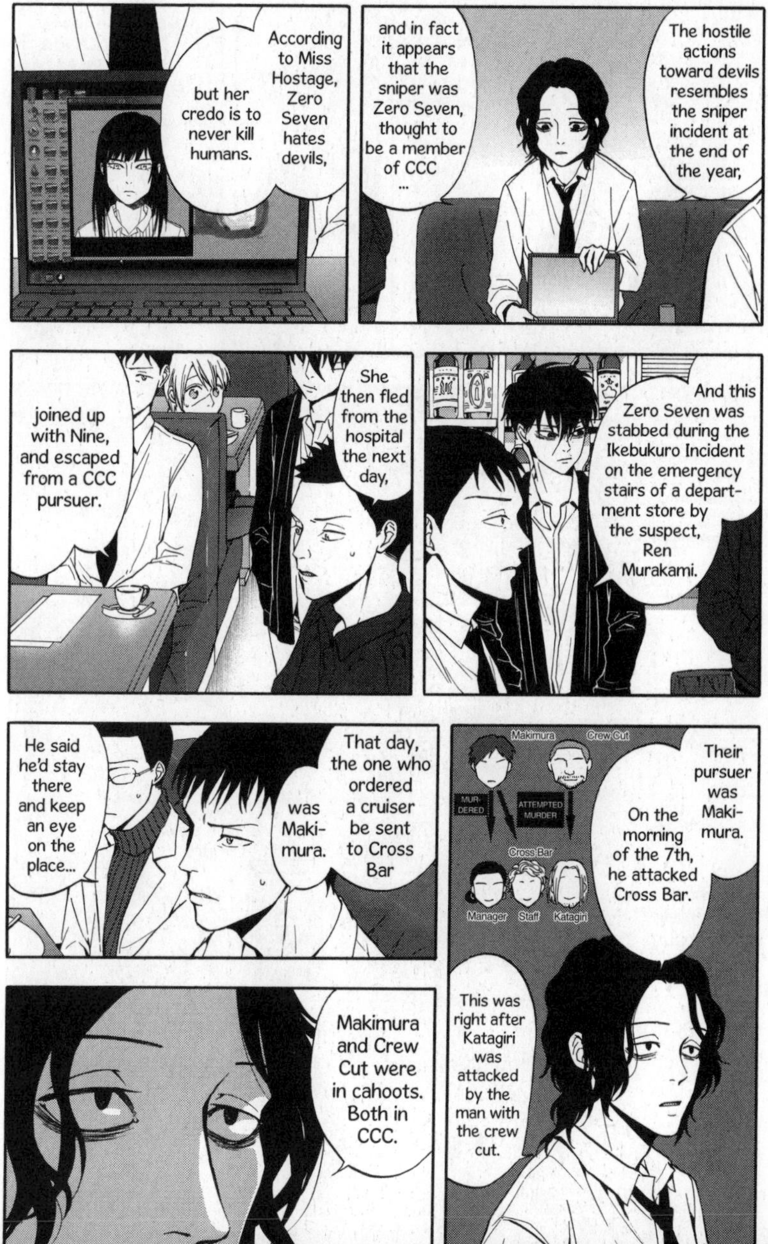
The hostile actions toward devils resembles the sniper incident at the end of the year,
and in fact it appears that the sniper was Zero Seven, thought to be a member of CCC ...
According to Miss Hostage, Zero Seven hates devils,
but her credo is to never kill humans.
And this Zero Seven was stabbed during the Ikebukuro Incident on the emergency stairs of a department store by the suspect, Ren Murakami.
She then fled from the hospital the next day,
joined up with Nine, and escaped from a CCC pursuer.
Their pursuer was Makimura.
On the morning of the 7th, he attacked Cross Bar.
Makimura
Crew Cut
MURDERED
ATTEMPTED MURDER
Cross Bar
Manager
Staff
Katagiri
This was right after Katagiri was attacked by the man with the crew cut.
That day, the one who ordered a cruiser be sent to Cross Bar
was Makimura.
He said he'd stay there and keep an eye on the place...
Makimura and Crew Cut were in cahoots. Both in CCC.

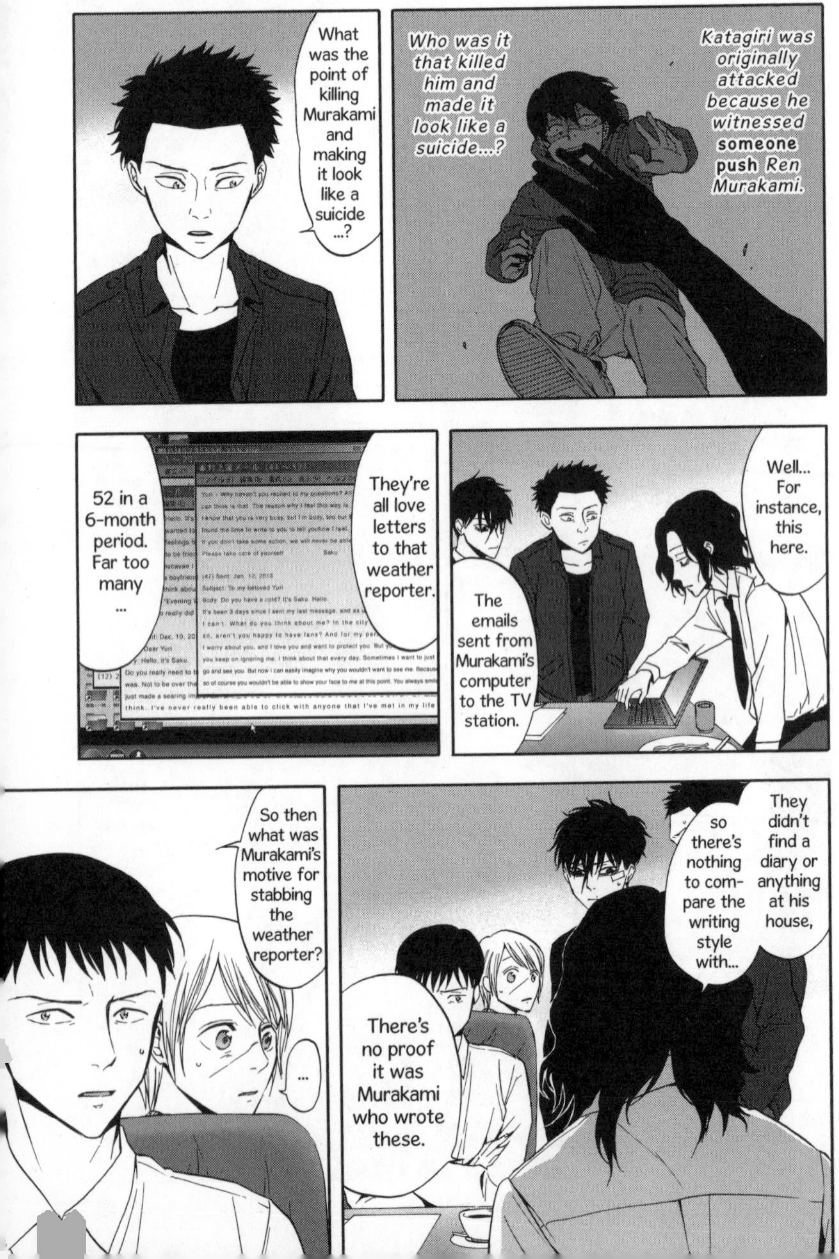
Katagiri was originally attacked because he witnessed someone push Ren Murakami.
Who was it that killed him and made it look like a suicide...?
What was the point of killing Murakami and making it look like a suicide ...?
Well... For instance, this here.
The emails sent from Murakami's computer to the TV station.
They're all love letters to that weather reporter.
52 in a 6-month period. Far too many ...
They didn't find a diary or anything at his house,
so there's nothing to compare the writing style with...
There's no proof it was Murakami who wrote these.
So then what was Murakami's motive for stabbing the weather reporter?
...

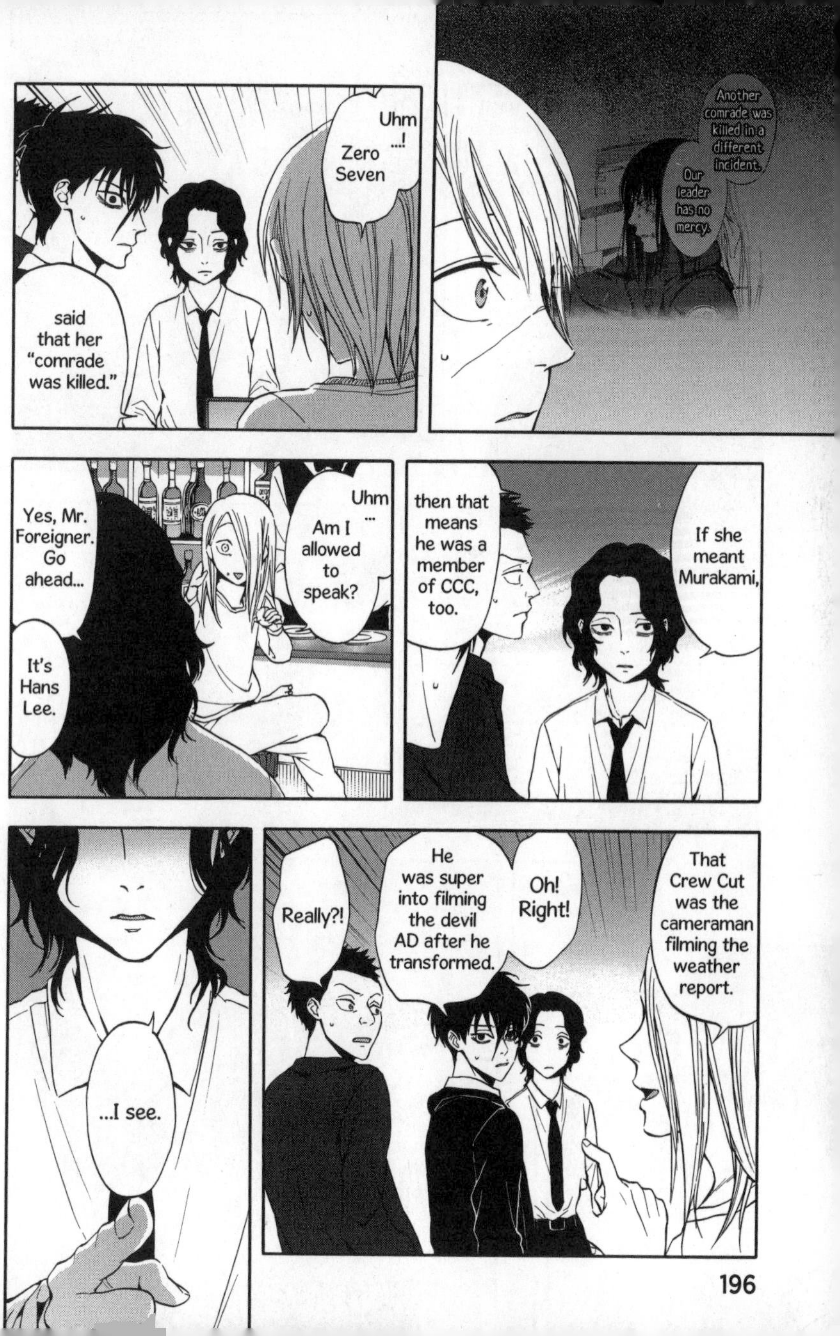
Another comrade was killed in a different incident.
Our leader has no mercy.
Uhm ...! Zero Seven
said that her "comrade was killed."
If she meant Murakami,
then that means he was a member of CCC, too.
Uhm ... Am I allowed to speak?
Yes, Mr. Foreigner. Go ahead...
It's Hans Lee.
That Crew Cut was the cameraman filming the weather report.
Oh! Right!
He was super into filming the devil AD after he transformed.
Really?!
...I see.

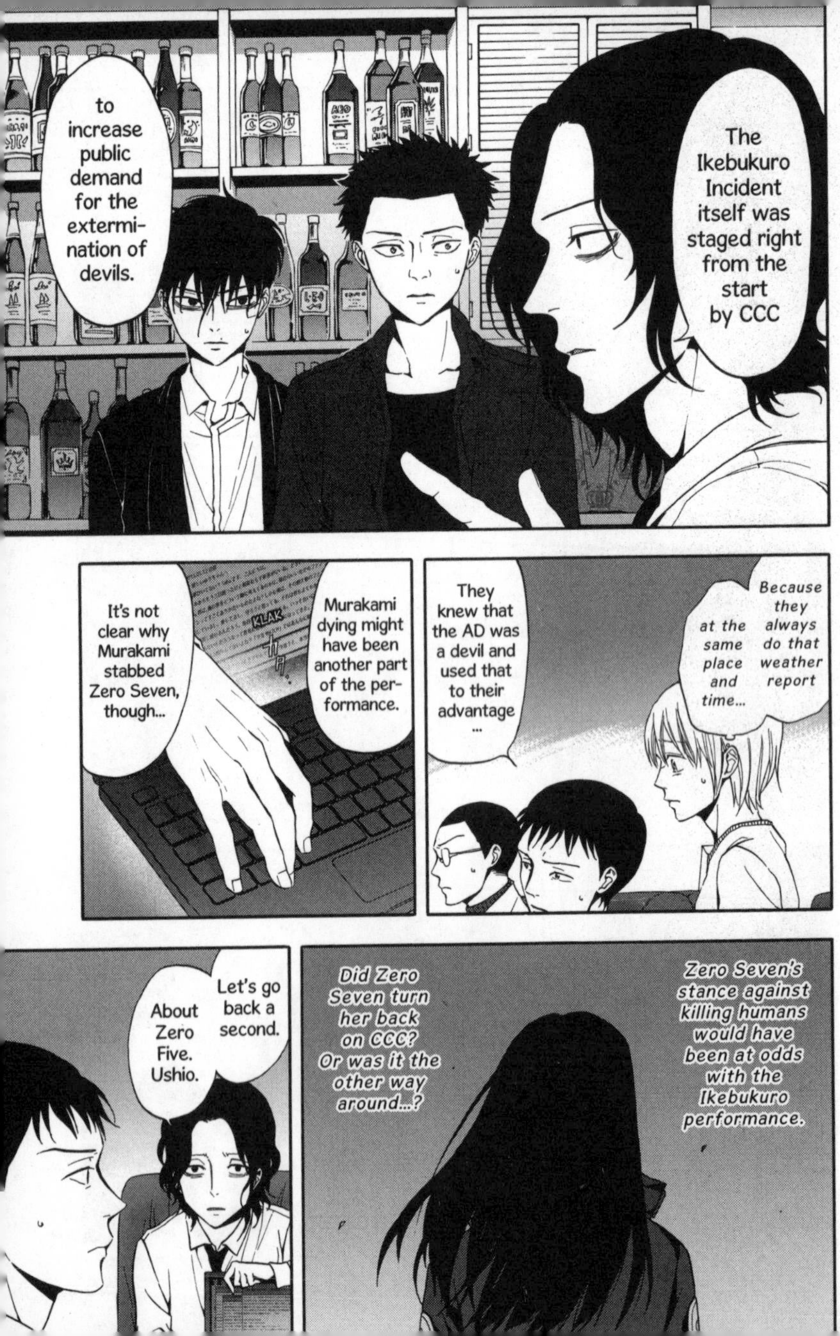
The Ikebukuro Incident itself was staged right from the start by CCC
to increase public demand for the extermination of devils.
Because they always do that weather report
at the same place and time...
They knew that the AD was a devil and used that to their advantage ...
Murakami dying might have been another part of the performance.
KLAK
It's not clear why Murakami stabbed Zero Seven, though...
Zero Seven's stance against killing humans would have been at odds with the Ikebukuro performance.
Did Zero Seven turn her back on CCC? Or was it the other way around...?
Let's go back a second.
About Zero Five. Ushio.

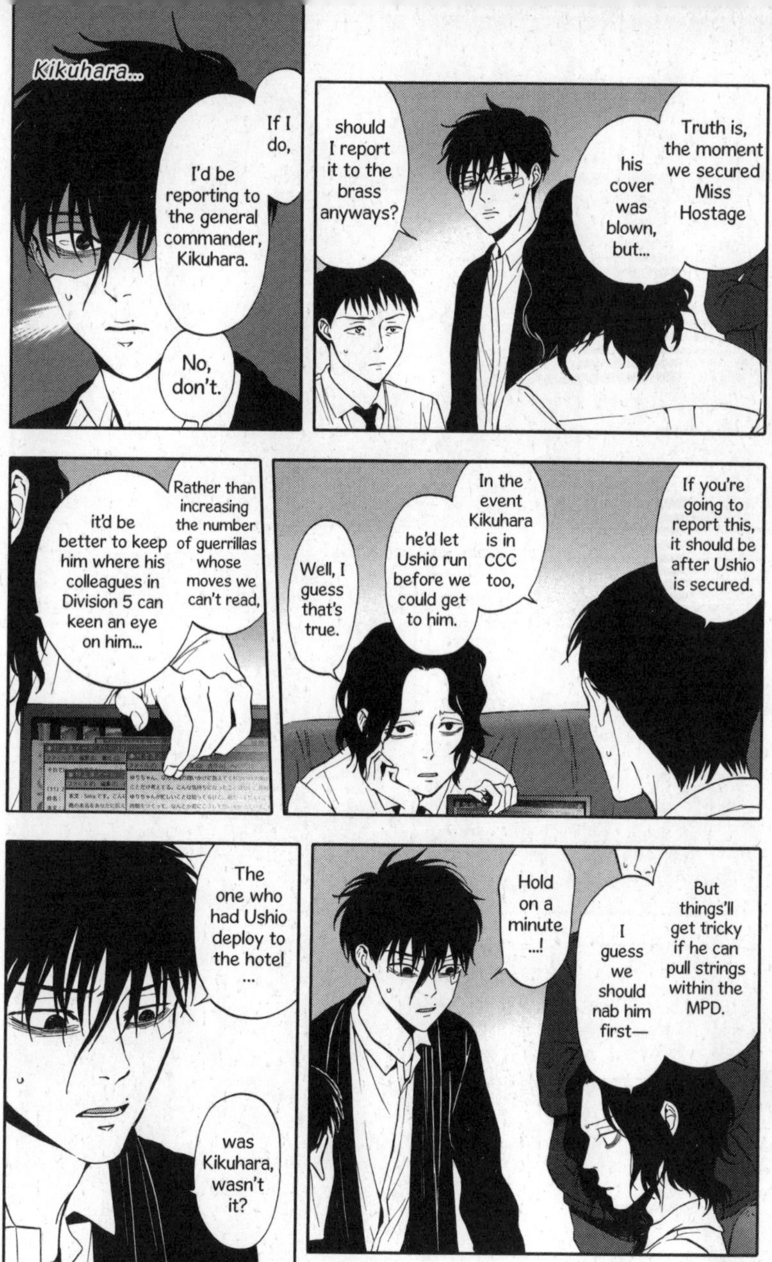
Truth is, the moment we secured Miss Hostage
his cover was blown, but...
should I report it to the brass anyways?
Kikuhara...
If I do,
I'd be reporting to the general commander, Kikuhara.
No, don't.
If you're going to report this, it should be after Ushio is secured.
In the event Kikuhara is in CCC too,
he'd let Ushio run before we could get to him.
Well, I guess that's true.
Rather than increasing the number of guerrillas whose moves we can't read,
it'd be better to keep him where his colleagues in Division 5 can keen an eye on him...
But things'll get tricky if he can pull strings within the MPD.
I guess we should nab him first—
Hold on a minute ...!
The one who had Ushio deploy to the hotel ...
was Kikuhara, wasn't it?

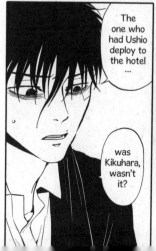

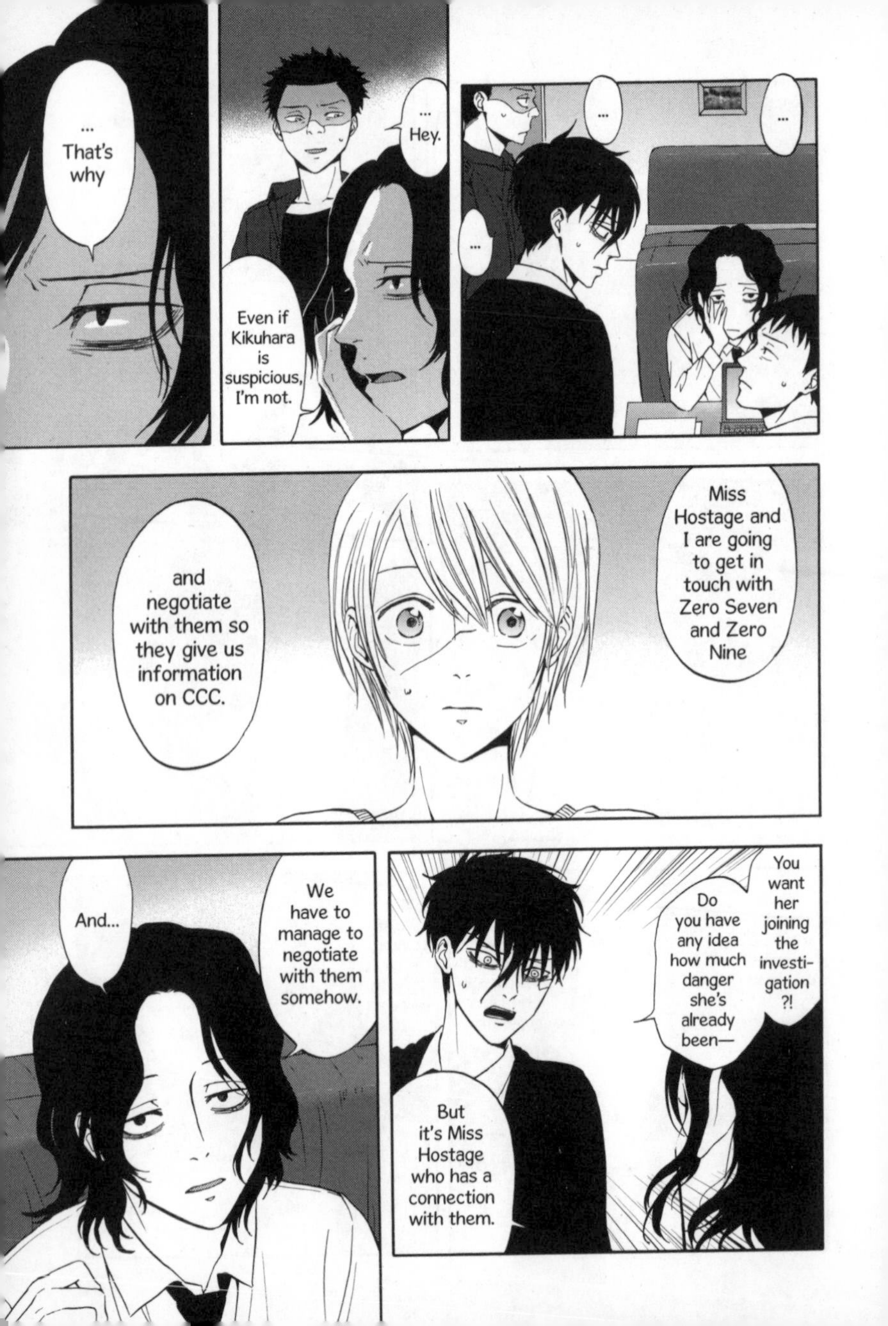
...
...
...
... Hey.
Even if Kikuhara is suspicious, I'm not.
... That's why
Miss Hostage and I are going to get in touch with Zero Seven and Zero Nine
and negotiate with them so they give us information on CCC.
You want her joining the investi-gation?!
Do you have any idea how much danger she's already been—
But it's Miss Hostage who has a connection with them.
We have to manage to negotiate with them somehow.
And...

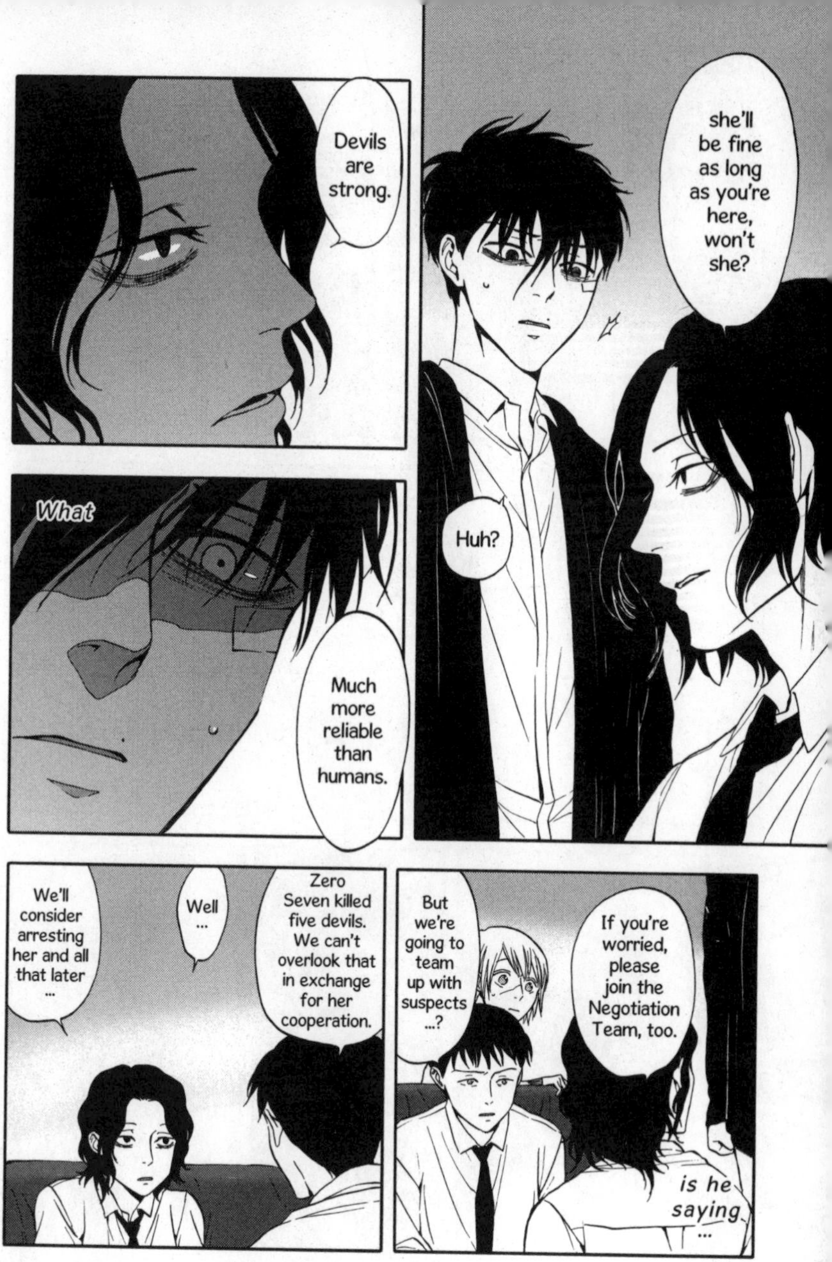

she'll be fine as long as you're here, won't she?
Huh?
Devils are strong.
What
Much more reliable than humans.
If you're worried, please join the Negotiation Team, too.
But we're going to team up with suspects ...?
is he saying ...
Zero Seven killed five devils. We can't overlook that in exchange for her cooperation.
Well ...
We'll consider arresting her and all that later ...

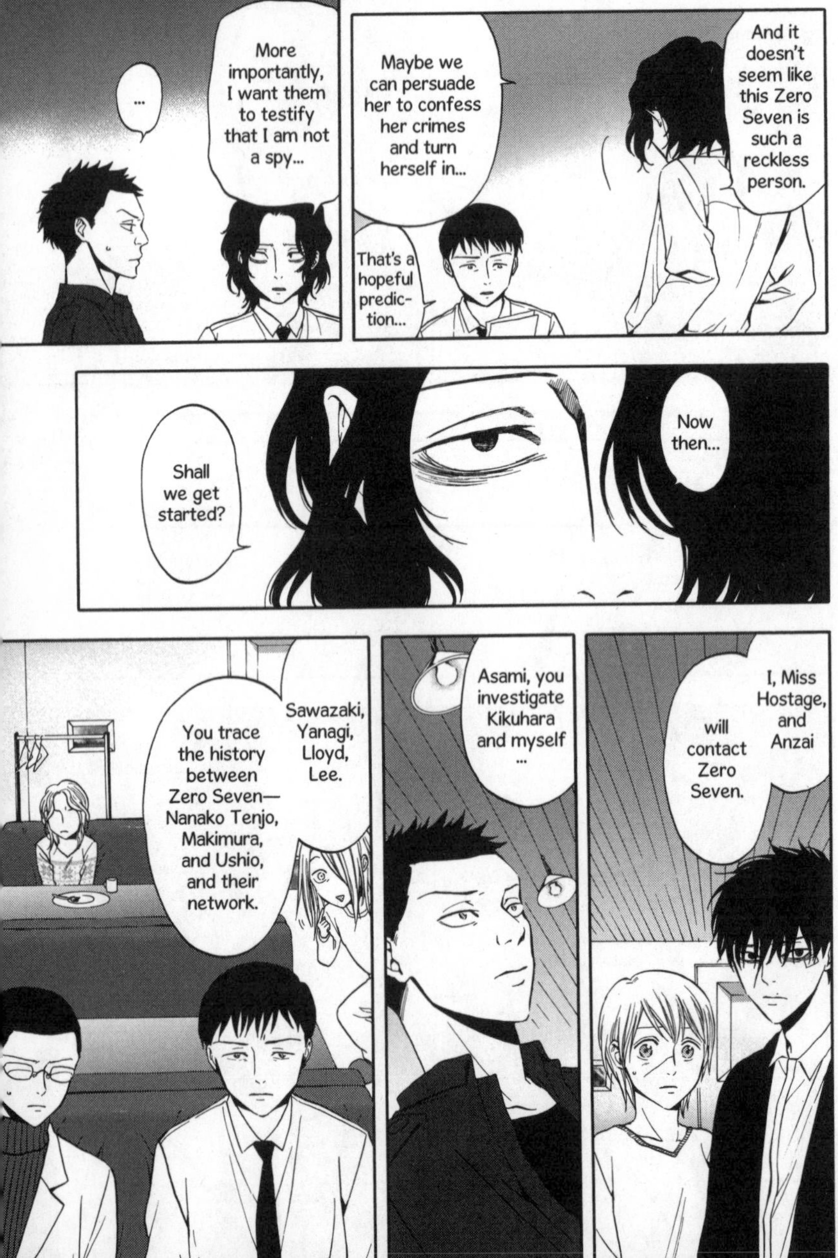
And it doesn't seem like this Zero Seven is such a reckless person.
Maybe we can persuade her to confess her crimes and turn herself in...
That's a hopeful prediction...
More importantly, I want them to testify that I am not a spy...
...
Now then...
Shall we get started?
I, Miss Hostage, and Anzai
will contact Zero Seven.
Asami, you investigate Kikuhara and myself ...
Sawazaki, Yanagi, Lloyd, Lee.
You trace the history between Zero Seven—Nanako Tenjo, Makimura, and Ushio, and their network.

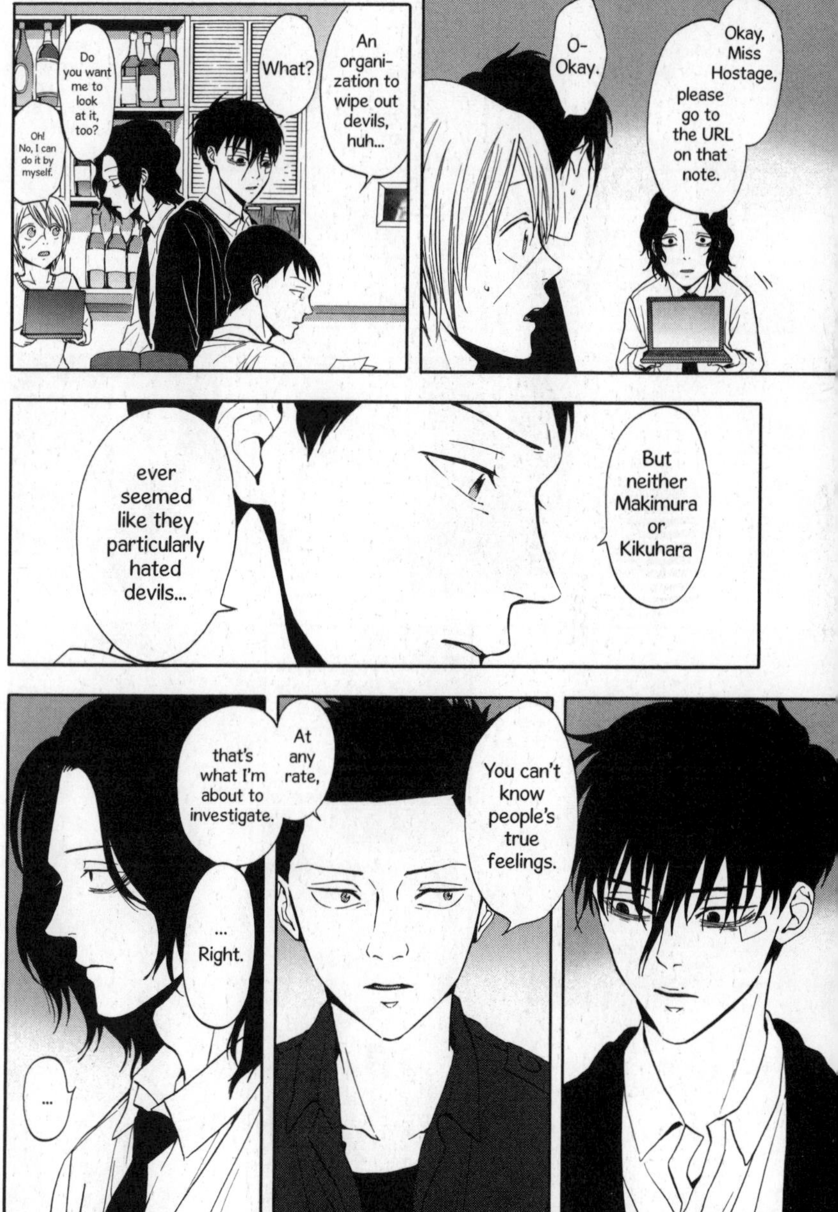
Okay, Miss Hostage, please go to the URL on that note.
O-Okay.
An organization to wipe out devils, huh...
What?
Do you want me to look at it, too?
Oh! No, I can do it by myself.
But neither Makimura or Kikuhara
ever seemed like they particularly hated devils...
You can't know people's true feelings.
At any rate,
that's what I'm about to investigate.
... Right.
...

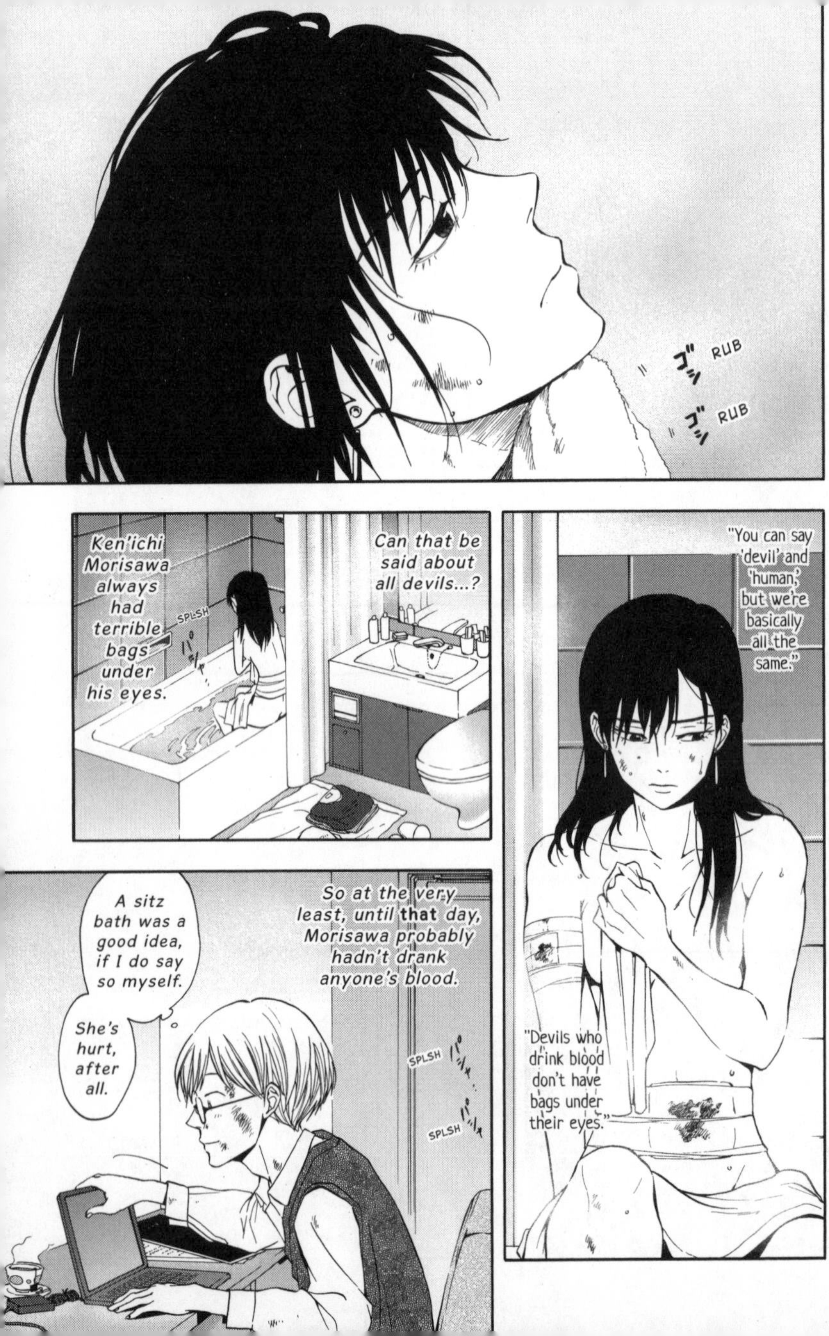
RUB
RUB
"You can say 'devil' and 'human,' but we're basically all the same."
"Devils who drink blood don't have bags under their eyes."
Can that be said about all devils...?
Ken'ichi Morisawa always had terrible bags under his eyes.
SPLSH
So at the very least, until **that** day, Morisawa probably hadn't drank anyone's blood.
A sitz bath was a good idea, if I do say so myself.
She's hurt, after all.
SPLSH
SPLSH

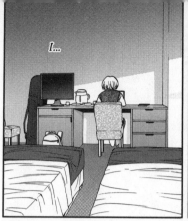

layout
layout(2)
07sleeping_face
Did I actually save that to this computer? The picture of her sleeping...
I...
I thought the only thing I could do
was take sneaky pictures of her.
layout(2)
KLIK
From now on, I'm going to
07sleepin
Open (O)
Browse in Aperta Ver.5
Share (H)
Restore previous version
Search with S-Security
be a real friend...
Search with S-Security
Detailed setting options
Add to Library (I)
Send (N)
Cut (T)
Copy (C)
Create shortcut (S)
Delete (D)
Properties (P)
KLIK
JOLT
I'm done, Nine.
You take a bath, too.

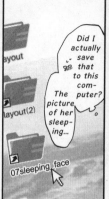

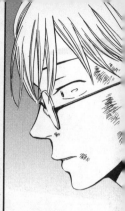

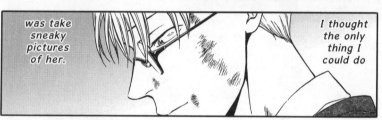

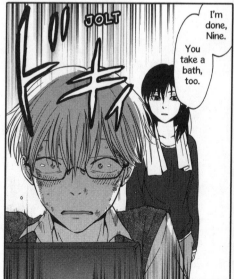

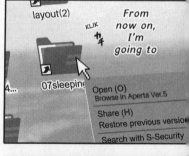

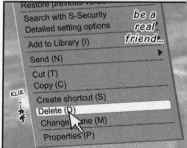

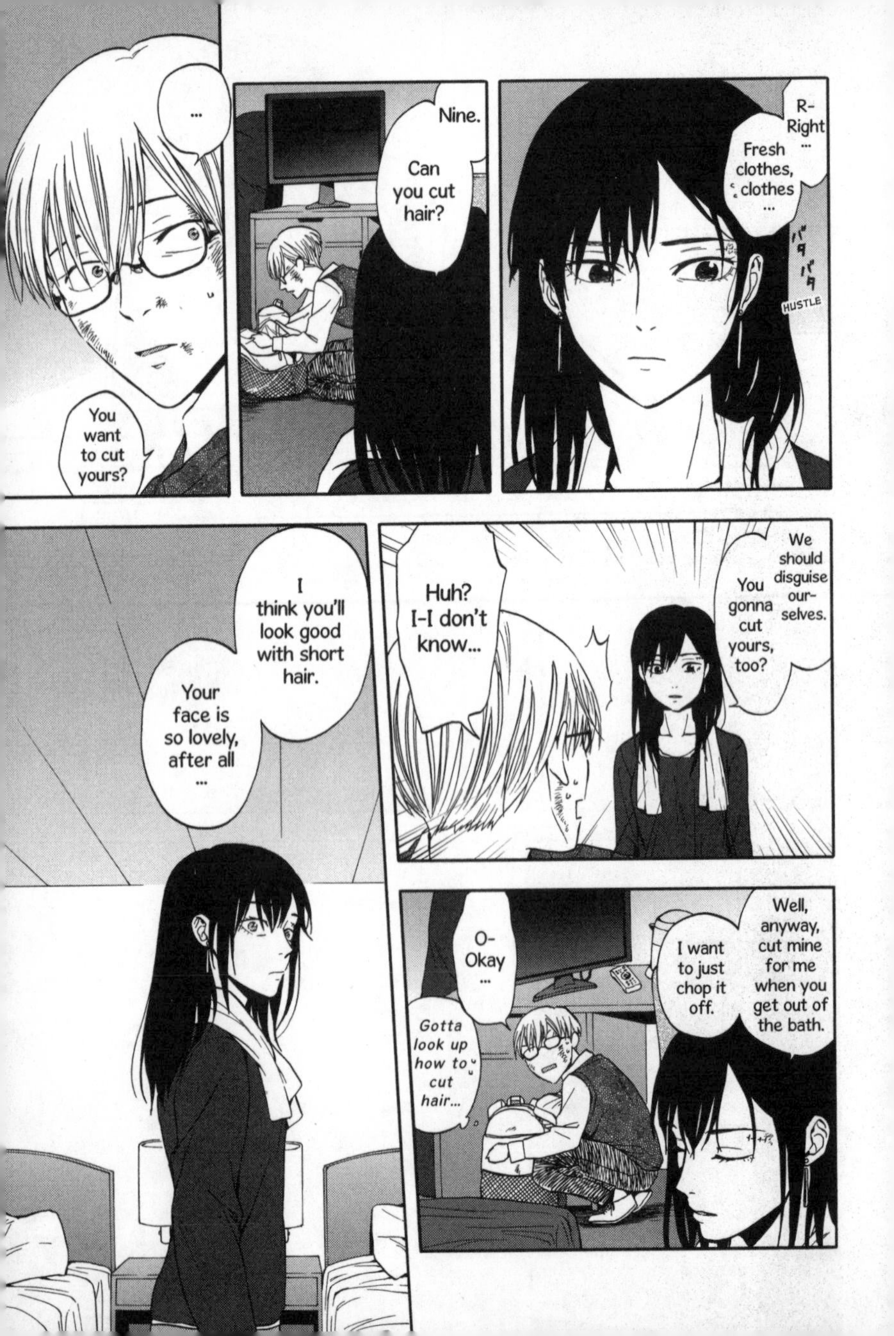
R- Right ...
Fresh clothes, clothes ...
HUSTLE
Nine.
Can you cut hair?
...
You want to cut yours?
We should disguise our-selves.
You gonna cut yours, too?
Huh? I-I don't know...
Well, anyway, cut mine for me when you get out of the bath.
I want to just chop it off.
O-Okay ...
Gotta look up how to cut hair...
I think you'll look good with short hair.
Your face is so lovely, after all ...

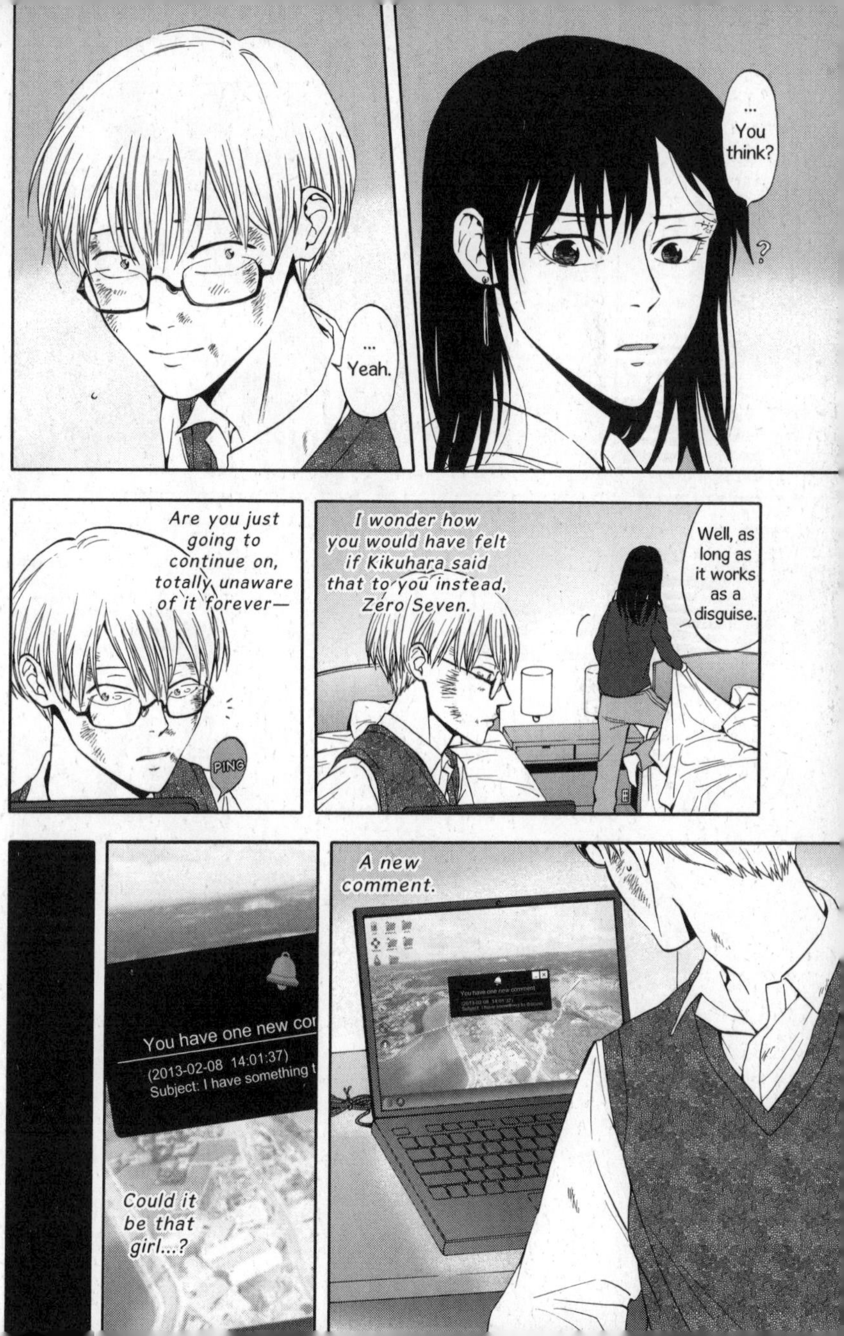

... You think?
... Yeah.
Well, as long as it works as a disguise.
I wonder how you would have felt if Kikuhara said that to you instead, Zero Seven.
Are you just going to continue on, totally unaware of it forever—
PING
A new comment.
You have one new com
(2013-02-08 14:01:37)
Subject: I have something t
Could it be that girl...?

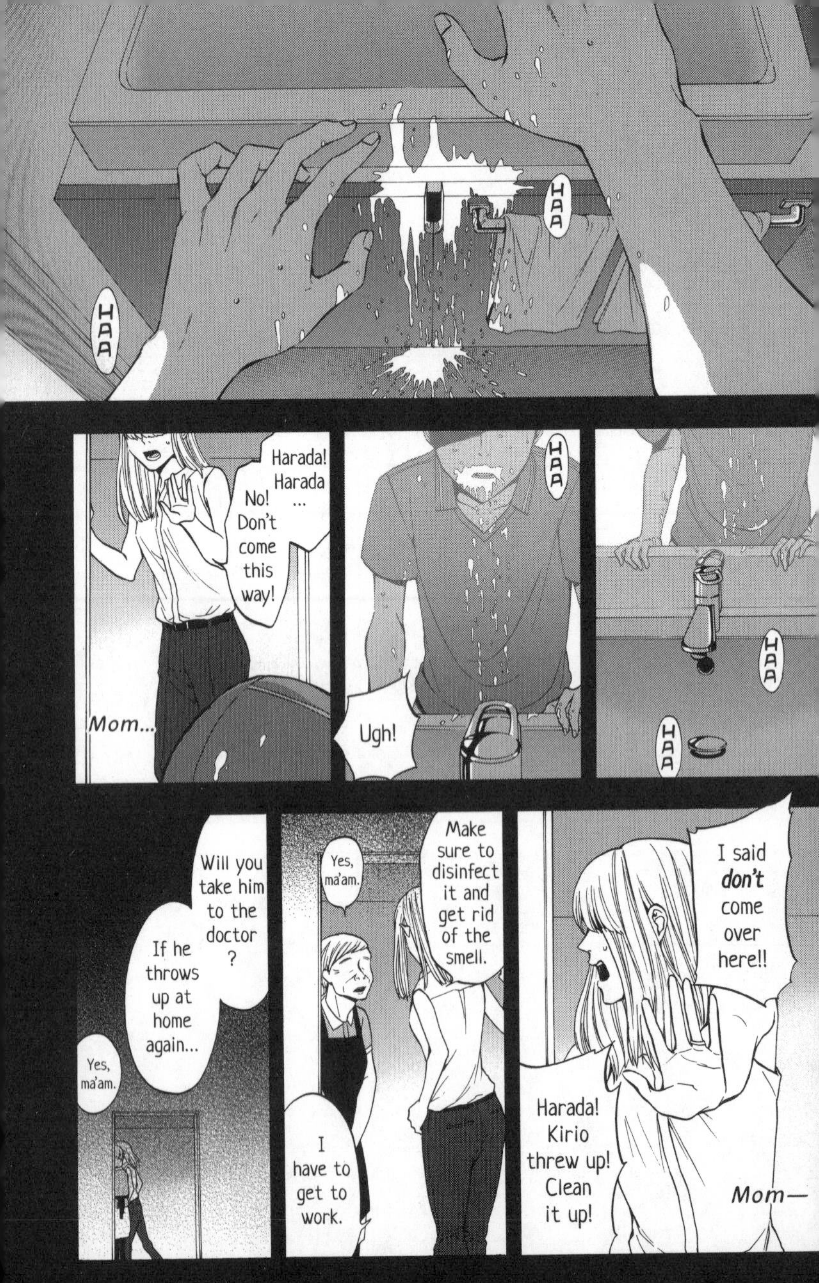
HAA
HAA
HAA
HAA
HAA
Ugh!
Harada! Harada...
No! Don't come this way!
Mom...
I said **don't** come over here!!
Harada! Kirio threw up! Clean it up!
Mom—
Make sure to disinfect it and get rid of the smell.
Yes, ma'am.
I have to get to work.
Will you take him to the doctor?
If he throws up at home again...
Yes, ma'am.

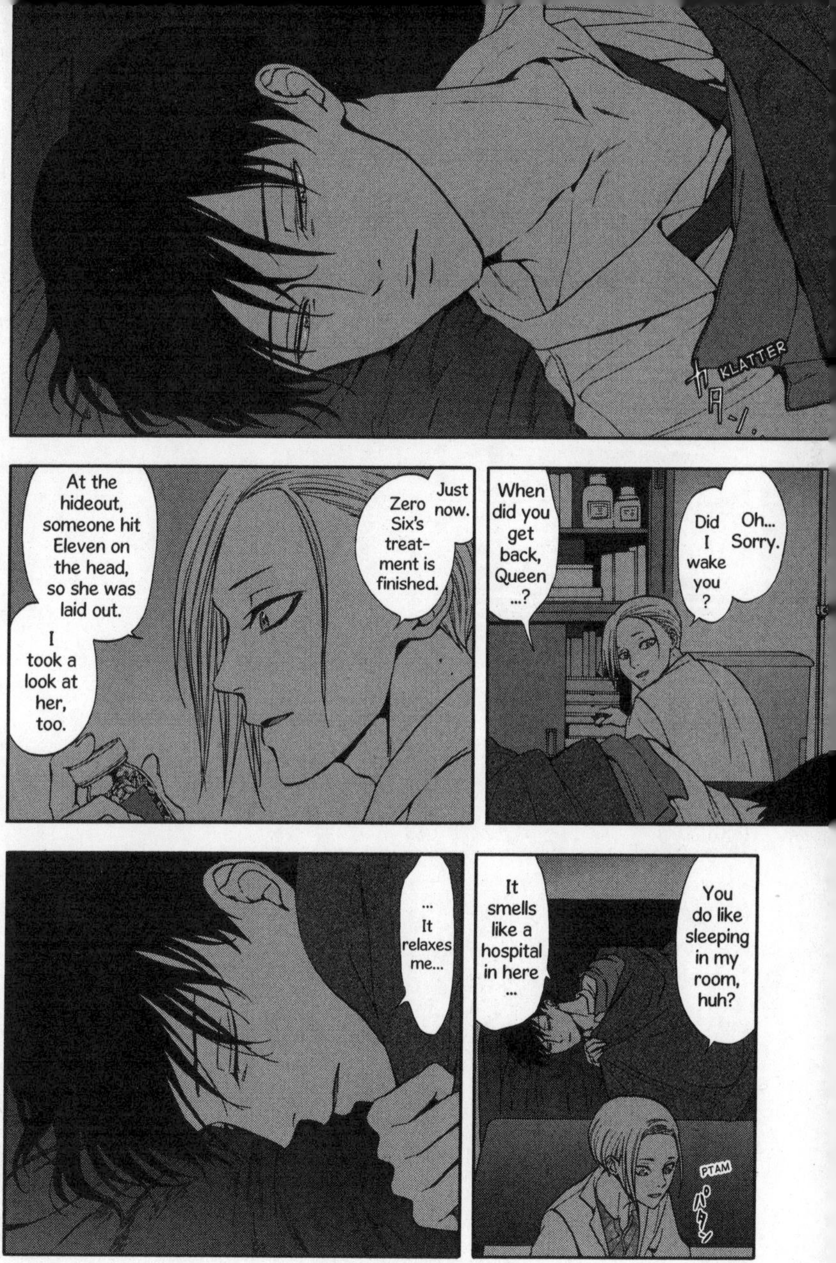
KLATTER
Oh... Sorry.
Did I wake you?
When did you get back, Queen...?
Just now.
Zero Six's treatment is finished.
At the hideout, someone hit Eleven on the head, so she was laid out.
I took a look at her, too.
You do like sleeping in my room, huh?
It smells like a hospital in here...
PTAM
... It relaxes me...

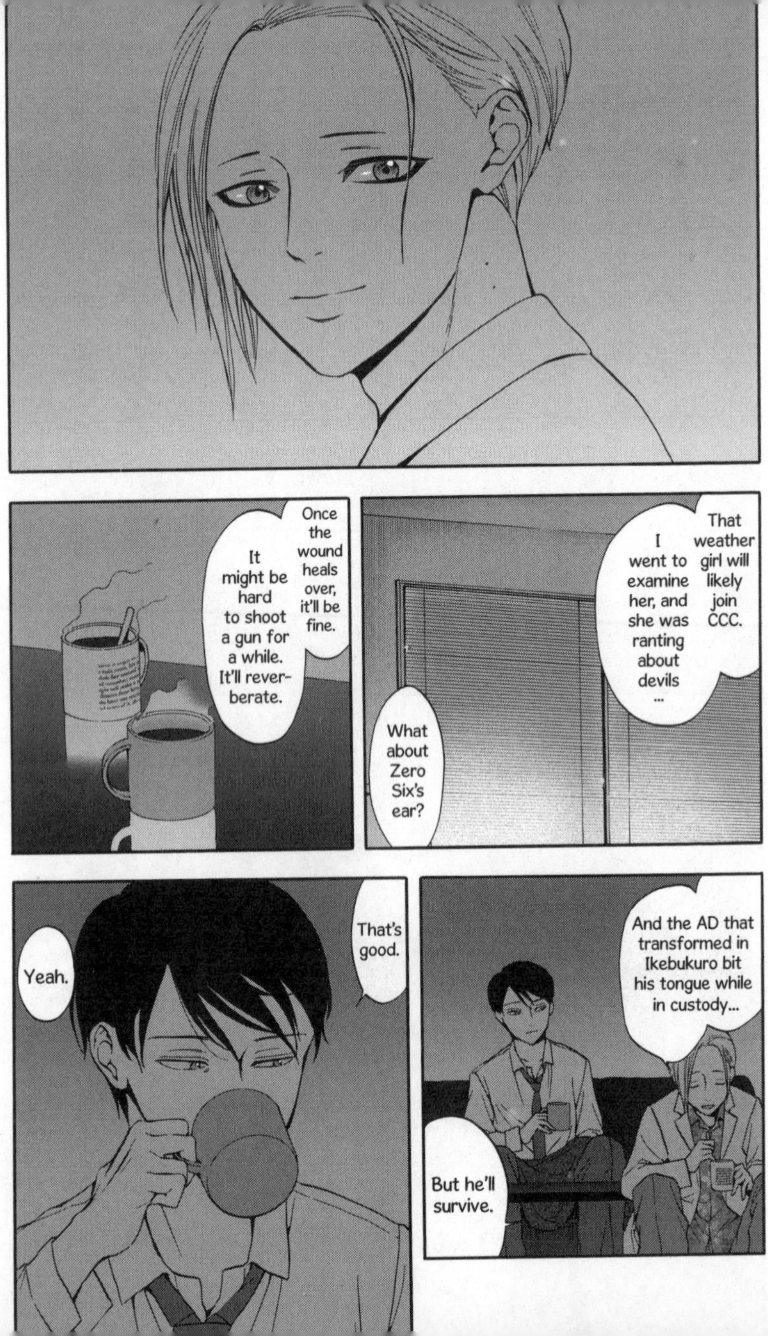
That weather girl will likely join CCC.
I went to examine her, and she was ranting about devils...
What about Zero Six's ear?
Once the wound heals over, it'll be fine.
It might be hard to shoot a gun for a while. It'll reverberate.
And the AD that transformed in Ikebukuro bit his tongue while in custody...
But he'll survive.
That's good.
Yeah.

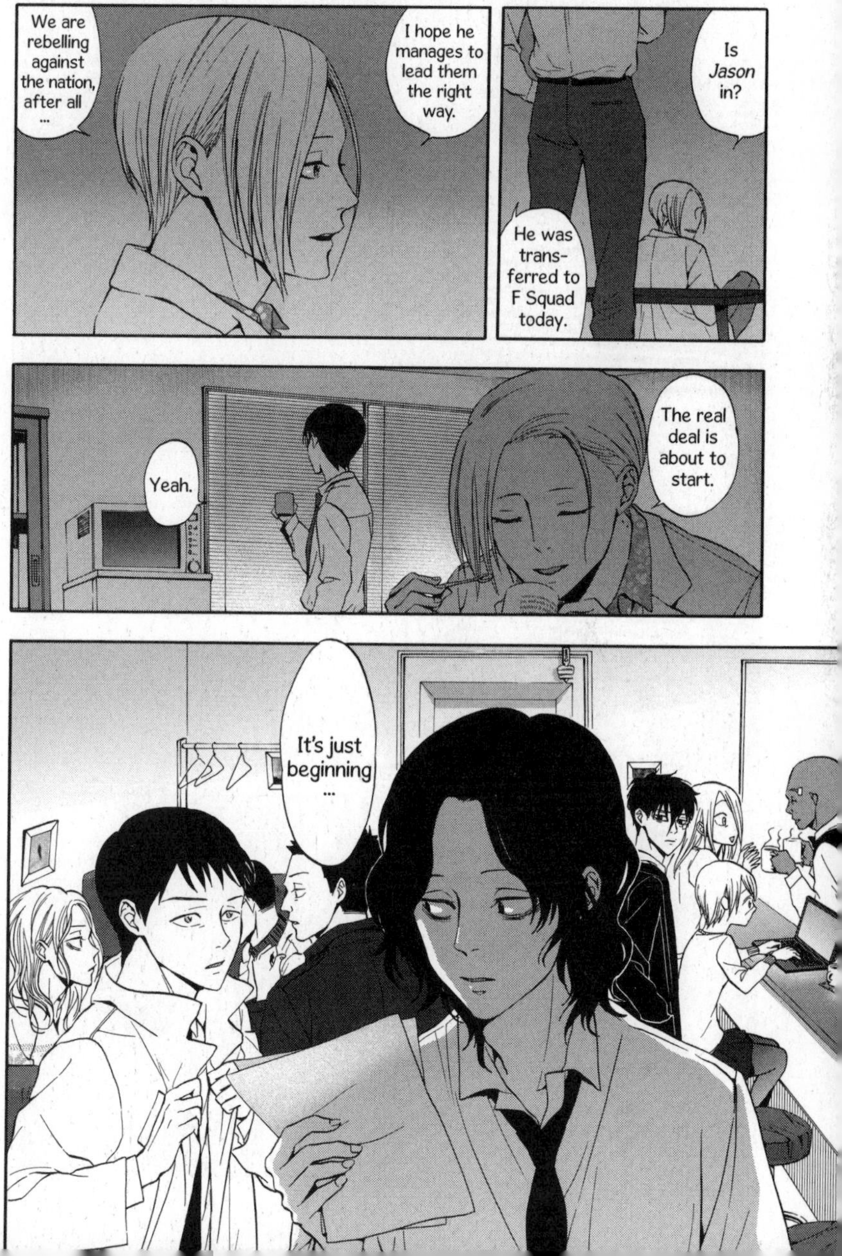
Is *Jason* in?
He was trans-ferred to F Squad today.
I hope he manages to lead them the right way.
We are rebelling against the nation, after all ...
The real deal is about to start.
Yeah.
It's just beginning ...

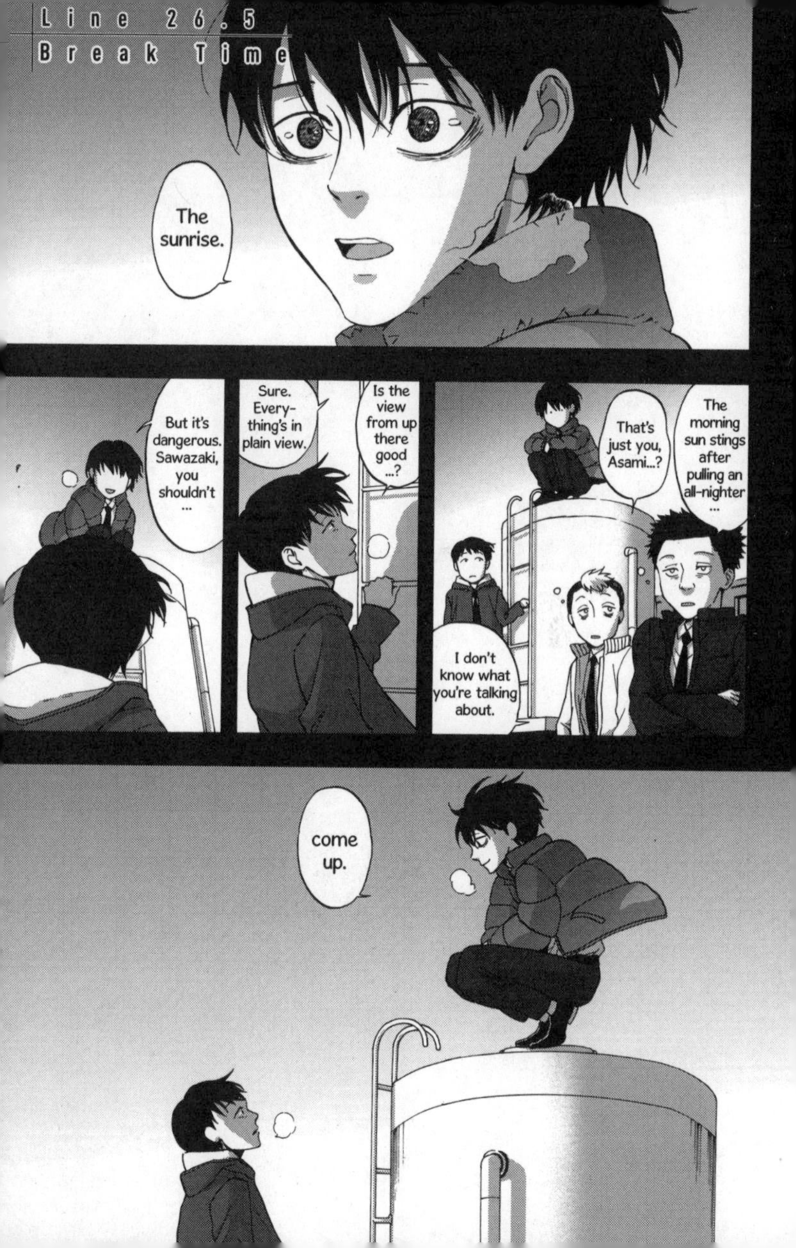
Line 26.5
Break Time
The sunrise.
The morning sun stings after pulling an all-nighter ...
That's just you, Asami...?
I don't know what you're talking about.
Is the view from up there good ...?
Sure. Everything's in plain view.
But it's dangerous. Sawazaki, you shouldn't ...
come up.

Line X Break Time

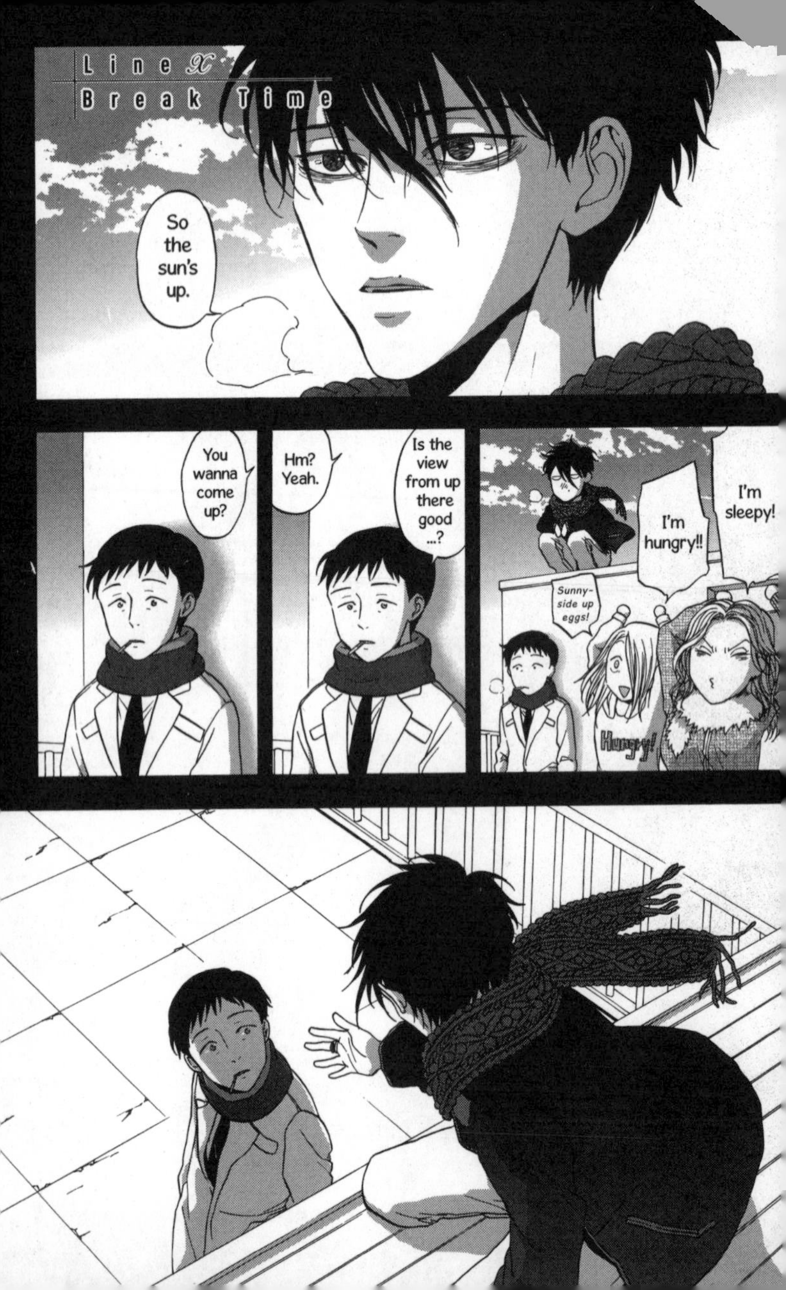

So the sun's up.
I'm sleepy!
I'm hungry!!
Sunny-side up eggs!
Hungry!
Is the view from up there good ...?
Hm? Yeah.
You wanna come up?

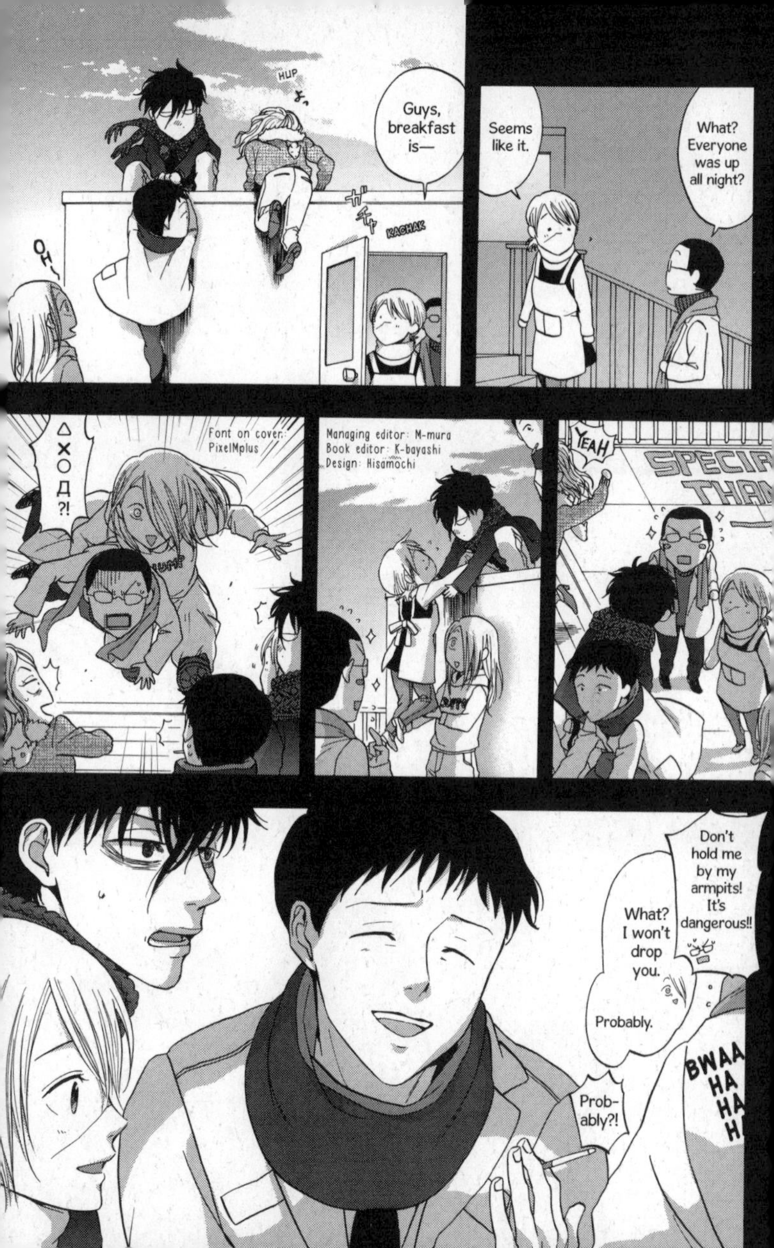
What? Everyone was up all night?
Seems like it.
Guys, breakfast is—
HUP
KACHAK
OH
YEAH
Managing editor: M-mura
Book editor: K-bayashi
Design: Hisamochi
Font on cover: PixelMplus
△×○Д?!
Don't hold me by my armpits! It's dangerous!!
What? I won't drop you.
Probably.
BWAA HA HA H
Prob-ably?!

AS OF FEBRUARY 2013

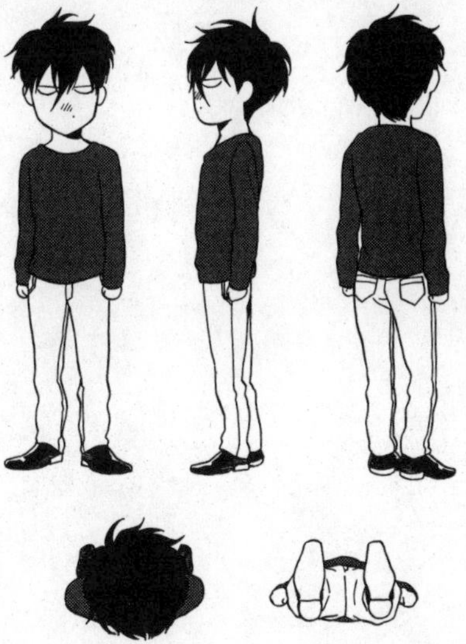

YUUKI ANZAI

Birthday: January 15 (21 years old)
Permanent residence: Hokkaido
Class: Hybrid

Height: 5′ 9″
Eyesight: Left 3.5; Right 3.4
Average sleeping time: 6 hours
Favorite foods: Chocolate, milk

Features: He is not aware of it, but he's basically a perv at heart. He prefers slip-on shoes.

Combat strength: 60/100
Skills: Transformation
Class 1 driver's license (from 2010)

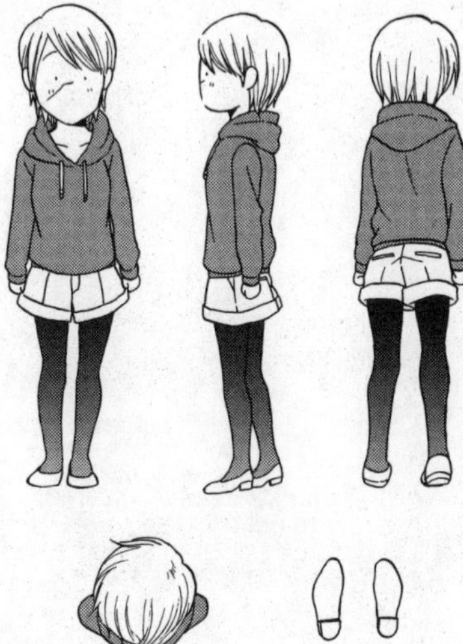

Shoe size: 5

TSUKASA TAIRA

Birthday: March 20 (22 years old)
Permanent residence: Kagawa Prefecture
Class: Human

Height: 5′
Eyesight: Left 1.2; Right 1.4
Average sleeping time: 7.5–8 hours
Favorite food: Sardines with grated daikon

Features: Gentle personality. Her instincts aren't bad, but she's very slow on the uptake when people like her. She likes cooking and crafts.

Tolerance: 90/100
Skills: Class 1 driver's license (from 2009) ※ Never drives
TOEIC score of 690 (2011)

AS OF FEBRUARY 2013

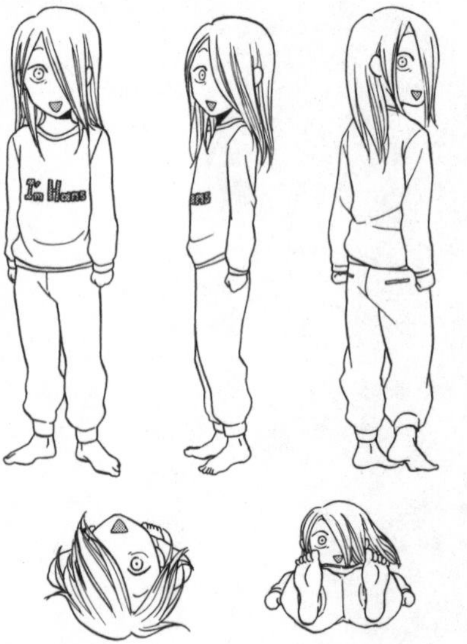
I'm Hans

HANS LEE (JOHANNES KLEEMAN)

Birthday: January 18 (21 years old)
Permanent residence: Germany
Class: Hybrid

Height: 5′ 11″
Eyesight: Left 0.2; Right 4.8
(Left 4.6 when transformed)
Average sleeping time: 4 hours
Favorite foods: Anything

Features: Sunny and brimming with curiosity. Eats a lot. Occasionally says things that cannot be taken as either the truth or a joke.

Combat strength: 80/100
Skills: Just-right level of transformation
Making flip books

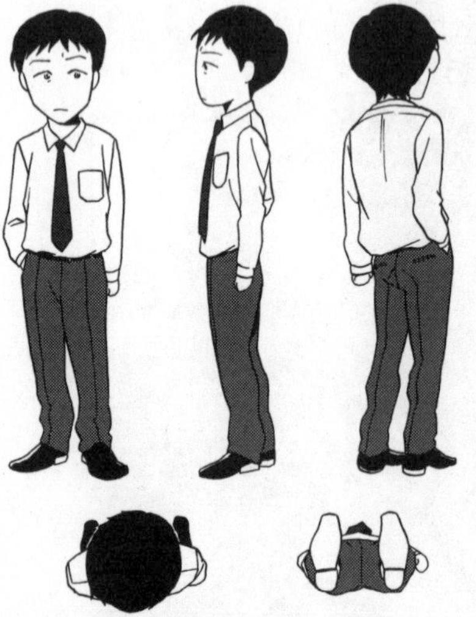

(Not good at standing out)

TAKASHI SAWAZAKI

Birthday: November 20 (38 years old)
Permanent residence: Chiba Prefecture
Class: Human

Height: 5′ 9″
Eyesight: Left 0.8; Right 0.9
Average sleeping time: 5 hours
Favorite food: Boiled gyoza

Features: He′s always worried about his subordinates. He′s maybe always been a bit dense when it comes to relationships?

Combat strength: 50/100
Skills: Class 1 driver′s license (from 1993)
EIKEN English certification level 2 (1992)
Junior High/High School teaching license (social studies, civics) (1997)

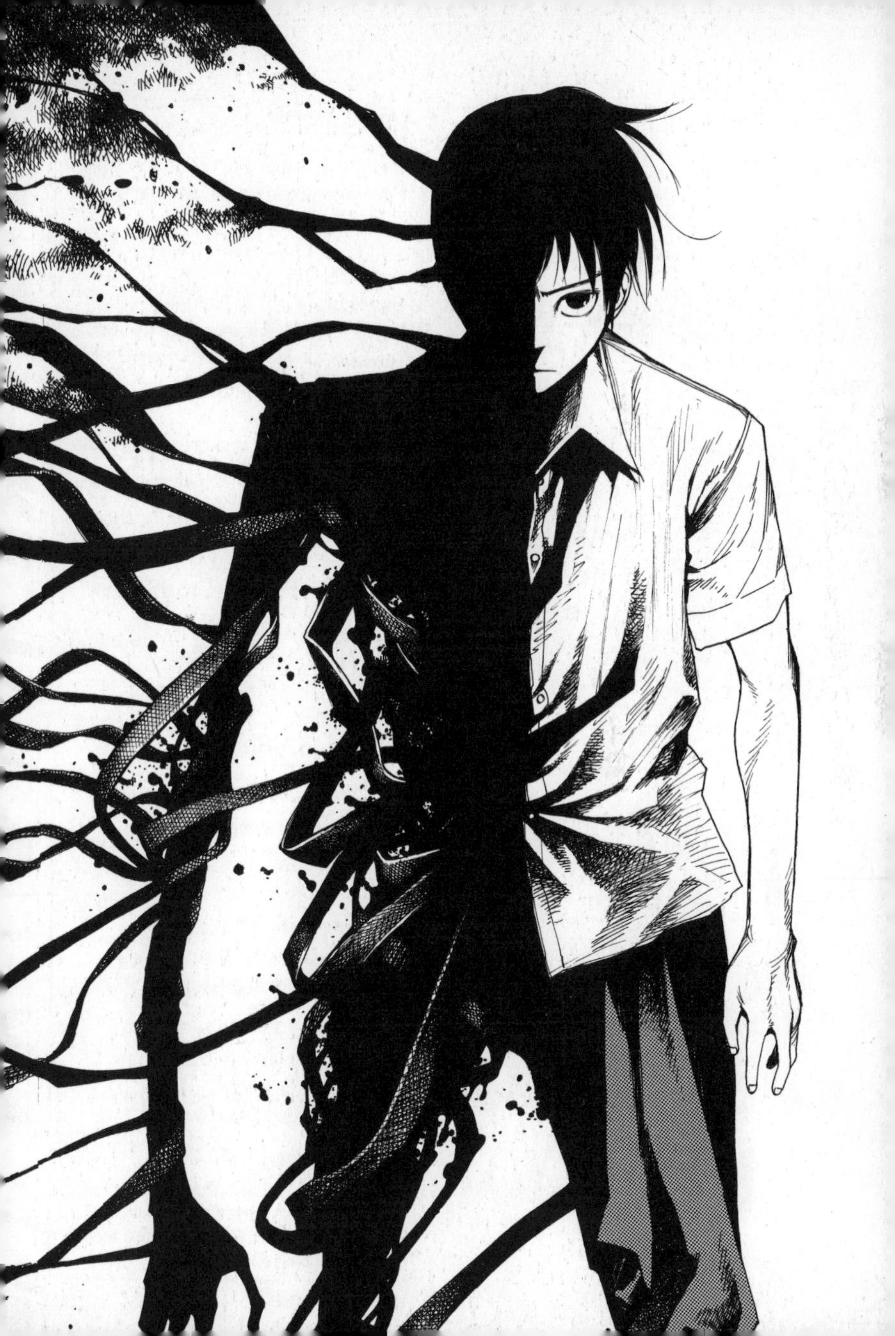

AJIN
DEMI-HUMAN

GAMON SAKURAI

SAY YOU GET HIT BY A TRUCK AND DIE. YOU COME BACK TO LIFE. GOOD OR BAD?

FOR HIGH SCHOOLER KEI—AND FOR AT LEAST FORTY-SIX OTHERS—IMMORTALITY COMES AS THE NASTIEST SURPRISE EVER.

SADLY FOR KEI, BUT REFRESHINGLY FOR THE READER, SUCH A FEAT DOESN'T MAKE HIM A SUPERHERO. IN THE EYES OF BOTH THE GENERAL PUBLIC AND GOVERNMENTS, HE'S A RARE SPECIMEN WHO NEEDS TO BE HUNTED DOWN AND HANDED OVER TO SCIENTISTS TO BE EXPERIMENTED ON FOR LIFE—A DEMI-HUMAN WHO MUST DIE A THOUSAND DEATHS FOR THE BENEFIT OF HUMANITY.

APOSIMZ

TSUTOMU NIHEI

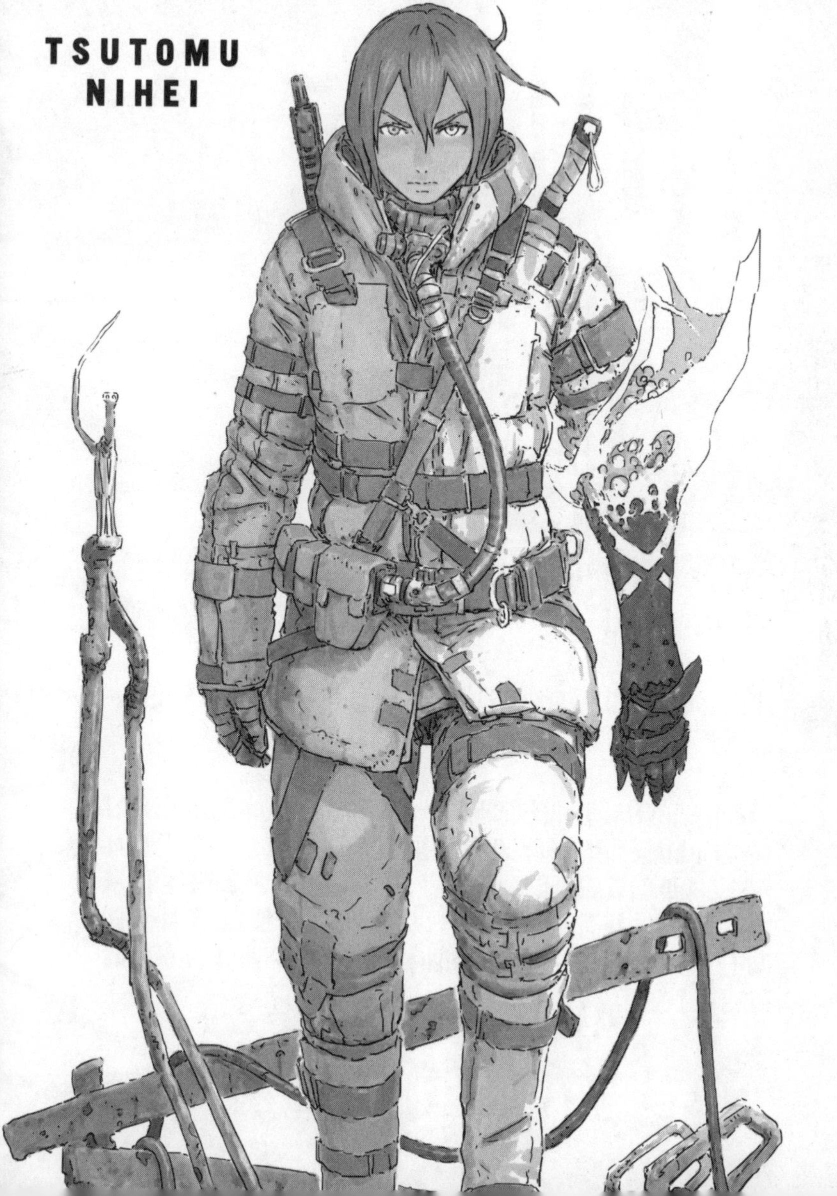

This story takes place on the frigid, massive artificial planet known as Aposimz.

Eo, Biko and Etherow, residents of the White Diamond Beam, are in the middle of combat training when suddenly a girl appears, Rebedoan Empire soldiers in hot pursuit. The girl asks for their help in keeping safe a "code" and seven mysterious "bullets." This chance encounter marks a major shift in the fate of the entire planet...

The curtain rises on a grand new adventure from Tsutomu Nihei, the author of *BLAME!* and *Knights of Sidonia*.

VOLUMES 1-7
AVAILABLE NOW!

PREVIEW FOR NEXT VOLUME:

Public Safety Division 5's F Squad is now under the command of Ishimaru. Strength is imperative in the batt
Awaken your inner devil...

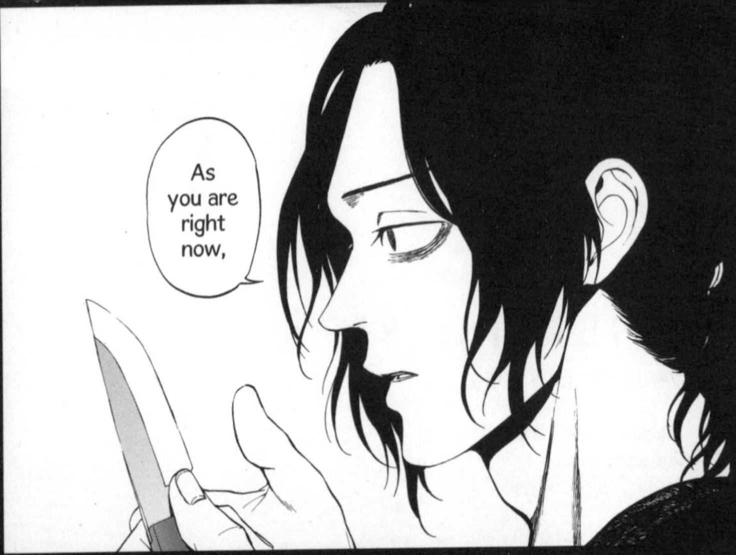
As you are right now,

Be prepared to discard kindness.

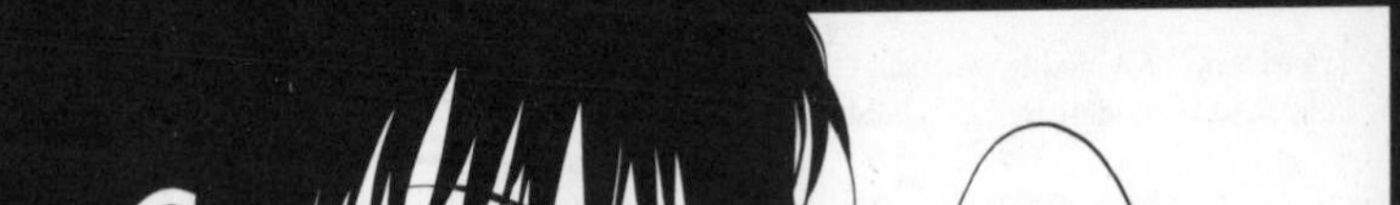
you won't be able to defeat *anyone.*

DEVILS' LINE 5

A Vertical Comics Edition

Translation: Jocelyne Allen
Production: Risa Cho
Lorina Mapa

First published in Japan in 2015 by Kodansha, Ltd., Tokyo
Publication rights for this English edition arranged through Kodansha, Ltd., Tokyo
English language version produced by Vertical Comics, an imprint of Kodansha USA Publishing, LLC

Translation provided by Vertical Comics, 2017
Published by Kodansha USA Publishing, LLC, New York

Originally published in Japanese as *Debiruzurain 5* by Kodansha, Ltd., 2015
Debiruzurain first serialized in *Morning two*, Kodansha, Ltd., 2013-2019

ISBN: 978-1-942993-62-9

Manufactured in the United States of America

First Edition

Fourth Printing

Kodansha USA Publishing, LLC
451 Park Avenue South
7th Floor
New York, NY 10016
www.kodansha.us

Vertical books are distributed through Penguin-Random House Publisher Services.

REX JONES
SPIN OFF

by Jonny Zucker

illustrated by Enzo Troiano
Cover Illustration by Marcus Smith

Librarian Reviewer
Marci Peschke
Librarian, Dallas Independent School District
MA Education Reading Specialist, Stephen F. Austin State University
Learning Resources Endorsement, Texas Women's University

Reading Consultant
Mary Evenson
Middle School Teacher, Edina Public Schools, MN
MA in Education, University of Minnesota

STONE ARCH BOOKS
Minneapolis   San Diego

First published in the United States in 2007
by Stone Arch Books,
151 Good Counsel Drive, P.O. Box 669,
Mankato, Minnesota 56002.
www.stonearchbooks.com

Originally published in Great Britain in 2005
by Badger Publishing Ltd.

Original work copyright © 2005 Badger Publishing Ltd
Text copyright © 2005 Jonny Zucker

Library of Congress Cataloging-in-Publication Data
Zucker, Jonny.
    [DJ Fight]
    Spin Off / by Jonny Zucker; illustrated by Enzo Troiano.
    p. cm. — (Keystone Books (Rex Jones))
    Originally published: Great Britain: Badger Publishing Ltd., 2005,
under the title D.J. Fight.
    Summary: When fifteen-year-old Rex Jones's mysterious cell phone
transports him to a contest for disc jockeys, he becomes the target of a
cheater and must take some risks even to compete.
    ISBN-13: 978-1-59889-333-5 (library binding)
    ISBN-10: 1-59889-333-5 (library binding)
    ISBN-13: 978-1-59889-429-5 (paperback)
    ISBN-10: 1-59889-429-3 (paperback)
    [1. Adventure and adventurers—Fiction. 2. Disc jockeys—Fiction.
3. Contests—Fiction. 4. Cellular telephones—Fiction.] I. Troiano, Enzo,
ill. II. Title.
PZ7.Z77925Spi 2007
[Fic]—dc22   2006026735

1 2 3 4 5 6 12 11 10 09 08 07

Printed in the United States of America

TABLE OF CONTENTS

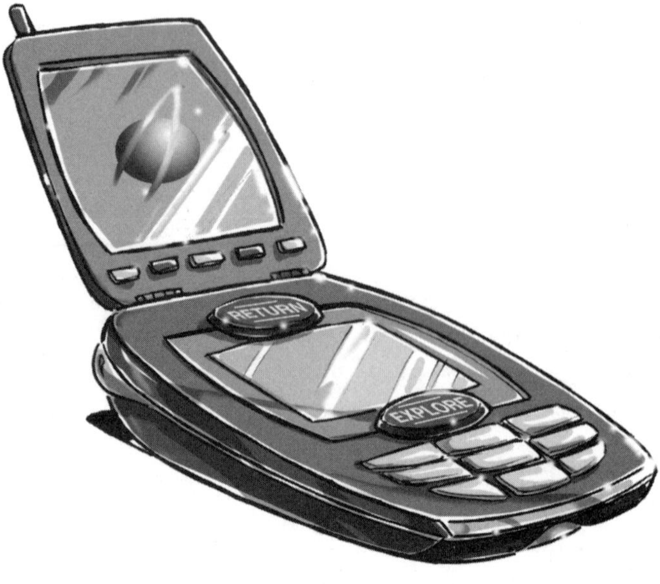
RETURN
EXPLORE

HOW IT ALL BEGAN

Fifteen-year-old Rex Jones used to have a pretty normal life. He went to school. He hung out with his best friends, Carl and Dave. He played sports. He watched TV. Normal stuff.

Then, a few months ago, Rex bought a new cell phone. It was the last one the store had. Rex had seen the phone in a magazine, but his new phone was different in one way.

It had two extra buttons. One said EXPLORE and one said RETURN. The man in the store said that none of the other phones had those buttons.

The phone worked fine at first. Rex forgot about the extra buttons.

One day the phone started to make a strange buzzing sound. When Rex looked at it, the green EXPLORE button was flashing.

He pressed it, and suddenly found himself in an incredible dream world of adventures. Each adventure could only be ended when Rex's phone buzzed again and the flashing red RETURN button was pressed.

He never knows when an adventure will begin, and he never knows if it will end in time to save him.

Chapter 1

THE CLUB

Rex's music class had a special guest, DJ Emerald, who was teaching them about turntables.

Suddenly, Rex's cell phone buzzed and its green EXPLORE button flashed.

Rex pressed it quickly. There was a flash of white light and he found himself in a small, hot room. A sign on the door said BACKSTAGE.

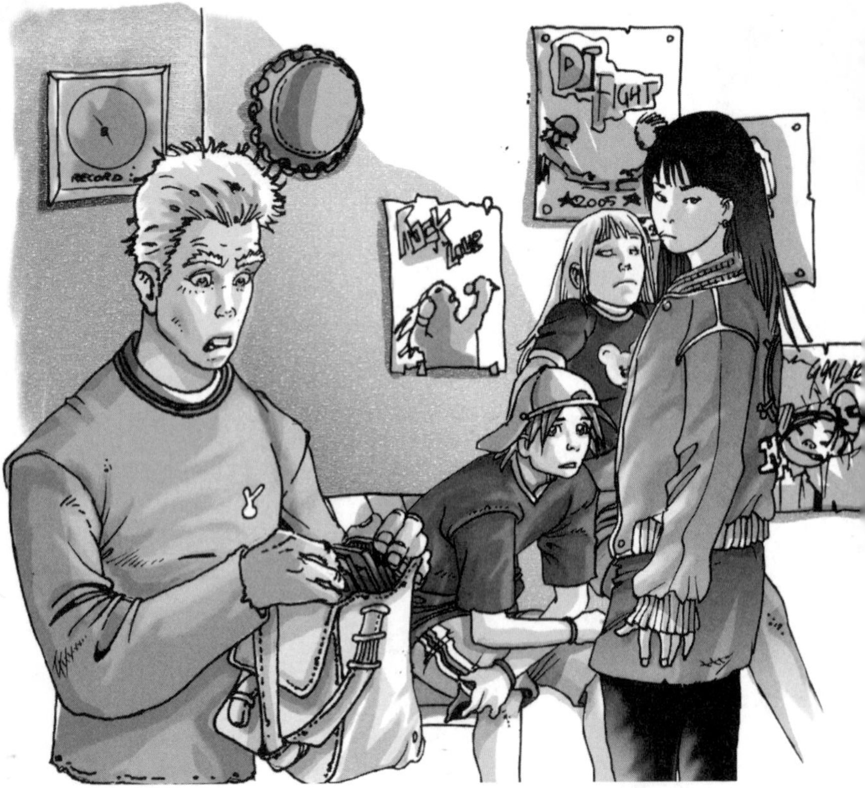

DJ FIGHT
2005

There were nine kids his age in the room, five boys and four girls. Each of them had a record bag stuffed with records.

There was a full record bag on Rex's shoulder. He also found a pair of headphones in his pocket.

An older girl started talking. "I'm Cat," she told them. "Welcome to the Beat Club DJ contest. The best DJ wins a spot at the coolest nightclub in town. Here's the order for the contest."

Cat taped a list on the wall. Rex was ninth, after a girl named Liz and before a boy named Paul. This was amazing. Rex was dying to try out his DJ skills on a live audience.

The ten kids left the room. The guy named Paul walked over to a boy waiting outside and turned to face Rex.

"This is Baz," said Paul. "He's my main man. Does anything I tell him to. He's the only one who knows my secret trick. No one will beat me."

Chapter 2

CHEAT

Two hours later, the club was packed. "Okay," shouted Cat. "The contest is ready to start! Suzie, you're on first!"

Suzie nervously pulled on her headphones and went out to face the crowd. Rex listened to Suzie's set from the side of the stage. She was good.

A boy named Kareem was on next. Rex thought he was sort of boring. Not as good as Suzie.

Next on was a girl named Liz. As she lined up her first record, Rex went off to find the bathroom. He walked along a dark hallway and pushed open the first door he found.

Paul and Baz were inside the room, sitting at a table. The door opening had startled them. The music player they were listening to fell off the table and clicked open.

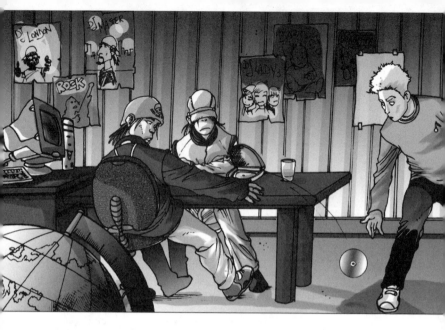

A CD fell out of it and rolled across the floor. Rex picked it up.

"Give that back!" snarled Paul.

Rex ignored him.

'Finished DJ Contest CD' was written on the CD in black pen.

"So this is your great trick," Rex said coldly. "You play this perfect CD and pretend you're doing it live? You are a cheat."

Paul lunged at Rex. Rex fell over, and the CD flew out of his hands. Paul grabbed it.

"Come on, Baz," Paul shouted.

Paul and Baz ran out the door. Rex stood up to go after them, but the door slammed shut. He pushed against the door but it wouldn't move. He was locked inside.

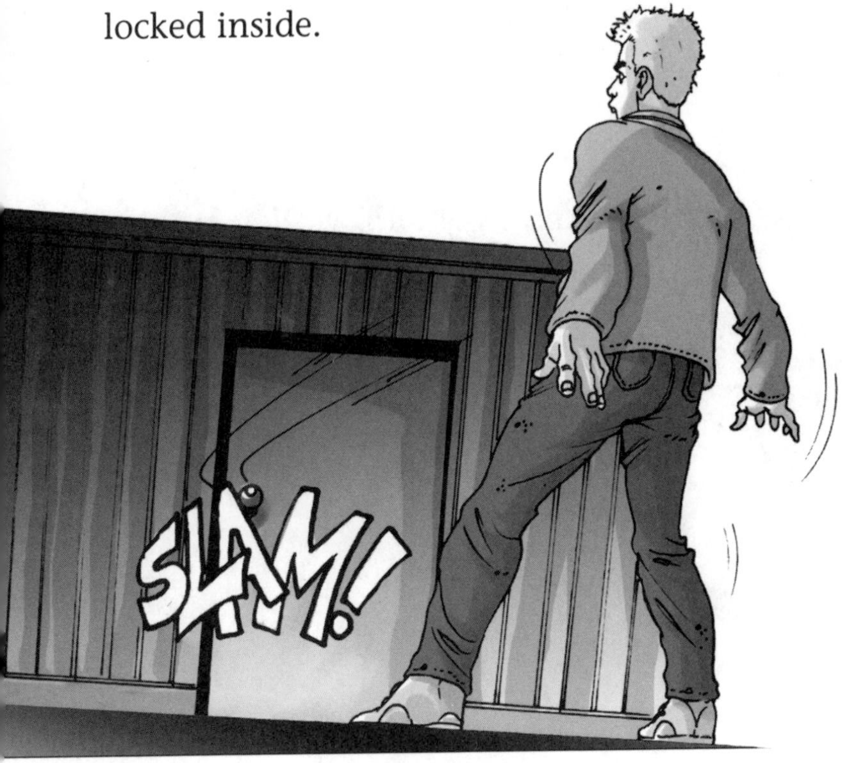
SLAM!

Chapter 3
LOCKED IN

Rex tried the door again but it was no use.

He looked around the room and spotted a small skylight window on the ceiling.

There were some wooden crates in the corner of the room, and Rex started piling them up. They made a wobbly, wooden tower.

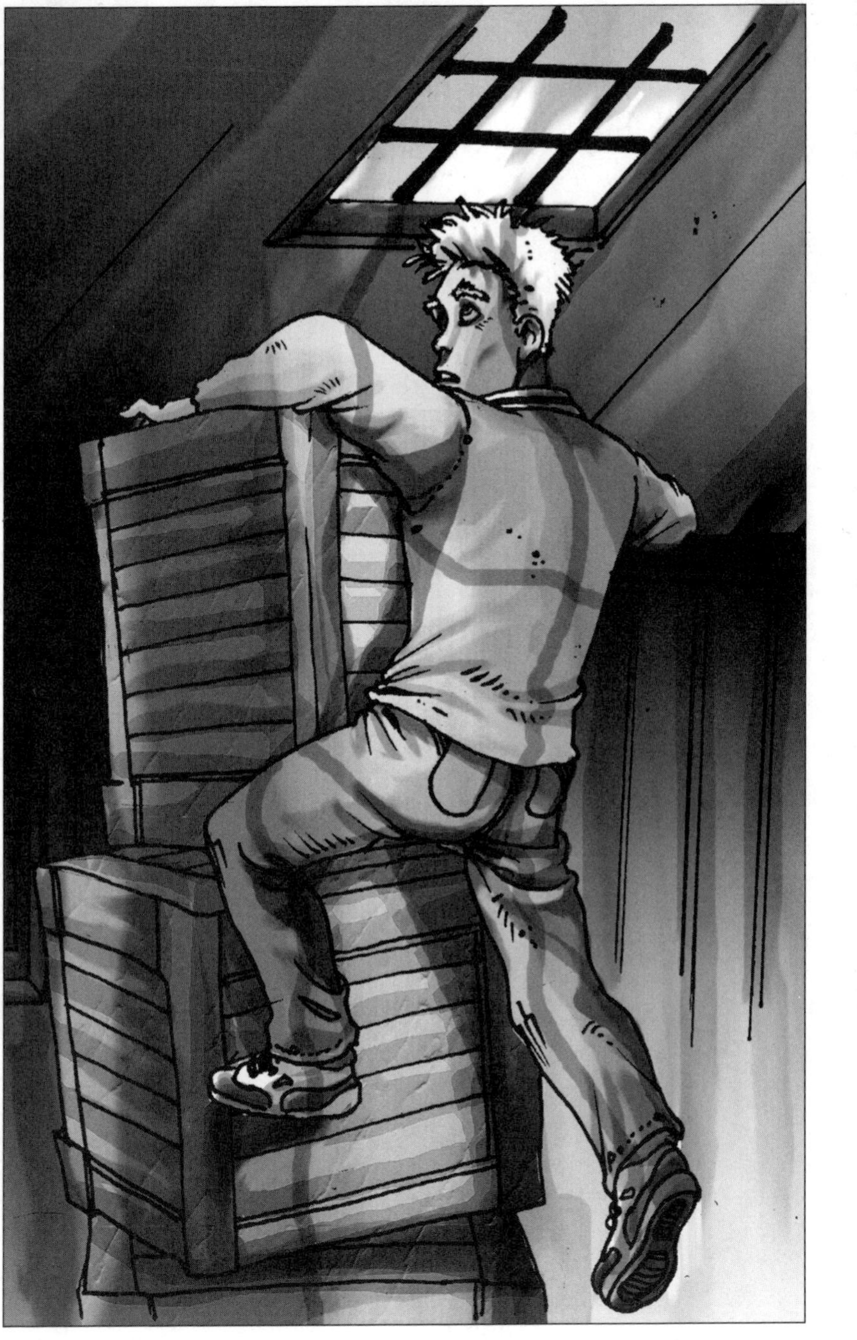

The first time Rex tried to climb the tower, he fell down.

But the second time was better. He spotted a tiny latch underneath the window.

He flicked it and the window opened. He reached up and slowly pulled himself through.

Rex was on top of the Beat Club roof. He was too high up to jump to the ground. Cars sped by on the road below.

At least I tried, Rex thought as he prepared to climb back down through the window. Then he heard the low rumble of a truck. It was coming around the corner. Its back was piled high with sand.

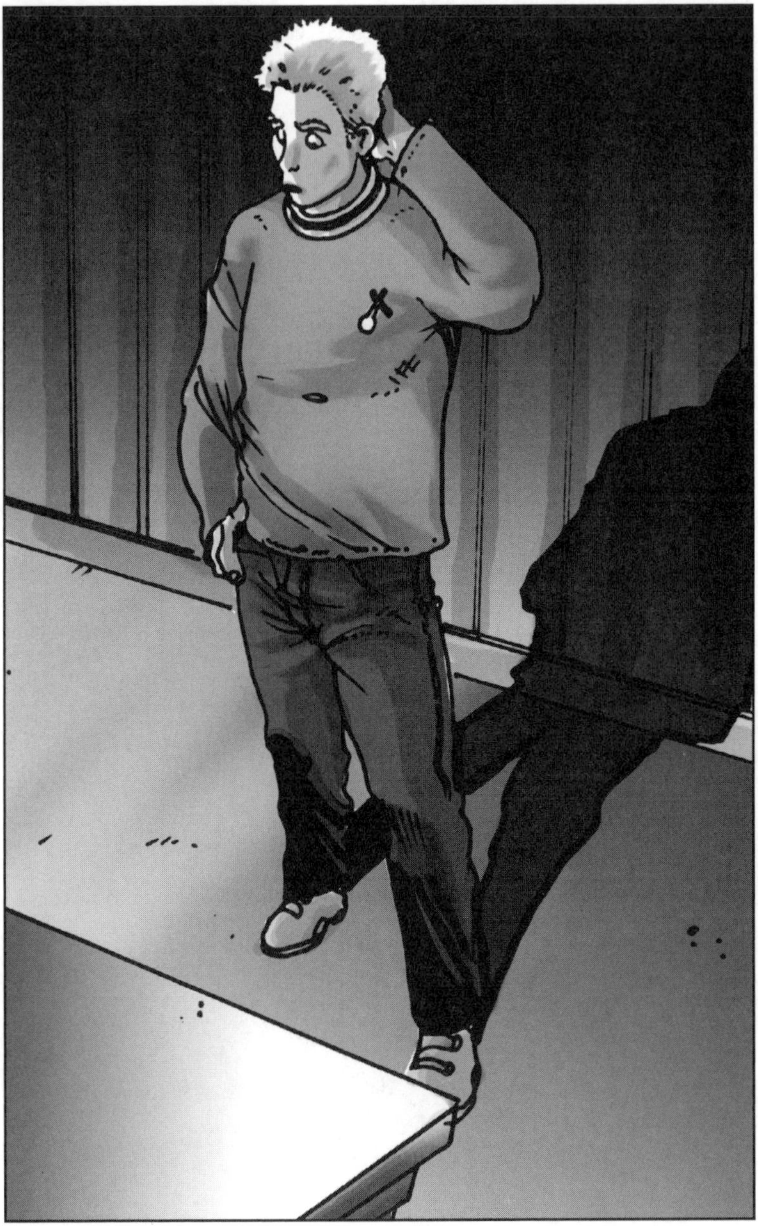

Rex didn't have time to think about it. He ran across the roof and jumped as far as he could, landing with a thud on the back of the truck.

He waited until the truck stopped at a nearby set of traffic lights. Then he jumped down onto the pavement.

Rex ran back into the club.

He headed for the backstage room to get his record bag. When he got there he froze. His record bag and all of his records were gone.

Chapter 4
TIME RUNS OUT

Rex ran up to some of the other DJs and started asking if he could borrow some of their records. He was on in twenty minutes.

Rex felt a tap on his shoulder. It was Cat.

"Rex," she said, "you know the rules. You can't borrow other people's records. If you don't have your own records, you can't enter the contest."

"But I did have my own records," Rex replied, "I just don't know where they are now."

"I'm sorry, Rex, that's the way it goes," Cat said. "Try again next year."

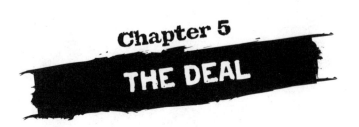

Chapter 5
THE DEAL

Rex had never felt so angry. He stormed off down a hallway. He needed to get some fresh air. At the end of the hallway there was a fire exit. Rex pushed open the fire exit door and walked out into the cold night air.

As soon as he stepped outside he saw something shocking. Baz was standing on a low wall and throwing something into a huge garbage can.

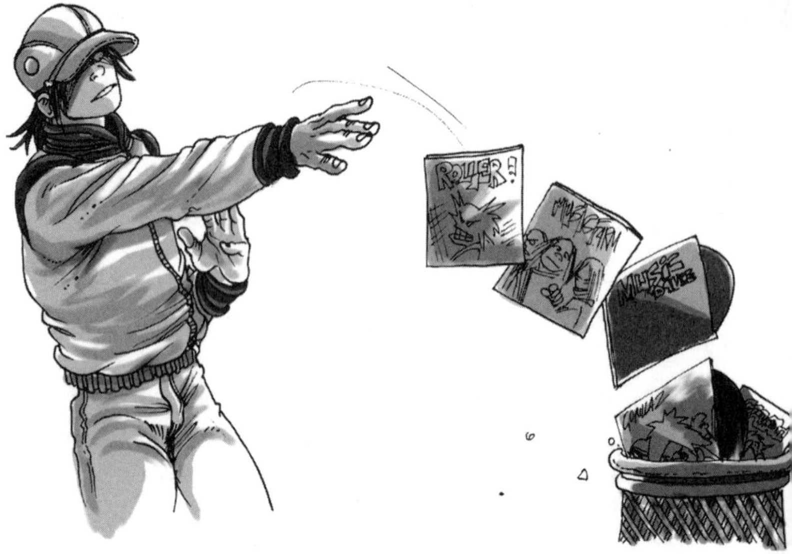
ROLLER!

It was Rex's records.

"Hey, what do you think you're doing?" Rex yelled.

"Paul told me to do it," replied Baz, turning red in the face.

"What's in it for you?" snapped Rex. "Do you always let Paul boss you around?"

Baz shrugged his shoulders. "Paul really wants to win this contest. He will do anything to win."

Rex climbed up onto the wall next to Baz. "Listen, Baz," he said, "if you give me my records back, maybe we can make a deal."

Baz listened to what Rex had to say. When Rex was finished talking, Baz nodded. "Okay, I'll do it," he said. He tipped over the garbage can. Piles of trash fell out. So did Rex's records.

Chapter 6

CHASED

Rex and Baz ran over to the fire exit door. But it had locked on the inside after Rex had come out of it.

Baz checked his watch. "Hurry up, man," he shouted. "You are supposed to be on in two minutes."

Rex and Baz ran around the side of the building and up to the front door.

A security guy blocked their way. "Who are you two?" he asked.

Just then, a girl in the line started shouting at someone. The security guard stepped toward the screaming girl. Rex and Baz pushed past him and ran inside.

"Hey, you two!" the guard yelled. "Get back here now!"

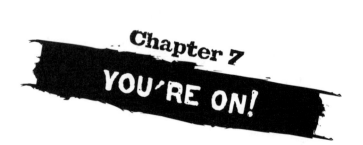

Chapter 7
YOU'RE ON!

The huge crowds of people slowed them down, but Rex and Baz went as fast as they could. The guard was close behind them. On stage, Liz was winding up her set. Rex was due on next, but Cat was pointing at Paul. "Rex blew it," she shouted. "You are on next, Paul."

But Rex leapt up on to the stage and shouted at Cat. "I got my own records back!"

Cat looked surprised. Paul looked furious. "You're on!" Cat yelled to Rex.

"Stop that boy!" shouted the guard.

Cat tapped the guard on the shoulder. "It's okay," she said, "he's with me."

Liz moved out of the way. Rex pulled his headphones out of his pocket and lined up his first record.

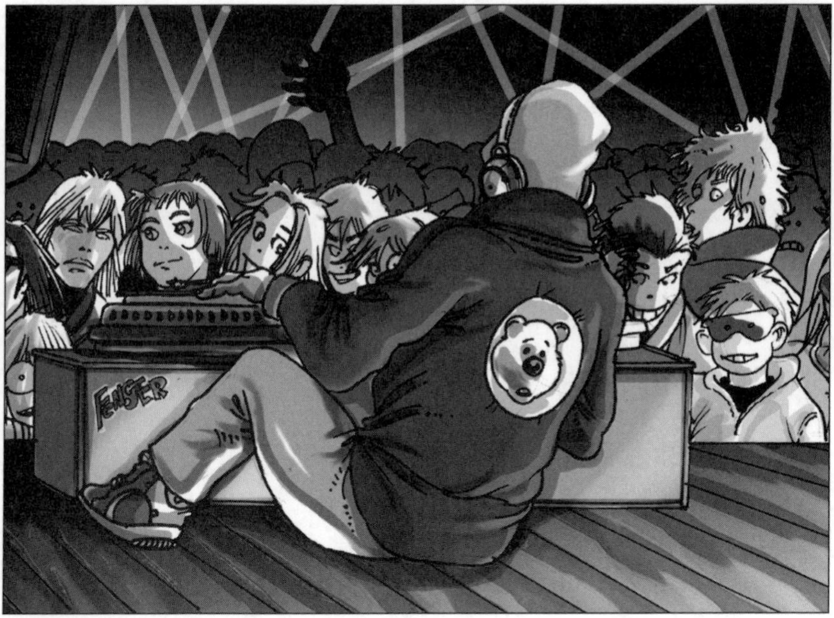
FENDER

Chapter 8
WINNER

Rex's set was amazing. The crowd loved it.

Then it was Paul's set. It was okay, but the crowd had already chosen a winner.

When Paul finished, Cat ran back on stage and held Rex's arm in the air.

"Tonight's winner is Rex Jones!" she screamed.

The crowd went crazy.

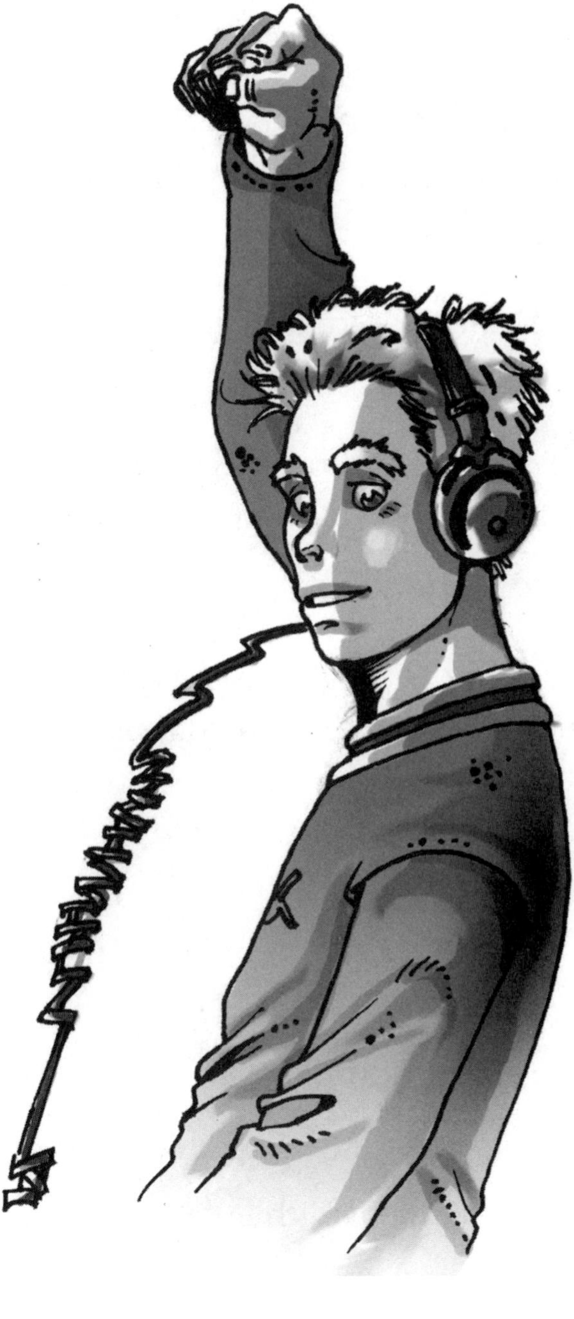

Rex was putting a record down onto the turntable when Baz appeared at his side. Baz slapped him on the shoulder.

"Thanks for your help, Baz," Rex said, grinning.

Paul stomped over to them. "Baz, why did you help him?" he asked meanly.

"I'm tired of being bossed around by you," said Baz. "I help you, but I get nothing back."

"So?" said Paul.

"So, Rex said I should do some gigs with some of the other DJs and split the money with them."

"Who would want to work with you?" said Paul with a cruel laugh.

At that second, Suzie, Kareem, and
Cat walked up. They had heard what
was going on. "We'll all work with you,
Baz," Cat said, smiling.

Paul looked like he was going to cry.
He turned and ran offstage.

Rex dropped the needle on the
record. As the sound boomed out of the
speakers, the red RETURN button on
his phone lit up.

"I have to go, Baz," he called. "Good luck with those gigs!"

There was a flash of white light and Rex found himself back in the school music room.

DJ Emerald laughed. "Give it some time, Rex," he said, as Rex dropped a record onto the turntable. "You are not a great club DJ yet."

Rex just smiled.

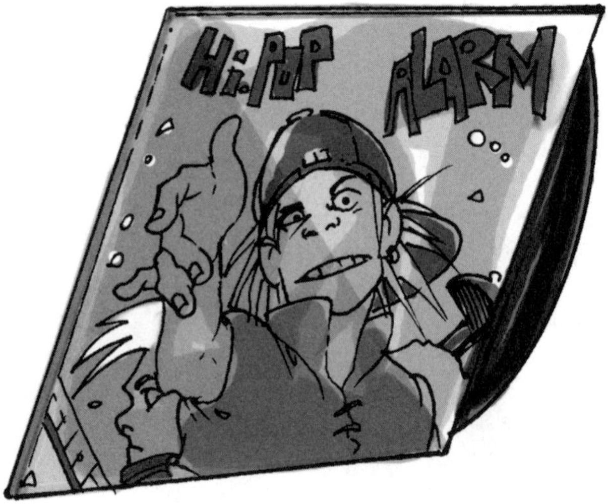
Hi-Pop
ALARM

ABOUT THE AUTHOR

Even as a child, Jonny Zucker wanted to be a writer. Today, he has written more than 30 books. He has also spent time working as a teacher, song writer, and stand-up comedian. Jonny lives in London with his wife and two children.

ABOUT MARCUS SMITH

Marcus Smith says that he started drawing when his mother put a pen in his hand when he was a baby. Smith grew up in Chicago, where he took classes at the world famous Art Institute. In Chicago he also designed band logos and tattoos! He moved west and studied at the Minneapolis College of Art and Design, majoring in both Illustration and Comic Art. As an artist, Smith was "influenced by the land of superheroes, fantasy, horror, and action," and he continues to work in the world of comics.

GLOSSARY

audience (AW-dee-uhnss)—the people who watch or listen to a performance

club (KLUHB)—a hip, cool place, that often has dancing or shows

DJ (DEE-jay)—short for "disc jockey," a person who plays music, usually records or CDs

fate (FAYT)—what will happen to a person

furious (FYOO-ree-uhss)—very angry

gig (GIG)—a scheduled performance for a musician in public

headphones (HED-fohnz)—small speakers that are worn in or over the ears

needle (NEE-duhl)—on a turntable or record player, the long, thin part that touches the record

record (REK-urd)—a disk with grooves on which sound is recorded

set (SET)—one person's part of a performance

turntable (TURN-tay-buhl)—a revolving surface, used to play records

winding up (WYND-ing UHP)—finishing

DISCUSSION QUESTIONS

1. Paul is a bully, but Baz does what Paul says. What are some of the reasons Baz obeys Paul? Have you ever been in a similar situation?

2. When Rex's records go missing, Cat says he won't be allowed to go onstage. Why do you think this is? Do you think it's fair or unfair? What could Rex have done to try to change Cat's mind?

3. On pages 30-31, Paul tells Baz that no one else will want to work with him, but many of the other DJs say that they will work with Baz. This upsets Paul. Why does Paul become upset? How can you explain his behavior?

WRITING PROMPTS

1. Rex is transported to the club during music class, where he had been learning about turntables. Write a story in which you are transported to a location or an event you've learned about in school. Where is it? What do you do there? If you like, you can create other characters to meet.

2. It isn't fair that Paul planned to play a CD and pretend that it was him. But if you could create the perfect mix CD, with all of your favorite songs, what would it be? List the songs and the performers, and what feeling each song gives you. Don't forget to give your perfect CD a title!

ALSO BY JONNY ZUCKER

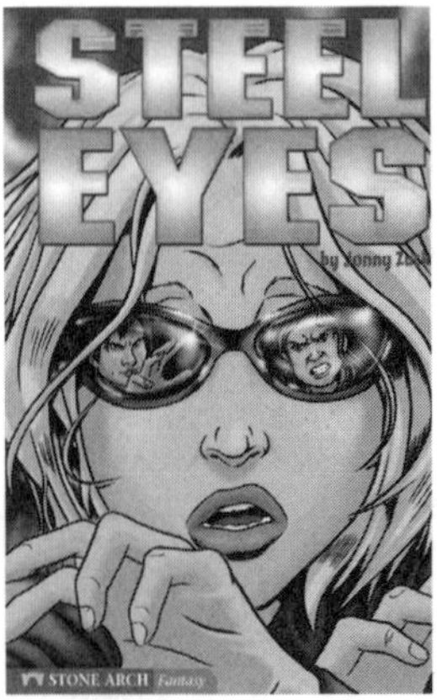
STEEL EYES
STONE ARCH Fantasy

Steel Eyes

Emma Stone is the new girl in school. Why does she always wear sunglasses when the others can't? Gail and Tanya are determined to find out, but Emma's cold stare is more than they bargained for.

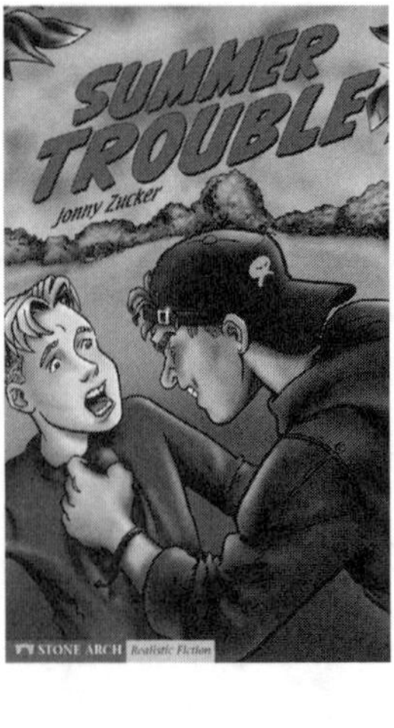
SUMMER TROUBLE
Jonny Zucker
STONE ARCH Realistic Fiction

Summer Trouble

Tom's summer plans change when his cousin Ben decides to visit. Tom believes his entire vacation will be ruined, unti Ben comes to his rescue in a tight situation!

MORE REX JONES ADVENTURES

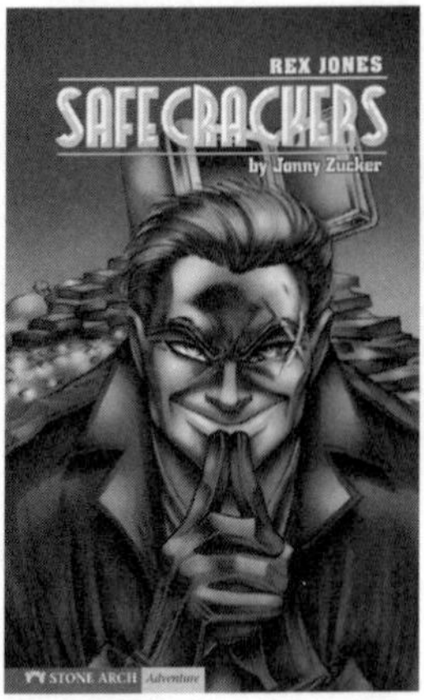
REX JONES
SAFECRACKERS
by Jonny Zucker
STONE ARCH Adventure

Safecrackers

Rex Jones's cell phone sends him and his friends to the high-powered security center of a bank. The three boys are in charge of making sure that Razor Bell, a bank robber who's a master of disguise, can't steal the bank's hundred million dollars!

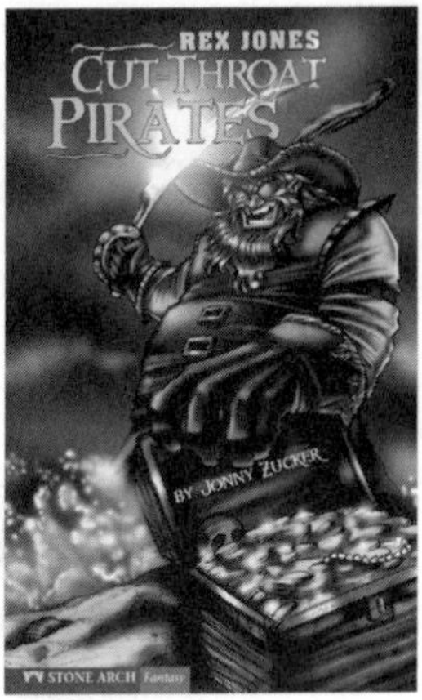
REX JONES
CUT-THROAT PIRATES
BY JONNY ZUCKER
STONE ARCH Fantasy

Cut-Throat Pirates

When Rex Jones's mysterious cell phone flashes, Rex, Carl, and Dave are transported to the deck of a pirate ship. Evil Eric has planned a raid and he asks the boys to help him. Can Rex, Carl, and Dave survive on Eric's ship, or will they walk the plank?

INTERNET SITES

Do you want to know more about subjects related to this book? Or are you interested in learning about other topics? Then check out FactHound, a fun, easy way to find Internet sites.

Our investigative staff has already sniffed out great sites for you!

Here's how to use FactHound:

1. Visit *www.facthound.com*

2. Select your grade level.

3. To learn more about subjects related to this book, type in the book's ISBN number: **1598893335**.

4. Click the **Fetch It** button.

FactHound will fetch the best Internet sites for you!